Challenging nu

Manchester University Press

Challenging nuclearism

A humanitarian approach to reshape the global nuclear order

Marianne Hanson

MANCHESTER UNIVERSITY PRESS

Copyright © Marianne Hanson 2022

The right of Marianne Hanson to be identified as the author of this work has been asserted by them in accordance with the Copyright, Designs and Patents Act 1988.

Published by Manchester University Press
Oxford Road, Manchester M13 9PL

www.manchesteruniversitypress.co.uk

British Library Cataloguing-in-Publication Data
A catalogue record for this book is available from the British Library

ISBN 978 1 5261 6509 1 hardback
ISBN 978 1 5261 8259 3 paperback

First published 2022
Paperback published 2025

The publisher has no responsibility for the persistence or accuracy of URLs for any external or third-party internet websites referred to in this book, and does not guarantee that any content on such websites is, or will remain, accurate or appropriate.

Typeset by Newgen Publishing UK

In memory of
Yolande Mary Pamela Roberts Lacey
3 November 1922–25 February 2021

Contents

Foreword viii
Acknowledgements xi
List of abbreviations xiii

Introduction 1

Part I: The dominance of nuclearism

1 Identifying the elements of nuclearism: the traditional framings that normalized nuclear weapons 11
2 Nuclearism today: modernization, the persistence of deterrence, and ongoing dangers 43
3 Pushing for disarmament: a fruitless exercise 67

Part II: The transition – from the Humanitarian Initiative to the prohibition treaty

4 The humanitarian context: drawing lessons from earlier disarmament campaigns 95
5 Creating the Treaty on the Prohibition of Nuclear Weapons 117

Part III: Rejecting nuclearism

6 Rejecting nuclearism I: changing the discourse; bringing humanitarianism back; empowering new voices and actors; challenging material spending 133
7 Rejecting nuclearism II: disrupting the nuclear order 160

Part IV: Ending nuclearism?

8 Challenges to and likely impacts of the Treaty on the Prohibition of Nuclear Weapons 189
Conclusion 204

References 214
Index 254

Foreword

This book explores the origins and the potential impact of the recent process to make nuclear weapons unequivocally illegal and illegitimate. It examines how the achievement of a treaty banning these weapons, for all states, has come to pose a substantial challenge to the prevailing global nuclear order. This order had been constructed and sustained by a select handful of states over several decades, enabled by a process of what came to be called 'nuclearism'. While nuclearism has been, so far, impossible to dislodge, it is now under an extraordinary level of scrutiny, and is being, I argue, rejected by a growing number of states.

Numerous non-nuclear states and civil society actors have been involved in challenging the global nuclear order established by these powerful states, and their sense of injustice against the nuclear weapon states has been rising for years. In 2017, their grievances were channelled into the creation, at the United Nations, of the Treaty on the Prohibition of Nuclear Weapons (TPNW). This treaty, which entered into force on 22 January 2021, delegitimizes the possession, manufacture, deployment, transfer, or use of nuclear weapons, for all states. Together with the processes that created it, and the actions which will follow it, the treaty refutes the elements of nuclearism which have enabled the untrammelled dominance of the nuclear weapon states for over seven decades.

The puzzling question is how and why a group of relatively weak actors in international politics have been able to achieve the formal prohibition of a weapon which is deemed central to the security doctrines of powerful states, and how they have been able, with this new treaty, to challenge the traditional nuclear order by using humanitarian arguments. In many ways, it seems an unlikely feat that small and middle-sized states, together with non-governmental organizations, have been able to defy the wishes of the great powers and act against them by delegitimizing a weapon that the nuclear weapon states see as essential to maintaining their security, prestige, and power.

The new treaty, of course, faces several obstacles. It has been denigrated by leaders of the nuclear weapon states, who argue that it is disruptive (which it is) and that it will not lead to the elimination of nuclear weapons (which is also correct: it will not, at least not by itself). But it is a significant normative development nonetheless, and is one which is likely, I argue, to have several important consequences in the medium to long term.

It is necessary for me to note at the outset of this work that I believe that eliminating nuclear weapons will be a positive and useful step in international security, and that despite the challenges of doing so, aiming for a de-nuclearized world is a preferable strategy to persisting with the status quo, where the world is threatened by the continued existence of over 13,000 nuclear weapons, many of these hundreds of times more powerful than the Hiroshima bomb. Readers should not be surprised to find that I am deeply critical of the way that nuclear policy has been developed and implemented over the decades, and that I make a clear call for phased, mutual, monitored, and verified disarmament.

I can also say that I am in good company. A number of strategic experts and political leaders have examined this issue and have concluded, especially since the ending of the Cold War, that retaining nuclear weapons is a dangerous and unnecessary practice. Among those who have drawn attention to the urgent need to reduce and then eliminate them are Henry Kissinger, Robert McNamara, and William Perry, former Secretaries of Defense in the United States, General Lee Butler, former Head of US Strategic Command, General Colin Powell, former US Secretary of State, and Australian Professor Robert O'Neill (former Director of the International Institute for Strategic Studies in London, and Chichele Professor of the History of War at Oxford University, whose careful thinking on this subject has come to influence my own position).

Unsurprisingly, some consider it 'unrealistic' to adopt the view that nuclear weapons should be eliminated, and are convinced that the global nuclear order should remain unchanged. They dismiss calls for disarmament as Utopian or destabilizing, supported only by those who apparently know little about *realpolitik* or the putative benefits of nuclear deterrence. I do not deny that there is a strong belief and faith in the idea of nuclear deterrence and that this fuels the retention of nuclear weapons. But with a background in strategic studies, three decades of researching these issues and working with several diplomats and political leaders, I believe that this faith in nuclear deterrence is misplaced, and that change is long overdue. For those who believe that nuclear restraint can always be counted on to avert catastrophe, that nuclear deterrence has kept the peace, and that it will continue to keep the peace – all debatable assumptions – and that disarmament is therefore not necessary, there is still the awful spectre of accidental or inadvertent use, together with the possibility that these weapons might come into the hands of terrorist or other sub-state groups. We have come perilously close to accidents in the past, and our luck will not hold indefinitely. A continuing faith in nuclear weapons may therefore itself be unrealistic: to think that we can continue to have many thousands of nuclear weapons in existence without them ever being used again reflects a degree of hubris and short-sightedness, the consequences of which could lead to disaster. Certainly the military and political strategists I mention above have stressed these dangers.

Thus I cannot claim to be 'objective' in this debate, or at least any more objective than those who are in favour of retaining nuclear weapons are seen as 'objective'. As the editor of the respected journal, *The Bulletin of the Atomic Scientists*, noted in its issue offering practical advice on nuclear matters to the incoming US president in 2016, 'The *Bulletin* is non-partisan, but it does have an unapologetic bias toward science, expertise, and the long-term preservation of humanity' (Mecklin 2016). So too is this book non-partisan, but biased towards science, expertise, and the preservation of humanity.

I thus remain confident of my claims. I know that achieving a world without nuclear weapons will require a substantial rethinking of current policies, a great deal of political good-will, the sustained building of trust between nuclear adversaries, and judicious management of regional security fears during any process of de-nuclearization. It will need to be carefully balanced and phased, and occur in a strictly monitored and verified manner. As I and many others argue, all of these things are feasible.

I thus do not succumb to a view that nothing can be changed. Military conflict might never be eliminated from international politics, but pursuing a security order where the option of global or even regional nuclear annihilation is removed is an urgent necessity. As such, I offer these chapters in a spirit of humility, but with some confidence also, and with a wish that they might persuade readers to re-examine the entrenched doctrines within nuclear policies, and to seek answers to global insecurities which do not rely on this most destructive weapon of mass destruction.

This book therefore explores how and why we have got to the stage where, seventy-seven years after their invention, nuclear weapons have come to be prohibited under international law, regardless of the views of the nuclear weapon states and regardless of their existing military doctrines. I hope to do justice to this important achievement by telling this story. At the same time, there is a real need to consider what the new Treaty on the Prohibition of Nuclear Weapons can and cannot do. In addition to examining the intriguing origins of this new treaty, then, exploring its implications and outlining its potential impact is therefore also a goal of this book.

Acknowledgements

I owe a debt of gratitude to numerous colleagues who have helped to shape my thinking on international security issues over the years. In Oxford, Andrew Hurrell, Robert O'Neill, Adam Roberts, William Wallace, Geoff Wiseman, the late Geoffrey Best, and the late R. John Vincent, were all invaluable mentors. At the University of Queensland, Chris Reus-Smit and Roland Bleiker have been unfailingly supportive and generous with their time, and I am very much in their debt. They, together with Stephen Bell, Alex Bellamy, Ian Clark, Richard Devetak, Dan Druckman, Tim Dunne, Sebastian Kaempf, Matt McDonald, Jacinta O'Hagan, Andrew Phillips, Heather Rae, Richard Shapcott, and others have all proved to be wonderful colleagues and friends. In other forums, Ken Booth, Anthony Burke, Andy Butfoy, Joseph Camilleri, Gareth Evans, Trine Flockhart, Michael de Hamel, Jenny Neilson, Tanya Ogilvie-White, Nick Ritchie, Maria Rost Rublee, Richard Tanter, Nicholas A.J. Taylor, Ramesh Thakur, and Nicholas Wheeler have been influential and important collaborators on issues of global security.

Numerous other analysts and scholars have also shaped my thinking and assisted me in this book. I am grateful for interviews and discussions with John Borrie, John Burroughs, Tim Caughley, Thomas Doyle, Trevor Findlay, the late Malcolm Fraser, Paul Ingram, Rebecca Johnson, Hans Kristensen, Richard Lennane, Patricia Lewis, Benoit Pelopidas, Matthew Rowland, Randy Rydell, Tom Spies, Alyn Ware, and Ward Wilson. Margie Beavis, Dimity Hawkins, Daryl Le Cornu, Ruth Mitchell, Gem Romuld, Tilman Ruff, Jemila Rushton, Dave Sweeney, Sue Wareham, Tim Wright, and others from the International Campaign to Abolish Nuclear Weapons (ICAN) Australia have been very helpful and kind, as have Annette Brownlie, Del Cuddihy, Wendy Flannery, Chris Henderson, Valerie Joy, Norma Forrest, and many others in Brisbane. In New Zealand, those who have influenced my thinking greatly – although I did not appreciate it fully at the time – included the late Harold Evans, and the late Bridget Farrell.

All of the above deserve credit and grateful thanks for their insights and experience, upon which I have called many times. None bear any responsibility for any flaws or shortcomings that might be present in this book.

The editorial team at Manchester University Press have been immensely helpful, and I am very grateful for their guidance and help. This work on the subject of eliminating nuclear weapons would not have been possible without the generous assistance of the Royal Norwegian Ministry of Foreign Affairs and its grants programme supporting research on disarmament. I was privileged to receive funding for hosting a conference in Brisbane, for travel to conduct interviews and research, and for a one-year post-doctoral assistant. Tor Martin Moller, Adviser, Section for Disarmament and Non-Proliferation, together with his colleagues, worked with me for several years as I completed this book, and I remain very grateful for their assistance. In a world where many nation-states declare themselves to be supporters of peace and justice, Norway stands out as one country which takes these responsibilities seriously and which makes an enormous contribution to a better world. By enabling scholars to conduct and share their research on nuclear politics, the government of Norway demonstrates its serious commitment to addressing some of the most pressing issues in global politics today. For their excellent work – in development assistance, with landmine-clearing activities, diplomatic endeavours to promote conflict resolution, among other things – Norway and its people remain a beacon of hope in a troubled world. For their commitment to a nuclear-free world, and their generous funding of the research for this book, I note here my deep and humble thanks. I look forward to the day that Oslo will join the TPNW.

The late Kenneth and Joyce Hanson always encouraged me, and for this I remain truly grateful. My father Frank and my siblings (Tim, Tony, and especially Julie, Pamela, and thoughts of Lisa) have kept me grounded and supported. Last, I wish to note the loving support of my mother, Yolande Lacey, and my dear children, Lorraine and Christopher Hanson.

List of abbreviations

CCW	Convention on Certain Conventional Weapons
CD	Conference on Disarmament
CEND	Creating an environment for Nuclear Disarmament
CSA	Comprehensive Safeguards Agreement
CTBT	Comprehensive Test Ban Treaty
FMCT	Fissile Material Cut Off Treaty
HINW	Humanitarian Impact of Nuclear Weapons
IAEA	International Atomic Energy Agency
ICAN	International Campaign to Abolish Nuclear Weapons
ICBL	International Coalition to Ban Landmines
ICC	International Criminal Court
ICJ	International Court of Justice
ICNND	International Commission on Nuclear Nonproliferation and Disarmament
ICRC	International Committee of the Red Cross
IPNDV	International Partnership for Nuclear Disarmament Verification
IPPNW	International Physicians for the Prevention of Nuclear War
JCPOA	Joint Comprehensive Program of Action
MAPW	Medical Association for the Prevention of War
NAC	New Agenda Coalition
NAM	Non-Aligned Movement
NGO	Non-Governmental Organisation
NPT	Non-Proliferation Treaty
OEWG	Open Ended Working Group
OPCW	Organisation for the Prohibition of Chemical Weapons
OSCE	Organisation for Security and Cooperation in Europe
P5	Permanent Five members of the United Nations
PNND	Parliamentarians for Nuclear Non-proliferation and Disarmament

RevCon	Review Conference
SIPRI	Stockholm International Peace Research Institute
SANE	Smarter Approach to Nuclear Expenditures
START	Strategic Arms Reduction Treaty
TPNW	Treaty on the Prohibition of Nuclear Weapons
UNIDIR	United Nations Institute for Disarmament Research
UNODA	United Nations Office for Disarmament Affairs

Introduction

The history of nuclear weapons has been a strange one: these weapons have been both revered and feared, desired and shunned, proliferated and renounced. They have conferred status, at different times both prestige and pariah. Perhaps the most paradoxical aspect of their existence is that they were acquired and have come to constitute the core of security strategies for a small group of states, yet remained – realistically speaking – impossible to use. At the same time that vast resources have been spent on developing and modernizing nuclear weapons, on refining and targeting them for war planning, it was implicitly understood that these weapons should not be used. The nature of nuclear deterrence demanded that one had to promise to use nuclear weapons, and to be completely convincing in threatening unparalleled devastation against an opponent, but at the same time understand that such weapons should never be launched. Nuclear weapons have been the subject of intense ethical concern, yet they continue to be fixed firmly in national and international security policies. Their use would clearly violate international humanitarian law, but for over seventy years there was no explicit legal prohibition against them. At the same time that they have been shown to be almost worthless as military instruments, they remain the core element around which certain states have built their military doctrines. Their holders have promised publicly and unequivocally to eliminate them, but privately retain an unyielding determination to keep them. Nuclear weapons have been presented as very normal elements of politics and security at the same time that they represent one of the most abnormal undertakings in human history.

These various paradoxes make it difficult to find a way to proceed with the management of nuclear weapons in global politics; indeed they have rendered it almost impossible to dislodge the prevailing global nuclear order established by the nuclear weapon states, and to create a world free of nuclear weapons. Notwithstanding the calls, especially over the past few decades, for the elimination of nuclear weapons, their very longevity seems to have conferred upon these weapons a sense of permanence and inevitability that persists well beyond their actual utility, and indeed beyond any rational assessment of their purpose.

The juxtaposition of the deep valuing of nuclear weapons on the one hand, and the need to reduce nuclear dangers on the other, provides the context for this book. At its heart, the book explores the following questions: How was 'nuclearism' established and how has it been sustained for so long? How, in the face of continued possession of nuclear weapons by a few states, have advocates of disarmament responded? How has the accumulation of seventy-seven years of acceptance and 'normality' shaped efforts to prevent nuclear catastrophe? In short, can the traditional casting of nuclear weapons as valuable strategic assets (for some, at least) be countered by arguments that cast them as militarily impractical, inhumane, and illegal?

The fact is that such arguments have *not* troubled the nuclear weapon states – at least not until recently. The concept and practices of nuclearism remained dominant, and enabled the nuclear weapon states to continue with the status quo, regardless of the fact that the Cold War – ostensibly the very reason these weapons were seen as essential for the largest nuclear weapon states – ended over thirty years ago. The nuclear order has been stunningly resistant to challenge or change.

From 1968 onwards, with the adoption of the nuclear Non-Proliferation Treaty (NPT), the United States, the Soviet Union, and Britain, consolidated a nuclear order which privileged their possession, as well as France and China's possession, of nuclear weapons, on the basis that these five states had tested nuclear weapons prior to January 1967. As the Permanent Five members of the UN Security Council, or simply, the P5, their use of the NPT has been one of the ways in which they have been able to keep their nuclear arsenals, even though Article VI of the NPT calls clearly for these states to move in good faith towards nuclear disarmament. At the same time, all other states were exhorted not to acquire nuclear weapons, in exchange for assistance with the peaceful use of nuclear materials, and the pledges by the P5 states that they would, eventually, disarm.

The global nuclear order, therefore, is *inter alia* one where questions about which state may possess nuclear weapons 'legitimately', and which states would be considered violators if they dared to proliferate, have been determined by a treaty which the two superpowers and Britain (and later the other P5 members) embraced as a means of solidifying their position as the accepted possessors of nuclear weapons, while at the same time denying any such 'right' to all other states.[1] This order has been variously described as inequitable, as a means whereby large and powerful states continue to keep potential proliferators at bay, and as perpetuating a system of 'nuclear apartheid'.[2] At the same time, the order implies that these select nuclear weapon states act always in the interests of the world at large, that they are 'responsible', trustworthy, nuclear weapon states, and that their management of the global nuclear order is a safe, stable, and unquestionable one.

Since 1991, when the Cold War ended, there have certainly been substantial reductions in the number of nuclear weapons, and the nuclear weapon states continue to pledge their commitment to eliminate their arsenals. But the pace of reductions has been slow and is now stopped, and advocates of elimination fear that such pledges will never be honoured. Moreover, relations between key nuclear weapon states, especially the United States, Russia, and China, deteriorate, and fears of a regional nuclear conflict – in Europe, in South Asia, or in Northeast Asia – continue to grow.

One of the key factors that has enabled the nuclear weapon states to sustain the global nuclear order and thus their possession of nuclear arsenals has been their success in perpetuating a system of 'nuclearism' which firmly embedded nuclear weapons within a 'strategic imperative', and which – in the name of security – had defied any serious challenge to its dominance. For this reason, there had never been a clear legal ruling which outlaws the possession and use of nuclear weapons, for all states. The nuclear weapon states, as the chief architects of the prevailing nuclear order, have long been able to sustain their exclusive control over the contours of this order, and have easily resisted any efforts by states and citizens seeking the elimination of these weapons. Especially through their position in the NPT, the great powers – the US, Russia, China, Britain, and France – have successfully deflected any grievances against their privileged place in the global nuclear order.

This has now changed. A formal process began after 2010, with a very deliberate challenge mounted against the nuclear weapon states, aiming to change the discourse surrounding nuclear weapons to one which is fundamentally humanitarian-, rather than security-, oriented. This challenge involved a programme of humanitarian advocacy, the imposition of a process of what is sometimes called 'humanitarian arms control', designed to stigmatize and delegitimize particular weapons as a vital step towards their eventual elimination. It was labelled the 'Humanitarian Initiative'. This development was a significant one, because for the first time, at a widespread and *state*-driven level, the traditional security-led framing of nuclear weapons was passed over by a large group of countries, who sought to put a new construction in its place. This happened despite the efforts made by the great powers to prevent it.[3] The Humanitarian Initiative moved rapidly, and by 2017, 122 non-nuclear weapon states, strongly supported by an extensive civil society network, gathered at the United Nations in New York to adopt the new Treaty on the Prohibition of Nuclear Weapons (TPNW) (UN 2017), making these weapons unambiguously illegitimate, on the basis of international humanitarian law.

This book considers why this has come about, and why it came about when it did. What were the factors that allowed for this new recasting of nuclear debates? How were various key actors able to bring this perspective to the table when for so long, the matter of nuclear weapons and their global impact was one overseen by those few states which had possession and which, *ipso facto*, were the self-appointed custodians of our collective nuclear future? What were the dynamics that allowed the debate to be moved to a level which clearly was unwanted by the nuclear weapon states? In effect, how have the building-blocks of nuclearism been rejected by the new treaty? Have the processes associated with the treaty shaken the elements which have sustained nuclearism for so long?

Moreover, can this shift – a shift which many argue is long overdue – sustain its momentum and assist the move towards a nuclear weapon free world? If there is no participation by the nuclear weapon states, what impact, if any, is the TPNW likely to have? Has nuclearism been seriously weakened? Are the nuclear weapon states losing control of the nuclear weapon debate, and with it their standing within the global nuclear order, and if so, what might this suggest about the new forms of diplomacy and agency in global arms control and disarmament efforts? These questions have only recently come to the fore, and they drive the investigations of this book.

'Humanitarian advocacy'

Given that the insertion of humanitarianism into the nuclear weapon debate has been so important, it is necessary to note briefly here what is meant by the terms 'humanitarianism' and 'humanitarian advocacy', in order to understand how these have been applied to weapons control generally and to nuclear weapons specifically. A good starting point in any description of humanitarianism is provided by the International Committee of the Red Cross (ICRC) and particularly the Geneva Conventions of 1949 and the Additional Protocols of 1977, which embrace four well-established humanitarian principles, namely, those of humanity, neutrality, impartiality, and operational independence. (The ICRC also identifies two further tenets, namely voluntary service and universality, to be applied in its daily operations.) The four foundation principles are firmly anchored in international humanitarian law, and all governments have affirmed these principles through their acceptance of United Nations resolutions (notably UN General Assembly Resolutions 46/182 in 1991, and 58/114 in 2004). A short definition of what is meant by each of the four principles is offered by the UN's Office for the Coordination of Humanitarian Affairs (OCHA): First, the principle of humanity means that 'human suffering must be addressed wherever it is found; the purpose of humanitarian action is to protect life and health and ensure respect for human beings'. Second, neutrality is taken to mean that those engaging in humanitarian work 'must not take sides in hostilities or engage in controversies of a political, racial, religious or ideological nature'. Third, impartiality requires that humanitarian action 'must be carried out on the basis of need, giving priority to the most urgent cases of distress and making no distinctions on the basis of nationality, race, gender, religious belief, class or political opinions'. And finally, operational independence requires that humanitarian action 'must be autonomous from the political, economic, military or other objectives that any actor may hold with regard to areas where humanitarian action is being implemented' (UN 2012). Thus 'humanitarianism' has typically come to be associated with the protection of human beings, especially during military conflict, and with responding to the needs of human beings following disasters. Indeed, it is most likely that the layperson would take the term to mean the activities carried out by humanitarian organizations like the Red Cross, particularly in terms of disaster relief. In essence, humanitarianism is about saving lives and alleviating existing suffering.

But if we are seeking to explain more fully what is meant by humanitarianism and humanitarian action, those descriptions are a starting point only, suggesting that humanitarianism is for the most part a reactive process, activated only when crises have already occurred, and marked by strict impartiality. Our present understanding of humanitarianism is broadening considerably, and it is clear that traditional applications – protection in war and responding to crises – are no longer the only goals and activities inherent in a humanitarian approach.[4] A new, more proactive, understanding has become evident, and it can be conceived of as 'humanitarian advocacy'. This broadened description sees humanitarianism take various concrete forms. Practical measures include publicizing pain and suffering, initiating legal agreements, lobbying governments to adopt particular courses of action or to comply with various treaties, and campaigning to prevent war and other calamities (rather than merely responding to them). These are all part of a broader involvement of varied actors in international relations, reflecting a more proactive and holistic approach to security, designed to prevent a crisis or other event which would cause widespread suffering and death. The most common labelling of groups advocating at the international level, is of course that given by Keck and Sikkink (1999), who explored the formation and evolution of what are called 'transnational advocacy networks'.

Essentially, humanitarian advocacy goes beyond what has been typically considered humanitarian work, which, by employing the practices of neutrality and impartiality, implicitly remained more or less *outside* the political process. Humanitarian advocacy brings into closer alignment political and humanitarian agendas. It respects impartiality but is not averse to politicization; indeed it is very deliberately a proactive process that seeks to engage political players: as Neil MacFarlane (2000: 5) suggests, 'the humanitarian imperative is best served not by avoiding the political process but by consciously engaging it'.

In line with this broadened view then, this book is concerned with how humanitarian advocacy, practised by states, civil society actors, and international organizations, came to outlaw the possession and use of nuclear weapons, and how it retained as its focus the need to protect human life and the environment. In this sense, what has been termed 'humanitarian arms control' takes the form of creating new international norms and limitations governing the practice of warfare and proscribing the use of specific weapons. Central to the process of adopting a humanitarian approach to arms control and disarmament, of course, is a recognition of the provisions of international humanitarian law as they apply to weapons, within the context of *jus in bello*. These include the principles of distinction protecting civilian populations, of proportionality and balancing the needs of military necessity with humanitarian considerations, and the requirement that armed attacks must avoid superfluous injury and unnecessary suffering.

This book's focus on humanitarianism in arms control is also driven by the fact that humanitarian action has had a significant effect on a number of international issues (including the landmines and cluster munitions conventions). In recognition of this new 'turn' towards humanitarianism, the United Nations Institute for Disarmament Research (UNIDIR) held a special conference in October 2000 on 'Disarmament as Humanitarian Action'. The conference developed a research project which aimed to 'reframe multilateral disarmament negotiation processes in humanitarian terms' and 'formulate practical proposals to apply humanitarian concepts to assist disarmament negotiators' (UN 2004; Borrie and Martin Randin 2006). This resulted in a number of publications explicitly linking the problem of restricting or eliminating weapons which raised humanitarian and human security concerns.

Structure of the book

This book is divided into four parts.

Part I, 'The dominance of nuclearism', examines the ways that nuclearism has been sustained in world politics, and the efforts made to dislodge it. Chapter 1 examines the traditional global nuclear order, whereby a process of nuclearism has driven an unchanging focus on nuclear weapons as essential for international security. This nuclearism has been characterized, I argue, by five key factors. Chapter 2 canvasses briefly the continuation of nuclearism today, primarily by looking at the current actions of the nuclear weapon states. Chapter 3 examines the attempts made since the end of the Cold War to reduce and eliminate nuclear weapons, to counter the sense of normality that nuclearism had created, by appealing to the nuclear weapon states to fulfil their disarmament obligations. The chapter looks at the meagre impact that these efforts have had.

Part II, 'The transition – from the Humanitarian Initiative to the prohibition treaty', explores the advent of the process of 'humanitarian arms control', which has come to influence the creation of the new nuclear prohibition treaty, the TPNW. Chapter 4 addresses the history of 'humanitarian arms control', and outlines the processes and actors involved especially in the landmines ban, suggesting that significant lessons from this period were applied to the case of nuclear weapons also. Chapter 5 explores the formation of the 2017 Treaty on the Prohibition of Nuclear Weapons and its key provisions.

Part III, 'Rejecting nuclearism', assesses how each of the elements of nuclearism explored in Part I has been challenged by the new treaty. Chapter 6 considers how the dominant discourse of security, and the lack of a humanitarian view – what I have called a 'humanitarian-free zone' – have been challenged and rejected by the new treaty. This chapter examines the way in which new actors and new processes allowed a wide range of voices into the nuclear debate, voices which are fundamentally different to those drawn from the traditional realms of the national security elite, and which are challenging government decisions and spending on nuclear weapons. Chapter 7 argues that the new treaty, in its challenge to the structures of the prevailing global nuclear order, constitutes an unambiguous rejection of nuclearism.

Part IV of this book, 'Ending nuclearism?' considers the extent and potential impact that the rejection of nuclearism is likely to have on the nuclear debate. Chapter 8 considers the problems the new treaty is likely to face, as well as its limitations; it suggests that overall, and despite these challenges, the treaty has already begun to change the dynamics of the global nuclear order. The book's Conclusion notes that while the treaty has rejected the long-entrenched elements of nuclearism, this alone may not be sufficient to achieve the elimination of nuclear weapons; it is, however, the best hope we have of moving in that direction.

Notes

1 There have of course been challenges to this order. India, perceiving the inequity of the NPT, refused to join, as did Pakistan. Israel refuses to confirm or deny that it possesses nuclear weapons, and North Korea withdrew from the NPT in

2003 and proceeded openly to develop its nuclear arsenal. These states remain firmly outside the NPT, and while they are therefore not seen as 'recognized' nuclear weapon states, their proliferation has nevertheless come to be seen as a *fait accompli*. They do not hold the kind of authority that the P5 states do in the NPT, but they nonetheless have become absorbed into the nuclear club. Certainly they are seen as part of the wider nuclear problem by those advocating the elimination of nuclear weapons. To complicate the unequal nature of this nuclear order further, the reaction shown by members of the P5 to nuclear proliferation has been inconsistent, and has at times violated the letter and the spirit of the NPT. After initial criticism of India's and Pakistan's nuclear tests, for example, the United States has gone on to support India's civil nuclear programme, in defiance of NPT rules. Israel's nuclear arsenal is tacitly accepted. But any suspected intent to proliferate on the part of 'pariah' states has brought opprobrium, sanctions, and even threats of military intervention.

2 This term was first used by Indian diplomat V. M. Trivedi in the late 1960s, in response to US–Soviet preparations for the NPT.
3 These five states dominate the picture of nuclear possession. The four additional states that also possess nuclear weapons, albeit in much smaller quantities than do the P5 states, but remain outside the NPT are: Israel, India, Pakistan, and North Korea. By late 2021, nuclear weapons were held by the following countries at these estimated numbers: Russia – 6,257; the United States – 5,550; France – 290; China – 350; Britain – 225; Pakistan – 165; India – 156; Israel – 90; North Korea – 40–50 (Arms Control Association 2022).
4 On the evolving nature of humanitarianism and its practice, see Barnett and Weiss (2008), Barnett (2005), Carpenter *et al.* (2014) and MacFarlane and Weiss (2000).

Part I

The dominance of nuclearism

1

Identifying the elements of nuclearism: the traditional framings that normalized nuclear weapons

For decades, nuclear weapons have been portrayed as essential to the security of the few states that possess them, and as an established and very normal part of national and international security. This has been the case, despite the fact that these weapons have not been used in warfare since 1945, and that there seems to have arisen a 'taboo' against their use (Tannenwald 1999). Notwithstanding this history of non-use, nuclear weapons came to be the hallmark weapon of the Cold War era, the instrument into which certain states placed their faith, their finances, and their technological endeavours, coming to rely on atomic weaponry as *the* key element of their military doctrines, their position in the world, and their national security. These states proceeded to roll out enormous programmes of acquisition and expansion, all the while persuading their publics that this was a normal and necessary way to achieve national security. Yet the construction and the success of this 'normality' has been a puzzling phenomenon; it is based on what I argue are highly problematic foundations, laid by a select few whose everyday repetition and rehearsing of particular discourses and practices constituted what was meant to be, simply, 'common sense'.

The term 'nuclearism' captures this broad and entrenched acceptance of nuclear weapons. But even as it has been an essential concept in modern history, the term nuclearism has not been particularly well-researched or well-defined at a scholarly level beyond the description given by its original framers (Lifton and Falk 1982). Most of us know instinctively what 'anti-nuclearism' is, but nuclearism, even as it has affected the entire nuclear age and shaped the global nuclear order, has remained a vague and largely unexplored concept within academia.

In the absence of detailed examinations of nuclearism, I have determined a set of elements which I argue go some way towards constituting what is meant by the rather sweeping notion of nuclearism. This chapter explores the elements that I believe have enabled and supported nuclearism over the past seventy-plus years, in order to distil certain beliefs, practices, and institutional arrangements which have been key to the longevity and success of nuclearism. The building of nuclearism can be seen as parallel to and intertwined with the creation of a nuclear hegemony, one that has allowed for the imposition of a particular global nuclear order. While the terms 'nuclearism' and the 'global nuclear order' are not synonymous, there is a commonality to them. I argue that the elements of nuclearism that I explore in this chapter have all been intrinsic components and reinforcements of what I call broadly the global nuclear order.[1] Later chapters will show how each of these elements has come to be challenged by the processes involved in creating the Treaty on the Prohibition of Nuclear Weapons as well as by the actual contents of this treaty. For now, this chapter focuses on how each of these elements has been allowed to flourish, and how they have been instrumental in entrenching a view of nuclear weapons as acceptable elements of international security, resistant – at least until recently – to serious challenge.

Nuclearism

At the height of the Cold War, in a landmark book entitled *Indefensible Weapons*, Robert Jay Lifton and Richard Falk used the term 'nuclearism' to explain what they saw as the 'psychological, political, and military dependence on nuclear weapons, the embrace of [these] weapons as a solution to a wide variety of human dilemmas, most ironically that of "security"' (1982: ix). As noted, although rarely examined in-depth, the term came to imply the complete faith in nuclear weapons as the primary means for achieving security.

For Lifton and Falk, there was a deep psychological, even mystical, character to nuclearism: they intuitively noted that the bomb was embraced as a new 'fundamental', and as a 'source of salvation'. More recently, Falk (2018) has stated that he applied the term nuclearism to what was the 'association between the hardware dimensions of the weaponry and their various software dimensions', with these latter ranging from the strategic doctrines of the nuclear states to the 'infatuations of powerful men with their awesome destructive capabilities'. While the term was used less often after the 1990s, it remained a useful shorthand for describing the peculiar attributes of the atomic age.[2]

The term nuclearism thus holds great potential for helping us to define what it was that kept so many in the thrall of nuclear weapons, what it was that allowed policy planners to accept the 'rationality' of a system of extreme destruction, and what constituted the day to day activities of such a state of being. Political, bureaucratic, technical, and social factors noted by Lifton and Falk all contributed to nuclearism, as of course did the real fear of threat from the enemy. But perhaps what was really important was that nuclearism was also the means by which nuclear weapons and plans for nuclear war-fighting came to be seen as natural, normal, and as the way the world simply had to be, at least for those states involved. For Falk (2018), nuclearism established 'the rationality of irrationality' and enabled the concept of mutually assured destruction as well as ever larger and ever more destructive nuclear arsenals.

Following Lifton and Falk, Bryan C. Taylor has added to our understanding of what nuclearism is: the result of 'a potent mixture of ideologies including bureaucracy, nationalism, religious fundamentalism, militarism, technological determinism, and instrumental rationality' (Taylor 2007: 677). Nuclearism created a sense of certainty for its advocates, with no room for any who might question or resist its imposition. For Raymond Williams (1980: 26), the bomb, 'as fact or slogan', has operated in culture and society 'as a static if terrible entity, provoking resignation, cynicism or despair'.

Broadly speaking then, nuclearism can be seen as the 'dependence' on nuclear weapons, the 'embrace' of these weapons as the answer to insecurity, the 'rationalization of the irrational', and as a self-reinforcing 'potent mix of ideologies'. But we should add an important factor here: nuclearism is also the *justification* for having these weapons and for maintaining the present global nuclear order. Nuclearism creates and perpetuates the 'need' for nuclear weapons, but its very dangers are seen as the reason why the status quo should continue.

A number of elements compounded the rise of nuclearism and made it difficult to dislodge the view of nuclear weapons as being normal, and essential, for national and international security. Krieger (2013) points to several developments which, at a broad level, help to explain why nuclear weapons were acquired and sustained, and why it has been so hard to shift entrenched views. On one hand we can see a level of complacency on the part of the general public, often with a resigned deference to authority, accompanied by a sense of powerlessness or marginalization – the view that an individual cannot do anything to challenge the unstoppable march of the nuclear age. On the other hand, there are the practices of elites, the secrecy that surrounds nuclear policy-makers, their unerring belief in the infallibility of technology, and their optimism that deterrence will inevitably work; this is what Krieger has called the 'tyranny of experts'. All these factors, and the state of nuclearism itself, have come to be co-constitutive, each reinforcing the other.

While it is interesting to explore further what nuclearism *is*, the purpose of this chapter is to draw out some of the key elements of practice and policy which have enabled nuclearism to develop in the first place, and which have kept it alive in all its vastness. From the broad range of factors noted above, it is possible to distil certain key elements that have helped to establish, reproduce, and reaffirm nuclearism. They may not be a comprehensive accounting of what has led to and sustained nuclearism over the decades, but they nonetheless seem to me to be most relevant.

These elements have for years enabled nuclear weapons to be seen as 'normal', almost 'conventional', 'natural', and beyond question.[3] They are interrelated, and are identified as follows: First is the language used to describe the role of nuclear weapons and the overall discourse that this has created over several decades. Second, and very closely related to the first point, is the suppression of humanitarian concerns about nuclear weapons, and the deliberate avoidance of acknowledging the implications of nuclear weapons' use. By holding off, for decades, any serious consideration of the humanitarian consequences of nuclear weapons' use, policy-makers have been able to present this option as something manageable, acceptable, and perhaps not greatly different from conventional warfare. A third element is the decision-making processes and the 'exclusivity' which has enabled national security elites to plan for nuclear war largely free from public oversight; this has served to limit involvement with, and knowledge about, nuclear issues, in essence denying any real democratic deliberation on the topic within the state, and generally insulating decision-makers from external questioning. A fourth element is the material costs devoted to nuclear weapons programmes; that is, the expenditure of enormous sums of money on nuclear projects, which has served to elevate the status of these weapons almost beyond question, and which has created patterns of government spending more or less impervious to change. The fifth element identified here is the way in which the P5 nuclear states have used the nuclear Non-Proliferation Treaty and its associated non-proliferation regime to ensure that the global nuclear order remains essentially static, always favouring themselves, the 'recognized' nuclear states, as the hegemons of this order.

Establishing the abnormal: a discourse of security, strategy, and rationality normalizes nuclear weapons

Since 1945, nine states have elevated the most lethal weapons ever created into ones considered essential for (their) security. This study focuses to a large extent, but not exclusively, on developments within the United States, because it is the national security elites and nuclear experts from that country who have, arguably, exercised the most influence in constructing the nuclear 'world' and the way that we think about it. This is not to suggest that the other nuclear weapon states, both within and outside the NPT, do not share in the creation of this overarching paradigm – merely that it has found its most dedicated builders among policy-makers, nuclear scientists, and strategic experts in the very first state to have developed, and the only state to have used, nuclear weapons. As Taylor *et al.* (2008) in their study of communicative processes in the US remind us, *how* individuals talk about nuclear weapons, or how they do not talk about nuclear weapons, have been important factors in creating the nuclear world understood by the United States and its Western allies, but also in turn by other nuclear weapon states.

When nuclear weapons have been discussed within politics and government, this has invariably been within strategic and technological contexts; rarely have they been assessed and debated – by states – within explicit humanitarian contexts, or within the broader contexts of morality, or even of utility and rationality, notwithstanding the privately held fears of individuals or constituents regarding them. Ideas about strategic necessity, parity, nuclear preponderance, 'prevailing' in, and even 'winning' a nuclear war,[4] have characterized much of the thinking and research in this field. As Ritchie (2013) and others have observed, the nuclear weapon states have exhibited a long-standing and deeply entrenched *valuing* of nuclear weapons, a traditional framing of nuclear arsenals which was, first and foremost, about 'security', strategy, deterrence, and war-fighting, but rarely about what the actual impact would be of any nuclear weapons' use.

Unsurprisingly, challenging the dominant discourse – built up over several decades – has been very difficult. A full history of how this discourse was constructed and how it continues to prevail – in some national security circles, at least – is extensive and complex, and only a brief overview can be presented in this chapter.[5] Nonetheless, this overview will help us to understand why it has been difficult, until now, to apply a humanitarian framework to the question of nuclear weapons, and will assist us in understanding the recent challenges to these traditional views as a serious contestation of prevailing policies.

What is meant here by the 'normalization' of nuclear weapons is the creation of that state of affairs where their possession came to be construed by their owners as 'natural', and almost without question. This involved cultivating a faith in nuclear weapons and presenting it to the layperson as an inevitable and essential part of national security, notwithstanding that these weapons are highly abnormal in terms of their destructive capability, and that their actual military utility is limited.[6] The paradox of nuclear weapons has been that they are always viewed with both 'faith and fear': at the same time that we see an overwhelming reliance on nuclear weapons for security, so too do these weapons invoke an existential sense of fear and dread (Ungar 1992).

To contextualize this concept of normalizing further, the words of Lewis Mumford are useful. He wrote in 1946 of the growth of the US nuclear weapons programme, the 'undeviating motions' which 'soberly, day after day', were conducted and which were 'so stereotyped, so commonplace, that they seem the normal motions of normal men, not the mass compulsions of people bent on total death'. This normalizing meant that even while living with the perpetual threat of impending destruction, we have kept, for the most part, what Mumford (1946: ix) called a 'glassy calm'.

Normalizing these weapons does not suggest that their enormous power was not recognized. It is rather that these bureaucratic and strategic everyday practices by the leaders and strategists of the nuclear states built a nuclear context that replicated itself easily, and strengthened its presence every day. Gamson (1987: 16) has written of a 'nuclear forgetting', where 'sustained governmental efforts' successfully softened atomic dangers, and where the impacts of a nuclear strike were invariably downplayed. Nuclear forgetting provided a sanctuary, where ordinary people could avoid confronting the reality of what would be entailed in a nuclear war (Ungar 1992: 5). For Boyer (1985), this 'forgetting' meant the deliberate suppression of fear and the diversion of attention away from the nuclear threat; this was the outcome of a contest in which state interests and national security came to eclipse the ever present but successfully submerged public fears of nuclear war. Ken Booth spoke of a 'nuclear amnesia' or an 'escape from memory' (1999: 12) which seems to have affected the broader public, whose perception of the likelihood of nuclear war is that it is improbable. (In a somewhat different approach, strategists like Herman Kahn (1962) openly acknowledged the horrors that nuclear war would bring, but argued that the United States nevertheless would be able to absorb the deaths of tens of millions of people, and still emerge victorious.) Thus, normalizing is seen here as the amelioration or even defusing of nuclear anxieties and the implicit conferring of a sense of everyday legitimacy (Ungar 1992: 9; Hanson 2018) onto the 'fact' of nuclear strategy.

This does not mean that the 'normal' nature of nuclear weapons was never challenged.[7] From the early periods of the nuclear age, peace and disarmament activists, groups of scientists and public intellectuals – notably of course Lifton and Falk (1982) – have questioned the assumptions behind the acquisition and retention of such arsenals on a number of grounds, especially moral.[8] But this had not resulted in any serious challenge to the dominance of a belief which continued to privilege an ontological acceptance of weapons which might be considered, under other circumstances, abhorrent and unacceptable. Opposing views were often considered 'radical', 'leftist', or unpatriotic, and in any case, these actors wielded little power over government policies. (Moreover, much of the opposition there was against nuclear weapons for many decades did not emerge formally from *states* or groups of states. In this sense, the formal campaign – by a large number of states – to make nuclear weapons illegal is what makes the current development all the more remarkable.)

Crucial to this persistence of nuclearism from the 1950s onwards, and after the Cold War also, was the creation of the language and dominant discourse which allowed daily planning for what was termed the 'unthinkable' (Kahn 1962, 1984), the use of nuclear weapons against not just the leaders and armies of an enemy state but also against – and indeed *primarily* against – its people and cities. That one's security was now inevitably tied up with nuclear weapons, and that nuclear weapons were henceforth seen as essential for national security, was built into a discourse that saw such weaponry elevated to new heights. Constructing this security discourse not only made the use of nuclear weapons 'more or less thinkable'; they also, as Borrie *et al.* (2016) remind us, 'empowered particular interlocutors'.

The building of this particular discourse presents us with a series of first-order questions: how is it that the meanings and practices associated with nuclear weapons allowed the 'ordinariness' of a system which under a different perspective might have produced different results? How did nuclear weapons come to be embraced as central pillars in the security doctrines of certain states (even as there was a parallel and growing norm of non-use, and even a 'taboo' status, demonstrated by the fact that at the same time that their presumed use was deeply enshrined in the doctrine of nuclear deterrence, their actual use was held to be undesirable)? In other words, thinking and planning for the allegedly unthinkable was all too common, and even the growth of a norm of non-use was never enough to produce an outright rejection of what had become, in fact, quite thinkable.

Part of the answer to these questions lies in an analysis of how nuclear threats and responses were constructed and how strategic calculations were made, almost totally disconnected from the realities of political and social life and the effects of nuclear weapons on the human body. The discourse surrounding nuclear weapons' acquisition and policy was removed from considerations of humanitarianism, of participatory democracy, and of the optimal allocation of national resources. This occurred at the same time that we were witnessing what Weart (2012) called 'the rise of nuclear fear', where publics became generally aware of the dangers but where this fear did little to inhibit deterrence policies and nuclear war-planning. The development of what has been called 'nukespeak' enabled a distortion of the debate on nuclear weapons, using jargon, metaphor, and euphemism to deflect attention away from the reality of horrific injury and death (Hilgartner *et al.* 1982). Discussions revolved around strategy and military security. Bryan C. Taylor observes that the language of nukespeak was designed to suggest 'mastery and control', by glossing over contradictions, 'by normalizing the presence and use of nuclear weapons, by obscuring attribution of agency (and thus accountability) ... and by inhibiting ethical reflection about consequences' (Taylor 2007: 677). This successful construction of a set of beliefs and practices, talked about often in abstract and unemotional language, allowed nuclear doctrines to flourish, insulated against meaningful external scrutiny and assessment, and permitting its adherents to intensify and replicate their own dominant discourse and practices. For Ken Booth (1979), strategic analysis, at least during the Cold War, was 'ethnocentrism writ large'.

One of the most compelling observations of this development was provided by Carol Cohn in 1987, and although hers is a well-known and oft-quoted account, it is nevertheless worth recalling here. Describing how an assumed language and patterns of belief constructed a legitimacy around nuclear weapons among 'defense intellectuals' in the United States during the Cold War, Cohn stated that she was 'gripped by the extraordinary language used to discuss nuclear war'. She noted 'the elaborate use of abstraction and euphemism, of words so bland that they never forced the speaker or enabled the listener to touch the realities of nuclear holocaust that lay behind the words' (Cohn 1987: 690).

This language was the core of a nuclearism which informed and legitimized nuclear strategic practice in the United States (Cohn 1987: 688). It was not only self-evident to its creators, but was also unexamined and unquestioned within the confines of strategic planning. As someone closely involved in US nuclear war planning, General Lee Butler later drew attention to the extent to which a 'nuclear priesthood' continued to determine the most fundamental decisions over life and death, with little heed to the human costs of such policies (Butler 2000). Indeed the 'technostrategic language' that was used was done so as 'to articulate the perspective of the users of nuclear weapons', but never that of the victims' (Cohn 1987: 786). Cohn *et al.* (2005: 5) observed that defence personnel neglected 'the emotional, the concrete, the particular, human bodies and their vulnerability, human lives and their subjectivity'. Paul Chilton has also observed of nukespeak that it rendered nuclear weapons sanitized and almost beyond human control:

> The wide use of abstractions, technical jargon, acronyms, metaphors, playful euphemisms, meaning-laden weapons names and titles, and the wide use of passive voice, has been likened to a form of propaganda that makes nuclear weapons more acceptable, thus acculturating a society to their presence while linguistically domesticating their dangers. (Chilton 1982)

This linguistic taming of the dangers of nuclear weapons, complete with its opaque machinations and its extensive jargon, was perfectly at home within the academic stream of 'strategic studies'. Long critical of the way that this had developed during the Cold War, Ken Booth argued forcefully that:

> nuclearism had its sacred texts and high priests; nuclear deterrence had become a dogma, proclaimed as true by its exponents; alternative ways of thinking

were silenced as far as possible by indoctrination, socialisation, loyalty tests and exclusion; critics were cast as heretics or the 'useful idiots' of the communist devil; and Strategic Studies in general and nuclear deterrence theory in particular was believed to be a faith to be embraced, not a politics to be contested. (Booth 1999: 44–45)

Confronting or oppositional discourse on the role of nuclear weapons was seen not only as uninformed, but also as disruptive to national security. Challenges to the role of nuclear weapons were not taken seriously, and in any case were always disadvantaged by the prevailing discourse which claimed a monopoly over knowledge and technical expertise, reinforced by jargon, formulations, and acronyms.

The core practice that this discourse served to protect was, of course, the idea of nuclear deterrence, the threat to use nuclear weapons against an adversary to dissuade that adversary from taking any undesired action, and especially to deter it from attacking one's own state and allies.[9] Deterrence rested on a delicate psychological balance and if it failed, would bring unparalleled disaster not only to the states concerned, but likely also to the wider world. Deterrence required, if it was going to be effective, clear communication between adversaries, a capacity to inflict the damage promised – that is, the actual nuclear weapon capability – and the credibility that indeed such punishment would be undertaken. It also required that each state was to remain vulnerable to attack from the other, if strategic 'stability' was to be maintained. Rarely did we see leaders and war-planners talk about the carnage and destruction that such an attack would bring; instead, the concept of deterrence was held up as the primary means by which this could be averted, even as it promised to deliver such a fate to millions if it failed.

There remains no clear consensus among practitioners or scholars about the usefulness, workability, or moral standing of the policy of nuclear deterrence during the Cold War. Whether it was the determining factor that prevented war between the great powers, or whether it was ever truly reliable as a strategy, remain contentious questions.[10] Nonetheless, the concept and practice of nuclear deterrence became institutionalized by strategists who shaped it as a logical, workable, and reliable procedure, complete with its language of 'delivering' nuclear strikes, 'maintaining' strategic parity, 'prevailing' in a nuclear war, and other neutral terms. This was not, of course, only the American experience: implicit in the programmes of all the nuclear weapon states was a persistence of the belief that their arsenals were rational and necessary, that they could and would deter the use of others' nuclear weapons against them, and also prevent conventional weapon attacks. In sum, nuclear weapons were seen only within the prism of strategic requirements.

Enabling the abnormal: the disregard of humanitarianism

That the leaders and strategists of the nuclear-armed states successfully avoided any humanitarian framing from being applied to their nuclear weapons, effectively turned the arena of nuclear policy-making into what I term a 'humanitarian-free zone'.[11] Nuclear weapons rely for their effectiveness on the promise of widespread civilian destruction, yet explicit humanitarian considerations played no part among states in determining the possession, deployment, or potential use of these weapons.[12]

There had been an awareness that the use of nuclear weapons was transgressing a moral code, even though widespread conventional bombing of civilians had been the hallmark of the Second World War. Using nuclear weapons implied that the legal principles restricting warfare would be more explicitly rejected, especially those requiring discrimination between civilians and combatants, those of proportionality, and those against weapons causing excessive injury and unnecessary suffering.[13] But for over seventy years, this disquiet was unable to be translated into a formal legal prohibition of the possession or use of these weapons. Opponents of nuclear weapons had long sought to publicize the profoundly disturbing humanitarian implications of nuclear weapons. While at a general level, members of the public were aware of the horrors of nuclear weapons' use through the Hiroshima and Nagasaki bombings, and also through the impacts of nuclear weapons-testing,[14] this was never able to be articulated forcefully in an explicit way and at a widespread level.[15] As one organization has observed, rather than being prohibited and eliminated, nuclear weapons have been 'protected—with great tenacity. It is as if they have been granted immunity from basic moral values and ethical practices' (PAX 2016b). It suited governments of the nuclear weapon states not to encourage any close examination of the consequences of nuclear weapons' use. This was so despite the fact that the fundamental tenets of international humanitarian law were sure to be breached with any use of nuclear weapons. Not only was there an absence at the state level of discussion of the humanitarian consequences of a nuclear strike, there was also little consideration given to what would be the unprecedented realities that would have to be faced by domestic and international communities in the event of any such strike.[16] The details of how to provide effective assistance, and how to address radioactive spread, for example, were absent.

It can be argued of course that most instances of warfare have violated international humanitarian law, and that the twentieth century saw the rapid rise of civilian deaths in warfare, relative to the number of combatants killed. Very rarely have we seen a clear regard for the upholding of the fundamental principles of the laws of war. But there are two important points to note here. The first is that nuclear weapons, by their very nature (remembering that today they are invariably much more powerful than the bomb dropped on Hiroshima) constitute a qualitatively different capacity for human destruction, when compared against conventional weapons and conventional warfare. The second point is that notwithstanding violations of humanitarian law in the past, we are seeing expectations that warfare must now abide by these guidelines (Solis 2016). That is, even where war is deemed to be legitimate, it is not the case that protagonists have recourse to unlimited ways of fighting. Civilian deaths, in particular, are increasingly being seen as regrettable and states are (at least sometimes) being held accountable – even if they are not always able to be prosecuted – for civilian deaths caused as a result of warfare. While the current conflicts in Iraq, Syria, Yemen, Ukraine, and elsewhere would suggest that states continue, brutally, to violate humanitarian law with impunity, there has nonetheless been a stronger than ever focus on the need to avoid civilian casualties.[17] Nuclear weapons have long been seen – by civil society actors at least – as a serious contravention of international humanitarian law. In terms of their targeting indiscriminately both civilians and combatants, their disproportionality as weapons of attack or revenge, and the undisputed level of human suffering they would cause, arguments against their use are not difficult to make. It is also telling that proponents of their use, or at least the threat of their use, have not sought to defend their views against the laws of war, citing instead reasons more aligned with alleged strategic necessity.

Given that nuclear weapons were used by the United States in 1945 in the war with Japan, and that the USSR acquired its nuclear capability in 1949, it is unsurprising that America would not concede that nuclear weapons should be proscribed on humanitarian grounds in the early stages of the nuclear era. The use of American nuclear weapons was presented as 'evidence' of hastening the end of the war in the Pacific – regardless of the accuracy of this assertion (Alperovitz 1996; Wilson 2007, 2014) – and this allowed them to be incorporated into strategic doctrines as essential elements of US, and later of other states', security. This was despite the fact that, if used again – and particularly given the vast destructive power that newer bombs would deliver – the effects of these weapons were likely to be 'far beyond what most people would consider acceptable' (Article 36 2013a). Analysts have applied the perspective of genocide studies to the question of nuclear weapons, with Robert Jay Lifton and Eric Markusen (1990) likening policies of nuclear deterrence to what they term a 'genocidal mentality'.[18] These scholars believed that many of the elements which facilitated involvement in mass killing projects – that is, 'the role of ideology, dehumanization, euphemistic language, professional socialization, inter-organizational rivalries' – can be found in the field of national security nuclear weapons policies also (Maguire 2007a: 355).

Various scholars had, of course, addressed the issue of nuclear ethics and international law.[19] Drawing on the work of prominent ethicist and Catholic priest J. Bryan Hehir, who had written of the 'exile' of an ethical analysis of nuclear strategy in government, Doyle (2010: 287) reiterated Hehir's claim that 'the price of error on this issue' would be 'catastrophic', and urged the adoption of clear moral perspectives in strategic planning. An 'exile' of ethics presumed that such a thing existed substantially in the first place, but it is hard to see where this was evident in US policy after 1945, or in Soviet policy after 1949. Nuclear weapons posed a unique threat, a view expressed well by Australian Foreign Minister Gareth Evans in his testimony to the International Court of Justice, when that body was deliberating the legality of nuclear weapons:

> The fact remains that the existence of nuclear weapons as a class of weapons threatens the whole of civilization. This is not the case with respect to any class or classes of conventional weapons. It cannot be consistent with humanity to permit the existence of a weapon which threatens the very survival of humanity. (Evans 1995)

If humanity was to be held hostage to the security requirements of a handful of states, then we would expect that this construction would have been examined, challenged, and rejected. Yet the practitioners of the nuclear age have remained largely insulated from any meaningful scrutiny on humanitarian and ethical grounds, and nuclear planning has been able to continue relatively unchallenged. While this was a result also of inertia and complacency on the part of many citizens, it enabled the threat of such destruction to become ordinary and incorporated into everyday life.

Imposing the abnormal: exclusivist voices in decision-making

A third factor examined here is how nuclear policy and war planning came to dominate strategic thinking, driven by an elite group which remained largely beyond the influence and control of the broader population. This has certainly been true in non-democratic states such as the USSR and China, and in contemporary North Korea, where political decisions were always divorced from public involvement, and is evident also in the quasi-democratic or authoritarian states of Russia, India, and Pakistan. But this practice was also implicit and entrenched in the nuclear weapon programmes of democratic, Western states, raising profound questions about the nature of civil–state relations and the constitutional requirements of participatory democracy when it comes to life and death issues such as nuclear war. Lifton and Falk (1982) were early observers that nuclearism was only made possible by decision-makers departing from the democratic process.

The world of defence planning brought with it its own legitimacy and authority, a self-reinforcing system that kept the control of weapons of massive destruction firmly in the hands of a select group of individuals wedded to the status quo. Once embarked on the drive for such arsenals, the leaders and national security elites of these states were not likely to question, let alone renounce, the 'natural' strategic choices that they had made. Benoit Pelopidas has observed that not only did these men occupy 'a privileged place' in the nuclear debate; their self-arrogated authority and legitimacy also had, and continues to have, important political effects: first, by providing largely unquestionable assessments of past policies, and second by foreclosing the possibility of political innovation or any reorientation of security needs (Pelopidas 2011: 297).

In Western democracies, almost everyone, except a small group of 'experts', has deliberately been kept away from having any input into nuclear decision-making, and this has been done ostensibly on the grounds of maintaining national security (Benedict 2011). Fred Kaplan, whose seminal work on 'the small group of men who have devised the plans and shaped the policies', has described those who informed US nuclear policies in the 1950s as 'the strategists in power', the 'wizards of Armageddon', who occupy a secret world (1983: 390). And while we might expect to find several studies on this important issue, it becomes clear that civilian control and democratic accountability of nuclear weapons is in fact a domain which has been and continues to be relatively neglected (Born 2006; see also Born *et al.* 2010).

Essentially, small groups of individuals had and continue to have the ability to shape the decision to inflict unparalleled destruction not just on their adversary, but, via the logic of deterrence, on their own populations, and potentially on other parts of the world. Within nuclear weapon states, it is only a minute proportion of the population which formulates nuclear policy, and there are fewer still entitled to make the decision actually to use nuclear weapons. Not only is this group of individuals proportionally tiny within the population of each of the nuclear states, but the number of nuclear states is also small, globally: this nuclear coterie is made up of only nine out of some 193 states, reinforcing this sense of un-representation.[20] This does not sit well with notions of democracy, transparency, and accountability.

Decisions about nuclear weapons have been taken in closed circumstances, with few effective review processes available for public scrutiny. (This is changing, to a small extent, in the United States and Britain, where debates on renewal and modernization of weapons is undergoing some parliamentary and congressional review, but public regulation has not been the norm, and it was not present when individuals made the decisions that their states would acquire nuclear weapons in the first place.) It is curious that such exclusivist decision-making came to be accepted as compatible with liberal democratic practices, at the same time that it limited public input and oversight and denied any real accountability to those citizens whom nuclear deterrence was designed to 'protect'. Profound existential decisions were left to a select group of individuals whose world was largely closed to criticism and who operated with little or no obligation to justify their doctrines and strategies to the broader community. Essentially, citizens have been encouraged to leave vital issues about life and death to the select few entrusted with these tasks. As Becker *et al.* (2008: 810) remind us, 'nuclear weapons are the most powerful means of warfare', and as such they 'present a crucial field for inquiring into the relationship between democracy, arms, and arms control'. Yet these fundamental questions are not put by governments to the broader public.

At best, we see a default position which – in the West at least, with circumstances far worse in the non-democracies – allowed something like a system of 'stewardship' to manage and determine vital security policies. Critics argue, however, that instead of a well-functioning stewardship, where a range of specialists with appropriate knowledge and wisdom are entrusted with such decisions and are cognizant of and responsive to broader public opinion, we have seen instead the evolution of something like a 'nuclear despotism' (Deudney 2007). In the early 1980s, Richard Falk warned that political leaders in the United States had repeatedly failed to consult with, or even to disclose to the public 'the occasions on which the use of nuclear weapons was seriously contemplated' (Falk 1982a: 3). We know today that there were several instances when this occurred (Lewis *et al.* 2014).

Commenting on these nuclear decision-makers, Kennette Benedict observed that:

> this special class of people is being given sole responsibility for deciding whether or not to kill millions and destroy vast areas of the planet by firing nuclear weapons – without any participation by the people who paid for the weapons with their taxes or by those who voted for the leaders who give the final orders. This is not delegation of authority … this is alienation from authority. Once citizens no longer feel qualified to participate in decisions about their very survival, the connection between the governing and the governed is severed. It is hard to see where the democracy is in this. (Benedict 2012)

There are surely questions to be asked about how governments – or more likely, just a few individuals within a government – are able to deliberate on issues of such enormity and reach the conclusions that they do, allowing nuclear war-planning to take place in a remote world where ordinary citizens hold little sway. Robert Dahl argued in 1985 that when it comes to nuclear weapons, 'we have in fact turned over to a small group of people decisions of incalculable importance to ourselves and mankind, and it is very far from clear how, if at all, we could recapture a control that in fact we have never had' (1985: 6–7). Democratic deliberation was excluded even though the threat posed by nuclear weapons would, one might expect, demand much more from leaders in terms of consultation, legitimization, and accountability. The nuclear elite responsible for forging plans that promised annihilation was arguably afforded more secrecy than any other decision-making branch of government, at the same time that it was given a free hand in developing plans which, if they were implemented, could mean the end of the state itself.

Daniel Deudney takes this argument further with his focus on state leaders, suggesting that all the nuclear weapon states, regardless of their constitutional provisions, have become 'nuclear monarchies', where such decisions seem to have been placed into the hands of one individual, an 'absolute monarch' (Deudney 2007: 255–256). This is certainly true in the United States where the president can launch nuclear warheads without consulting Congress or indeed any individual or branch of government (Perry and Collina 2020). Deudney (2007: 255–256) suggests that the need to make decisions quickly, and the fact that these decisions are often in the hands of one individual, results in a despotism prone to fallibility and corruptibility. Similarly, Elaine Scarry warns about a 'thermonuclear monarchy', one that violates the US Constitution and the broader social contract: 'Millions of people reside at the receiving end of the injury; only a handful of people reside at the end where injury is authorised: the voices of millions – both foreign and domestic – are excluded' (Scarry 2014: 13–14).[21] In a compelling essay, Bryan C. Taylor argues that, besides posing other critical issues, nuclear weapons 'embody technological autonomy and institutional indifference to democratic deliberation' (Taylor 2007: 667). Drawing on the work of a number of other observers, he concludes that the 'oppressive conditions' surrounding the development of nuclear weapons 'subvert the capabilities of citizens to acquire, deliberate, and act on information concerning nuclear policy'. The end result of this is that the public is

> fragmented, alienated, uninformed, and unable to participate in deliberation with forceful and reasoned discourse. Commonly listed elements in this indictment include: an official regime of secrecy which suppresses and distorts nuclear information; official cultivation of a climate of permanent emergency that promotes public inertia and acquiescence to authoritarian rule; undue deference by nominal agents of congressional oversight to the interests of military elites and corporate defense contractors; a timid and amnesiac news media; and official demonization of anti-nuclear dissent as extreme, irrelevant, and unpatriotic. (Taylor 2007: 671–672)

A common argument is that the wider public cannot, and should not, be privy to the details of security threats or knowledgeable enough to determine how such threats should be addressed. Public input into security and defence decisions, even in democracies, has always been limited, and the 'high politics' of national security is understood to be one largely controlled by a select group of individuals bestowed with the authority to make decisions on behalf of the state. This seems to be an accepted area of governance where citizen input has not been integrated into decision-making, except at a fairly nominal level via public consultative committees or by parliamentary bodies. It might also be argued that nuclear decision-making requires even greater levels of secrecy, and less transparency, than do other areas of national security.

There is some merit to the argument that the public has given decision-making privileges to those elected (in democratic societies, at least) to provide security for the state, and that they cannot therefore expect a place at the table where important decisions about nuclear policy are made. But unfortunately, the degree of public exclusion is most pronounced in the realm where high-stakes life and death decisions are at their most profound, and where, arguably, there should be extensive deliberation rather than minority control. The public generally lacks access to information and a detailed knowledge of these issues. And as Taylor notes, the very presence of secrecy in the nuclear realm itself 'limits public knowledge of nuclear matters'; in turn, this limitation is 'used to justify excluding an "uninformed" public from subsequent deliberation' (Taylor 2007: 673). These arrangements enable and replicate patterns of exclusivity within decision-making and heighten the element of 'mystery' surrounding all things nuclear. Born (2006: 28) has observed that while democratic oversight is denied on the basis of confidentiality, complexity, and time pressures, 'not all decisions are taken under acute time pressures, require highly specialist nuclear weapons knowledge or other military insight'. Moreover, nuclear procurement and deployment decisions have other implications also, namely 'financial, moral and environmental consequences', making it essential that a system of democratic accountability is put in place (Born 2006: 28). What has happened, however, is that nuclear issues have remained 'highly sequestered' from external scrutiny, and demands for more consultation, legitimacy, and accountability have invariably been discounted or suppressed (Rojecki 1999: 12). Examining what he calls the evolution of the 'national security state', forged by what he identifies as strong elements of 'secrecy, centralization, repression and distortion', Hudson (2004) has suggested numerous ways in which various American administrations have used the 'instrumentalities of secrecy' to hold off any serious attempts at penetration of the closed circles making foreign policy and security decisions. For some

Identifying the elements of nuclearism 27

(e.g. Taylor 2007: 676) this is an 'illegitimate stranglehold' on what should be a robust public deliberation, enabled in part by nuclear weapon states maintaining unreasonable and persistent 'threat exaggerations'.

The way that initial decisions were taken by states to acquire nuclear weapons is especially problematic. Simpson and Nielsen (2010), for instance, note that Britain's choice to develop nuclear weapons was made by 'a small group of key cabinet members in private' and that subsequent British governments have continued to take most nuclear decisions this way (see also Maguire 2007b).[22] The very first decision to use a nuclear weapon – against Hiroshima – was apparently decided by the US president without any formal approval or recommendation from the Joint Chiefs of Staff (Alperovitz 1996: 322). Even allowing for the fact that some secrecy might be necessary for security purposes, it is hard to escape the conclusion that such processes and the way they have continued are designed chiefly to inhibit public scrutiny. The Manhattan Project, resulting from a wartime climate of urgency, was presented to the American public as 'a *fait accompli*, rather than as a potential innovation requiring collective authorization of its development' (Taylor 2007: 673); covert planning during wartime has simply continued as secrecy forever. While there is some British parliamentary and US congressional oversight of nuclear issues, there is little real political questioning of nuclear policy or of the decision to become a nuclear weapons state; still less debate is offered to civilians. Speaking of Britain's Trident programme, Nick Ritchie (2006) concludes that this justification of limited debate 'is often used to render decisions about Britain's nuclear future unaccountable', if not to Parliament then to the British public at large.[23] Indeed, as Eric Schlosser (2013b) notes, Britain has never had a 'full, vigorous debate about its nuclear weapons'; neither, for that matter, have any of the other nuclear weapon states.

Another concern is that the scale and destructive power of nuclear weapons remain evident long after the Cold War ended, fostered and driven by national security elites and weapons manufacturing corporations. Not only did military planning remain unassailable, but the destructiveness of nuclear forces grew substantially.[24] Lynn Eden observes, for example, that 'the lethality of the US missile force increased more than three times from 1985 to 1990', as the Cold War was ending; it continued to rise, peaking in 2002, more than twelve years after the USSR had collapsed (Eden 2011: 73). Eden also shows that while the United States in 2009 possessed around the same number of deployed warheads that it did in 1969, the lethality of this force, some twenty years after the Cold War ended, 'was more than seven times greater' than that of its 1961 arsenal (Eden 2011: 73). All of this suggests a massive and unreasonable capacity for overkill, which was arguably illogical during the Cold War but which continued to be viewed as not just logical but also essential, regardless of its suitability for meeting recognized threats or for addressing changed circumstances once the superpower confrontation had ended.

Anthony Burke points to the illogical nature of nuclear war-planning, arguing that we must 'acknowledge the fundamental impossibility of nuclear strategy as a system of reason: one that has never been able to connect nuclear means and security ends in a way that is either viable or legitimate' (Burke 2009). Again, this illogicality and lack of legitimacy does not seem compatible with norms of democratic deliberation or indeed of a normal and reasonable political process. That such practices continue more than thirty years after the Cold War ended confirms the essentially closed nature of defence planning when it comes to nuclear weapons. This internal logic put in place doctrines and programmes which then took on a life of their own, impenetrable to ideas of sufficiency or reasonableness. As Eden notes, 'the logic of nuclear war planning sets the terms by which threat is understood' rather than the other way round (Eden 2011: 81), whereas a sober assessment of current threats should result in a more rational calculation of defence requirements.

Governments were skilful in keeping nuclear decision-making isolated from public oversight at the same time that they threatened (and, perversely, invited) destruction through their policies of nuclear deterrence. Ken Booth has pointed to the cumulative and disturbing effects of this arrangement: nuclear policies undermined democracy because of the unprecedented secrecy that these brought, but there was a disturbing psychological cost also: nuclearism takes a toll on human culture because it conditions us to the idea that 'national security can only ultimately rest on genocidal threats' (Booth 1999: 21). In other words, not only were – and are – democratic values and institutions at risk by the insulation of decision-making elites from public oversight, but rendering as 'normal' the securing of one's interests largely at the expense of mass slaughter of others itself erodes liberal principles, and institutionalizes a nihilistic, zero-sum security outlook. While in various ways and to differing extents this has always been the case with war, it becomes profoundly more problematic when we are contemplating nuclear warfare.

Once nuclear weapons were acquired by the nuclear states, they soon became central to the security doctrines of their owners and came to dominate strategic thinking and international affairs in a way that no other weapon has ever done. But never before could so much destruction be promised by so few individuals, and done so within the most restricted confines of what was called 'strategic planning'. Nuclear war-planning from the 1950s onwards was remarkable in that it brought with it a promise of widespread destruction on a scale never seen before in history. The Cold

War was synonymous with the ever-present threat of nuclear war, and the analyses and calculations of nuclear planners was conducted against a backdrop of the massive upward spiral in the numbers of nuclear weapons. Even as the number of weapons has dropped since the Cold War ended, such planning continues, and remains confined to select groups of policy elites.

Reinforcing the abnormal: material spending

A fourth and related factor noted here is how the expenditure of public money on the nuclear project has over several decades helped to consolidate and reify a view of nuclear weapons as normal, rational, and essential. The allocation of a high level of material resources seems to have conferred a sense of legitimacy and necessity onto these programmes, creating a pattern of government behaviour which is difficult to challenge, and which became in time self-reinforcing. No matter whether a state's nuclear policies might be illogical, devoting vast sums to these weapons endowed them with an aura of untouchability and framed them as highly 'special' possessions.

The sums of money allocated to nuclear arsenals represented an extraordinary level of spending, often approved with minimal oversight or questioning regarding the value and benefits that it would bring. Maintaining nuclear weapon programmes required the commitment of budgets that were passed relatively easily and which escalated in line with the vertical proliferation of nuclear weapons over the decades of the Cold War. These budgets were largely uncontested in circumstances which saw nuclear weapons as the essential response to security threats, notwithstanding that these weapons were of limited utility against most threats, even during the Cold War. The more that was spent on building up, modernizing, and maintaining nuclear weapons, the less it seemed possible to challenge such spending or to query the very projects for which these resources were destined.

Notable here too, specifically within the United States, was the close association between weapons manufacturing corporations, scientific and technical laboratories, and the branches of government responsible for national defence, where continuing research and development, and the monetary rewards that these brought, required the perpetuation of a particular strategic culture demanding a growing revenue. Hans Kristensen notes that military and defence contractors 'have largely succeeded in preventing significant changes to the nuclear force structure' (2015: 574). Here we certainly *have* seen the involvement of civilians in nuclear issues, but these have been drawn from a narrow section of society, one which had a clear financial interest in sustaining high levels of spending on military programmes and nuclear research laboratories, thus adding to the overall 'exclusivity' of nuclear decision-making. Kevin Martin and Jay Coghlan point out that research laboratories and production facilities 'have long enjoyed a privileged existence, thanks to powerful supporters in Congress, presidential administrations, and weapons corporations', and that those involved in this have not been required to account for how funds are spent or programmes are run (Martin and Coghlan 2013).

Additionally, at least in the United States, many politicians and Pentagon staff take up lucrative positions in the defence industry after leaving office, leading to what is called the 'revolving doors' syndrome. Attempts to restrict the ability of former staffers from profiting in roles with defence contractors were evident at least as early as the Carter Administration (Wilson 1977; Proxmire 1985), but the Proxmire Law, which sought to impose a two-year waiting list on former officials joining defence contractors, was largely ineffective, and in any case was repealed in 1996. That persons from a restricted elite which makes decisions about nuclear weapons policy should be the same persons who advocate for vastly expensive nuclear projects is disconcerting. As William Hudson notes:

> The congressional clout of the defense industry has continued in the post-Cold War period, as it has campaigned vociferously for policies that expand arms sales. Industry lobbying has been very effective in getting Congress to fund weapons programs, *even those the Pentagon does not want* ... this power has been used to bias public policy in favor of large levels of defense expenditure. (Hudson 2004; emphasis added)

This favouring of expensive weapon systems, regardless of their suitability, is especially evident in the realm of nuclear weapons. Twenty-five years after the end of the Cold War, the United States continued to spend more on its nuclear weapons programmes than it ever did (Rinna 2015). While there are different views on what counts as nuclear weapons spending (see Cohn and Rumbaugh 2012), there is general agreement that these figures have nevertheless been extremely high. A useful, if conservatively estimated, statistic to remember is that in the first decade of this century, the nine nuclear weapon states spent an amount of approximately US$105 billion, annually, on their nuclear weapon programmes (Global Zero 2011; Archer *et al.* 2016). For its part, NATO spending on ensuring the security of US tactical nuclear weapons deployed in Europe has doubled: since 2000, US$80 million has been spent in shoring up the storage sites housing these weapons, but a further US$154 million was requested from the 2015 Pentagon budget for additional upgrading (Kristensen 2014).

By far, it is the United States which spends the most on its defence and nuclear weapons. One study calculates that the United States spent at least US$5.5 trillion on its nuclear weapons programmes between 1942 and 1996 (Schwartz and Choubey 2009). Others have put this figure higher, revising it to US$7.5 trillion (Krieger 2011). A Stimson Center Report (Cohn and Rumbaugh 2012) in June 2012, which focused on US strategic nuclear forces only, estimated that at least US$390 billion would be spent over the subsequent decade, with this rising steeply if taking into account all US spending on nuclear weapons, strategic and tactical. Indeed, the Report carried the strong message that, if anything, there has been a substantial understatement of the actual costs the United States has incurred. It has been estimated that over the next three decades the United States will spend over one trillion dollars to maintain and upgrade its current nuclear arsenal and to purchase replacement systems (Reif 2018a). Plans for upgrading – what John Mecklin (2015: 59) has called the 'modernization tide' – are forecast to continue for at least the next thirty years and reinforce a solid faith in nuclear 'solutions'.

There are also the opportunity costs associated with nuclear weapons spending, especially in light of the Global Financial Crisis in the first decade of this century. As one study surveying spending by all nine nuclear weapon states has noted:

> Against the backdrop of increasing budgetary austerity and widespread cuts in health and social spending, such allocations for weapon systems appear not only exorbitant, but also counter to the economic and social needs of the nuclear-armed States. In order to spend such large budgets on nuclear weapons, they are forced to reduce the budgets in other areas such as health, education, environmental protection and welfare. (Archer *et al.* 2016)

These opportunity costs are all the more significant for the poorer nuclear states, India, Pakistan, and North Korea, where intense poverty and famine are frequently encountered. Zulfikar Ali Bhutto, the architect of Pakistan's atomic programme, asserted that 'if India builds the bomb, we will eat grass, even go hungry, but we will get one of our own' (cited in Archer *et al.* 2016, see also Cramer 2009).

Bloated nuclear weapons budgets also have a negative impact at a global level. The staggering amounts allocated to these programmes could easily fund domestic and international social, environmental, and economic problems. It is a statement of the obvious to say that even a small portion of the roughly US$70–80 billion spent each year on nuclear weapons[25] would go a long way towards implementing the United Nations' Sustainable Development Goals or towards mitigating the effects of climate change, or towards resisting the spread of deadly pandemics, all of which are urgently needed. The nuclear weapon states also have an obligation to consider the effects of their military spending against global moral requirements: Article 26 of the UN Charter places responsibility on the Security Council to facilitate disarmament 'in order to promote the establishment and maintenance of international peace and security with the least diversion for armaments of the world's human and economic resources' (UN 1945).

There have been efforts to scrutinize and constrain these budgets, at least in the nuclear weapon states that are democracies. In the United States, for example, a group of legislators supported by civil society groups and former military officials in 2004 and 2005 were successful in ultimately denying the Bush Administration's funding requests for development of the 'Robust Nuclear Earth Penetrator', a new type of nuclear weapon commonly known as the nuclear 'bunker buster'. This sustained opposition resulted in the US Congress abandoning the expensive and controversial proposal. In 2016, a group of ten US Senators, led by Ed Markey and Dianne Feinstein, sought to deny Air Force funding for a new Long Range Stand-Off nuclear capable cruise missile, arguing that this capability could increase the risk of nuclear war (Fleck 2016; Mehta 2016). Senator Markey has also been instrumental in initiating proposals for reductions in the nuclear programme, urging that funds saved be directed to domestic health and social needs as well as to the new kinds of security threats the United States faces, via the Smarter Approach to Nuclear Expenditures (SANE) Act, described as key opportunity to cut the bloated US nuclear arsenal (Archer *et al.* 2016). It is strongly backed by Darryl Kimball, Director of the Arms Control Association, who urged that 'Congress can and should pursue these proposals to avoid wasting taxpayer dollars on rebuilding a massive, Cold War-sized nuclear arsenal, which is poorly suited for today's threats, including nuclear terrorism' (cited in Markey 2015). Senator Markey made the case well: 'We are robbing America's future to pay for unneeded weapons of the past … it makes no sense to fund a bloated nuclear arsenal that does nothing to keep our nation safe in the 21st century.'

In Britain, the high cost of the Trident submarine and its nuclear weapons delivery systems has been a focal point for public discontent, especially among those affected by the cutting of state funding to education and other social services. Various civil society groups have raised concerns about the utility and the full cost of Trident renewal, estimated to cost between 167 billion pounds sterling (Mortimer 2016) and 205 billion pounds sterling (Stone 2016). Nevertheless the British Parliament voted in 2016 with a comfortable majority to renew Trident. In France meanwhile, where the nuclear budget has typically been unquestioned (Archer *et al.* 2016), there has been some, admittedly small, movement in raising awareness of these issues.

In none of these cases, however, can we expect to see real change. The SANE Act, which was introduced into the US House of Representatives and then to the Senate in 2016, languished for four years without sufficient support. It has been reintroduced in 2021 (Markey 2021b), but its opponents are many, and are drawn not just from within Congress but from defence contractors and industries. It is likely that this important – and relatively modest – call for new thinking about nuclear weapons will fail, a clear example of how difficult it is to rethink or challenge prevailing attitudes towards nuclear weapons, regardless of their actual utility in today's world or their value for money.

Cementing the abnormal: appropriating the Non-Proliferation Treaty to uphold an unequal global nuclear order

The nuclear NPT, negotiated within the UN's Conference on Disarmament between 1965 and 1968, is widely regarded as one of the most successful treaties achieved within the realm of international security, and deservedly so. Its membership is almost universal (only five states out of 193 – Israel, India, Pakistan, and North Korea, all nuclear weapons holders, and South Sudan – remain outside the treaty). It has been the cornerstone of global attempts to manage and limit the spread of nuclear weapons. But while it is credited with limiting horizontal nuclear proliferation by force of its legal argument and its strong normative foundation, it has been unsuccessful as a mechanism for the elimination of nuclear weapons. Even in its formation, it was perceived as an unequal treaty, effectively creating two categories of membership, the nuclear 'haves' (those states which had tested a nuclear device before January 1967, which all of the P5 states had done, were recognized as existing nuclear weapon states) and the nuclear 'have-nots'.[26] And while the majority of states were willing to accept this two-tier structure, in the belief that it was a temporary arrangement which would be redundant once the P5 eliminated their weapons, the latter states have used the NPT's structure and provisions to control the global nuclear order while retaining their own privileged position within that order. In particular, since working in 1995 for the NPT to be extended for an indefinite period of time, the nuclear weapon states have been able to manipulate the treaty to their own advantage.

These states have consolidated an inequitable nuclear order by continuing to retain their arsenals, despite the legal requirement in Article VI of the NPT to pursue effective measures to cease the nuclear arms race and to embark on nuclear disarmament. (While only the United States, the Soviet Union, and Britain were original depositary states, with China and France not acceding to the NPT until 1992, Article VI's provisions were to be applied to all those states recognized as nuclear weapons states by virtue of having tested a nuclear device before January 1967.) While they are aware of the requirements of Article VI, it would appear that the P5 see the NPT as having legitimized their nuclear weapons' possession as an indefinite fact.

Typical of this belief was a statement made by British Prime Minister, Tony Blair, that 'the NPT makes it absolutely clear that Britain has the right to possess nuclear weapons' and that 'those who are the major nuclear powers can remain nuclear powers' (as cited in UK 2006: column 34).

This is partly a result of the poor wording of the NPT itself, which lists no date by which disarmament must occur. But it is also because, for these countries, their status and authority as permanent members of the United Nations Security Council (UNSC) and their role as great powers has become conflated with their nuclear status. These states portray themselves as 'responsible' nuclear players in a global order, presenting their arsenals as normal elements of an international security order which is reserved for them exclusively (see for example the Joint Press Statement by all P5 states (US Mission to the UN 2017)).

Permanent membership of the UNSC (and its concomitant, prized, veto power) had never been determined by nuclear status: it is worth reminding ourselves that when the UN and its Security Council were founded in 1945, the United States was the sole nuclear weapon state; the Soviet Union, Britain, and France, all made permanent members in 1945, did not develop their nuclear capabilities until 1949, 1952, and 1960, respectively.[27] Thus there was nothing automatic about the prestige and responsibility associated with permanent membership of the UNSC and a country's nuclear status. Nevertheless, and as Richard Maguire (2007a: 354) reminds us, nuclear weapons became 'instituted as the currency for establishing a hierarchy of state power'. Maguire points out that this conflation, has been 'unremarked, unanalysed, and taken for granted'. Rather than questioning this assumed correlation of nuclear possession with permanent Security Council membership, most analysts and national security and political elites have simply concurred that this was 'the correct reading of reality' (Maguire 2007a: 354). The P5 states remain privileged by both their UNSC status and their recognition as nuclear weapon states existing prior to 1967, within the NPT.

The NPT has served the world well in limiting the proliferation of nuclear weapons to other states. But while the majority of its signatories saw it as a potentially transformative mechanism which would help move the world towards the eventual elimination of all nuclear weapons, it has become increasingly obvious that the P5 states regard the NPT as a vehicle to entrench their own positions, and as a means of negating any nuclear aspirations shown by non-nuclear states. Even as this pact between the nuclear and non-nuclear states was coming into existence, the nuclear weapon states showed no intention of limiting their arsenals: from around 40,000 nuclear weapons at the time of the treaty entering into force in 1970, the NPT's nuclear weapon states' arsenals increased dramatically, to a high point of around 70,000 by the mid-1980s, with the majority of these held by the

United States and the USSR (Bulletin of the Atomic Scientists 2015). Thus the NPT not only recognized the P5 states' possession of nuclear weapons as a *fait accompli*; it soon also became clear that this agreement could do nothing to limit the massive vertical proliferation of nuclear weapons. In essence, the NPT made the world safe for the persistence of a highly unequal global nuclear order.

This 'order' has also meant that the security and future of non-nuclear states would continue to depend on the nuclear states' successful control of their precarious nuclear relations with each other. The risks and calculations of a small group of states are likely to have profound consequences for overall global security. Although many non-nuclear countries formed themselves into nuclear weapon free zones – incorporating around 115 states to date – this has hardly minimized the global dangers posed by the few states wielding nuclear weapons. Thus, the NPT, while generally upheld by its members and seen by the nuclear have-nots as the only arena where they could press the P5 to disarm, has served only to reinforce the original inequalities inherent in its structure, having no provision to compel the nuclear weapon states to uphold their end of the 'grand bargain'. For the nuclear states, the NPT was the ideal mechanism in which to push for non-proliferation: any instance of horizontal proliferation – that is, the spread of nuclear weapons to other states – was now prohibited. The NPT became the permanent institution by which the established nuclear order would be sustained. It kept the position of the P5 states intact, while denouncing proliferation by others.[28]

The difficulty in sustaining this order was always apparent: at the same time that they were constructing and normalizing nuclear weapons for themselves, the P5 states had to convince others that any attempt they might make to acquire nuclear weapons was unnecessary, abnormal, and destabilizing to international security.[29] Tellingly, leaders of the P5 states had successfully avoided the terminology of 'weapons of mass destruction' being applied to their own weapons (Mutimer 2000; Cooper 2006: 365), even though nuclear weapons remain the quintessential weapon of mass destruction. Speaking of the nuclear aspirations of others, leaders, especially in the United States, would refer to would-be proliferators as acquiring 'weapons of mass destruction', while not attaching this label to their own arsenals. As Cooper has observed, 'the "WMD" label now lies at the very heart of the dominant discourse on proliferation to others ... In contrast, the discourse on domestic nuclear armouries is less likely to be burdened with this kind of sobriquet' (2006: 356). Cooper went on to note that:

> the combined effect of such linguistic devices is to ensure that 'our' WMDs are framed as nuclear whilst 'their' nuclear technologies are framed as 'WMDs', thus de-linking discussion of 'our' technology from the acute moral opprobrium and heightened images of threat and danger that are currently constructed around the term 'WMD' in popular culture. (Cooper 2006: 356)

A cursory look at the way nuclear weapons holdings are described in official military policies in the nuclear states confirms this: one's own weapons are 'nuclear weapons', representing a 'nuclear capability', the natural element of an international security order which is nevertheless reserved for the nuclear states exclusively. Other states should not seek these weapons, even as a deterrent measure against their adversaries.

This meant that the nuclear weapon states had to perform two contradictory tasks (which remain irreconcilable even today): to continue with their nuclear possession on the basis of an assumed sagacity and a perceived strategic necessity, while at the same time casting attempts made by other states to acquire nuclear weapons as unnecessary for their security, and in violation of a global norm against such weapons. As William Walker (2000: 703) has noted, the nuclear weapon states shaped the nuclear order and preserved their favoured positions by persisting with a 'managed system of deterrence' while at the same time preaching a 'managed system of abstinence' to others. And the NPT was the chief framework within which this could be justified: it was an excellent non-proliferation treaty, highly useful to the P5 states in limiting horizontal proliferation. Yet because its disarmament obligations were not bound by any timeframe, it has not been able to achieve the objective wanted by its non-nuclear signatories.

Even with the ending of the Cold War, it was evident that this treaty had no power to assist disarmament. While anti-nuclear arguments during the Cold War were given no heed, the persistence of the nuclear age well beyond the ending of the Cold War reflects the extent to which nuclearism had become entrenched in world politics. Despite a peaceful process which saw the demise of the Soviet Union and relatively cordial relations between Russia and the United States, it was soon evident that there would be no reassessment of what would be the most appropriate security needs in a dramatically changed international landscape. Rather, as the 1990s passed and the new century advanced, it was clear that the world would have to continue to live with an indefinite nuclearism, with the NPT sustaining the privileged position of the P5 states, and unable to produce radical change.

Moreover, since the Cold War ended, the NPT can be seen as having been hijacked by the P5 nuclear states, in two ways. First, they pushed successfully for the indefinite extension of the treaty in 1995, despite the reservations of significant numbers of non-nuclear states. Second, the United States and Britain, with sometimes the tacit backing of the other P5 states, came to adopt a policy of geopolitical 'management' of the non-proliferation regime, which arguably goes well beyond their legitimate role as NPT nuclear weapon states. The United States, and to a lesser extent Britain, have accorded to themselves the right to deny, forcibly, nuclear weapons to states even suspected of seeking such a capability. From the late 1990s, military action was taken against suspected proliferators, framed as a justified outrage against 'rogue' states. Richard Falk (2017) has pointed to this as a further misuse of the NPT; for him the nuclear non-proliferation regime has become simply a 'managerial one', where the managing is conducted by the United States, United Kingdom, and sometimes France, and this is all but accepted by China and Russia, because it protects their nuclear interests also. Falk argues that the NPT has been 'unilaterally supplemented by a geopolitical regime of Western powers', led by the United States, something which goes beyond the provisions of the NPT accepted by the majority of its member states (Falk 2017).

Essentially, at the same time that they show no sign of moving to disarmament, these states have wielded their power and authority to regulate and enforce what is, for them, the required nuclear order. The US and UK bombings of Iraq in the late 1990s, and their invasion of Iraq in 2003 are obvious examples of this, but there are other cases worth noting. These include US threats against North Korea (which in 2006 went on to develop a nuclear arsenal); a long-standing aggressive policy towards Iran which was suspected of seeking a nuclear weapon, and President Trump's withdrawal from the 2015 Joint Comprehensive Program of Action (JCPOA) together with renewed threats of force, on the spurious grounds that Iran was not complying with the JCPOA; and the support for Israeli attacks on suspected nuclear reactors in Iraq, Iran, and Syria. This selective enforcement of the non-proliferation rule reveals a nuclear order which is administered inequitably, allowing some states to remain as 'accepted' nuclear weapon states while demonizing others which might seek the same status. This 'excessive enforcement' (Falk 2018) of the non-proliferation norm not only goes beyond the provisions of the NPT, but it also violates the UN Charter's limitation on the legitimate use of force. When military action is taken to enforce the non-proliferation requirements of the NPT by the same states which continue to ignore its disarmament requirements, it is hard not to conclude that the treaty and the broader non-proliferation regime have been subverted by the nuclear weapon states to perpetuate their own nuclear order indefinitely.

Conclusion

Certain practices, self-propagating ideas, institutions, and policies over the decades have coalesced and resulted in a situation where nuclear weapons 'have become enshrined in myths and hardened into an orthodoxy' (Wilson 2014: 4), creating a nuclearism resistant to change, and a nuclear order driven by a select group of states. This chapter has only briefly outlined some of the reasons why this has occurred, and there remains more to be done to provide a satisfactory explanation of why we see the presence of a tightly controlled, inimically undemocratic, and vastly expensive project, which carries with it the prospect of global annihilation, notwithstanding claims about the benefits of nuclear deterrence. There has been some important research on how ideas are propagated, and how large-scale beliefs – even if these are misleading ideas and beliefs – arise over a period of time in various populations.[30] Erroneous claims and ideas can become accepted and resistant to 'rational' or 'logical' interrogation. The work of Ward Wilson comes especially to mind here: he argues that, as far as nuclear weapons are concerned, 'a series of powerful myths' – some of them deliberately fostered – 'have shaped our thinking, distancing us from the facts and undermining pragmatic policy making' (Wilson 2014: 10). For him, the arguments of those in favour of nuclear weapons have been built on 'myth, misperception, exaggeration and error' (2014: 3).

This chapter has attempted to show how particular practices and elements have been important in reinforcing the view that nuclear weapons were essential, unquestionably so, for the states that possessed them, creating a dense condition of nuclearism resistant to change. In reality, the regime upheld by the NPT nuclear states underpinning the global nuclear order has been a static regime, impenetrable to transformation and allowing these states to exercise a hegemonic control over the ideas and practices surrounding nuclear weapons. The following chapter demonstrates the enduring nature of nuclearism, with many thousands of these weapons remaining firmly entrenched in the doctrines of the nuclear weapon states.

Notes

1 Although this work argues that the processes pushing for the prohibition of nuclear weapons represents a significant challenge to the prevailing global nuclear order, I do not explore in any great depth here the various nuances within this order. For my purposes in this book, I have inferred that the elements I identify in this chapter, the particular elements of nuclearism, have shaped – and are shaped by – the broad contours of this order, even as this order has evolved over time. I refer those interested in a more detailed approach to the question of nuclear order to Kutchesfahani (2019), Ritchie (2019), Horsburgh (2015), Biswas (2014), Walker (2000, 2004, 2012), and Bull (1976).
2 Stuart Allan (1992), Ken Booth (1999), Piyush Mathur (2001), and Sheldon Ungar (1992) have all used the term in various ways, and as a backdrop to studying particular developments in nuclear policy. There has been some renewed interest in the term recently: in 2019, the London School of Economics hosted a panel which examined *70 Years of Nuclearism*, with Falk himself publishing 'Rethinking Nuclearism' (2018).

3 We must remain alert, of course, to the paradox created when policy-makers have sought to cast these weapons as 'normal', while at the same time treating them as 'special', as unlike any other weapon, and as weapons which have rightfully been accorded a sense of 'taboo' (Tannenwald 1999, 2007). Some have questioned Tannenwald's use of the word 'taboo', suggesting that a more simple norm of 'non-use' might be more appropriate, especially given that the declaratory positions of all the nuclear weapon states is that they *will* use their nuclear weapons (Paul 2010).
4 Perhaps the most influential works proposing a winnable nuclear war were those by Kahn (1962), and Keith Payne and Colin Gray (1980), the latter titled 'Victory is Possible'. Even today, the idea of fighting and winning a 'limited' nuclear war is evident (see Borger 2020).
5 In addition to the authors cited in this chapter, excellent works that address these issues include Stegenga (1988), Allan (1992), Deudney (1995), Meyer (1995), Nadel (1995), Gusterson (1999, 2001), and Hecht (2003).
6 Useful accounts of the limited utility of nuclear weapons can be found in the *Report of the Canberra Commission* (1996) and its large selection of Background Papers.
7 Clearly, not all world leaders, or the general public, approved of nuclear weapons. But their ongoing existence has come to be seen as the norm, even though these same individuals and communities will have had little or no role in acquiring nuclear weapons.
8 For excellent accounts of public activism against nuclear weapons, see the works of Lawrence S. Wittner, especially *Confronting the Bomb* (2009). Early opposition to nuclear weapons emerged in the 1950s, by individuals from the scientific and intellectual community (mainly via the Federation of Atomic Scientists, the Russell-Einstein Manifesto, and the Pugwash Conferences), and the formation in Britain in 1957 of the Campaign for Nuclear Disarmament. This emerging opposition grew at a global level, driven by various NGOs such as Greenpeace and Friends of the Earth. Much of the anti-nuclear weapon sentiment was also a result of concern about the impacts of nuclear testing. It was also fuelled by, and sometimes conflated with, strong views against nuclear power as a result of accidents such as those at Three Mile Island in the United States and Chernobyl in the Soviet Union.
9 Classic works on nuclear deterrence include Quinlan (2009), Schelling (1966), Schelling and Halperin (1961), and Freedman (2004).
10 Useful critiques of the role of nuclear weapons in the Cold War include those made by MccGwire (1985), Lebow and Stein (1995), and by Price and Tannenwald (1996), with some even pointing to what has been called the essential 'irrelevance' of nuclear weapons as a determining factor in preventing war between the superpowers (Mueller 1988). It is worth remembering that US–Russian nuclear deterrence did not prevent Russian aggression against Ukraine in 2022. Some might argue that nuclear deterrence has meant that the US/NATO dare not defy Russia on this issue. It is likely, however, that even in the absence of nuclear weapons on all sides, the US/NATO would not risk even a conventional war with Russia.

11 My phrasing here reverses the well-known term which defines those zones, in various cities, states, and regions of the world, where the development, possession or use of nuclear weapons has been nominally prohibited, as Nuclear Weapon Free Zones. Describing the past seventy-seven years of nuclear weapons' development and nuclear strategy as being characterized by a *lack* of humanitarian considerations therefore not only suggests that there is a need to think differently about these weapons; it also recasts the tradition of a largely unquestioned acceptance of nuclear weapons and places a burden on current thinkers to reverse the traditional strategic and national security approaches to nuclear weapons, applying instead a long-absent focus on the inhumane effects of these weapons.

12 An interesting exception to this was the work of Michael Quinlan, Permanent Secretary at the British Ministry of Defence, who as a devout Catholic weighed carefully the moral dilemmas of maintaining a nuclear deterrent. He was a notable thinker on international law, the Just War tradition, and the ethical aspects of nuclear politics, who nonetheless believed that on balance, nuclear deterrence against a totalitarian Soviet Union was morally acceptable. Quinlan's thinking stands out among strategists as some of the most carefully considered and informed on the subject of nuclear weapons (Quinlan 2009; see also Ogilvie-White 2014). On the whole, however, little attention was paid by strategists to issues of humanitarianism and law.

13 Even as the first nuclear weapon was being assembled in the United States, some of the Manhattan Project scientists expressed their concerns about its use to the president, and Robert Oppenheimer, in particular urged Truman not to continue with atomic weapons' development. See the contents of the Franck Report, written on 11 June 1945 (Franck *et al.* 1945). Truman dismissed Oppenheimer as a 'cry-baby scientist' (cited in Ham 2011).

14 Over 2,000 nuclear weapon tests were conducted between 1945 and 1996 (when the five nuclear weapon states ceased testing), causing substantial environmental damage and human trauma, and often resulting in populations being removed from their lands and subject to ongoing and devastating health concerns.

15 A harrowing account of the human impact of the Hiroshima bombing was provided by American journalist John Hersey (1946). Simply titled 'Hiroshima', it appeared in *The New Yorker*, on 31 August 1946. This was one of the few accounts made widely available for the general public, and it appeared only because its author managed to smuggle his writings out of Japan, unseen by US occupying forces who would almost certainly have censored or blocked them. For an account of how information about the bombings was restricted on the basis of military secrecy, see Janet Brodie (2015). A more recent account of the effects of the atomic bombings is provided by Paul Ham (2011).

16 There were some analyses of what a 'nuclear winter' might look like, undertaken by scientists during the Cold War, although these never became influential in policy formulation.

17 Several organizations have been established recently to monitor and publicize unlawful civilian deaths. Among the most prominent of these are Airwars, Iraq Body Count, and Every Casualty, which coordinates numerous sub-groups via its Casualty Recorders Network.

18 An excellent introduction to this field is provided in the 2007 special issue of *Journal of Genocide Studies*, entitled 'Nuclear Weapons, Liberal Democracy and Genocide: A New Field of Dialogue', 4(1).
19 See for example Moxley *et al.* (2010/2011), Hashmi and Lee (2004), Ward (2001), Granoff (2000), Kahn (1998/1999), Lee (1985), and Nye (1986). For an excellent overview of the current field see Doyle (2010, 2020).
20 The case can be made, of course, that measured in terms of the world's population, the nuclear weapon states, which include China and India, represent a sizeable majority of the planet's people; however, one can still point to the fact that nuclear decision-makers within these states are but a tiny fraction of these states' populations.
21 The point that nuclear war can be initiated by only the president in the United States has prompted lawmakers to introduce a Bill (in 2016 and again in 2021) which would eliminate the ability of the president to conduct a nuclear first strike without an explicit declaration of war from Congress. Senator Ed Markey and Representative Ted Lieu note that the current approval process, which gives the decision to potentially end civilization to a single individual, is 'flatly unconstitutional' (Lieu and Markey 2016; Markey 2021b).
22 The decision in Britain to acquire the bomb was made primarily by Foreign Secretary Ernest Bevin, who insisted that 'we've got to have this thing [the nuclear bomb] over here, whatever it costs. We've got to have the bloody Union Jack on top of it!' (cited in *The Economist* 2010). Nuclear weapons would provide, as Margaret Gowing (1974: 63) observed, a 'passport to first-class military rank'. She also writes that this decision 'had become a matter not only of prestige and status, but of basic self-respect' (Gowing 1973).
23 The British Parliament, of course, has had direct input into the debate on retaining the UK's nuclear deterrent system, with Trident renewal easily secured in the July 2016 vote.
24 Lethality is calculated on the basis of both yield and accuracy of a nuclear weapon, with increased accuracy delivering the same effect as increasing the yield (see Eden 2011).
25 In 2019, it was estimated that the nine nuclear weapon states spent roughly US$72.9 billion on their nuclear arsenals (ICAN 2020).
26 This has prompted Maddock (2010) to describe the NPT as a 'treaty to castrate the impotent'.
27 The People's Republic of China became a nuclear power in 1964, but it was not given its place on the UNSC until 1971, displacing the Taiwanese Republic of China.
28 Israel's proliferation has been quietly permitted, and although Indian proliferation was initially denounced, the United States later formed a nuclear partnership with India, indicating that such outrage has been felt very selectively.
29 By way of example, responding to India's nuclear testing in May 1998, US President Clinton asserted that he was 'deeply disturbed' at India's actions, and that when it came to a nuclear arsenal, 'they clearly don't need it to maintain their security' (Clinton 1998). For its part, China stated that India, by acquiring nuclear weapons 'runs against international trends and is detrimental to the peace and stability' (cited by Khan and Sullivan 1998).

30 Aaron Lynch, for example, in his 1996 work, *Thought Contagion: How Beliefs Spread through Society*, sought explanations for why both true/useful *and* false/unprovable notions could become accepted and widespread beliefs. He concluded that the 'contagiousness' of particular ideas was not necessarily dependent on their 'truth value', and that regardless of their veracity or logical application, even improbable or undesirable practices and processes can be replicated and widely accepted. Irving Janus (1972) also examined the pressures that have led to what he called 'groupthink', and its suppression of dissent and alternatives, in foreign policy decision-making.

2

Nuclearism today: modernization, the persistence of deterrence, and ongoing dangers

If the concept of nuclearism and the elements which shaped it gained hold during the Cold War, how might we characterize the position of the nuclear weapon states, and especially the P5 states, today, in 2022? What explicit doctrines and practices prevail more than thirty years after the collapse of the Soviet Union, an event which brought widespread relief that we had escaped mutually assured nuclear destruction? Importantly, has nuclearism diminished?

The simple answer to the last question is 'no'. Despite hopes that the ending of the Cold War had brought an end to the heavy reliance on nuclear weapons, the current policies of the nuclear weapon states, the modernization of their nuclear forces, their continuing faith in nuclear deterrence, and their persistence in maintaining sizeable arsenals (especially Russia and the United States), with many weapons on high-alert status, all serve to demonstrate the entrenched nature of nuclearism. The picture today – seventy-seven years after Hiroshima, fifty-two years since the nuclear Non-Proliferation Treaty entered into force, and twenty-seven years since that treaty's indefinite extension – shows no sign that the elements which built and sustained the faith in, and reverence for, nuclear weapons have weakened. For the few states which possess these arsenals, there was no fundamental shift in thinking, despite the changed circumstances, and despite the emergence of new national and global threats against which such weapons will be unsuitable and irrelevant. There has been no serious downgrading of the role of nuclear weapons in the policies of these states, or any real reconsideration of their adherence to the policy of nuclear deterrence.

In the immediate post-Cold War era, there were substantial reductions in the numbers of nuclear weapons held by the United States and Russia, with some small reductions undertaken also by Britain and France. The P5 nuclear weapon states have pointed to the progress they have made: a joint statement in 2016 noted that 'global stocks of nuclear weapons are now at their lowest point in over half a century as the result of unprecedented efforts on the part of nuclear weapon states' (US 2016). The governments of these states, again especially the United States and Russia, point to the fact that the number of nuclear weapons has dropped from a high point of about 70,000, in the mid-1980s, to the 13,000-plus we see in 2022. But as Kristensen and Norris remind us, the bulk of these reductions took place in the 1990s and were often the deletion of old stock, that in any case contemporary nuclear forces are much more capable and destructive than they ever were, and that instead of planning for the elimination of their weapons, the nuclear-armed states appear to be planning to 'retain large arsenals for the indefinite future' (Kristensen and Norris 2021).

Proponents of nuclear weapons continue to venerate the idea of nuclear deterrence, bolstered by a history of decades of nuclear non-use and the conviction that nuclear deterrence has prevented war between the major powers. They do so despite the fragile and uncertain nature of nuclear deterrence, and the evidence of many 'close calls', with a confidence that nuclear deterrence will continue to hold successfully into the future. In sum, despite a changed world, and their NPT obligations, these states signal to the world that they have no intention of eliminating their nuclear weapons.

Endless modernization

Leaders in all the NPT nuclear weapon states have given a commitment to negotiate in good faith for nuclear disarmament. When the Cold War ended and the NPT was extended, at NPT Review Conferences, in the UN Security Council, and other forums, these states have all promised to disarm. For some of these states, at times, their leaders have been genuinely inclined towards disarmament; we saw, for example, Ronald Reagan proposing this with Mikhail Gorbachev in 1986, and Barack Obama in 2009 stating 'clearly and with conviction America's commitment to seek the peace and security of a world without nuclear weapons' (Obama 2009).

But against these (rare) glimpses of potential change, very little has altered, either in terms of doctrinal policy or strategic deployments. The persistence of nuclearism thwarted the attempts of even these highly influential men, with political and military establishments determined to resist change. Not only are nuclear weapons deeply valued (Ritchie 2013; Gandenberger and Acheson 2016), they are also exalted and fetishized (Harrington de Santana 2009; Biswas 2014), and all the nuclear states remain 'wedded to' (Higgs 1997; Miller 2002), 'addicted to' (Wolfenstein 1991; Flockhart 2013; *The Economist* 2015; Lennane 2015), and 'fixated on' (Mueller 1988, 2012) nuclear weapons and nuclear deterrence. Former Australian diplomat Richard Lennane has noted that, as with individuals hooked on illicit and dangerous behaviour, the 'addicted' nuclear weapon states, 'make promises and undertakings' to disarm but at the same time, they consistently undermine any progress towards their stated goal. They make excuses, drag their feet, rationalize, reinterpret, accuse others of misunderstanding, shift the blame, complain of persecution, behave secretively, succumb to irrational outbursts, lie to friends and family, and neglect their personal hygiene.[1] (Lennane 2015)

The standard narrative on nuclear weapons and the prospects for disarmament proclaimed by these states (especially from 1995 onwards) has been that they will disarm, that gradually the numbers will decrease, but that the world must be patient, and must wait for the 'right conditions' for this to happen. As they promise they will move to disarmament, they invariably raise a host of objections as to why they cannot fulfil this promise:[2] that the security situation has 'deteriorated'; that new or 'increasing' threats – which are never well-defined – have arisen; that nuclear weapons are somehow 'special', or 'different' (at the same time that they have been normalized); that we cannot expect to change easily the dominant views which have prevailed for over seven decades; that nuclear weapons bring (for them) strategic reassurance; and the circular argument that as long as any other state has nuclear weapons, they also must have them.

All the indicators suggest that these states will cling fiercely to their nuclear arsenals, and that there will never be, for them at least, 'the right conditions' in which to achieve the elimination of these weapons. This is despite the fact that what has been called for over the past thirty-odd years is a programme of phased and monitored steps, and not instant, unilateral, or unconditional disarmament. The world has asked them to take steps to minimize the immediate dangers of mistaken or accidental launches, to reassure the international community of their good intentions, and to discourage nuclear proliferation. Such steps are seen as necessary, but initial, components of a broader project, whose ultimate end-goal is the elimination of all nuclear weapons, under strict verification and monitoring.

The frustration felt by the non-nuclear states is compounded by the fact that every one of the nine nuclear weapon states is currently modernizing its nuclear arsenal. On the face of it, it is clear that nuclear-armed states would want to maintain the viability of their arsenals, as long as any other state has these weapons. The safety and reliability of their existing forces must be guaranteed by ongoing maintenance. However, these processes of 'maintenance' have evolved into the development of newer and more lethal weapons, signalling the continued valuing of these arsenals, and even a lowered threshold for using them. This is happening even as crises between NATO and Russia deepen against the context of Russia's invasion of Ukraine, where South Asia remains a high-risk zone for nuclear war, and where tensions in East Asia between the United States, China, and North Korea persist. Instead of minimizing their reliance on these deadly weapons and downplaying their role in security – especially given their limited utility in resolving these crises in an effective way – the nuclear states have worked to refine their nuclear capabilities.

From around 2010, they seem to have moved beyond ensuring the 'safety and security' of their arsenals and towards the creation of a new generation of sophisticated weaponry. These modernization programmes are not merely about maintaining safety and security but are about developing new capabilities which extend these weapon systems for decades into the future.[3] Modernization has accelerated in recent years, and for some of these states at least, there appears to be a greater willingness actually to use nuclear weapons, taking the purpose of nuclear arsenals beyond that of purely deterrence.

The case of the United States is especially illustrative. Despite President Obama's promising nuclear disarmament views, in reality his disarmament legacy was minimal (Joeck 2016). He had been able to achieve only minor reductions, through the NewSTART process. In return for congressional support for this treaty, he pledged billions of dollars to upgrade the US nuclear arsenal: every nuclear weapon delivery system in the US strategic nuclear arsenal was to be replaced, and the warheads carried by them updated. The Alliance for Nuclear Accountability (2016) has called this programme a 'Trillion Dollar Trainwreck', with harsher observers suggesting that Obama should return the Nobel Peace Prize, which was awarded to him largely on the basis of his visions for a nuclear-free world (Blechman 2016).

The American project on modernization has been enabled by the programme of 'stockpile stewardship', ostensibly for the safety and reliability of the existing nuclear arsenal. But this programme continues to be hugely expensive, is of debatable military value, and has metamorphosed into the capacity to develop new nuclear weapons. Taylor and Hendry suggest that by using the terminology of stockpile stewardship, proponents have cast themselves as 'guardians of nuclear resources' (2008: 304), when in fact their programmes are designed to retain these weapons forever.[4] In line with the element of exclusivity and restricted decision-making noted in the previous chapter, these national security elites have

> successfully defended themselves against undesirable change arising from public reconsideration of nuclear deterrence. As a result, this rhetoric has undermined the possibility of a genuine nuclear democracy based on adequate representation and deliberation of nuclear interests in the post-Cold War era ... The official rhetoric of stockpile stewardship has succeeded ... in sustaining nuclear weapons' institutions through the legitimation crises posed by the end of the Cold War. (Taylor and Hendry 2008: 304–305)

'Stockpile stewardship' transformed into nuclear modernization in the United States most evidently around 2010. Not only has this made US nuclear weapons 'more capable and effective'; it is also being accompanied by a 'refinement of strike plans' for the potential use of these weapons (Kristensen and McKinzie 2015: 568). Such programmes are rarely portrayed to the public as being designed actually for enhancing military capabilities (Kristensen *et al.* 2017). New technologies have been developed, including a 'super-fuze' ability for more accurate ignition of a nuclear warhead, which will increase the targeting capability and the overall destructive power of the US ballistic missile arsenal 'by a factor of roughly three' (Kristensen *et al.* 2017). Investigators have concluded that the United States has been able to do this 'under the veil of an otherwise-legitimate warhead life-extension program'. A focus on newer, smaller, and better targeted weapons suggests that the United States might be considering launching a surprise first-strike (Kristensen *et al.* 2017), indicating also a belief that it can launch and win against an adversary. In January 2020 it was revealed that the United States had deployed a low-yield nuclear weapon on its ballistic-missile submarines, something which might lower the threshold for actual use, and which could result in nuclear escalation (Arkin and Kristensen 2020).

Whether modernization is simply 'a hedge against the future' (Taylor 2010), an all-purpose 'comfort blanket' (Hanson 2002: 14; MccGwire 2006), all of the nuclear weapon states are paying significant attention to updating their arsenals, and the United States leads the way in these actions. Attempts to challenge or limit these modernizations have so far been fruitless, even in the wake of rising costs and national budgetary constraints. Thus even while the number of nuclear weapons has dropped substantially since START I was signed in 1991, we see the development of new warheads and missiles, some with enhanced lethality (Eden 2006, 2011), or as new, more 'useable' weapons. As Thakur and Evans observe, 'on the evidence of the size of their weapons arsenals, fissile material stocks, force modernization plans, stated doctrine and known deployment practices', every one of the nine nuclear states signals an indefinite retention of these arsenals and an ongoing central role for them in their security doctrines (2013: 4). One of the most surprising developments was the British announcement in May 2021 that instead of moving towards promised reductions, the UK would actually increase its arsenal by 40 per cent. The UK also appeared to lower the threshold for using nuclear weapons, and rejected the (previously favoured) idea of transparency in nuclear policies (UK 2021). In sum, and as Anne Harrington de Santana (2011) aptly noted almost a decade ago, the activities of the nuclear states contradict so clearly the commitment they have made to disarm, that they find it hard to maintain the 'credibility of an incredible pledge to disarm'.

No progress on steps to reduce risks, no downgrading the salience of nuclear weapons

If modernization is a stark reminder of the nuclear weapon states' priorities, so too is the absence of tangible progress on implementing steps to increase safety, to reduce the risks of accident or miscalculation, and to lessen the value of nuclear weapons in security doctrines. One of the primary requests made of the nuclear weapon states has been for 'no-first-use' declarations, where nuclear states will formally and explicitly declare that they will only use nuclear weapons in retaliation to another's use of these weapons, and that nuclear weapons will not be introduced into a conflict involving conventional weapons. Such declarations are meant to limit the conditions under which use of nuclear weapons might be considered, until such time that a nuclear-free world is achieved.

No-first-use is also a logical element of nuclear deterrence theory, at least if we accept that deterrence is all about preventing nuclear attacks, and not about the idea of actually *using* nuclear weapons to one's advantage: at its most fundamental level, nuclear deterrence involves the belief that the possession of these weapons will deter another nuclear weapon state from mounting a nuclear attack. In reality, then, the nuclear weapon states *should* implicitly have a no-first-use policy in place, as an element of their nuclear deterrence strategic stance.

Nonetheless, with the exception of China, and in a more qualified way India, the nuclear states reserve the option to use their nuclear weapons in a variety of circumstances, even if they are not attacked by nuclear weapons themselves, because they refuse to have an explicit no-first-use policy in place. Disarmament advocates and various strategists have asked the nuclear weapon states to make explicit their pledge not to be the first to use nuclear weapons, thereby limiting the utility of nuclear weapons only to that of deterring (and if necessary responding to) a nuclear attack by an adversary. A clear and explicit no-first-use pledge would signal to the world that the nuclear states are serious about limiting nuclear dangers, that they will confine their arsenals to deterrence only, and will confirm that their nuclear weapons will not be used if they themselves – or their allies – have not suffered a nuclear attack. There were hopes that towards the end of his presidency, Barack Obama would announce a formal 'no-first-use' policy statement, especially as he had signalled in his 2010 Nuclear Posture Review that the 'fundamental role of US nuclear weapons' was to deter nuclear attacks on itself, its allies or partners (US Department of Defense 2010: 15). In any case, this has been asked of all the nuclear weapon states, as part of the processes urged upon them by numerous studies (explored in the following chapter). Yet to date, China and India are the only states to have made this concession.[5]

Other nuclear states have vacillated between continuing with the implicit no-first-use element of nuclear deterrence, and renouncing it – that is, putting nuclear first-use clearly 'on the table'. Retaining the option to use nuclear weapons first, even in the absence of a nuclear attack, opens wide the possibility that these weapons can and will be used for a range of purposes including as a reprisal against conventional attacks, but also as a pre-emptive or punitive measure for a host of reasons. The ambiguity resulting from the absence of formal no-first-use pledges is seen as dangerous and destabilizing, creating uncertainty among all nuclear states about the intentions of other nuclear states (Gerson 2011; O'Hanlon 2016; Tierney 2016).

It is evident that some of the nuclear states have been willing to use nuclear weapons first, and to do so even against an adversary which is not a nuclear weapon state. President George W. Bush's 2001 Nuclear Posture Review was perhaps the most obvious example of this (Arkin 2002; Sagan 2009a), in which it was declared that the United States would be fully prepared to use nuclear weapons first, even against a range of non-nuclear countries. The Review stated that nuclear weapons 'provide credible military options to deter a wide range of threats, including WMD and large-scale conventional military force' (reprinted in NTI 2002). Obama's Nuclear Posture Review in 2010 modified this somewhat, but it still did not rule out the possibility that nuclear weapons might be used against an adversary even in the absence of a nuclear attack upon the United States.

For its part, Russia has declared that it reserves the right to use nuclear weapons in response to any large-scale conventional weapon aggression, and officials continue to suggest that nuclear weapons might be used in a variety of situations, including against ballistic-missile defence facilities (Kristensen and Korda 2019). The assessment is that Russia is willing to use its nuclear arsenal beyond the role of deterrence and is considering actual war-fighting strategies (Kristensen and Korda 2019). As tensions between NATO and Russia deteriorate, having an option of first-use is an unnecessary and dangerous practice (Kimball 2016; Reif 2016a). President Putin made the most overt indication that nuclear weapons would be used against even a conventional weapon attack in his executive order, the *2020 Basic Principles of State Policy of the Russian Federation on Nuclear Deterrence*, the first time that official Russian nuclear policy had been made easily and publicly available.

By late 2016, it was evident that Obama would not adopt an explicit no-first-use policy, despite the fact that many had called for existing threat postures to be abandoned and replaced by clear and unambiguous pledges of no-first-use. The Parliamentary Assembly of the Organisation for Security and Cooperation in Europe (OSCE), for example, urged the formal implementation of no-first-use policies (OSCEPA 2016), as did Parliamentarians for Nuclear Non-proliferation and Disarmament (PNND), a cross-party network of politicians from over ninety countries. The OSCE Parliamentary Assembly declaration was especially significant because the delegations supporting this call were drawn from fifty-four countries in the OSCE including Russia, and all NATO states – that is, including the nuclear weapon states Russia, the United States, Britain, and France – and the former Soviet-controlled states. In the end, a number of Obama's advisers disagreed that a formal declaration was necessary, and even US allies Japan and South Korea, in private warnings, urged the president not to change existing policy (Chang 2016; Quilop 2016).[6]

No-first-use is also closely tied up with the need to reduce the role of nuclear weapons in security policies generally. There have been numerous requests for the nuclear weapon states to reduce the salience of nuclear weapons and to downgrade the central role that these weapons continue to play in their security doctrines. Recognising this, Obama had stated that he would 'reduce the role of nuclear weapons in our national security strategy and urge others to do the same'. Nonetheless, neither in the United States nor in any of the other nuclear weapon states can we see any serious downplaying of this role. After softening somewhat the role of nuclear weapons when the Cold War ended, NATO has, at the urging of its newer East European members, revived the centrality of nuclear weapons in its doctrines, with calls even for a renewed and deliberate reliance on the nuclear option (Kroenig and Slocombe 2014; Durkalec 2015). Regretting the fact that since the ending of the Cold War, NATO, in his view had 'de-emphasized nuclear weapons in its defence policy and posture' nuclear advocate Kroenig (2016) has argued that it is time for the Alliance to develop a 'serious' policy of nuclear deterrence. Yet NATO's 2010 Strategic Concept had reaffirmed very clearly that NATO was indeed a 'nuclear alliance'.

Following the election of Donald Trump to the US presidency, the Heritage Foundation, in December 2016, sponsored an event titled, *How to Make US Nuclear Weapons and Missile Defense Policy Great Again: What Should the Trump Administration Do?* The Heritage Foundation claimed that a 'dangerous geopolitical environment' required the re-evaluation of America's nuclear posture, which the organization believed 'currently minimizes the role of these weapons in the US national security strategy'. In December 2016 a Pentagon panel, the Defense Science Board, urged the incoming Trump government to make the American nuclear arsenal more capable of a 'limited' nuclear war (see Donnelly 2017). The claims that nuclear weapons have been minimized in national security strategy is somewhat spurious: nuclear weapons remain central in US and Russian doctrines, and as noted in the previous chapter, receive billions of dollars in funding. Making US nuclear weapons 'great again' does not suggest that the salience of these weapons is being lowered. If anything, it suggests a perennial reliance on what Colin Powell (2010) has called 'useless' weapons. Trump's 2018 Nuclear Posture Review called for more weapons, and especially 'low yield' weapons in the face of what were described as dangerously worsening security conditions, and alleged beliefs in Russia and China that the United States was not going to be willing enough to use its nuclear weapons (Feinberg 2018). Yet as critics have pointed out, the United States already has a large number of low-yield weapons, and its existing capabilities, including conventional capabilities, are sufficient to meet security needs (Weir, cited in Feinberg 2018). For his part, Russian President Putin has shown that there is no likelihood of downgrading the importance of nuclear weapons to Russian security either: in October 2016, and amid serious differences with the United States and NATO (regarding Syria as well as Russian aggression in Eastern Ukraine) Putin provocatively moved nuclear-capable missiles close to Poland and Lithuania (De Luce and Standish 2016). And as the invasion of Ukraine began in February 2022, Putin made the most explicit threat yet actually to use nuclear weapons.

We continue to see strong identification with nuclear weapons in other regions also: in East Asia, where North Korea has conducted a destabilizing set of nuclear tests and missile delivery systems, and in South Asia, where perennial tensions between India and Pakistan have resulted in the rapid growth and modernization of these states' nuclear arsenals; the rate of growth of nuclear arsenals in these states is the highest in the world. Within the European sphere, France continues to assert that its nuclear arsenal is 'the most vital element in its defense capabilities' (cited in Lewis *et al.* 2014: 25), and the United Kingdom, describing itself regularly as 'a responsible nuclear weapon state' (Rowland 2016), insists that it reserves the right to use nuclear weapons; this would be even as a 'pre-emptive, initial strike' (Fallon, cited in Merrick 2017), dispelling any hopes that the United Kingdom would adopt a no-first-use policy. As noted above, the United Kingdom has recently moved to reify, rather than diminish, the salience of nuclear weapons in its security policy.

As Nick Ritchie observes, the changes made to numbers and doctrines has been a process of 'surface devaluing' only, which has left intact the fundamental policies that prevailed during the Cold War. He summarizes this surface devaluing as follows:

> It has left the logic of nuclear deterrence relatively undisturbed, the perceived legitimacy of threatening massive nuclear violence intact, and the idea of nuclear prestige largely untouched. It is a process centred on the technocratic and managerial orientation to arms control developed during the Cold War. It privileges ... a firm belief in the necessity and efficacy of nuclear deterrence.
> (Ritchie 2014b: 1)

No-first-use, and reducing the salience of nuclear weapons in security doctrines, are but two of the many steps that the nuclear weapon states are currently resisting. Other steps urged on the nuclear states include the request to provide negative security assurances to non-nuclear states, to promise them that nuclear weapons will not be used against them; to take nuclear weapons off the dangerous launch-on-warning alert status (where missiles can be launched within minutes of incoming news of an apparent attack); for bringing into force the Comprehensive Test Ban Treaty and the negotiation of a Fissile Material Cut-off Treaty; for the United States to eliminate the long-range, nuclear-armed cruise missiles that provoke fears of first strikes in China; and for Russia and the United States to take strong action on reducing nuclear dangers, with a view especially to eliminating the approximately 2,000 short-range or tactical nuclear weapons still deployed in Europe (the vast majority of which are held by Russia). Critics might counter that the relations between Washington and Moscow have deteriorated so much that this is unlikely to happen. This should not, however, be taken as evidence that these states *cannot* cooperate on security agreements. The experience of the thirty years since the Cold War ended has shown that even in times when relations between these great powers were relatively cordial, none of them was willing to downgrade seriously the role of nuclear weapons. None of them has undertaken a fundamental rethinking of nuclear weapons or of what Acheson *et al.* (2014: 18) term 'the collective dangers of a nuclear-armed world'. Compounding this already grim picture, both Russia and the United States have been willing to discard a number of arms control agreements very recently, the most important of which was the Intermediate Nuclear Forces Treaty.

A continuing reliance on nuclear deterrence

There has been no lessening of the faith in nuclear deterrence. While an adherence to deterrence might have been justified during the Cold War, and strategic calculations based on nuclear retaliation may well have played a part in averting direct war between the major states, it is more difficult to make a case for nuclear deterrence today. A nuanced understanding of the costs and dangers of deterrence was provided by Michael Quinlan, who accepted that maintaining a credible nuclear deterrent was a necessary step during the Cold War standoff (see Jones 2013; Ogilvie-White 2014). Yet even this 'high priest' of nuclear deterrence, as he was known, believed that changes in international circumstances – such as the ending of the Cold War – required us to think afresh about appropriate defence and deterrence needs. This has not happened. As Shannon Kile, Head of the SIPRI Nuclear

Weapons Project, reminds us, every one of the nuclear weapon states continues 'to prioritize nuclear deterrence as the cornerstone of their national security strategies' (Kile 2016), regardless of the fact that Cold War deterrence conditions cannot simply be replicated in today's world.[7]

Nuclear deterrence has of course been 'vindicated' for some by the fact that no state has used a nuclear weapon in conflict since 1945, constituting the norm of non-use and defined as 'an internalized moral restraint on detonating a nuclear weapon' (Freedman 2013: 96). Atomic advocates argue that this 'internalized restraint' proves that deterrence has worked. As such, deterrence is seen as carrying with it no real costs, and instead provides the benefit of deterring attack against oneself.[8] Many strategists continue to argue that the norm of deterrence has kept the peace, because of the hesitation to resort to launching nuclear weapons against an adversary. Freedman determines that this hesitation 'stems from prudence, proportionality, and a general sense that such a step would be so momentous, so terrible, so extreme as to preclude it' (2013: 96). The implication is that prudence, proportionality, and rationality will prevail in the future. Advocates of nuclear deterrence hold fast to these beliefs, even in the knowledge, much of it recently uncovered, of the many breaches of security and close calls that the world has faced when nuclear weapons were very nearly used.

The view that deterrence is essentially defensive in nature reinforces this faith. So too does the view that nuclear weapons are seen, as James E. Doyle, in his critique of deterrence (2013: 10) notes, as 'weapons of acceptable risk'.[9] The following statement is illustrative of this view of these weapons as an acceptable, and even benign, risk:

> For decades, nuclear weapons have safeguarded US and allied security from an outside threat and contributed to assurance of allies ... There is no substitute for nuclear deterrence. In the words of General Larry Welsh (USAF), 'The nuclear deterrent is the only weapons system I know of that has worked perfectly without fail, exactly as intended, for [its] entire life span. And because [it has] been so successful, then there may be some who have forgotten why we need [it]'. (Spring and Dodge 2013)

In this same paper, Keith Payne is cited as linking the decrease of casualties in combat as a percentage of world population (both civilian and military) with the advent of nuclear weapons (in Spring and Dodge 2013). In other words, the undeniable decline of inter-state war, as well as the reduction in battle deaths since 1945, are attributable to the power of nuclear deterrence.

That nuclear deterrence can be seen as essentially a benign practice is something that has worked to the advantage of the nuclear weapon states. It is indeed fortunate that nuclear non-use has been the case since 1945. But this has allowed the nuclear states to conclude that (their) possession of nuclear weapons is 'safe', 'acceptable', even unremarkable, because the tradition of non-use is likely to continue (notwithstanding the inconsistencies which arise when these same states reject a policy of no-first-use or when they explicitly threaten first-use). Their argument suggests that alarm about their retention of nuclear weapons is misplaced, that nuclear deterrence is an entirely justifiable policy, and that the continuation of the status quo brings with it no actual harm: the weapons are not being 'used', thus they pose no real danger to global security. The nuclear states should be left to continue with their long-held policies, on the basis that deterrence will continue to work, and that their possession of nuclear weapons is a safe and desirable practice.

But arguments for nuclear deterrence, even if they carried weight during the Cold War, are difficult to sustain today (Berry *et al.* 2010). Jeffrey Lewis (2016) has described Cold War deterrence policies as 'the most absurd moments of the cold war, when nuclear strategists followed the logic of deterrence over the cliff and into the abyss'. Deterrence was rarely problematized during the Cold War, but its continued application to the post-Cold War era is even more puzzling. Not only is there an over-confidence about the efficacy of deterrence during the Cold War; there is also an unquestioned and continuing doctrinal attachment which is difficult to dislodge (Herzog 2013), especially given the changed circumstances of global politics since the Cold War ended. Among other analysts, Brad Roberts (2015) believes that US nuclear policy has indeed been adapting nuclear deterrence to the circumstances of a greatly changed world and he argues strongly for the retention of the US nuclear arsenal. Yet it is not easy to see how this can in reality be applied to all threats, or how a *nuclear* weapon, rather than any other kind of weapon, is necessarily the essential element in preserving American security. Roberts and others note that Russian nuclear policies, especially, remain threatening to the United States; however, this threat is at least partly fuelled by US practices themselves.

Nuclear deterrence is a highly complex issue, and this chapter cannot hope to address the nuances, psychology, and uncertainties inherent in this doctrine. The reader is directed to a number of useful sources which examine the relevance, complexity, and efficacy of nuclear deterrence.[10] Recognizing that this can never be a full critique of nuclear deterrence, the section below nevertheless suggests some of the flaws implicit in the doctrine. These flaws alarm the non-nuclear weapon states, who urge the elimination of these weapons rather than the persistent reliance on nuclear deterrence. For non-nuclear states, ongoing reliance on nuclear deterrence and the often bellicose rhetoric that accompanies nuclear statements simply reaffirms the ongoing nature of nuclearism and its unswerving faith that these weapons provide security against every kind of threat to their possessors.

A first point is that during the Cold War, these weapons were targeted against *states*, where the enemy was a known quantity, and where a precarious but somewhat stable relationship was managed between the two superpowers. As prominent statesmen Shultz, Kissinger, Perry, and Nunn remind us, 'it is not possible to replicate the high-risk stability that prevailed between the two nuclear superpowers during the Cold War' (Shultz *et al.* 2011). There are now more nuclear weapon states, multiplying the dangers of miscalculation.

Not only are there more nuclear weapon states now than during the Cold War, but threats emanate also from non-state actors. Using nuclear weapons against actors such as Al Qaeda or ISIS, whose whereabouts may be unknown, and whose numerous cells may in any case be scattered geographically, cannot be seriously contemplated. Even if a terrorist cell's whereabouts could be located, and we could be assured that its complete network would be effectively destroyed – itself unlikely – a nuclear strike is likely to kill thousands (or more) of civilians, and destroy large parts of the environment. This is not likely to be tenable even under the pressure to devise successful counter-terrorism measures.

A second point, when weighing up the utility of nuclear deterrence, is the fact that these weapons are hardly practical as instruments of warfare. As the Canberra Commission Report noted decades ago, they have 'long been understood to be too destructive and non-discriminatory to secure discrete objectives on the battlefield' (Australian Government, Department of Foreign Affairs and Trade 1996). As weapons of mass destruction, likely to kill friendly as well as enemy forces, and probably large numbers of civilians, their use would almost certainly negate whatever perceived military or political benefit prompted it. Their use as a retaliatory strike is also problematic. This is not to say that these weapons will not or cannot be used; rather, it is to say that the moral calculations and costs incurred in using such weapons make them less useful than other options. In short, nuclear weapons will be very good at indiscriminate and massive destruction, but much less effective at targeting military objectives (Allen 2015: 390). They have not been, and are not likely to be, the rational choice of weapon when seeking specific military goals.

Third, and following from the previous point about the utility of nuclear weapons, it is far more likely to be the increasingly sophisticated *conventional* weapons which will be used in contemporary and future military campaigns. Even deliberate counterforce strategies, where nuclear targeting is aimed at military rather than civilian establishments, are unlikely to be practicable: restricting damage to precise areas and differentiating between civilians and combatants is not possible with weaponry that is diffuse, rather than discrete, in its impact. One of the peculiar consequences of the entrenched nature of nuclear weapons and the persistence of nuclearism more generally, is that conventional weapons – the weapons that *are* actually acquired and used by states, for defence, for deterrence, or for waging war – receive much less attention, even though they are the default choice when states face military threats. The nuclear 'debate' amongst strategists rarely touches on conventional weapon sufficiency and suitability. It is the highly expensive focus on nuclear arsenals which is seen as imperative and which generates enthusiasm; the more prosaic, but far more useful, conventional weapons raise much less interest by comparison. This is so despite the fact that conventional weapons have been, and are likely to remain, the weapons of choice for states, notwithstanding the advent of atomic weaponry in 1945.

In line with the overwhelming faith in nuclear weapons which is part and parcel of nuclearism, the fascination with maintaining their nuclear arsenals has often overridden sensible thought about the kinds of military hardware that are actually required in the modern world if we are to address contemporary security challenges effectively (or for that matter whether the application of military force is even the right choice in all cases). As Doyle (2017) has argued, 'nuclear deterrence is a blunt instrument that cannot be tailored to evoke particular responses in particular situations'. With the development of ever-more complex conventional weapons able to provide discrete strategic targeting, the more indiscriminate and unpredictable nature of a nuclear strike is hardly a suitable option.

There is also no clear reason to assert that it is *nuclear* weapons which must be retained in order to counter any threats or attacks of a chemical or biological nature. Yet regardless of the limited military utility of nuclear weapons, an implicit linkage appears to have been made which assumes that a weapons of mass destruction (chemical or biological) threat or attack requires a weapons of mass destruction (i.e. a nuclear) deterrent/response. Conventional weapons are more likely to be chosen as a response to this issue. Massive (or even limited) nuclear arsenals may not be helpful for either deterrence or retaliation. The political, humanitarian, and strategic consequences attendant on using nuclear weapons in military scenarios makes it difficult to argue that they possess real utility. In recognition of this, George Shultz and his fellow writers have urged that it is necessary for states to move forward to create 'a series of conceptual and practical steps toward deterrence that do not rely primarily on nuclear weapons or nuclear threats to maintain international peace and security' (Shultz *et al.* 2011).

That each of the nuclear weapon states possesses significant conventional weaponry underlines this point. Even without their nuclear arsenals, they will be seen as powerful military entities. Generals Charles Horner and Colin Powell have repeatedly stated that US conventional weaponry was sufficient to achieve America's military goals, with Horner noting that the US conventional arsenal was more credible than a nuclear threat against Saddam Hussein in 1991, even to deter against chemical or biological attack (cited in Daley 2010: 135). Nuclear weapons, Powell wrote, 'were trouble-prone, expensive to modernize, and irrelevant in the present world of highly-accurate conventional weapons' (Powell 1995: 540). Or to put it in the words of Tad Daley (2010: 137), 'our conventional weapons can accomplish anything that nuclear weapons can accomplish. And for those objectives that conventional weapons cannot accomplish – such as winning hearts and minds ... – nuclear weapons offer us no help at all'. It is the question of military utility that is important to remember here. By way of example, rather than NATO 'beefing up' its nuclear capabilities, relying on its substantial conventional weapon capabilities will be a better and in any case more realistic policy choice (Sauer 2016).

Given the likely default position – that conventional weapons are the weapons that are used – the credibility of extended nuclear deterrence is also problematic. Of course US allies in NATO, and Japan, South Korea, and Australia, seek strategic reassurance from the United States. But, as Sauer points out, any military assurances given should meet at least two conditions: they should be credible, and, in the case of Europe, they should not unnecessarily antagonize Russia:

> The question is whether nuclear weapons are a credible means of reassuring Eastern European member states. Tallinn is fully aware that NATO is not going to use nuclear weapons, even in the extremely unlikely event of a Russian occupation of Estonia. Updating NATO's policy of extended nuclear deterrence should therefore not be on the agenda ... There is an alternative that is much more credible than nuclear weapons, namely the forward deployment of usable weapons. That would mean conventional weapons and troops, even if on a rotational basis. That is exactly what NATO has been doing until now. (Sauer 2016)

The overwhelming sense that they *have* to rely on nuclear weapons is perhaps one of the most peculiar aspects of nuclearism displayed by the nuclear states. In reality, the inapplicability of these weapons for use against contemporary threats, and their unsuitability for war-fighting, renders them essentially 'useless' (Powell 2010). Yet at the same time, they continue to be revered by those who hold them and (to varying degrees) by their allies. Calls for protection which insist ultimately on a nuclear response reflect a belief that nuclear weapons have some kind of a magical property, that they bring benefits and have uses that no other weapon has or can provide. Nuclearism has ensured that these weapons have achieved a legendary status, but this does not mean that their actual usefulness should go unquestioned.

Rejecting calls for nuclear – as opposed to conventional – deterrence is not an indication of strategic naivety. Lawrence Freedman has suggested that 'the rhetoric of disarmament insists that mankind [*sic*] is on either of two tracks: one route leads to continued conflict and eventual disaster, while the other leads to disarmament and greater international harmony' (Freedman 2013: 99). But this is a highly contrived dichotomy. As has been noted earlier in this book, many in favour of nuclear elimination argue from a strategic perspective, based on their own experiences in nuclear policy. They do not suggest that conflict will disappear or that 'greater international harmony' will prevail. Rather, they assert that there are numerous alternatives to relying on nuclear weapons to address these conflicts. Freedman insists that 'proponents of disarmament ... must explain why this particular approach must now have priority over the thus far successful combination of non-use, deterrence, and non-proliferation'. This is, however, a sanguine view of the status quo which is seen as both benign and a predictable indicator of future 'success'. It also discounts the potential role of ever-more capable conventional weaponry in achieving strategic objectives. MccGwire (1985: 55) has referred to what he calls the 'dogma of deterrence' – a key manifestation of nuclearism – which by the 1950s 'came to crowd out other long-established ideas, becoming at times a virtual substitute for both foreign and defence policy'. Assertions that nuclear weapons must be retained forever to deter attack or because of some vague and undefined necessity continue to be repeated like a refrain, as if no other policy choice could ever be contemplated.

The one argument within deterrence thinking that does carry significant weight is the belief that possessing nuclear weapons can deter nuclear attack by another nuclear state. Indeed this is the cornerstone of nuclear deterrence (notwithstanding that some nuclear states appear to have expanded the role of the bomb beyond this limited utility). We cannot easily discount the importance of this strategy in Cold War and even in contemporary thinking. The position that nuclear weapons must be retained as a strategic necessity might be upheld if we were to accept that nuclear weapons serve the sole purpose of deterring a nuclear strike from an adversary. But this argument is still subject to the following logic: any such utility would disappear if all nuclear weapons were eliminated, particularly as calls are for a phased, balanced, and verifiable process of elimination, with strategies devised to address the security concerns of nuclear states as they move towards a position of zero. Again, the presence of large and sophisticated conventional weapons' arsenals in all of the nuclear weapon states should not be underestimated as being useful deterrents in their own right.

Fourth, the claims that nuclear deterrence provides unique and valuable benefits which are unable to be secured any other way – which is effectively what the possessors of nuclear weapons are saying – must accept the logical extension of this argument, and agree that *all* states who value their security should also have access to nuclear weapons. If nuclear deterrence does indeed keep the peace, then we should not be concerned about nuclear proliferation. For Kenneth Waltz (1981), 'more is better', even to the point where Iran should get the bomb (Waltz 2012). However, expansion of the nuclear 'club' is unlikely to be seen as a positive development for global security, either by the existing nuclear states or by the international community more broadly. Arguing that they must keep their weapons for deterrence purposes will surely mean that the existing nuclear weapon states cannot retain their monopoly on these weapons forever, and that they must expect proliferation as the natural extension of their own policies. The difficulty for the nuclear weapon states as they cling to nuclear deterrence is that they have to strive to retain their arsenals at any cost and deny nuclear weapons to others, or else accept that their claims that nuclear weapons provide unique security benefits will be adopted also by other states. Waltz's position, that 'the measured spread of nuclear weapons is more to be welcomed than feared' (Waltz 1981: 30) has not been seen as desirable. It is rightly viewed as multiplying nuclear dangers; indeed the very existence of the Non-Proliferation Treaty rejects such a notion.

Fifth, nuclear deterrence, if it is to be effective, relies on a delicate psychological balance. It requires all parties to act rationally, and to be restrained by the inherent fear of nuclear annihilation. There is no guarantee that any future holders of nuclear weapons, or even the leaders of the existing nuclear weapon states, will always act rationally. Deterrence cannot be seen as a foolproof instrument for preventing a nuclear strike. A dependence on rationality and the good intentions of one's own leaders is problematic enough, but reliance on the leaders of *other* nations is also required. Apart from suggesting an over-confidence in the abilities of human beings, advocates of deterrence seem untroubled by the many times when technological failures, glitches, 'acts of God', or inadvertent human actions have resulted in catastrophes. (Notable incidents that come to mind include the 2011 Fukushima disaster, the 1985 Chernobyl meltdown, the 2010 Deepwater Horizon explosion, seen as the worst environmental disaster in the United States, and the 1986 Challenger spacecraft accident, caused by the failure of a very minor component which had not been designed to perform in the severely cold conditions approved by the experts in the field). It defies logic to think that humans will never fail in the requirements for deterrence, or that our creation of technology will always serve to prevent disaster. Robert Oppenheimer noted at the outset of the nuclear age that 'it would be visionary in the extreme, and not practical, to hope that methods which have so sadly failed in the past to avert war will succeed in the face of this far greater peril' (Oppenheimer 1946). Humility, a sense of proportion, and alertness to the risk of failure all seem to be absent in calculations of deterrence. As one writer, coming from an ethical Christian perspective notes, 'Christian understandings of human fallibility represent an intractable problem for acceptance of both nuclear optimism and a long run policy of nuclear deterrence' (Allen 2015: 373).

Deterrence comes with several illogicalities. At the same time that their holders believe that nuclear weapons should never be used, they are expected to convey to their adversary that they *will* indeed be used. Deterrence requires forbearance from execution, but also the promise of that very execution. Proponents are content to proceed with the practice of deterrence, bolstered by the non-use of these weapons and ongoing nuclear constraint, viewing deterrence as a useful security blanket that they are loath to give up. After all, these weapons are not being *used*. But as Gilinsky (2016) reminds us, deterrence cannot easily be divorced from use: 'that is why trained and dedicated officers in nine countries operate in shifts, waiting for orders to release their weapons'. Non-use is predicated on oneself and one's adversaries never using their nuclear weapons, while at the same time preparing most ardently for that very action.

This psychological uncertainty and the assumption of rationality bring other problems also: nuclear deterrence poses an unprecedented difficulty for citizen–state relations. John Herz (1958) was one of the first to observe the impact of nuclear weaponry on the idea of the territoriality of the state. Noting that the advent of nuclear weaponry overwhelmed the functional role of governments, which was the protection of the state and its people, he wrote of a new 'condition of permeability' or vulnerability never before experienced by societies (Herz 1958). With a failure of deterrence, the state becomes immediately vulnerable to utter devastation, representing a strategic environment unlike anything encountered previously. Continued survival now depends not only on the actions of our own government, 'but on the continued sanity of [our] opponents' leaders' (Harknett 1996: 142). This would seem to be an unacceptably risky strategy but it remains the central component of nuclear deterrence.

Sixth, in any case, a number of historians and scholars question the extent to which nuclear deterrence 'worked' during the Cold War (see, for example, Mueller 1988; Garthoff 2000; Wilson 2008). That no nuclear weapons were used during this time has been taken as incontrovertible proof of the effectiveness of nuclear deterrence. Victor Gilinsky, noting the number of instances where these weapons were very nearly used, asks, 'what conclusions can be drawn from the decades of non-use of nuclear weapons for the future? None we can be sure of' (Gilinsky 2016). To accept uncritically that it was nuclear weapons and their deterrent qualities that kept the peace between the great powers after 1945, and to use the Cold War experience to argue the need to keep nuclear weapons today, at once attributes too much value to their deterrent qualities and pays insufficient attention to the dangers attendant on their very existence. Nuclear deterrence, as Pelopidas (2015) summarizes, is very much a 'bet', but it has been 'portrayed as a certainty'. Yet the nuclear states continue to assert the deterrent value of these weapons, even in the face of a history which should rather dictate extreme caution.

Undeniably, the ongoing threat of nuclear confrontation between the nuclear states cannot simply be wished-away. But the argument is that with sufficient commitment and a closely monitored and verified process of mutually balanced, gradual, and verified elimination, these uncertainties can be managed and can result in a safer kind of security than is achieved by relying on the vagaries of nuclear deterrence. Certainly, resorting to the view that 'our adversary has them, so we must have them too' entrenches nuclearism further and is likely to prompt proliferation by other states. The nuclear weapon states' claim that they must retain their weapons for deterrent purposes has worn thin as far as many non-nuclear states are concerned, and this has added to the latter's frustration with the prevailing nuclear order. Retaining the nuclear option is unconvincing, both logically or strategically, and for non-nuclear states it is also morally untenable. Thus a fundamental aspect of nuclearism – what Lifton and Falk (1982) recognized as the unwavering faith in nuclear weapons to provide security – remains strong, and the impasse remains.

Ignoring instances of near-use and the risks of accidents

That nuclearism continues to prevail is difficult enough for non-nuclear states to accept. This state of affairs is only compounded by the fact that these weapons, far from being benign or 'not used', pose serious risks to international security. Reflecting this frustration, Ken Booth notes that the nuclear weapon states insist on 'worst-casing' or playing-up 'the risks they believe will come with nuclear abolition'. At the same time, they 'best-case' the 'condition of living indefinitely with thousands of nuclear weapons', playing down and even dismissing the risks of nuclear conflicts, accidents, miscalculations, and nuclear terrorism, that come with retaining these arsenals (Booth 1999: 18).

And these risks are very real. Nuclear weapons designed to provide 'national' security carry the danger of compromising global security, should deterrence fail. This danger, Falk argues, requires us to challenge the 'mental armour of nuclearism … its associated myths and rationalisation', and its 'moral myopia' (Falk 1982b: 251). Such risks have long been evident. It is worth remembering that where prominent individuals – such as Henry Kissinger, Robert McNamara, and William Perry – have changed their minds about the usefulness of nuclear weapons, this has been done not on the basis of 'dovish' sentiments, but because of 'strategic reasoning, a recalculation of the balance of risks, and a re-thinking of the axioms' attendant on nuclear deterrence (Booth 1999: 15).

Yet the nuclear states continue to rely on a system that is fraught with dangers. Adhering to nuclear deterrence not only glosses over the many problems associated with deterrence and nuclear weapons' use; it also perpetuates a nuclear 'culture' in which the very existence and modernization of nuclear arsenals increase the risk of accidental or what we might term 'irrational' use. Long-time observers of nuclear politics have warned that the norm of non-use, or the taboo against nuclear weapons, might fail accidentally (Butler 2000; Arbatov and Dvorkin 2006; Wilson 2008; Ritchie 2014a; Perry 2015; Perry and Collina 2020). There are several documented occasions when deterrence very nearly did fail (sometimes saved only by the actions of a single military officer). Hedley Bull had noted his belief as early as 1961 that 'the danger of nuclear war by accident is more serious than that of deliberate and premeditated attack' (Bull 1961: 207). Numerous close-calls have occurred, and continuing with sanguine policies will not save us from disaster (Schlosser 2013a). One report has published 270 publicly known military incidents which had occurred over a period of twenty-one months involving nuclear weapon states or their allies. A troubling proportion of these were deemed to be either 'provocative', or 'high risk', and any one of these could have escalated tensions and resulted in accidental or deliberate nuclear use (Global Zero 2016).

A report prepared by the European Leadership Network documented a number of serious incidents between nuclear-capable NATO forces and Russian military forces. The report paints a 'disturbing picture of violations of national airspace, emergency scrambles, narrowly-avoided mid-air collisions, close encounters at sea, simulated attack runs and other dangerous actions happening on a regular basis' (Frear *et al.* 2014). Recent research, especially the 2017 report, *Playing with Fire: Nuclear Weapons Incidents and Accidents in the United Kingdom* (Nuclear Information Service 2017) allows us a clearer understanding of the many occasions when disaster was narrowly averted. Eric Schlosser outlines the times that accidents occurred in the United States. He claims that while the Pentagon's official list of nuclear weapon accidents comes to thirty-two, his research shows that 'just between the years 1950 and 1968, there were more than 1,000 accidents involving nuclear weapons' (Schlosser 2014). These include the occasion in January 1961, when the US Air Force accidently dropped two thermonuclear bombs on North Carolina; each of these bombs had yields of between two and four megatons (that is, between 130 and 260 times more powerful than the Hiroshima bomb, which was about 15 kilotons). In one weapon all the safety switches worked to prevent detonation; in the other, three out of the four safety switches failed, and it was only good luck that the fourth held, preventing a disaster which would have engulfed most of the eastern United States. At the time, the government denied there had been any risk of explosion, but Freedom of Information requests subsequently showed that indeed a single switch prevented detonation. Schlosser reminds us of the tenuous nature of human control over technological developments. One of the themes of his book is about 'how we are so much better at creating complex technological systems than we are at controlling them' (Schlosser 2014).

Lapses in safety and security are increasingly coming to light. One report notes thirty-two 'broken arrow' incidents between 1950 and 1980 which jeopardized the safety and security of US nuclear weapons (Shultz and Drell 2012). While these poor practices have occurred in the United States, we can assume that standards of safety and security of nuclear materials might be far worse in nuclear weapon states like Russia, Pakistan, India, China, or North Korea. There are also the many cases where nuclear weapons were nearly used deliberately. Patricia Lewis and her team (2014) documented thirteen cases where nuclear use was seriously contemplated, in the United States, Soviet Union/Russia, the United Kingdom, Israel, India, and Pakistan,[11] as a result of miscommunication, misperception (often relating to military exercises), miscalculation, or simply poor management. And Ira Helfand and Robert Dodge remind us that there were at least five occasions since 1979 when either Washington or Moscow mistakenly believed that the other had launched a nuclear attack, and prepared to retaliate in kind; in each of these situations, nuclear war was averted by a matter of minutes (Helfand and Dodge 2016).

There is also the possibility that cyber-attacks against a nuclear state will cause an unauthorized launch of a nuclear weapon (Fritz 2009; Unal and Afina 2020). In June 2015, former Head of Strategic Command James Cartwright, addressing a meeting of the Ploughshares group, warned that terrorists and others might hack into the command and control systems of the United States or Russia, sparking a wider nuclear calamity (cited in Cirincione 2015). For his part, William Perry has noted that at least during the Cold War, there was little danger of cyber-attack, but today's circumstances make this a dangerous possibility (cited in Borger 2016). As late as 2013, there had been no proper assessment of the cyber-vulnerabilities of US nuclear weapon control systems. Noting the weak level of 'cyber hygiene' within the Department of Defense and its networks and systems, a task force has singled this issue out as one of the most pressing threats facing the department (US Department of Defense 2013).

Conclusion

Nuclearism, the faith that nuclear weapons are essential for security, continued even after the Cold War, and is evident in the policies of the nuclear states today. The nine nuclear states, and especially the United States and Russia, remain wedded to their weapons of mass destruction, refusing to undertake even relatively straightforward measures which would reduce the risks of nuclear dangers, continuing to place faith in nuclear deterrence, no matter how precarious this might be, and regardless of the very real threats of accidents, misperception, and human frailty.

The research on risks and dangers will be known to the leaders of the nuclear weapon states, but the continuation of nuclearism leads them to ignore or sweep aside these dangers.[12] Nuclearism allows for the belief that the status quo can be maintained indefinitely, and that the risks involved in nuclear deterrence are either barely existent, or so low that the alleged gains outweigh them. Nuclearism suggests a disregard for the probabilities of catastrophic danger. It downplays evidence-based assessments, favouring instead unproven 'certainties' that these weapons are useful and that they can be managed rationally, repeating the mantra that nuclear deterrence assures a state's security.[13] In this sense, those who continue to rely on nuclear weapons to keep the peace, traditionally labelled in International Relations scholarship as 'realists', and who appear not to be worried by the prospect of accidental or terrorist use that the ongoing retention of nuclear weapons could bring, might be better described as idealists who seek to perpetuate a nuclear future built on a dangerously shaky past.

This apparent disregard for the many risks and dangers, the absolute faith in nuclear deterrence – and even a willingness to use nuclear weapons first – all signal that nuclearism is very much alive and well today. The nuclear-armed states have been remarkably successful in retaining their arsenals, much to the frustration of many of the non-nuclear countries, and it is clear from their current modernization programmes, doctrines, and statements that they intend to continue with this course.

Notes

1 'Hygiene' presumably refers here to the questionable standards of safety and security surrounding nuclear weapons, even in the 'advanced' Western democracies.
2 Parrish and Bond Graham (2009) have pointed to what they call 'anti-nuclear nuclearism', whereby the nuclear states, and especially the United States, have been 'rhetorically calling for what has long been derided as a naïve ideal: global

nuclear disarmament'. De-emphasizing the 'offensive' nature of nuclear weapons, anti-nuclear nuclearism disingenuously professes to understand the need for disarmament, while at the same time ensuring that such a development will never take place.
3 Among the best analyses of these modernization programmes are those conducted by Warren and Baxter (2020), Woolf (2020), Kristensen and Korda (2020a, 2020b), Kristensen et al. (2017), Reif (2018a), and Acheson et al. (2017), who have outlined in detail what these programmes entail. The nuclear arsenals of all nine nuclear weapon states currently 'are designed to inflict specific, calculated damage on potential adversaries. This ranges from the use of a few nuclear weapons against more vulnerable or "soft" targets such as a city to the simultaneous or highly orchestrated employment of many hundreds of weapons against military forces, including damage-resistant or "hardened" missile silos and underground command and control centres' (Kristensen and McKinzie 2015: 566). Gilinsky (2016) notes that 'India seeks a submarine-based strategic force, Israel already has one and is expanding it, North Korea is building more weapons and is experimenting with submarine-launched missiles, and Pakistan is introducing short-range nuclear weapons to counter a possible Indian conventional attack'.
4 The term 'stockpile stewardship' is itself troubling: as Taylor and Hendry (2008: 304) argue, 'the articulation of "stewardship" with "nuclear weapons" is potentially incongruous. Stewardship traditionally refers to the preservation of unambiguously beneficial resources', and connotes elements of 'care, responsibility, and sustainability', especially in the interests of future generations. Appropriating this word therefore not only obscures the ongoing modifications to nuclear weapons in the United States; it also distorts the very meaning of the word 'stewardship'.
5 North Korea's leader in 2016 announced a no-first-use policy (Murphy 2016), but the sincerity of this is tested by other assertions he has made claiming the right to a preventive nuclear strike.
6 Their fears were fuelled by North Korean conventional military postures, which would be encouraged, they felt, if Kim Jong-un believed that the United States would not respond with nuclear weapons.
7 Notable individuals engaged in defending and continuing American nuclear possession, regardless of the end of the Cold War, have included Donald Rumsfeld, Charles Krauthammer, Richard N. Haas, Edward Luttwak, and Keith B. Payne.
8 In reality, possession of nuclear weapons has never meant invulnerability for nuclear armed states. There have been several attacks against these states, as well as conflicts where nuclear weapons could not be used.
9 Doyle had worked for the Los Alamos Laboratory in New Mexico for seventeen years, but after publishing his article in 2013 ('Why Eliminate Nuclear Weapons?') was dismissed from his post. He believed that 'the world must reject the myths and expose the risks of the ideology of nuclear deterrence if it is to meet the challenges of the twenty-first century'. He believes that his

dismissal was 'part of a Washington-inspired campaign of retribution for his refusal to stay on message and support the lab's central mission, namely its continued development and production of nuclear arms' (cited in Birch 2014).
10 An excellent work is the collection of essays edited by Shultz and Goodby (2015), especially the chapter by Benoit Pelopidas. Other notable works include MccGwire (1985), Larkin (2008), Anderson (2016), and Berry *et al.* (2010).
11 The authors note that the omission of cases from China or North Korea is due to lack of publicly available information, and that it should not suggest that these states are exempt from cases of near inadvertent use or nuclear risk (Lewis *et al.* 2014: 2).
12 A notable exception was President Obama's Nuclear Security Summits, held between 2010 and 2016, aimed at reducing the possibility of nuclear terrorism by securing global stocks of nuclear material.
13 In the context of Russia's 2014 war against Ukraine, the argument was heard that Ukraine would have been safer if it had not returned Soviet nuclear weapons to Moscow in 1994. But this is, as Rublee (2015) argues, a counterfactual 'fantasy'. Rublee and others point out that Ukraine was unlikely to have been able to maintain these weapons reliably; even if Ukraine had been able to do so, the long-term safety of these weapons would have been in doubt. Retaining them would have produced untenable political, military, and technical risks. Rublee also suggests that far from these weapons being a deterrent, if Ukraine had kept them for its own purposes, Russia would have annexed Crimea well before 2014. In the context of the 2022 war, the presence of additional nuclear weapons would only increase the chances of their use and the catastrophic damage that would result if any of them were detonated, deliberately or inadvertently.

3

Pushing for disarmament: a fruitless exercise

Previous chapters have noted how nuclearism has been sustained for decades and how it continues, even as the risks of reliance on nuclear deterrence, the limited utility of these weapons, and the ongoing dangers of accidents and misperception suggest that a new approach is needed. There have been several attempts since the ending of the Cold War to persuade these states to move to eliminate these weapons. That is, well before the achievement of the Treaty on the Prohibition of Nuclear Weapons in March 2017, numerous formal efforts had been made to change the dynamics of nuclearism and to implement a process of disarmament via a series of mutual, balanced, phased, and verified steps. These have been put forward by various states and state groupings and have been endorsed by civil society actors. A brief history of these activities is provided here to demonstrate the extent and persistence of the efforts made over recent decades to push for the elimination of nuclear weapons, and because they provide an explanatory context for the growing sense of frustration felt by many non-nuclear weapon states.

Non-nuclear states and civil society groups acknowledge that while the number of weapons has dropped from its high level during the Cold War to just over 13,000 today (Arms Control Association 2022), this figure is still high and simply extends the ongoing dangers associated with nuclear weapons. Prime responsibility for cuts falls on the two largest nuclear powers, Russia and the United States, who hold over 90 per cent of this global tally, but these two states appear unwilling to negotiate any further reductions, and their strategic relationship has deteriorated significantly in recent years. Moreover, none of the other nuclear weapon states – Britain, France, China, India, Pakistan, Israel, and North Korea – are showing any willingness to eliminate their weapons. Non-nuclear states fear that despite the promises made to disarm, every one of the nuclear weapon states shows instead a determination to retain their arsenals. As one report noted in April 2017, instead of disarmament, we are seeing instead 'assured destruction forever' (Acheson *et al.* 2017).[1]

Promoting the elimination of nuclear weapons: a short history

The very first resolution of the United Nations General Assembly, in January 1946, called for the elimination of nuclear weapons, through the appointment of a commission whose terms of reference were, *inter alia*, to make specific proposals 'for the elimination from national armaments of atomic weapons and of all other major weapons adaptable to mass destruction' (UN 1946). In 1968, the Non-Proliferation Treaty itself opened with 'the need to make every effort to avert the danger of [nuclear] war', and urged all nuclear weapon states to take seriously their obligation to disarm. Largely because of the vagaries of superpower confrontation, these proposals were ineffective, and we saw instead only a dramatic increase in the numbers of these weapons, even after the NPT entered into force. Promoting a nuclear-free world during the Cold War was simply ineffective, despite activities and campaigns undertaken over the decades.

When the Cold War ended – unexpectedly, almost abruptly, but with much relief – the opportunity arose to take stock of the position in which the world now found itself, and to reconsider those assumptions and policies that had prevailed in international security for the previous four decades. This profound change in the structure of world politics – the move away from bipolarity and the ending of a confrontation which had threatened nuclear annihilation – allowed policy-makers a chance to reflect seriously on what kind of a world we now lived in, and what steps would be necessary to sustain and consolidate the peace which the ending of superpower hostility had brought. In reality, however, this did not happen, at least not in any systematic or deliberate way. Many of the troubled issues which existed during the Cold War – such as the Israeli–Palestinian conflict, the simmering resentment against Western, and especially US, policies and presence in the Middle East more broadly, the grave inequalities between states and people of the world where extreme poverty and vulnerability existed for many and immense wealth and political influence prevailed for some, and even the growing warnings on climate change – did not receive the attention they deserved, now that the threat of nuclear annihilation seemed to have passed. To be fair, the world seemed overwhelmed in the 1990s by the rise of ethnic conflicts, in parts of Eastern Europe, in the Balkans, and in parts of Africa, and by the rise of a new kind of terrorism from 2001 onwards.

Nonetheless, little effort was made by political leaders to secure lasting positive relations between East and West, and some of the blame for this can be placed on the United States, which appeared to see the ending of the Cold War as its own 'victory', and which manifested what realist author Stephen Walt (2016) has called 'a textbook combination of both hubris and bad geopolitics'. There seemed no need to consolidate the peace, to reform or replace security organizations, to revise old military doctrines, and to create a safer world. This was especially true in two key and interrelated areas: Russia was more or less isolated and antagonised after the Cold War as NATO expanded eastwards at an unwise pace (Kamp 1995; Eland 1998; Hanson 1998; Walt 2016),[2] and nuclear weapons continued to remain the central pillar in security policy for the nuclear weapon states, even though the *raison d'être* for these arsenals – certainly for Washington and Moscow – should have been a thing of the past.

We had, however, seen the glimmer of an alternative nuclear future during negotiations for the Intermediate-range Nuclear Forces Treaty conducted between Ronald Reagan and Mikhail Gorbachev in Reykjavik, Iceland in 1986. There, and before the Cold War ended, both leaders had advanced the idea that it was not only possible, but indeed feasible and desirable, to seek the elimination of all nuclear weapons. Disagreements over various issues, especially plans for US missile defence, resulted in a more modest achievement – the elimination of intermediate range nuclear forces – but, as Nikolai Sokov (2007) notes, the meeting at Reykjavik had 'become a symbol of sorts – an example that nuclear disarmament is within reach as long as political leaders have courage to make such a decision and break through bureaucratic politics and the maze of arcane nuclear balance theories'. Reykjavik thus came to represent a tantalising opening for the elimination of nuclear weapons, led by the two superpowers,[3] but it was an opening that was not taken seriously and pursued at the time; nor was it revived by leaders in the nuclear weapon states even when the Berlin Wall fell and the East–West confrontation came to an end three years later.

The immediate post-Cold War world

Nevertheless, the idea that international security could be maintained without relying on nuclear weapons was kept alive by some: the Pugwash Conferences on Science and World Affairs produced a seminal work examining the desirability and feasibility of a nuclear-free world (Rotblat *et al.* 1993), while in 1994 the Henry L. Stimson Center, established in Washington, DC in 1989, launched a substantial project on this same idea, examining the conditions under which the world might move towards the balanced and progressive elimination of nuclear weapons. Its Steering Committee brought out three important reports (Stimson Center 1995a, 1995b, 1997). Among those on this Steering Committee of this think-tank were Robert McNamara, US Secretary of Defense from 1961 to 1968, and General Andrew Goodpaster, Supreme Allied Commander, Europe (SACEUR), from 1969 to 1974. The presence of such individuals from the policy and military fields was an important element in this new process.

The 1995 Review and Extension Conference of the Nuclear Non-Proliferation Treaty

When it was time to hold the first NPT Review Conference (RevCon) since the ending of the Cold War, there were confident hopes that disarmament would now be taken seriously. This particular RevCon would be important for a number of reasons: not only was it was the first to be held after the Cold War; it was also the first time that all five of the nuclear weapon states recognized as such by the NPT would participate as members. And it was also, coincidentally, the occasion at which the future of the treaty was going to be decided. The NPT had entered into force in 1970, and was initially to last for a period of twenty-five years; in 1995, it would be up to the states parties to the treaty to decide on its future, its text specifying that a majority of states could decide 'whether the Treaty shall continue in force indefinitely, or shall be extended for an additional fixed period or periods' (UN 1968). Thus the 1995 meeting would be termed the NPT Review and Extension Conference (NPTREC).

In addition to deciding on the future of the NPT, the central 'bargain' of the treaty – that is, the promise by non-nuclear states to forego nuclear weapons, in exchange for the P5 states assisting them with the peaceful use of nuclear technology and the P5 moving firmly to eliminate their nuclear weapons – would be coming under intense scrutiny. These three elements of the bargain had been reflected in the three 'pillars' of the NPT: non-proliferation, the peaceful use of nuclear technology, and nuclear disarmament. Clearly, it was the first pillar which was most important to the nuclear weapon states, while the latter two pillars were of concern chiefly to the non-nuclear weapon states. In particular, it was Article VI of the NPT which exercised the minds of delegates from the non-nuclear states. Article VI had stipulated that all states parties must 'undertake to pursue negotiations in good faith on effective measures relating to the cessation of the nuclear arms race at an early date and to nuclear disarmament' (UN 1968). Thus while the document had been formally termed the 'Non-Proliferation Treaty', this did not mean that non-proliferation was its sole focus, and non-nuclear states were keen to hold the P5 to their promise of disarmament. At this time, therefore, the existing NPT machinery was seen as the best mechanism to facilitate a process of disarmament, especially now that Cold War hostilities had lifted.

While there was a general acceptance that the NPT had been a useful element in international security, with Joseph Cirincione (1995: 201) noting that it had successfully created 'an international standard against the spread of nuclear weapons, changing the acquisition of such weapons from a source of national pride to an object of official denial', there were, already by 1995, signs that some non-nuclear states were becoming impatient with the nuclear weapon states and the 'apartheid' system regarding the management of the global nuclear order (Biswas 2001; Maddock 2010; Thakur 2016b). For some, the NPT reflected another instance of domination of smaller countries by powerful states, simply perpetuating a hierarchical global order (see Biswas 2014). For them, this discriminatory approach had

Pushing for disarmament

been a cause of concern ever since the NPT had been negotiated, and it had resulted in a determination by some of them – most notably India – not to sign a treaty which had created a two-tier approach to the possession of nuclear weapons (Pilat and Pendley 1990: 1).

There were bound to be questions about the future of nuclear weapons in the post-Cold War era, now that the primary reason for their existence – the superpower confrontation – had ceased. But no clear policy review took place. An early and disappointing indication that things were not likely to change appeared when the United States, in 1994, released the first of its Quadrennial Reviews of its nuclear forces (a process that has subsequently grown into the US Nuclear Posture Review). The review continued to reaffirm the central role of nuclear deterrence, signalling to the world that global changes notwithstanding, Washington, whose lead would likely influence the other nuclear weapon states, would not be revising its security doctrines or its weapons policies (Pilat and Pendley 1995). This indicated, ahead of the 1995 NPTREC, that any serious move to the elimination of nuclear weapons on the part of the United States was unlikely. Although the United States and Russia were engaged in nuclear reductions through the START agreements, these were not comprehensive, and in any case did not constitute a fundamental reappraisal of the role of nuclear weapons in national and international security, a questioning of whether these weapons held any utility for new security challenges, or whether they were relics from a Cold War era very different to the world of the early 1990s.

Importantly, there had been long-standing calls for the nuclear weapon states to negotiate and bring into force a comprehensive nuclear test ban treaty (CTBT), amidst global concern for the ongoing hazards posed to humans and the environment by the more than 2,000 nuclear weapons tests which had been conducted by the five nuclear powers since 1945.[4] From the early 1990s, the United States, Britain, and Russia had observed a self-imposed moratorium on nuclear testing, and while this was welcomed, it was seen as not enough to convince the world of the good intentions of these states. Additionally, there had been calls for a Fissile Material Cut-Off Treaty (FMCT). An FMCT and a CTBT, it was argued, would be important for both disarmament and for non-proliferation efforts, limiting as they would the availability of nuclear material and the possibility of testing nuclear devices, precursors to a functioning nuclear weapons capability. But the body charged with negotiating such agreements, the UN's Conference on Disarmament (CD), showed no signs of being able to produce these treaties, constrained as it was by the rule of consensus where a single member state could prevent agreements from being reached. Indeed, disappointment at the slow progress of the CD in general was another element of unease between those states which enjoyed dominance in security affairs (the nuclear weapon states and their allies) and the non-nuclear weapon states. All this formed the background in the years leading up to the 1995 NPT Review and Extension Conference.

The significance and standing of the NPT should not be underestimated. As Richard Butler has observed, in the absence of nuclear weapons being addressed in the Charter of the United Nations – which had been drawn up before the first use of these weapons in August 1945 – the NPT served to fill this space by creating and consolidating a legal and political norm that states should not possess nuclear weapons. The NPT, together with the International Atomic Energy Agency (IAEA), had become for many what Butler called the 'compact', which would proscribe these weapons, and it was hoped that the 1995 extension of the NPT was going to become 'the foundation stone of a new nuclear compact' (Butler 1996). Most states agreed that the NPT had been vital in limiting the number of nuclear-armed states since 1970; it had after all created a strong norm against proliferation, and all but a handful of states remained outside the treaty.

Yet there was ongoing disquiet about its discriminatory nature and whether the P5 states would in fact comply with Article VI. Some countries used the opportunity of the upcoming NPTREC to indicate their concern. The Nigerian Foreign Minister, for example, criticized not only the huge numerical increase in the nuclear weapon states' nuclear arsenals after the superpowers had pressed the NPT onto the world to restrain any other would-be nuclear states, but also the technological improvements that they had made to these weapons, where warheads now carried ever greater destructive capabilities (cited in Kelle 1995: 40). Critics also took aim at the record of disarmament since the Cold War ended: this was notable, but it did not indicate a genuine wish to disarm on the part of the nuclear states (Kelle 1995: 40). Some argued that as proof of their commitment to their disarmament obligations, the nuclear weapon states should set a timetable for elimination, so that at specified periods they would be able to demonstrate the achievement of particular goals, leading to the eventual elimination of their weapons (see, for example, the speech of Indonesian Ambassador Ibrahim, cited in Kelle 1995: 40). Above all, there had been concern as early as the 1960s that the P5 states seemed to 'arrogate to themselves that [nuclear] status for all time, while prohibiting other states from acquiring it' (Shaker 1990: 19).

Therefore while there was no doubt about the value of the treaty, by 1995 it was recognized by the non-nuclear states that their adherence to the NPT was the only real leverage they had over the P5 states, in terms of holding the latter to account for their pledges to disarm. In particular, states from the Non-Aligned Movement (NAM) were reluctant to extend indefinitely an agreement which bound them to a permanent non-nuclear status but which at the same time allowed the established nuclear powers to retain their arsenals with no stipulated date for disarmament. Simply extending in perpetuity the NPT would be to give up whatever legal influence and control the non-nuclear states might have over the issue of disarmament.

In addition to their misgivings about the nuclear states' lack of commitment to undertake disarmament within a time-bound framework was a concern about the lack of universal adherence to the NPT (that is, the fact that Israel remained a nuclear state outside the treaty). Many Arab states, already dissatisfied with the double-standard inherent in the treaty, were resentful of Israel's and that its nuclear facilities were not subject to IAEA safeguards. The NAM expressed strong reservations about allowing this inequitable situation to continue. That Israel's allies had acquiesced in that state's nuclear aspirations, but had at the same time prohibited other states from acquiring these weapons, was seen as inconsistent and unfair. As the Egyptian Foreign Minister noted, there had been unsuccessful attempts in the previous decades to bring Israel into a closer alignment with the non-proliferation regime. He asked,

> Is it logical, politically correct or even responsible for the States in the region to agree to support the indefinite extension of the treaty, whereas a state within its region is benefitting from an exemption allowing it to maintain a nuclear programme outside the boundaries of international legitimacy? (Cited in Kelle 1995: 41)

Nevertheless, after considerable diplomatic wrangling and substantial pressure from many Western states (Dhanapala and Rauf 2016: 36), NPT member states agreed, without a vote, to extend the treaty indefinitely.[5] In three landmark provisions, the decision allowed for indefinite extension, for a new mechanism for 'Strengthening the Review Process for the Treaty', and for a set of 'Principles and Objectives for Nuclear Non-Proliferation and Disarmament'. These provisions were designed to give the Treaty 'permanence with accountability', with the latter two focused on moving the nuclear states towards disarmament. Together with these decisions, and prompted by NAM members' concerns regarding Israel, the NPTREC also adopted a 'Resolution on the Middle East', which reaffirmed the importance of 'universal adherence to the Treaty' and, *inter alia*, called upon all states in the Middle East to accede to the NPT, and to take practical steps towards the establishment of a zone free of weapons of mass destruction in that region.

While some states had preferred that the Conference's outcome should be determined by a vote, it was generally felt, especially by Western states, that putting extension of the treaty to a vote would be too divisive, and might result in a substantial number of states voting against indefinite extension.

As with many of the NPT Review Conferences, the outcome was reached on the basis of a unanimous agreement, without a vote taken or any obstructing veto used. An accord reached 'unanimously' did not necessarily mean overwhelming or equal support for proposals from all states, but it did indicate that no one state or group of states was willing to obstruct proceedings. In the end, states wary about their loss of leverage over the NPT were not willing or able enough to prevent the outcome of indefinite extension in 1995.

But it was also clear that extension had been granted by the non-nuclear states primarily as a result of the new proposals for furthering disarmament and the resolution on the Middle East. They trusted that these would pressure the nuclear weapon states to disarm, and to seek universal adherence to the treaty. As Dhanapala and Rauf (2016) remind us, the decision to extend the treaty was secured through this 'interlinked, inseparable and irrevocable, package of three decisions and a resolution'. The decision for extension was granted on the promise of a strengthened review process and enhanced accountability, the enunciation of a clear set of principles and objectives for measuring progress on nuclear non-proliferation and disarmament, and the resolution on establishing a conference to consider a zone free of nuclear and other weapons of mass destruction in the Middle East (Dhanapala 2013).

Western states, especially the United States and its allies, had lobbied hard for this outcome, and overall, this result was well-received. While concern remained about the loss of leverage over the nuclear weapon states (Dhanapala and Rauf 2016: 46), it was generally felt that the world could now expect the nuclear states to move to disarmament. After all, by 1995, there had already been a promising drop in the number of US and Russian nuclear weapons and it was hoped that this bilateral process would continue, in turn leading to the other nuclear weapon states also implement deep reductions. Non-nuclear states would continue to push for concrete steps to be taken towards disarmament and were emphatic that indefinite extension of the NPT should not become 'a *carte blanche*' for these states to retain their monopoly and privileged position forever (Dhanapala and Rauf 2016: 13). Various observers were keen to reinforce this message. In his closing statement as President of the Conference, Ambassador Dhanapala noted:

> The permanence of the Treaty does not represent a permanence of unbalanced obligations, nor does it represent the permanence of nuclear apartheid between nuclear haves and have-nots. What it does represent is our collective dedication to the permanence of an international legal barrier against nuclear proliferation so that we can forge ahead in our tasks towards a nuclear weapon-free world. (Dhanapala cited in Dhanapala and Rydell 2005: 176)

Indefinite extension of the NPT was clearly one of the most important US foreign policy goals at the time and its success was warmly welcomed. Yet, as US Ambassador Thomas Graham, who led the US delegation to the NPTREC, warned at the time, it was 'important to understand that a [P5] failure to meet the obligations of the Statement of Principles and Objectives – especially reductions in nuclear weapons – will endanger the permanent status of the NPT or even the NPT regime itself' (Graham 2002: 292). Several influential ambassadors from the NAM had made this point to him privately, emphasizing that they 'were only willing to remain second-class states under the NPT temporarily as negotiated disarmament proceeded' (Graham 2002: 291). One publication noted what it called the 'victory arrogance' of the nuclear weapon states after 'achieving their objective of "consensus" on indefinite extension' (Acronym Institute 1998). It also registered the 'concomitant anger' in a group of non-nuclear states from the NAM, who 'felt cheated by the adoption of the indefinite extension decision without a vote' (Acronym Institute 1998). The Indonesian Ambassador, for instance, argued that pressure had been put on non-aligned states, and that promises and even threats had been made by certain nuclear weapon states, in particular the United States, but also from other Western states (cited in Welsh 1995). The fact that many felt coerced into indefinite extension, and that the decision was taken without a vote, led some states to believe that the means by which the extension was reached was neither welcome or democratic (Welsh 1995).[6]

Neither did it reassure the non-nuclear states when US President Clinton's statement on the day of the agreement stressed the importance of extension for the cause of non-proliferation, but failed to make any mention of the nuclear weapon states' obligation to disarm. He perceived the agreement as the 'community of nations' remaining 'steadfast in opposing the dangerous spread of nuclear weapons' (Clinton 1995). The decision was 'to confront the nuclear danger by rejecting nuclear proliferation' (Clinton 1995). Clearly, what was 'nuclear danger' for nuclear states and their allies was proliferation, but what was 'nuclear danger' for the majority non-nuclear states was the refusal of the nuclear powers to fulfil their obligations to disarm. China proceeded to conduct tests of nuclear weapons, barely three days after the Review and Extension Conference ended.

Soon after the extension of the NPT, there was a further historic decision reached regarding nuclear weapons. In its 1996 *Advisory Opinion*, the UN's International Court of Justice (ICJ) reiterated the fact that the nuclear weapon states had a legal obligation to negotiate nuclear disarmament in good faith. The ICJ's deliberations had been the result of the 'World Court Project', a campaign pushed largely by individuals and non-governmental organizations (NGOs) in New Zealand, which expanded to civil society groups in other states, and which came to be taken up by a range of non-nuclear states within the United Nations. The World Court Project sought to achieve a legal ruling on the illegality of nuclear weapons, motivated by the fact that there was no explicit treaty which outlawed nuclear weapons (Dewes and Green 1999). In the end, the ICJ was not able to determine conclusively that the use of nuclear weapons in very limited circumstances would necessarily be illegal (although Judge Christopher Weeramantry in his *Dissenting Opinion* (1996) outlined his strong view that the use of nuclear weapons would be illegal 'in any circumstances whatsoever').[7]

Notwithstanding its indeterminate statement, the Court was nevertheless very clear in its unanimous ruling that the nuclear weapon states had an overriding obligation to curb the arms race and to move to eventual elimination. Coming so soon after the NPTREC, this ruling served to consolidate the expectation that disarmament should occur.

Commissions, studies, and further reports: attempts to reorient the nuclear weapon states towards disarmament

The studies conducted by the Stimson Center and elsewhere had, by 1995, come to influence the thinking of Australian Labor Prime Minister Paul Keating and his Minister of Foreign Affairs, Gareth Evans. Their creation of the Canberra Commission reflected a sense of optimism that nuclear elimination was possible. The NPT had been extended indefinitely, and Australia had helped to bring about a treaty to eliminate another kind of weapon of mass destruction, the Chemical Weapons Convention, in 1993. Moreover, the Labor government at the time saw the country as an activist middle-power, a 'good international citizen' keen to rethink the role of nuclear weapons in international security in the post-Cold War era, even as it remained a loyal US ally. But the event which galvanized the government to create the Canberra Commission was the Chinese and French nuclear testing in 1996, especially that conducted by France in the South Pacific. Keating (1998) noted that,

> No image in the twentieth century has seared our collective consciousness like that of the mushroom cloud. And in our minds that image of the Bomb defined the Cold War ... We assumed that because the Cold War was over, the weapons that defined it had miraculously disappeared as well.

Keating and Evans brought together a group of prominent thinkers and practitioners to form an independent Commission tasked with assessing the options for a nuclear-free world. Keating noted that over the years, various anti-nuclear groups had campaigned for this, and had prepared many reports on nuclear dangers, but importantly, up until that time, no *government* had put its name to a report backing nuclear elimination. He stated:

> I wanted to put the authority of a sovereign government behind the push to rid the world of nuclear weapons ... I thought we had an unprecedented and possible unrepeatable opportunity to begin to move to a new strategic environment which offered not just a reduction in the number of nuclear weapons, but their elimination. (Keating 1998)

As one of the appointed Commissioners, Robert O'Neill noted, 'It was clear to me that the role of nuclear weapons had changed since the end of the Cold War and it was high time to re-examine their utility' (O'Neill 2007). Others among the seventeen Commissioners were former prime ministers, ambassadors, and civilian and military leaders. In particular, Robert McNamara, former Secretary of Defense, and General Lee Butler, former Commander in Chief of US Strategic Air Command, had worked in the upper echelons of the US political and military establishments. Field Marshall Lord Carver, Former Chief of the Defence Staff and head of British Armed Forces, was an additional military voice. The appointment of these authoritative individuals was quite deliberate: Keating recognized that the Report would need to demonstrate its credibility to the security and defence policy communities in the nuclear weapon states if it was going to be taken seriously.

Over the course of several months, the Commissioners met to consider ways to reduce the dangers that the ongoing retention of nuclear weapons posed. At the outset, there was no clear consensus among the Commissioners about the desirability of elimination or about the steps that should be taken. But after intense deliberation, and review of the technical and political issues canvassed by an extensive range of Background Papers, the Commissioners' collective view presented in their Report was that a balanced, phased and verified nuclear weapons elimination process was clearly feasible and necessary (Australian Government, Department of Foreign Affairs and Trade 1996).

The Report's essential message was as follows: as long as any one state has nuclear weapons, other states will want them also; as long as nuclear weapons exist, there is a chance that they will be used, either deliberately or by accident; and, that any use of nuclear weapons would be catastrophic (Australian Government, Department of Foreign Affairs and Trade 1996). The Report examined the strategic, technological and political arguments usually put forward in support of retaining nuclear weapons, and made a comprehensive and persuasive case against them. It argued that without elimination, the world faced increased threats of proliferation, nuclear terrorism, and nuclear use.

As part of the debate on the issue of elimination, the Report consolidated and extended the view that the utility of nuclear weapons – an issue that was never wholly resolved even during the Cold War – was even less convincing in the 1990s.[8] Moreover, the new kinds of security threat faced by the world in the post-Cold War era meant that nuclear weapons and nuclear deterrence were at best redundant, and at worst, obstacles to international security (Hanson 2002). The only utility accorded to nuclear weapons was that they might deter against a nuclear attack by another nuclear state. But even in this case, it was argued, the phased and balanced elimination of these weapons would be a positive gain. If nuclear weapons served no useful purpose, then retaining them would be costly, would invite further proliferation, and could result in them being used. The Report warned that while the world had not seen a nuclear strike, either deliberate or inadvertent, after 1945, this good fortune could not be counted on indefinitely.

While urging that as strategic circumstances change, so too must strategic thinking change, the Canberra Commission Report, following the Stimson Center Reports, laid out a series of immediate, reinforcing, and final steps which could be taken to move towards a nuclear weapon free world. Practical steps – such as devaluing the role of nuclear weapons in security policies, taking nuclear forces off high-alert status, removing warheads from delivery vehicles, hastening reductions between the United States and Russia, negotiating a CTBT and an FMCT, and providing mutual no-first-use pledges – were all steps that the Commissioners believed the nuclear weapon states could take, without damaging their security prospects (Australian Government, Department of Foreign Affairs and Trade 1996).

The Commissioners agreed that while nuclear weapons could not be 'un-invented', it was feasible for states to devalue, phase-out, eliminate, and outlaw their possession and use. In the same way that prohibition regimes had been put in place for the other two kinds of weapons of mass destruction – chemical and biological weapons – prohibitions adhered to even by the most powerful states in the international system, so too could nuclear weapons be stigmatized and relegated to the annals of history. The fundamental thinking behind this concept was that humans have the power to determine their future and to seek a world in which security can be achieved without recourse to inhumane weapons which are bound to have disastrous global impacts if they are ever used. Crucial to this argument was the view that while we cannot rewind the clock and un-invent chemical or biological weapons, nor indeed the gas ovens used by the Nazis during the Second World War, human sensibility and condemnation can produce strong moral and legal constraints against what are increasingly seen to be inhumane and abhorrent practices. As the Commissioners pointed out, the sophisticated level of modern conventional weaponry was sufficient to make it the first choice for military action: deterrence can be achieved with conventional weapons, as can any response to aggression and/or to any instance of a state which seeks to develop nuclear weapons after a nuclear-free world has been achieved.[9]

The Report received only a lukewarm reception in the key nuclear states. Additionally, the Australian government had changed during the course of the Commission's deliberations. The new, conservative, Liberal government was reluctant to promote the Report widely or to disturb the alliance with the United States. Notwithstanding this, various analysts recognized the value of the Canberra Commission Report as a sober and independent analysis of the nuclear issue by a group of distinguished and hard-headed experts.[10]

The Report presented an excellent opportunity for the nuclear weapon states to evaluate strategic requirements in the aftermath of the Cold War and to recalibrate their security postures accordingly. But its message – which, it must be emphasized, called for *mutual* measures to be undertaken, and only in a phased, balanced, monitored, and verifiable way, paying heed to the security concerns of all the nuclear states – was largely lost as leaders in the nuclear weapon states continued with the status quo, as members of the public remained generally unaware of continuing nuclear dangers, and as the world moved to address numerous other security considerations emerging in the 1990s. As with the NPT result in 1995, it did little to change the prevailing situation, leaving non-nuclear states increasingly frustrated by the continuation of policies based on nuclearism.

The Commission had made the point that a world which was divided into states that had nuclear weapons, and those that did not, was unsustainable, that while the normative power of the NPT had limited the number of states that possessed nuclear weapons, this discriminatory situation could not be sustained indefinitely. As John Simpson (1996) noted, 'the core of the disputes over the NPT is the demand that the division between nuclear and non-nuclear weapon states be eliminated'. The five nuclear weapon states within the NPT could not reserve to themselves the security benefits that nuclear weapons allegedly brought, while at the same time denying these to other states. This paradox showed itself very clearly in May 1998 when India and Pakistan tested nuclear devices and joined the nuclear 'club'.

India had long denounced the unequal nature of the NPT and the system which allowed the P5 states to retain their arsenals while denying nuclear weapons to any other states. This sense of injustice, and the 1995 extension of the NPT which consolidated this inequality, together with the rise to power of the hard-line Bharatiya Janata Party, led to India conducting nuclear tests in mid-May 1998. Pakistan followed suit later that month. The South Asian tests raised concerns throughout the world. They were denounced by most states, including the nuclear weapon states, and prompted the then Prime Minister of Japan, Ryutaro Hashimoto, to establish in August 1998 a new commission, the Tokyo Forum for Nuclear Non-Proliferation and Disarmament. This Forum met four times and produced its report in July 1999, *Reducing Nuclear Dangers: An Action Plan for the 21st Century* (Japan, Ministry of Foreign Affairs 1999). The Forum's members agreed that the proliferation recently seen in South Asia was a harbinger of future dangers, and that renewed attention had to be given to the issue of nuclear weapons. The Forum differed from the Canberra Commission, in that it was a direct response to India's and Pakistan's actions, and it focused more on the dangers of nuclear proliferation, rather than on disarmament, but essentially, it reiterated the measures recommended by the Canberra Commission three years earlier.

If the Canberra Commission appeared at a time of substantial optimism in world politics, the Tokyo Forum was a response to a deteriorated security landscape. Its first Key Recommendation was that the world must reaffirm the NPT's central bargain (Japan, Ministry of Foreign Affairs 1999). To do this, the nuclear weapon states were urged to demonstrate 'tangible progress in nuclear disarmament', and non-nuclear states pressed to work actively to discourage any further nuclear proliferation. The practical steps outlined in the Canberra Commission were repeated but there was an additional focus on stopping and reversing the proliferation now evident in India and Pakistan; specific attention was also paid to the dangers of missile proliferation. The Tokyo Forum essentially amplified the Canberra Commission's message further.

None of these messages made any difference to the nuclear weapon states, who maintained unchanged nuclear policies. Security conditions worsened in subsequent years, with the rise of jihadi-driven terrorism against the West and accompanying turmoil within the Middle East, the decision taken by North Korea to withdraw from the NPT and develop nuclear weapons in 2006, and the deterioration of US–Russian relations. While the United States and Russia continued with modest bilateral reductions, the relatively cost-free practical steps and recommendations enunciated in Canberra and Tokyo – both key US allies – were not taken, much to the concern of non-nuclear states.

A number of other studies reiterated the points first made prominent by the Stimson Reports and the Canberra Commission. These included the Canadian Parliamentary Report, *Canada and the Nuclear Challenge: Reducing the Political Value of Nuclear Weapons for the Twenty-First Century*, which had appeared in December 1998, and the *Weapons of Mass Destruction Commission Report: Weapons of Terror: Freeing the World of Nuclear, Biological and Chemical Arms* (commonly known as the

Blix Report) of July 2006. There was also the 2005 Norwegian-sponsored Seven Nation Initiative, an attempt to revive nuclear disarmament negotiations after the failure of the 2005 NPT Review Conference, and a further attempt in Australia to address these issues, when a new Labor Prime Minister, Kevin Rudd, established the joint Australia–Japan International Commission on Nuclear Non-proliferation and Disarmament (ICNND 2010). Prominent individuals invited to the Commission's Advisory Board included Henry Kissinger, Sam Nunn, and George Shultz, as well as George Robertson (former British Secretary of Defence and Secretary-General of NATO). The ICNND's Report essentially reinforced the recommendations made earlier about the urgency of addressing nuclear matters at a time when complacency threatened global security (ICNND 2010). Australia was also one of eleven members of the Non-Proliferation and Disarmament Initiative (NPDI) established in 2010. Several of its members were allies of the United States, resulting in some non-aligned states being cautious about the sincerity of the disarmament objectives held by that bloc (Ogilvie-White 2013).[11]

Further studies on the feasibility and desirability of a world without nuclear weapons included the Five Point Proposal for Nuclear Disarmament put forward by UN Secretary General Ban Ki-moon in 2009, and the work of numerous academics and analysts within various think tanks. These scholars have provided an array of literature on the problems posed by nuclear weapons and the need to move towards a nuclear weapon free world.[12] Military leaders and current and former politicians havealso contributed substantially to the debate,[13] and numerous non-governmental bodies had also been instrumental in producing analysis and commentary.[14]

These numerous reports and other activities conducted by these individuals and 'advocacy states' (Hanson 2012) were all a reaction to the slow progress with disarmament, and the need to fulfil the conditions of the NPT and especially its extension conference in 1995. They were motivated by both humanitarian and strategic concerns, mindful of the dangers of nuclear deterrence as well as proliferation, the possibility of accidental use of nuclear weapons, and the prospect of sub-state groups gaining access to nuclear material. They investigated the utility and the dangers of nuclear weapons and all made a strong case for complete nuclear disarmament.

Added to these were the important strategic arguments in favour of elimination first made in 2007 by the authoritative American figures George Shultz, William Perry, Henry Kissinger, and Sam Nunn, in the *Wall Street Journal*. In a series of notable editorials, these 'Four Horsemen' as they came to be known, have urged the United States, Russia, and other nuclear weapon states to act to prevent a serious nuclear accident or deliberate strike from occurring and to prevent further proliferation (Shultz *et al.* 2007,

2008, 2011). These editorials were emulated by numerous other writers and politicians around the world, including in Britain, France, and Russia, and can be read in the document published in 2013 (Shultz *et al.* 2013). They have reinforced the same message: that nuclear weapons presented more dangers than advantages, and that all nuclear weapon states must take urgent action to prevent the use of these weapons and to dissuade proliferation. They pointed to the risks of nuclear materials falling into the 'wrong hands', and urged strong measures to secure arsenals and nuclear materials from potential nuclear terrorists (see also LALN 2016). But they were also very keen to state that nuclear deterrence was at best 'precarious', that it was unpredictable and potentially catastrophic, and that 'reliance on this strategy is becoming increasingly hazardous' (Shultz *et al.* 2013). For them,

> continued reliance on nuclear weapons as the principal element for deterrence is encouraging, or at least excusing, the spread of these weapons, and will inevitably erode the essential cooperation necessary to avoid proliferation, protect nuclear materials and deal effectively with new threats.

These statesmen have also been closely involved in the Nuclear Security Project affiliated with Stanford University, and former Secretary of Defense William Perry, in particular, expanded his activities to detail how his thinking about nuclear weapons changed over the years. However, not even these eminent analysts have been able to disrupt nuclearism or influence the policies of the nuclear weapon states. While their op-ed pieces in the *Wall Street Journal* provided a useful context for President Obama's publicized views on a world without nuclear weapons, the essential positions of the nuclear weapon states remained unchanged.

Notwithstanding their limited impact on the nuclear states, these reports and contributions have been useful in bringing about a rethinking of the role of nuclear weapons to an informed and concerned public audience, and have played a part in the affirmation of the goal of a nuclear weapon free world by numerous state leaders, military personnel, and notable others. They have been vital in keeping this issue alive and in providing clear goals for the steady phasing-out of all nuclear arsenals. Every one of them has urged a reconsideration of prevailing assumptions about the utility of nuclear weapons, and the role of nuclear arsenals. The specialists involved in putting these together had decades of experience behind them, and have all argued that nuclear abolition was not a naive or strategically unwise goal. By being willing to reconsider the role of nuclear weapons in a changed strategic landscape, they provided prudent assessments and a clear course to follow. Reversing previous thinking on the utility of these weapons would undoubtedly have required some courage and a willingness to risk the ire of peers who continued to hold fast to old doctrines. Nonetheless, not even their efforts have had a marked effect on the determination of the nuclear weapon states to retain their arsenals,[15] nor has there been any reconsideration of the practices associated with nuclearism: daily nuclear planning, devoid of humanitarian considerations, and involving vast expense, continues.

The NPT after extension: continued calls for disarmament

While the various studies and reports examined above were appearing, the five-yearly Review Conferences of the Non-Proliferation Treaty continued to be held, and these were the occasions at which states sought to evaluate progress on disarmament, on non-proliferation, and on the peaceful use of nuclear materials. If the Conference in 1995 had been somewhat awkward because of antagonism towards the nuclear states, the subsequent meetings were fraught with considerably more tensions. As Tariq Rauf predicted, the challenge would be 'to reconcile the high expectations and ambitious agendas of many NNWS [non-nuclear weapon states] with the conservatism and obstructionism of most of the NWS [nuclear weapon states] – especially the United States' (Rauf 2000).

In 2000, there was, unsurprisingly, concern at the slow progress of disarmament and more non-nuclear states came to believe that they had acquiesced too easily to the indefinite extension of the NPT five years earlier. The three Preparatory Committee (PrepCom) meetings ahead of the main Review Conference which had been mandated in 1995 as part of the strengthened review process had ended ominously, indicating that it would be hard to reach consensus in 2000. The context for the 2000 Conference was marked by the nuclear tests in South Asia two years earlier, deteriorating relations between the major powers, US missile-defence plans, and the refusal of the US Senate to ratify the CTBT which had been negotiated, finally, in 1996. (With no American ratification, and with China, India, Pakistan, and Israel also refusing to accede to the CTBT, this treaty is yet to enter into force.)

The 2000 NPT RevCon was marked especially by the formation of the New Agenda Coalition (the NAC), a grouping of nine non-nuclear weapon states aiming to foster cooperation between the nuclear and the non-nuclear groupings. The NAC was useful in building a bridge between these groupings, and the Final Document of the Conference included stronger language on nuclear disarmament and the need for universal adherence than had been agreed to in previous Conferences. Additionally, a series of 13 Steps, 'practical steps for the systematic and progressive efforts to implement Article VI', of the NPT were agreed. These steps focused heavily on disarmament obligations, calling for an 'unequivocal undertaking by the nuclear-weapon States to accomplish the total elimination of their nuclear arsenals leading to nuclear disarmament to which all States parties are committed under Article VI'. The 13 Steps also sought to diminish the role of nuclear weapons in security policies, recommended signing and entry into force of the CTBT and creation of an FMCT – all requests made in 1995, and reiterated by the reports made since then. As Rebecca Johnson has noted, these steps are complementary and reinforcing, 'a multi-stranded approach of unilateral, bilateral, plurilateral, and multilateral measures which needs to be addressed in parallel as part of the overall process of reducing the legitimacy of and reliance on nuclear weapons' (Johnson 2000c).

These measures were again raised by the non-nuclear states at the 2000 NPT Review Conference precisely because the 1995 agreements on Principles and Objectives on Non-Proliferation and Disarmament, and the strengthened NPT review process had failed to deliver any substantial impact in the intervening years. Overall, the 2000 Conference was salvaged by the inclusion of the new '13 Steps', and because the five nuclear weapon states made an 'unequivocal undertaking' to abolish their nuclear weapons.

The 'delicate and hard-won compromise between divergent and sometimes conflicting positions' as the President of the 2000 NPT Review Conference had called it (cited in Johnson 2000a), was not, however, to be replicated at the 2005 Review Conference. Since coming into office in 2001, the George W. Bush government had made it clear that American commitment to multilateralism was waning and that it was in no mood to consider disarmament, particularly as the United States came to be engaged in its global war against terrorism. The 2005 NPT Review Conference ended with no progress at all in terms of moving the disarmament agenda forwards (Hanson 2005a). The dissatisfaction with the 2005 conference led to further civil society action. At the urging of Malaysian physician Ron McCoy, the International Campaign to Abolish Nuclear Weapons (ICAN) was formed in Australia by a group of medical and other professionals, presaging the growth of an umbrella group for anti-nuclear NGOs. By 2008, and with President Barack Obama in power, there was some optimism that the 2010 Review Conference would be able to make progress that the antagonistic 2005 meeting had failed to do.

The 2010 NPT Review Conference was thus marked by a real sense of optimism; at no time in its forty-year history had there been such high expectations that the NPT might work as it was intended to do, and this was largely because of the change in US politics under Obama. But there was still a growing impatience with the nuclear weapon states' unwillingness to implement the 1995 agreements or the 13 Steps outlined in 2000. Nevertheless, the Conference was able to conclude with an outcome document which advanced thinking on nuclear disarmament. It included a clear recommitment to the basic 'bargain' of the NPT, and noted 'the reaffirmation by the nuclear-weapon States of their unequivocal undertaking to accomplish, in accordance with the principle of irreversibility, the total elimination of their nuclear arsenals leading to nuclear disarmament' (UN 2010).

The outcome document also included a sixty-four point 'Action Plan' on non-proliferation, disarmament, and the peaceful uses of nuclear energy, and, importantly, a way forward for implementing the 1995 Resolution calling for work towards a WMD Free Zone in the Middle East. The Action Plan outlined specific, measurable activities that states were asked to take in support of all three pillars of the NPT. As Deepti Choubey (2010) notes, these 'were drafted in a way to serve as a scorecard for measuring progress and ensuring there would be accountability at future meetings', including a timeline whereby the nuclear weapon states should report on their disarmament activities ahead of the 2015 RevCon.[16] The Action Plan concerning the peaceful uses of nuclear energy was perhaps the most deliberate and emphatic affirmation of the right of non-nuclear states to access nuclear energy for peaceful purposes. The context for this was the tension between Iran and Western states (especially the United States) over the former's nuclear intentions and its failure to comply with its IAEA obligations. The document also specifically mentioned the importance of getting Israel to accede to the treaty, and the need for the placement of all its nuclear facilities under comprehensive IAEA safeguards. Similarly, the statement called on India, Israel, and Pakistan to accede to the NPT.

These were all reasonable achievements, but something else appeared in the Final Document of the 2010 RevCon which was unusual and of historical importance: the record of the Conference acknowledged that there had been 'new proposals and initiatives from Governments and civil society related to achieving a world free of nuclear weapons'. This was the first time that the phrase 'a world free of nuclear weapons' had been inserted into an NPT RevCon document, articulated as the goal of nuclear disarmament, in a clear and unambiguous way (UN 2010). The document also noted that many states wished to see 'negotiations on a nuclear weapons convention or agreement on a framework of separate mutually reinforcing instruments, backed by a strong system of verification' (UN 2010).[17] (The full significance of these is discussed in later chapters.)

This was a departure from previous documents, and it was won by the non-nuclear states keen to ensure that their wish for some kind of legal process was initiated. These states also insisted on recording the fact that many wished to see a time-bound commitment to such a process (UN 2010). During the Conference, many states had wanted the disarmament language to be stronger and more explicit, with clear time-bound commitments, but in the nature of the bargaining process inherent in the Review Conferences, this could not be achieved, as the nuclear weapon states firmly resisted it.

Nevertheless, a somewhat less ambitious language was agreed to, with the dissension of many states recorded in the final outcome document. Although it might seem a small thing, this was a considerable achievement, representing as it did in very explicit terms that while the eventual outcome was gained through consensus, significant divisions between the various groupings of states on the issue of disarmament were by now very evident and were being recorded.

The document also deliberately included concerns about the humanitarian impact of nuclear weapons and the importance of international humanitarian law. It noted the Conference's 'deep concern at the continued risk for humanity' represented by the possibility that these weapons could be used and the 'catastrophic humanitarian consequences that would result from the use of nuclear weapons' (UN 2010). The document made very clear the view that 'all States at all times' must 'comply with applicable international law, including international humanitarian law' (UN 2010). This was the first time that elements of humanitarianism and international law had been so explicitly included in Review Conference proceedings and reflected in the final document. This inclusion was the catalyst for the development of what came to be known as the Humanitarian Initiative against nuclear weapons, launched soon after the 2010 conference ended.

A further important aspect of the 2010 NPT Review Conference's final document was the recording of the disappointment at the lack of progress on discussing a Middle East WMD Free Zone, together with a directive to remedy this. This was by now a particularly pressing issue. The non-aligned states were clearly worried that this request was not being taken seriously.[18] This had become a key policy priority for Egypt, the chair of the Non-Aligned Movement at the 2010 NPT Review Conference and there was a strong sense among delegates that unless there was progress on this issue, support for other measures was unlikely to be forthcoming from what was essentially two-thirds of states present at the RevCon. Thus the 2010 final document called on the Secretary-General of the United Nations and the co-sponsors of the 1995 Resolution, in consultation with the states of the region, to 'convene a conference in 2012, to be attended by all States of the Middle East, on the establishment of a Middle East zone free of nuclear weapons and all other weapons of mass destruction'; this was to be done 'with the full support and engagement of the nuclear-weapon States' (UN 2010).

Again, we can see here the importance that was attached to this issue by the NAM states (especially the members of the Arab League). The promise was made yet again, and taken in good faith as a genuine commitment to the wishes of the NAM. It should be stressed that what was being asked for was a conference which would commence discussions on the establishment of a Middle East zone free of nuclear weapons and all other weapons of mass destruction. It was not expected that such a zone could materialize easily, but starting the process of dialogue and deliberation was seen as vital, especially if NAM resentment at the NPT's double standards was to be ameliorated.

That the Middle East region was beset by several security concerns was well recognized, but there had been hopes that despite this, working to reduce the dangers of biological, chemical, and nuclear weapons in the region was a worthwhile endeavour. At least two states in the region continue to have some level of WMD capability: Egypt has refused to sign the Chemical Weapons Convention and is known to possess chemical stocks, while Israel has signed but not ratified that Convention. Israel, in addition to its nuclear arsenal, has refused to sign the Biological Weapons Convention, while Egypt has signed but not yet ratified this instrument. Other states in the region – Iraq, Syria, Libya – have had a record of biological and/or chemical weapons' capability. Egypt appears determined not to accede to these global agreements until such time as a WMD Free Zone can be established in the Middle East, which would in turn require a nuclear-disarmed Israel to join the NPT as a non-nuclear weapon state. Given these factors, commencing talks on reducing the dangers of WMD was important. The promise made again in 2010 by the P5 states to convene a conference in the Middle East by the end of 2012 was seen as a further assurance to the NAM that their security concerns were being taken seriously.

Unfortunately, 2012 came and went, with no conference held. At the end of that year, the United States released a statement saying that the conference would not be held, 'because of present conditions in the Middle East and the fact that states in the region have not reached agreement on acceptable conditions for a conference' (Nuland, cited in Reuters 2012).[19] In a clear reference to its ally Israel, the United States stressed that it 'would not support a conference in which any regional state would be subject to pressure or isolation' (Reuters 2012). Iran and Israel had both raised objections to attending, but it was felt that more could have been done by the United States, Russia, and Britain to bring these parties to the table.

That the promised conference was not held – despite the best efforts of the UN and the Finnish Undersecretary of State named as Facilitator for the conference – boded ill for the entire NPT project and especially for the looming 2015 Review Conference. By 2014, Egypt had expressed its frustration by walking out of the third NPT PrepCom meeting (Karem 2013). The League of Arab States had also instructed the Arab group to put the 'Israeli Nuclear Capabilities' issue on the agenda of the upcoming IAEA General Conference (Kane and Mukhatzhanova 2013). Some Arab states had implied – either implicitly or explicitly – that they might reconsider their membership in the NPT given the slow progress on this issue.

By 2015, then, it was not surprising that tensions between the nuclear and non-nuclear states, and especially the grievances of the Arab states, would colour the NPT Review Conference proceedings. There was very clearly by now a sense that 'lip-service' to the goals of disarmament by the P5 would no longer be acceptable (Johnson 2013a).[20] Ultimately, the states participating in the 2015 Review Conference at New York could not agree on a final consensus document. The Middle East conference issue was a primary cause of the impasse, but so too was the sense that the P5 states were not going to be moved to take disarmament seriously. On the final day of the Conference, the United States and Britain (supported by Canada) stated that they would not accept the efforts of some who, they claimed, 'have sought to cynically manipulate the NPT', and that they refused to be bound by an 'arbitrary' (UN 2015) timetable to hold a Middle East conference. Many non-nuclear states were unhappy with the weak language in the draft document regarding disarmament, while the P5 refused to accept even this watered-down language. The P5 argued that disarmament proposals should be 'realistic', and implied that any process outside of the NPT itself could not be considered legitimate. In particular, the British delegation argued that an incremental 'step-by-step' approach was the *only* way that disarmament could be achieved (cited in UN 2015).

Conclusion

Clearly, the calls for disarmament – or at least serious steps *towards* disarmament – made by individuals, states, and groups of states, at NPT conferences, in special commissions, studies, and elsewhere have all been resisted by the nuclear weapon states. None of the calls have been for unilateral or precipitate action, and all of the studies and recommendations recognized the need to assure the security of nuclear weapon states as they move towards the goal of elimination.[21] Yet even these steps have been rejected by the nuclear states, leading to the charge that they will never voluntarily give up their arsenals. Reasoning with addicts, Lennane (2015) reminds us, 'is pointless'. All the 'studies, commissions, analyses, and carefully constructed arguments have failed to shift the nuclear-weapon states. They are powerless: their weapons own them'.

Essentially, nuclearism – especially the discourse of strategy and security – continued to inform the position of the nuclear weapon states. Although in 2010 non-nuclear states had been able to include in the final document the statement on international humanitarian law, this had been effectively forced upon the nuclear states. It did nothing to alter the way that they viewed, presented, and clung to their nuclear arsenals in 2015. P5 representatives at NPT and other diplomatic forums continued to voice the usual refrains of their national leaders: that nuclear weapons were untouchable assets, vital for state security. The modernization and deployment of nuclear weapons continues apace, with huge resources devoted to these processes. NPT meetings, notwithstanding the repeated pledges by the P5 states that they would disarm, have simply demonstrated that the status quo would continue, and that non-nuclear states would not be able to shift this state of affairs via the NPT. And as far as the nuclear states were concerned, the NPT was going to be the only 'game in town'.

Thus the realization of a nuclear-free world remained as elusive as ever, and thirty years after the Cold War ended, the policies preferred by the nuclear weapon states have prevailed. None of the efforts described above has been able to dislodge the mindsets and practices which make up the condition of nuclearism. Despite diplomatic negotiations and the major reports emerging from states and specialists in the field, things have remained essentially unchanged. Nuclearism remains dominant, and a discriminatory NPT has been unable to transform the nuclear order that favours the nuclear weapon states.

Notes

1 Rebecca Johnson observed as early as 2000 that far from inspiring real optimism, about disarmament, the reductions announced by the United States and Russia at the time were simply a means for them to 'rationalise their arsenals at levels still well above world overkill … and mainly intended to clear away enough of the oversized, obsolete junk to make room for new weapons for modern requirements' (Johnson 2000b: 2).
2 George Kennan himself offered the following opinion on NATO expansion, 'I think it is a tragic mistake. There was no reason for this whatsoever' (cited in Friedman 1998).
3 For useful accounts of these negotiations, see Bunn and Rhinelander (2007) and Goodby (2006).
4 Between 1945 and 1992, the United States had conducted 1,030 tests, the USSR/Russia 715 tests, France *c.*200 tests, the United Kingdom 45 tests, and China *c.*40 tests. India, Pakistan, and North Korea have tested, respectively, three (or four if its 'peaceful nuclear explosion' of 1974 is counted), two and six tests (Arms Control Association 2020).
5 For detailed accounts of the 1995 Review and Extension Conference see Onderco and Nuti (2020), Welsh (1995), and Rauf and Johnson (1995).

6 The fact that the NPT, always seen by India as an unfair treaty, had been extended indefinitely with little given in return by the nuclear weapon states, was likely to have been a key element in India's decision a few years later to become openly a nuclear weapon state.

7 Judge Weeramantry stated that there were precedents in international humanitarian law, namely the Geneva Gas Protocol of 1925, and Article 23(a) of the Hague Regulations of 1907, which would render any contemporary use of nuclear weapons clearly illegal.

8 For detailed examinations of the Commission's origin, arguments, and impact see Hanson and Ungerer (1998, 1999).

9 For more detailed analysis of the utility of nuclear weapons and how this in turn shaped the Commissioners' findings, see Hanson (2002, 2005b).

10 Indicative was the Bulletin of the Atomic Sciences' assessment which labelled the Report as a 'no-nonsense road map' (Moore 1996).

11 It was close allies of the United States – Japan, Australia, and Canada – which had driven the various reports noted above, but these were very much the product of particular governments in those states at particular times. This also helps to explain why those reports were not especially successful in influencing the nuclear weapon states; incoming and more conservative governments in every case reoriented their foreign policies more closely towards their chief ally, the United States, and were not willing to question the strategic decisions of the United States or to challenge nuclearism more overtly.

12 A small selection of these works include Blackaby and Milne (2000), Daley (2010), Huntley *et al.* (2004), Kelleher and Reppy (2011), Larkin (2008), Lewis *et al.* (2016), Ogilvie-White and Santoro (2012), O'Hanlon (2010), and Rotblat and Blackaby (1998).

13 See the *Statement by Generals and Admirals of the World Against Nuclear Weapons* (CCNR 1996), and also the work conducted by the Parliamentarians for Nuclear Non-Proliferation and Disarmament.

14 A selection of NGOs focusing closely on this issue and active in preparing reports and submissions include Reaching Critical Will, Article 36, ICAN, PAX Christi, Global Zero, Abolition 2000, and the Ploughshares Fund, while think tanks and professional organizations providing scholarly analyses include the Arms Control Association, the Nuclear Threat Initiative, the Bulletin of the Atomic Scientists, the Carnegie Endowment for International Peace, and the Federation of American Scientists.

15 Lest it be thought that avoiding responsibilities to devalue nuclear weapons and move to disarmament is characteristic of the five NPT-recognized nuclear weapon states only, it must be noted here that neither are any of the four non-NPT nuclear-armed states – Israel, India, Pakistan, and North Korea – taking any steps to reduce nuclear dangers or move their policies towards a lesser dependence on nuclear weapons.

16 Generally, the various proposals put forward from 1995 onwards to move nuclear states towards disarmament were very similar, albeit packaged somewhat differently at each new Review Conference, and in the case of the 2010

RevCon, called the 'Action Plan'. This is what Hoffman-Axthelm calls the 'ever-new packaging of the same old proposals'; he argues that this 'further underscores the absurdity' of believing that these would have any real effect: 'It used to be the "*step-by-step process*", which was adopted in 2000 as the "*13 steps*", and 10 years later again as the "*64 points*" of the NPT Action Plan. Pending their implementation, they were renamed "*building blocks*", and marketed again in 2015 as the "*full-spectrum approach*". In February 2016, those states that rely on nuclear weapons in their security doctrines claimed to have new ideas: the "*progressive approach*", which, you guessed it, contains the exact same steps' (Hoffman-Axthelm 2016).

17 The case for a Nuclear Weapons Convention had been made very clearly by Datan *et al.* (2007).

18 Proposals for such a zone had been raised in the United Nations as early as 1974. The United States and United Kingdom had invoked Article 14 of UN Resolution 687 in their formal justification for the 1991 Gulf War, as representing 'steps towards the goal of establishing in the Middle East a zone free from weapons of mass destruction and all missiles for their delivery and the objective of a global ban on chemical weapons'. Mukhatzhanova and Potter (2012) have explored in detail the background to the NAM's complicated relationship with the NPT: as they remind us, the NAM – with 120 full members and fifteen observer states, constituting more than two-thirds of the membership of the United Nations – is the largest political grouping of states in the world engaged with international security issues. They note that 'by virtue of its size alone, the movement has the potential to be a very constructive or obstructive force in dealing with many of the most pressing nuclear disarmament, non-proliferation, terrorism and peaceful-use challenges of the day' (Mukhatzhanova and Potter 2012: 9).

19 The Arab Spring which had started in late 2010, and the ongoing deterioration of the security climate in Iraq and Syria, did not bode well for this conference to occur. Other complicating factors included the lack of headway in resolving many of the seemingly intractable conflicts in the region, especially the Israeli–Palestinian conflict, the military procurement policies of regional powers, differing views on the feasibility and modalities of a Middle East WMD Free Zone, and the rise of Islamic State and Sunni-Shi'ite divisions. At heart was the view held by some, Israel included, that security conditions would have to be met *first*, and only then could talks commence about a WMD Free Zone. Others argued that it was possible to have mutually reinforcing, concurrent, security *and* WMD Free Zone processes.

20 It should be noted here that speaking of the 'nuclear weapon states' and the 'non-nuclear weapon states' at the 2015 RevCon over-simplifies things somewhat, chiefly because while their nuclear status unites each group, there nevertheless has been division and variations of emphasis within states in each of these groups. In 2015 especially, there was some disarray amongst the political and regional groupings present in terms of them projecting a common position, and the New Agenda Coalition states, as well as the NAM states, in particular,

were not as 'collective' as they had been in the past. The nuclear weapons states also were not rigidly united: Russia and China had expressed the view that they could live with the negotiated final document, but this was not something that the United States and Britain were willing to do. Similarly, within European Union states, there has been variation in the emphasis on disarmament, just as there has been a reluctance by allies of the United States – such as Australia, Japan, and Canada – to align themselves too closely to the more ardent supporters of disarmament within the non-nuclear state group.

21 The disarmament movement has not been requesting immediate, unilateral change, or 'unconditional' disarmament. (Doyle 2015: 25). They generally have asked for a series of steps, and accept that disarmament is likely to be a long-term goal; they also recognize the need to strengthen international institutions and to address the security concerns of states as they move to zero nuclear weapons.

Part II

The transition – from the Humanitarian Initiative to the prohibition treaty

4

The humanitarian context: drawing lessons from earlier disarmament campaigns

If the Cold War years, together with the decades after the Cold War, reflected an entrenched sense of nuclearism, there were nevertheless some novel conventional weapons arms control processes that were taking place in the background of global security politics. Even as the nuclear states continued to hold fast to nuclearism, a process of what has come to be known as 'humanitarian disarmament' was evolving, and was being applied, to certain weapons. There were some notable aspects of these disarmament processes which would, in time, come to have an important bearing on the way in which non-nuclear states worked to achieve the 2017 Treaty on the Prohibition of Nuclear Weapons.

As the previous chapter has shown, the lack of success in pushing for disarmament, despite the launch of studies and reports and by states working within the NPT, was becoming more and more evident. It was clear that none of these activities would be able to challenge seriously the elements of nuclearism which had sustained the nuclear states for so long. But the utilization of humanitarian arguments and the novel processes of diplomacy used to prohibit landmines (and later, cluster munitions) showed that there would be some value in applying similar arguments to nuclear weapons also, as a way of building a world without nuclear weapons.

The humanitarian context: limiting the 'calamities of war'[1]

The application of a humanitarian framework in the campaign to ban landmines appeared in the mid-1990s, in the aftermath of the Cold War period. The 1997 landmine ban – together with the 2008 cluster munitions ban, and arguably also the 2013 Arms Trade Treaty – marked a significant turning-point in the way that multilateral arms control and disarmament processes would be conducted. Indeed without these previous successes, and the way in which they disrupted traditional diplomatic methods, the humanitarian approach to the problem of nuclear weapons may not have emerged as and when it did. The experience of the landmines ban, and fifteen years of reflection on the success of that process and its role in reaffirming the place of international humanitarian law in weapons control, provided advocates with useful experience and an important background against which the matter of nuclear weapons would henceforth be framed.

But this humanitarian approach in the 1990s had itself drawn upon the tradition of restricting the conduct of armed warfare, dating back to the 1860s, which had evolved when the (European) community of nations had come to view the use of certain weapons and methods of warfare as unacceptable, because of their inhumane characteristics and consequences. In line with the growth of international humanitarian law, or the 'laws of war' as they are sometimes called, there arose a clear sentiment that the use of a particular weapon would be considered legitimate and permissible only if certain provisions were observed.

To be clear, we are talking here of the developments in international relations where the laws applicable to armed conflict were actually codified into international treaties and declarations, at a multilateral level. Of course there existed prior to the 1860s various traditions of thought and practice, drawn from philosophic, moral, or religious traditions all over the world, which informed the processes of armed conflict in particular regions. In Europe, for example, the evolution of notions of justice, chivalry, and mercy, together with elements of self-interest, led to several codes, suggesting the presence of natural law and at least a limited set of human rights.[2] And the ICRC reminds us that long before the 1860s, India, Greece, Rome, and states in the Middle East sought to prohibit poison weapons because of their excessive and injurious effects (ICRC 1999). But what is of relevance to this chapter are those instances, from the 1860s onwards, where multiple states agreed to codify and make explicit expectations at the international level regarding the use of weapons and the conduct of armed warfare, because it was these sentiments which were revived after the Cold War, which came to be applied to landmines and other weapons, and which came to influence the treaty prohibiting nuclear weapons in 2017.

Essentially, the humanitarian approach focused on the impacts of weapons, on the effects that they have on their victims, and on whether their use and effects are compatible with the laws of armed conflict.[3] As the ICRC argued, inhumane weapons were defined as those beyond which an honourable or 'civilized world' would accept (ICRC 1868).[4] The development of thinking about how wars – if they had to be fought – might be legitimately fought, and which tools of fighting were considered to be acceptable, was intimately connected to the growth of the laws of armed conflict, and specifically to the provisions of *jus in bello*. Only a very brief overview of this field and its impact on arms control in the late nineteenth and early twentieth centuries is presented here, but there are numerous sources addressing these developments more fully.[5] For our purposes, it will suffice to consider the motivating factors in these agreements.

Applying international humanitarian law

The first clear example of banning the use of certain weapons in war was the 1868 *St Petersburg Declaration Renouncing the Use, in Time of War, of Explosive Projectiles Under 400 Grammes Weight* (ICRC 1868). In the early 1860s, Russia had developed a musketball which, when it hit even a 'soft' target like a human body, would have fragmenting, explosive, or incendiary effects. This was seen as something which would merely aggravate the misery of warfare, and as not essential to the larger goal of achieving success in war-fighting. Banning these exploding bullets in 1868 because of the egregious wounds they would cause affirmed the principle that there were constraints on what weapons could be used legitimately in warfare, and that methods of fighting chosen by warring parties were not limitless. The 'landmark' nature of the Declaration was particularly evident in the impact of the wording of its Preamble.

This Preamble gave clear recognition to the view that 'there existed limits at which the necessities of war ought to yield to the requirements of humanity' and that 'the progress of civilization should have the effect of alleviating as much as possible the calamities of war' (ICRC 1868). Noting that exploding bullets would 'uselessly aggravate the sufferings of disabled men' (ICRC 1868), and stating the need to avoid unnecessary suffering (or superfluous injury) deemed to be gratuitous and illegitimate, the Preamble observed that 'the employment of such arms would therefore be contrary to the laws of humanity' (ICRC 1868).

The St Petersburg Preamble served as a declaration of fundamental principles at a broader level, and came to exert a significant influence on the formulation of the modern laws of war (Aldrich 1994: 50). It reflected, both explicitly and implicitly, three fundamental principles: those of distinction, the limits imposed on military necessity, and the prevention of unnecessary suffering (Aldrich 1994: 50). It was important in building the view that warfare, if it was to be considered legitimate, must be able to distinguish between combatants and non-combatants, must be proportionate in scale and purpose, and must not aggravate the already miserable calamities inevitably entailed by fighting.[6] Weapons could not be used indiscriminately, they should not violate the principle of proportionality in warfare, and they should not inflict superfluous injury or unnecessary suffering upon victims, not even on combatants. The Declaration was itself an evolution on the thinking of how warfare could legitimately be waged which had been tabulated in the American Lieber Instructions of 1863, the first modern codification of customs on warfare, drawn up at President Lincoln's request, to regulate the conduct of armed forces during the American Civil War (ICRC 1863). While the Lieber code was limited to that specific conflict, and was thus not an international agreement, and while it canvassed much more than weapons control, its provisions were nevertheless influential in subsequent thinking about the conduct of warfare, particularly at the Brussels Conference of 1874 and the Hague Conferences of 1899 and 1907 (Schindler and Toman 1988: 3).[7]

These latter conferences, two very important assemblies of world leaders, resulted in the formal agreement and acceptance of the modern laws of war. Specifically, the 1899 Hague Conference's *Declaration relating to the discharge of projectiles and explosives from balloons*, its *Declaration concerning asphyxiating gases*, and its *Declaration concerning expanding bullets* (what were commonly known as dum-dum bullets) all noted that the Contracting Powers to these agreements were 'inspired by the sentiments which found expression in the Declaration of St Petersburg' (ICRC 1899a, 1907). The regulations laid down in both Hague Conventions on land warfare are by now considered customary international law and are thus binding on all states, even those not parties to these Conventions at the time (Schindler and Toman 1988: 63).

The 1899 Hague Conference also resulted in the drafting of the 'Martens Clause', reiterated at the 1907 Conference, which specified that 'populations and belligerents remain under the protection and empire of the principles of international law, as they result from the usage established between civilized nations, from the laws of humanity, and the requirements of the public conscience' (ICRC 1899b: Preamble). The Clause had appeared due to unresolved differences between various states regarding the definition of lawful and unlawful combatants; in the end, its general thrust was to the effect that even where laws are incomplete, persons are to be protected by *implicit* laws of conscience and morality. As various international lawyers note (Ticehurst 1997; Cassese 2000; Meron 2000) there are competing interpretations of the Martens Clause, but the argument was that essentially – and given that it is unlikely that international treaties relating to the laws of armed conflict will ever be complete or able to cover new and emerging practices of warfare – the Clause was designed to counter any assumption that practices which were not (or not yet) explicitly prohibited by an existing treaty would be permitted simply on the basis that they had not been barred. The argument, more simply, was that a practice 'which is not explicitly prohibited by a treaty is not *ipso facto* permitted' (Ticehurst 1997). The clause has come to be incorporated into customary international law, was reiterated at the Nuremberg trials, and the 1977 Protocols to the Geneva Conventions, this time more simply as 'Recalling that, in cases not covered by the law in force, the human person remains under the protection of the principles of humanity and the dictates of the public conscience' (ICRC 1977). The Martens Clause has relevance to the regulation of weapons, in that existing law has not (yet) specifically outlawed some weapons or practices, or the rise of new kinds of weapons altogether.[8] This lack of a clear legal ban was particularly true of nuclear weapons until 2017; as such, the Martens Clause was used by those petitioning for the 1996 ICJ ruling on the legality of nuclear weapons.[9] The Clause has also been incorporated into several other weapons conventions (Nystuen and Casey-Maslen 2010). The Clause suggests, as Oberleitner (2015: 32) notes, that humanitarian law should evolve not just by means of treaty, but also by 'constant reference to natural law as an equally important source which complements and corrects a predominantly technocratic and positivist approach to humanitarian law'.

The Hague Conferences marked a high point in attempts to multilateralize norms regarding the conduct of war. A planned third Hague Conference did not eventuate, largely as a result of the breakout of the First World War. Following the destruction of this war, however, a conference was held, under the auspices of the League of Nations, as part of a move to regulate the international trade in armaments and ammunition. While the conference was not successful in this initial ambition, it did produce, as a separate protocol, a clear and unambiguous denunciation of the use of chemical and biological weapons in warfare. This prohibition, the Geneva Protocol of 1925,[10] and the sentiments which informed it had also been inserted into the Treaty of Versailles and other peace treaties reached in 1919, following the extensive use of gas warfare during the First World War. While it took several decades for these prohibitions to be codified explicitly – where not only use but *possession* also was condemned – in the Biological Weapons Convention (1972) and the Chemical Weapons Convention (1993) – the 1925 Protocol can be given considerable credit for stigmatizing these weapons of war and for reinforcing a culture where the use of such weapons would be, as the ICRC (1925) noted, 'justly condemned by the general opinion of the civilized world'. (Thus two of the three kinds of weapons which fall under the 'weapons of mass destruction' category were stigmatized very early, something which did not come to apply clearly to the third kind of WMD, nuclear weapons, until almost a century later.)

By the outbreak of the First World War then (paradoxical though this is, given the violations of many of these provisions during that hugely destructive conflict), the essence of the rules and restrictions on armed warfare had been well-articulated and codified, especially in the St Petersburg Declaration and the Hague documents. This pre-1914 period can thus be seen as a critical time when thinking about warfare came to reflect the clear requirement that its inevitable sufferings must be limited, in a legally codified way, and by multiple state parties. Oberleitner (2015: 28) writes of the period from 1868 as being one where the proponents of international humanitarian law perceived themselves as being almost on a *'mission civilisatrice'*. The limitations placed on waging war were no longer simply a religious imperative or one upholding older notions of chivalry, and they were not driven only by rational calculations; they could also be seen as part of a larger project, meant to demonstrate a 'desire to advance civilization' (Oberleitner 2015: 30). And they came to have a substantial influence on attempts to regulate the use of certain weapons after the Cold War ended.

Notwithstanding these European notions of 'advancing civilization', it is obvious that these humanitarian considerations were not greatly observed during the many wars of the twentieth century.[11] The key attempt during the Cold War period to incorporate the principles of humanitarianism as they related to the use of weapons was the achievement of the 1980 United Nations Convention on Certain Conventional Weapons (CCW), properly known as the Convention on Prohibitions or Restrictions on the Use of Certain Conventional Weapons Which May Be Deemed to Be Excessively Injurious or to Have Indiscriminate Effects, or more simply, as the Inhumane Weapons Convention (ICRC 1980). This included Protocols on the use of non-detectable fragments, landmines, booby traps, incendiary weapons, and blinding laser weapons, as well as the clearance of explosive remnants of war. While it set out some general provisions, it lacked an explicit prohibition of these weapons and practices (ICRC 1980). It was limited in its membership and impact and in any case did not attract many ratifications until after the Cold War had ended. Even now, it remains largely symbolic, and the implementation of its Protocol on landmines has been achieved not from adherence to this instrument, but rather by the new, more targeted, campaign developed in the mid-1990s.

Clearly then, the principles regulating the use of certain weapons outlined over a century ago lay largely dormant during the Cold War. But these were resuscitated in the mid-to-late 1990s, and have gathered pace since then, with clear implications for the attempts to make nuclear weapons illegal also. This 'thread'[12] of humanitarianism established the basis for allocating importance to certain criteria in post-Cold War weapons control.

The structural changes which the end of the Cold War brought allowed new dynamics, processes, and actors able to influence arms control and disarmament negotiations in a way that had not been seen in the preceding decades.[13] These new actors called upon the earlier tradition of characterizing certain weapons as inhumane. Essentially, the post-Cold War period marked an important shift in the way that debates and negotiations about arms control and disarmament came to be conducted; these have been influenced by a wide range of actors, most of whom had not been represented at negotiations, and they represented a striking shift away from the superpower-focused agreements of the Cold War decades.

The ban on landmines: reinserting humanitarian voices into weapons control

There is a considerable body of literature on the achievement of the treaty prohibiting the manufacture, transfer, and use of anti-personnel landmines, known as the Ottawa Convention (see for example Cameron *et al.* 1998; Short 1999; Hubert 2000; Monin and Gallimore 2002; Rutherford 2011). What is presented here is an assessment of how it denoted a significant break with processes utilized during the Cold War. Instead of a continuation of standard Cold War practices, the landmines process not only reflected elements which were evident a century earlier, but it also developed some altogether new practices. These have become consolidated over time, and have been applied to subsequent arms control and disarmament agreements, including to the ban on nuclear weapons.

In the early 1990s, it was estimated that there were more than 100 million anti-personnel landmines scattered in over sixty different countries, and that approximately 2,000 civilians were being killed or severely injured by them every month (Human Rights Watch Arms Project 1993: 11). The extent of the problem was made evident first to medical practitioners and other aid workers from NGOs based in Cambodia, Somalia, Angola, and other heavily mined states in the 1970s and 1980s, and these practitioners were instrumental in disseminating news of the catastrophic and overwhelming impact of landmines on mortality, health, and economic development. UN Secretary General Boutros-Ghali was also involved in alerting the world to the impact of mines in his seminal work, *An Agenda for Peace* (1992) and through an article in *Foreign Affairs*, two years later. He made it quite clear that the world was now facing an 'ongoing humanitarian disaster'. Urging states to take action to ban this weapon, he observed that if the true effects of landmines – and especially their effects on children and other civilians – were better known, they 'would undoubtedly shock the conscience' of humankind (Boutros-Ghali 1994: 13). The ICRC had also become closely engaged with this issue, publishing a report entitled *Mines: A Perverse Use of Technology* (ICRC 1993). These, together with the Human Rights Watch report of the same year, *Landmines: A Deadly Legacy* (Human Rights Watch Arms Project 1993), and a US Department of State (1993) report, *Hidden Killers: The Global Problem with Uncleared Mines: A Report on International Demining*, were authoritative voices in the early 1990s which influenced thinking on the need to tackle this enormous problem. Academics (Cahill 1995; Falk 1995) and individual state leaders were also becoming aware of the issue, with some of the latter taking unilateral measures to alleviate it. In October 1992 the United States announced a self-imposed moratorium on the sale, transfer, and export of anti-personnel landmines, an initiative followed by a number of other countries, with at least one, Belgium, passing national legislation in 1995 banning the production, transfer, and use of the weapon.

The first call to take action at a multilateral level came from France, in 1993. It should be kept in mind that the ending of the Cold War meant that conflicts in developing states, which had previously been cast largely in terms of superpower competition, could now, at last, be seen as 'conflicts in their own right' (Hubert 2000: 30), and that they could now receive attention and resources which might previously have been absent. This was accompanied by a new emphasis in international politics more broadly, from the 1990s, on conflict resolution, post-war reconstruction, and peace-building efforts. The removal of Cold War constraints allowed individuals, NGOs, states, and international organizations like the United Nations to direct their attention to long-standing problems, motivated by a concern for pursuing what was being called 'human security'.

The problem of using landmines – because of their indiscriminate nature and the suffering they cause, and because they remain active in the ground decades after the end of a conflict – had been recorded in the aforementioned 1980 CCW, under Protocol II (ICRC 1980). However, and as noted above, the provisions of the CCW were limited and it remained largely inactive during the 1980s. Nevertheless, in the mid-1990s, the CCW – a purely state-based legal forum – was the only existing setting in which any new action on landmines could feasibly be taken. The UN-established CD, which had been set up in 1979 to replace other Geneva-based arms control forums, was also a contender, but this body lacked any history of attention to landmines; it was seen as a forum whose focus was meant to be on nuclear, rather than conventional, weapons. Moreover, the CD, operating on the basis of consensus, was becoming increasingly moribund, with individual members able to block agreement on issues. In any case, the states most affected by the problems of landmines – mainly developing states – were not members of the CD, and even if that body was to take on the challenge of banning landmines, it was clear that negotiations would be painfully slow and cumbersome. Thus the CCW remained the only feasible venue for multilateral efforts to address the increasingly visible humanitarian disaster of landmines' use. The CCW (as with the CD), was a creation of the Cold War, and, as with the CD, it reached agreements – if they were reached at all – via consensus, which resulted in lowest-common denominator agreements, and both had very limited membership. Yet there was no alternative mechanism at the time. As such, the French government called for a Review Conference of the CCW to be held in October 1995 to address the landmines problem.

It was soon evident, however, that while some states wished to see an outright ban on these weapons, it was not going to be possible to achieve this by using the CCW. The Review Conference concluded in May 1996, but it accomplished nothing of significance as far as advocates of a clear ban were concerned. Simply put, the method of consensus decision-making meant that far-reaching and timely change was unlikely. Additionally, the provisions of the CCW's Protocols did not apply to non-international conflicts (civil wars) at the time.[14]

Importantly, but perhaps not surprisingly given that there had been no precedent for this in recent history, NGOs were not permitted to involve themselves in the CCW in any substantive way. And many states attending the Review Conference were not prepared to push for an outright ban on landmines, preferring only to tinker at the edges of the existing regulations. The Review Conference did produce a new Protocol on landmines, but this was, if anything, weaker than the original 1980 agreement. The nongovernmental International Coalition to Ban Landmines (ICBL), which had been established in the meantime, noted that, in the end, the CCW's Review Conference adopted only 'a weak amended protocol permitting continued use of antipersonnel mines' (ICBL 2012). Hopes that firm action would be taken by the CCW were dashed, and the body was seen by the ICBL as a 'humanitarian failure' (Hubert 2000: 16). The Review Conference had certainly been important in keeping the landmine issue positioned high on the global agenda, but at the end of the day, given the inherent limitations of the CCW, it was unable to provide any decisive and unambiguous agreement.

All of this confirmed that existing intergovernmental diplomatic mechanisms were not flexible enough to accommodate the demands being made by individuals, NGOs, and some states, in what was, by now, a very different political atmosphere to that which had prevailed only a few years earlier. There was also an increasing sense that the problem of landmines constituted a clear humanitarian crisis, and that as such, seeking change via the traditional arms control institutions was likely to be ineffective. For NGOs especially, this was no longer a national, or international, security issue, subject to the usual diplomatic negotiating and long drawn-out bargaining tactics employed by states as part of their national security calculations; rather, this crisis demanded a wholly different approach which would be guided first and foremost by humanitarian concerns (Hubert 2000: 20). If the use of landmines had become entrenched for many states, then change could only be achieved by using novel framings and unconventional methods. This same kind of reframing – away from entrenched views of the weapon as providing security, to a weapon deemed inhumane – came to be applied to nuclear weapons two decades later.

When it became clear to NGOs and those states in favour of a complete ban on landmines that their objective was not going to be achieved through any of the existing intergovernmental forums, the dynamics of the pro-ban movement changed. Impatient with the slow progress of discussions at the CCW, and discouraged from attempting to take their case to the Conference on Disarmament, civil society organizations and a key group of sympathetic states forged a new method for achieving a clear legal prohibition of this particular weapon. NGOs quickly identified those states in favour of a ban, noting Canada as a keen sponsor-state. Thus, when it was evident that the CCW would not be able to achieve a ban, the Canadian government delegation invited states to attend a new conference, to be held in Ottawa later that year. This was the point at which the campaign became known as the 'Ottawa process'. Unusually, NGOs were also invited to participate. At this new conference, then Canadian Foreign Minister Lloyd Axworthy announced his proposal for drawing up a complete ban, and he invited states to return to Ottawa in December 1997 to sign a treaty and bring it into law. It was up to individual states whether they would be a part of this movement or not. In this sense, Axworthy played an important entrepreneurial and normative role, recognizing the need for an innovative approach which would bypass the stagnant traditions of normal diplomacy. This fast-track process aimed to draft and produce a comprehensive ban and to attract signatures within fourteen months. It resulted in an international weapons treaty being created, presented to the United Nations, and entering into force, within record time.

The treaty attracted widespread support from a large proportion of states. Initially, it was expected that only forty or fifty states would come to Ottawa in December 1997 to sign, but on the day, 122 states attended and signed on immediately. Nevertheless, the Ottawa treaty was rejected by the large powers, the United States, Russia, and China, as well as by several other countries. While the United States had been willing to consider a tightening of the CCW regulations, it was not prepared to accept what ban advocates were by now clearly wanting, namely a complete prohibition of anti-personnel landmines, with no loopholes and no exceptions for any state. For the United States, this was a step too far: Washington wanted any forthcoming treaty to allow the United States to continue to use mines on the Korean peninsula, something which NGOs and pro-ban states were not prepared to allow.

Together with the ICRC, it was the NGO umbrella organization, the ICBL, which played a crucial role in making the treaty a reality. The ICBL had been formed in 1992, largely as a result of the activities of five key NGOs, whose staff were witnessing first-hand the deadly impacts of landmines, led by the efforts of Robert Muller, who had established the Vietnam Veterans of America Foundation. Over the next few years, the ICBL came to have 1,200 independent NGOs under its banner, and was operating in eighty countries.[15] Jody Williams (1999) noted that it was the field-based and medical experience of many of the NGOs which gave them credibility and influence with governments. With first-hand accounts of the gruesome impact of landmines, reminders that maimed individuals invariably had little or no access to health care, and confirming that the deaths and severe disabilities resulting from landmines were having detrimental effects on economic development and post-conflict reconstruction – all clear humanitarian arguments – their campaign called upon governments to join others in what would become a 'self-identifying pro-ban bloc' (Williams 1999). Its effect was to motivate sympathetic states – which might otherwise revert to the standard but unfruitful negotiating processes – and lead them into a new course of action which promised a quick and unequivocal outcome, namely a complete ban on landmines.

The features of this new process were enormously important. It was perhaps not realized at the time just how significant they were, and how they would influence later disarmament campaigns. As the president of the ICRC (Sommaruga 1997) noted just after the landmines ban had been signed, this was the first time that a weapon which had been 'in widespread use by armed forces' in many parts of the world was now being withdrawn or banished from the arsenals of the 122 states which signed the treaty at Ottawa. The use, development, production, stockpiling, and transfer of landmines were now all prohibited within the single agreement. For one landmine victim, writing just after the treaty was achieved, 'the [mine ban treaty] is unique in history. It bans a weapon in widespread use, and it is a blend of arms control and international humanitarian law. It is also the first time that civilized society has found a partnership with governments around the world to eliminate a conventional weapon' (Rutherford 2011: 4).[16]

New elements in humanitarian disarmament: novel framings and unconventional methods

Many observers of the Ottawa process (see, for example, English 1998; Price 1998; Rutherford 1999, 2011; Short 1999; Hubert 2000; Wisotzky 2009) have pointed to a range of specific factors instrumental in achieving a treaty which was created 'from below'. The following section draws heavily on these analyses, and examines these factors in some detail, because these same elements have continued to feature in subsequent attempts to outlaw or restrict particular weapons, and were taken up in the nuclear elimination campaign. These overlapping and mutually reinforcing factors are examined below; they help to address questions about the initiators of the process, the role of participants in the process, the nature of what was being sought by ban advocates, and how this was going to be achieved.

New initiators, new participants; bypassing the great powers

The first and most obvious point is that the search for a landmines treaty was initiated overwhelmingly by non-state actors, working in various non-governmental organizations. It was the direct actions of NGO workers, dealing with the deadly aftermath of conflict, which was instrumental in alerting the world to the crisis and in getting the ban process started. Without the clamour raised by NGOs working in mine clearance and victim assistance, it is unlikely that states on their own would have been motivated to take significant action, or to take it quickly. The authoritative studies conducted by NGOs – for example the ICRC and Human Rights Watch reports, and the various articles published in medical journals – were extremely important in raising global awareness.

The corollary of the fact that it was NGOs who activated the new mine-ban process is, quite simply, that it was the great powers, namely the P5 states, which did not. Until the early 1990s, the creation of arms control and global security treaties had been the result of decisions and preferences of the most dominant states in the international system. Not only did the large and influential states of the world not initiate the landmines process; ultimately, and after some hesitant early participation, they came to reject its final agreement altogether. The United States, Russia, and China rejected the Ottawa treaty, and some non-signatory states, including China and India, openly criticized the Ottawa process for side-stepping and undermining the 'legitimate' Conference on Disarmament (English 1998: 126).

Initiating a successful arms control and disarmament process was no longer something reserved exclusively for the large and influential states of the world, especially the superpowers, who would previously have conducted negotiations and sought legal instruments only when and how they wished. The process also showed that, henceforth, a successful treaty would not necessarily require their consent, support, or even involvement; the launch of a strong international agreement to outlaw a weapon in widespread use no longer depended on a 'permission slip' from the United States and other large powers before it could proceed. In this sense, Ottawa was a clear example of a process of forging weapons treaties from the bottom-up, rather than as something driven and controlled by the largest powers, the usual top-down mechanism employed by those powers.

This bypassing of the great powers was most evident in the case of the United States, which although originally sympathetic to the need for stricter regulations, was not prepared to accept the kind of comprehensive ban which advocates sought. In fact, it was Washington's declared resistance to the ban which became the very thing that allowed NGOs and pro-ban states to pick a new approach and to run with it, ultimately achieving what they wanted without waiting for the United States, or other influential powers like Russia, China, and India, to come on board. A key factor in the success of the Ottawa process was Washington's reluctance to engage with it. In early 1997, the United States still favoured the Conference on Disarmament as the mechanism for addressing the problem, even as it was by this time clear that no progress could be achieved there. The United States had pursued 'heavy-handed tactics' in Brussels and Oslo, earlier negotiation venues prior to the Ottawa signing (Hubert 2000: 38). These tactics only served to make others more determined to pursue a ban.

Certainly, NGOs and pro-ban states had initially sought great power support, but they also realized that the price for this could be a considerably weaker document than they wanted. In the to-and-fro-ing between ban advocates and US representatives, it had become clear that neither side would give way. Jody Williams (1999) observed that NGOs and smaller and middle-sized powers had 'for the first time ... not yielded ground to intense pressure from a superpower to weaken a treaty to accommodate the policies of that one country'. An unexpected result of this was that the final treaty signed in Ottawa included wording that was even stronger than the original draft proposed, when US engagement had first been sought. No longer needing to walk on the metaphorical eggshells that US demands represented, advocates were able to aspire to a stronger document than was originally envisaged. Being freed from the limitations of great power preferences seemed to have opened up thinking and allowed for more ambitious proposals which, earlier, might not have been considered achievable. Had pro-ban advocates continued to strive for the great powers to be brought into the treaty, we would not have seen the transformation from traditional processes of treaty formation to the new dynamics of policy-making that Ottawa came to represent in 1997.

Undoubtedly, some states underestimated the significance of what was happening at this time. Even when action switched decisively to the new Ottawa process, the United States continued to underestimate the momentum and 'cohesiveness of the pro-ban states' (Hubert 2000: 38), and were taken aback by the methods and fast-moving nature of the campaign. By the time the treaty had been achieved, it was too late for them to exert any real influence. Ken Rutherford (1999: 44) notes that:

> the attempts of major powers, especially the United States, to stop or weaken the treaty were limited. The United States did not take the Ottawa negotiations seriously until late in the process, when the treaty was already nearly completed. There was a belief among some in the US delegation that only arms control negotiations led by the United States could be successful.

It seems not to have occurred to the major powers that a legally binding security treaty could be achieved without their direct initiation, involvement, and support. Indeed, at the outset, all of the P5 states of the UN Security Council had been resistant to the idea of a complete ban; as the campaign progressed, Britain and France agreed to sign a total ban, largely as a result of domestic and EU influence, but the largest powers, China, Russia, and the United States, remained determined not to participate. In reality, their absence allowed middle-sized states to take the reins and develop a comprehensive ban without significant opposition. Many of these middle powers who signed in 1997 were close allies of the United States: Britain, France, Germany, Norway, Australia, and Canada, leading McFarlane (2000: xi) to observe that the Ottawa process was a 'rare instance where the United States was opposed on a matter of security policy by a number of its weaker allies and lost the battle'.

Choosing a single goal

The outcome at Ottawa can also be explained by reflecting on what exactly was being sought, and how this was going to be achieved. There was a clear and simple goal: advocates wanted a complete ban, with no loopholes, and no exceptions, for any state. The landmines example showed the importance of having a straightforward and clear objective, pursued by using simple and consistent arguments. Advocates would not be satisfied with just technical changes. For one thing, the CCW did not prohibit landmines use; it only limited how these weapons could be used. Rather than negotiating the complex articles and provisions of the existing CCW agreement, participants determined that a new approach would sweep away the loopholes and uncertainties of existing restrictions. What worked was 'the simplicity of the norm', a clear prohibition (English 1998: 30). Keeping the message short and uncomplicated allowed for easier internalization of the message, would require states to declare their intentions quickly based on the acceptance of a simple proposition, and would resist any state's attempt to create special conditions favourable to itself. The concept of an outright ban was easy to communicate politically, and the essence of its message would be understood in any language or state, allowing for a directness in diplomacy as well as a quick exposure of any given state's position. Existing legal mechanisms, including the landmines protocol of the CCW, were difficult to interpret and invited confusion rather than clarity about states' obligations and their practices (Rutherford 1999: 44).

Once the process was taken up by Canada, other supportive states, and NGOs, these participants did not swerve from their simple intention to achieve a comprehensive ban. Had they been willing to consider some states for special consideration, participants would have been drawn into the difficulties of managing the use of landmines and determining dispensations, rather than achieving an outright ban. Any attempt to regulate or manage landmines' use would have required a much more complex and contested process, would certainly have required longer than fourteen months of work, and in all likelihood would not have achieved anything more than the CCW already allowed.

Also eschewed in the process was the insertion of formal monitoring and verification procedures, not because these were deemed unimportant, but because negotiating these would take attention and energy away from the message of an outright ban. The urgency of achieving a ban in as little time as possible overrode any wish to specify the more technical and complex procedures of certification and monitoring. This again reflected the innovative nature of the Ottawa process: it was clear that momentum was building to create a ban. Placing attention and resources on this issue, rather than drawing up procedures for monitoring and verification, was essential. Once the treaty was established, the world could determine how to conduct monitoring and verification. In any case, many saw the task of monitoring and verification as one best taken up at a later date, and by NGOs, given that it was these actors who had been instrumental in de-mining efforts and in providing assistance to victims. Ensuring compliance could be best conducted by those citizens already active in the field and aware of a particular country's mine status. Securing a treaty, and leaving more complex provisions like verification and monitoring for later, has continued to be the preferred method in subsequent processes also.

Choosing stringent treaties for their cumulative normative effect

Related to the factors above, the pro-ban camp was faced with the dilemma of whether to lobby the great powers to join, which would give the resulting agreement a more 'heavyweight' character, or to disregard them and aim for a more stringent, 'no exceptions', treaty. It has to be conceded that there are drawbacks to not having the major powers, and especially the world's superpower/s, as signatories to an international treaty, particularly if these states are likely to continue to act in ways contrary to that treaty's provisions. The dissonance between widely held, legally codified norms and great power practices could lead critics to argue that a treaty lacking great power support is not worth very much.

In the end, it was felt that this need not have a negative effect in terms of the integrity of the treaty. If a substantial majority of states affirmed a particular code, this will be in itself an important normative statement. Reflecting on the trade-off between achieving a strong treaty (without the great powers) and achieving universal adherence (via a weak treaty), Hubert

(2000: 63–64) has noted that the strength of a legal agreement is usually dependent on *both* 'the stringency of the provisions and the breadth of support those provisions command'. In the past, many multilateral negotiations have been concluded through consensus decision-making, which is seen as a means of securing a wide level of support for the prescribed norm, even if this norm is only weakly enshrined. During the Ottawa process, most states showed that they preferred setting 'bold standards' and were willing to leave the achievement of universal or at least widespread support as a longer-term priority. For Hubert (2000: 63–64), the stringency of the provisions was more important than the level of support: 'effective humanitarian norms ... are more dependent on stringency than universality'.

In any case, the landmines treaty has come to have an undeniable long-term impact. The fact that the United States and some other states have not signed the treaty has not had a negative effect on the fortunes of that treaty, showing that a legally codified norm can – thanks to domestic and international pressure – come to have a constraining effect, over time, even on non-signatory and powerful states.[17] The strongly articulated norm against landmine use has meant that, in 2022, 164 states have joined the treaty. There has been no new use of mines by any state party to the treaty, and importantly, of the thirty-three states which have not signed the treaty, the government of only one of these – Myanmar – continues to use landmines (*The Landmines Monitor* 2020).[18] Since 1996, the manufacture and selling of landmines has ceased almost completely, and the number of persons injured or killed by their use has fallen (Wells 2016).

All of this would indicate that a secondary value of such treaties is the cumulative normative effect that they can produce, where their existence socializes other states into formal or informal acquiescence. And even when any state continues to use these weapons, the weight of moral opprobrium grows heavier against them. The treaty has arguably come to have a stronger long-term impact than was anticipated in 1997.

New methods for agreement

The Ottawa process showed that it was possible to create a treaty using a fast-track process. The advantage was that it did not rely on the glacial pace of diplomatic negotiations and wrangling over details of a treaty text, but kept a momentum going which in turn placed pressure on states to declare their position. As Rutherford (1999: 44) pointed out, the fast-track negotiating process reflected the view that 'public impatience will no longer tolerate long, drawn-out negotiations on an important issue'. It showed that where there appeared to be a serious and immediate crisis facing the world – something that health professionals and de-mining workers had been able to demonstrate – negotiations which took decades would no longer be acceptable to the general public. The key, therefore, seemed to be in publicizing widely the effects of landmines on ordinary people.

It was recognized in the mid-1990s that the means for achieving a quick treaty were limited: if standard practices such as seeking consensus were followed, getting a treaty swiftly would be impossible. It was becoming evident that in order to achieve a treaty at the earliest opportunity, and one that was stringent in its requirements, the principle of consensus needed to be jettisoned. Multilateral negotiations in international organizations were generally bureaucratic and slow, and subject to compromise. While the principle of consensus enables all parties to feel a sense of ownership of an agreement, which presumably would encourage greater compliance, it is inherently not democratic, and does not allow a majority opinion to prevail, regardless of how sound or strongly supported that opinion might be.

Throughout the negotiations for the landmine ban, as Williams (1999) notes, NGOs sought to ensure that their wish for a comprehensive ban would have little chance of being 'thwarted by compromise'. Ottawa was the first time that agreement on a major security treaty was achieved without striving for unanimity and a consensus agreement. This did not necessarily mean that decisions would be taken by a vote (although this remained an option); instead, it was felt that if a majority of the world's states sought a particular objective, then this ought to happen, without it being held up by obstructionist states and traditional diplomatic wrangling. At the most practical level, this enabled a quick treaty; at a more general level, this practice reinforced the view that concerned states were free to act, regardless of the lack of support or even opposition shown by the large and more powerful states.

A solely humanitarian framework

Equally important as the above factors was the framing of the problem within explicitly humanitarian terms. The clear message focused unambiguously on the impact of landmines on human beings simplified the issue and invited agreement (Larrinaga and Sjolander 1998). This was not an exercise in arms control, discussed in a clinical manner by national security officials. It marked a shift away from prevailing notions of state-based security concerns and acknowledged the actual physical impact of the armaments under question. This framing deflected discussions about national security objectives. It removed the prospects of a politically charged debate: prevailing discourses of security and strategic need were replaced by a simple call for humanitarianism. The focus on humanitarianism also privileged 'concrete knowledge about the practice rather than the theory of contemporary warfare', something with which field-based NGOs were much more familiar than were politicians or diplomats (Hubert 2000: 65).

This meant that arguments about military necessity would no longer automatically enjoy the dominant position they had held for so long. But this was not a guaranteed outcome: the prevailing view at the time was that weapons – especially those widely in use, as landmines were – were not likely to be banned unless a clear case could be made showing that they held little or no military utility. Landmines were generally considered to be useful in warfare (although the extent of this usefulness has been debated[19]). Their use in the Second World War was probably influential in the decisions of individual states to employ them in subsequent conflicts. Being relatively cheap and easily deployed munitions, they were beneficial in deterring an advancing army. As a result, ban advocates needed to emphasize the inhumane nature of landmines, and argue that these concerns should outweigh any calculations of military utility. In other words, even if these weapons were seen as useful in warfare, the emphasis on the elements of international humanitarian law needed to outweigh strategic calculations. This was indeed the conclusion reached by states that signed the treaty. As with the St Petersburg Declaration and the Geneva Protocol of 1925, there was a view that certain weapons needed to be proscribed, because their use would be 'justly condemned by the general opinion of the civilized world' (ICRC 1868). The 1972 Biological Weapons Convention in its preamble had referred back to this wording, the parties declaring that they are 'convinced that such use would be repugnant to the conscience of mankind and that no effort should be spared to minimize this risk' (UN 1972); the 1993 Chemical Weapons Convention also noted that the UN General Assembly has condemned all instances where states have taken actions contrary to the 1925 Geneva Protocol (OPCW 1996). All this suggested that the choice of weapons in warfare would likely be subject to a humanitarian test, and that there is now, as Price (1998: 614) notes, 'a moral calculus in the definition of national [security] interest'. With the landmines treaty explicitly noting in its preamble 'the role of public conscience in furthering the principles of humanity' (ICRC 1997), this was likely to become more influential than ever before.

Conclusion: carrying the Ottawa process forward

In sum, the landmines treaty in 1997 was the first time in the twentieth century that a global prohibitionary weapons regime had been achieved in a way that was quite different from that of prior treaties. It explicitly corralled humanitarian arguments, was driven by civil society groups forming a global coalition in partnership with key like-minded states, was achieved without the agreement of the largest powers (and indeed without their active involvement), was undertaken in new forums, and proceeded at a rapid pace.

It showed that arms control processes now could be initiated and implemented by small and middle-sized countries and civil society actors, they could be conducted outside the traditional diplomatic venues, and they could aim for disarmament, rather than just arms 'control'. The deliberate reintroduction of humanitarianism into questions of weapons control suggested that prevailing and largely unfettered exercises of state sovereignty and military practices was no longer seen as acceptable. Crucially, these campaigns also heralded a sense that such campaigns were now a part of global governance (Matthew 2003; Krause 2011) and that states should prepare for these kinds of processes to re-occur.

Had this achievement remained an unusual but ultimately isolated process, it might not have been so remarkable. But subsequent agreements, including the 2008 Cluster Munitions Convention and the Arms Trade Treaty of 2013, also showed a similar pattern to that of the landmine ban process (Borrie 2009; Corsi 2009; Hulme 2009; Bolton and Nash 2010; Bolton et al. 2014; Whall and Pytlak 2014). Ottawa marked the onset of an innovative set of practices. When the Nobel committee announced that the ICBL and Jody Williams had won the 1997 Nobel Peace Prize, it commended not only the achievement of the landmines ban, but also what it hoped might become 'a model for similar processes in the future', which 'could prove of decisive importance to the international effort for disarmament and peace' (Nobelprize 1997). Researchers have pointed to the ways in which elements of the landmines campaign could be applied to other disarmament projects (Borrie et al. 2009; Alcalde 2014; Mack 2014), signifying a clear hope that the Ottawa process would not be a 'one-off' exercise alone. And by 2015, when non-nuclear states realized that working with the nuclear-armed states through the NPT was not progressing nuclear disarmament, they moved quickly to achieve a nuclear ban using these same ideas and practices.

Notes

1 This phrase appears in the St Petersburg Declaration of 1868, properly the 'Declaration Renouncing the Use, in Time of War, of Explosive Projectiles Under 400 Grammes Weight', which states that 'the progress of civilization should have the effect of alleviating, as much as possible, the calamities of war' (ICRC 1868).

2 Useful studies on earlier codes include the works of Bederman (2009), Green (2008), and Oberleitner (2015).
3 As an aside, it is worth recalling here the words of Yves Sandoz, of the ICRC, who was responding to the critic's view that the Red Cross, by banning some weapons but making others permissible, serves to legitimize war. Critics do have a point when they argue that killing another human being with an inhumane weapon is banned, but killing a human with another kind of weapon is allowed, is fraught with contradiction and moral ambiguities. But this should not lead us away from the path of seeking to limit the effects of warfare as much as possible. While organizations like the ICRC are not able to build a world where warfare and killing are outlawed, they can play an important part in limiting the costs of such activities: it is essential, Sandoz noted, to continue to 'seek ways of limiting suffering caused by war, to develop humanitarian standards applicable to armed conflict, and above all, to make these standards known, accepted and respected' (cited in Rappert 2006: 18).
4 When the term an 'honourable' or 'civilized' state first appeared in an arms control statement, in 1868, it was applied only to European states at the time, and did not imply any obligations to restrict warfare against those persons outside the European community of states.
5 See for example, Friedman (1972), Best (1983), Roberts and Guellf (1982), and Solis (2016).
6 The St Petersburg Declaration had been preceded by the 1864 First Geneva Convention, on the *Amelioration of the Condition of the Wounded in Armies in the Field*, and it was the newly formed ICRC which was instrumental in pursuing the ban codified in the Declaration.
7 Strictly speaking, it was the Brussels Conference document (inspired by the Lieber Instructions) drawn up by the Russian government and presented by Czar Alexander II to a gathering of fifteen European delegations on 27 July 1874, as part of the Project of International Rules on the Law and Usages of War, which was the first attempt to draw up an international multilateral agreement on the laws and customs of war. The Brussels Declaration, as this came to be known, was never formally adopted, but its contents were incorporated, at a meeting in Oxford of the Institute of International Law (an independent body of interested individuals founded in 1873), into what became known as the *Oxford Manual of the Laws and Customs of War*, in September 1880. Both the Brussels Declaration and the *Oxford Manual* became the foundation of the two Hague Conventions on land warfare reached at The Hague Peace Conferences in 1899 and 1907 (Schindler and Toman 1988: 25). The *Oxford Manual* noted the need to codify what had become 'the accepted ideas of our age' regarding the conduct of warfare; that there 'are today certain principles of justice which guide the public conscience, which are manifested even by general customs, but which it would be well to fix and make obligatory'; and that the mutual acceptance of constraining rules would benefit all belligerents, 'rendering a service' to military personnel themselves (*The Laws of War on Land* 1880: Preface).

8 The development of drone warfare and lethal autonomous weapons systems (LAWS) are cases in point where the use of these has not yet been outlawed internationally.
9 Importantly, the ICJ in its advisory opinion affirmed that the Martens Clause 'has proved to be an effective means of addressing the rapid evolution of military technology' (ICJ 1996: para 78; see also Burroughs 1997).
10 This was officially titled the Protocol for the Prohibition of the Use in War of Asphyxiating, Poisonous or Other Gases and of Bacteriological Methods of Warfare.
11 Nonetheless, the 1899, 1907, and 1925 proposals prohibiting the use of chemical and biological weapons, although violated during the First World War, remained robust after this time, being largely observed during the Second World War.
12 This term is borrowed from Tim Caughley (2012: 2).
13 This is not to say that the conduct of warfare *itself* reflected humanitarian law in the immediate post-Cold War era. If IHL was coming to influence formal negotiations between states regarding what was considered an 'acceptable' weapon, such constraints were absent in the horrific wars that broke out in the aftermath of the Cold War. The 'ethnic cleansing' that we saw in the Yugoslav wars and in Rwanda, and indeed in previous and subsequent conflicts also, suggests that humanitarian constraints are far from being observed on the battlefield. It needs to be reiterated, therefore, that this work is examining those instances where multilateral diplomatic decisions are being made about particular weapons; it is not suggesting that humanitarian concerns have been observed in war in general, although the establishment of the International Criminal Court and the doctrine of the Responsibility to Protect do seek to prevent and address such violations.
14 The scope of the CCW's applicability was expanded in 1996 and again in 2001, but in the period of mounting concern at the landmines' toll, the CCW could not be applied to what were largely civil wars in Angola, Mozambique, Cambodia, and elsewhere. On the interplay between the CCW's Protocol II and the later landmines campaign, see Bryden (2013).
15 As one of its founders notes, there was no obvious 'leadership' in the ICBL, no secretariat, and no central office (Williams 1999). Despite this, the campaign's effectiveness was impressive, an achievement all the more remarkable given that much of their grassroots activities, public awareness campaigns, and lobbying of governments was done in the first half of the 1990s, before the popular advent of email and high internet use. It was the standard use of posted mail, fax, and telephone calls which established the ICBL and enabled its many coordinating activities. Only later, from about 1996, did extensive use of email begin.
16 Some have drawn very direct parallels between the Hague Conferences and the Ottawa achievement. In this sense, and to reiterate the chapter's earlier argument, the landmines campaign can be seen as 'revitalizing a pre-World War II style of disarmament negotiations rather than establishing an entirely new

approach to international diplomacy. From this perspective, it is the Cold War years rather than the 1990s that diverge from longer-term patterns in humanitarian advocacy' (Hubert 2000: 41). This writer also notes that banning dum dum bullets in 1899 occurred because of the actions of 'doctors with direct experience in the field and was subsequently picked up by a range of peace organizations' (Hubert 2000: 40).

17 President Trump announced in February 2020 that he was lifting the restrictions on landmines use by the United States, to allow 'smart' mines, which self-destruct after a specified period of time. This move was widely criticized, and incoming President Biden promised to reverse it.

18 However, non-state armed groups in at least six states have continued to use landmines in six countries, using improvised weapons.

19 One of the most respected studies was conducted by the ICRC, *Anti-Personnel Landmines: Friend or Foe?* (1996), which called on the expertise of numerous army personnel. See also the assessment of landmines' utility made by Monin and Gallimore (2002).

5

Creating the Treaty on the Prohibition of Nuclear Weapons

Cognizant of the approaches taken in the landmines case, certain states sought to apply the laws of war to nuclear weapons which had, for seventy years, evaded any clear legal prohibition. As noted in Chapter 3, there was a growing recognition that all the studies and reports which had been produced were not able to persuade the nuclear weapon states to take their promise to disarm seriously. From the earliest authoritative studies conducted by the Stimson Center in the early 1990s, informed groups and individuals had put forward measures and pathways for the nuclear states to move – gradually and in a phased, verified, manner – to a world free of nuclear weapons. None of these has had any real impact; if anything, we have seen in the past decade the 'unchecked resurgence in the saliency of nuclear weapons' (Rauf 2016: 209). Nuclear war, by accident or design, remains an ongoing concern. The continued absence of any humanitarian considerations in nuclear doctrines, the persistence of the 'security' discourse by the P5 states, and the failure of the NPT process to provide a more equitable global security order suggested instead that the world was destined to live with 'nuclearism forever' (Booth 1999), a 'nuclear eternity' (Pelopidas 2021).

This parlous state of affairs in the global nuclear order – with non-nuclear states increasingly despondent as the nuclear-armed states continued to affirm nuclear deterrence and engage in nuclear modernization programmes – came to a head at the Non-Proliferation Treaty Review Conference in May 2015. Beliefs that the NPT process would not be able to advance the prospects of a nuclear-free world reached their apogee at this Conference, especially on the final day when negotiations could go no further. By this time, it was clear that many non-nuclear states and civil society actors had come to place their faith in what was being called the Humanitarian Initiative on nuclear weapons as an alternative means of framing the nuclear weapons debate, and that they aimed to shift the discourse on nuclear weapons – and nuclearism more generally – away from purely strategic concerns. For many of these states, building on the earlier processes of humanitarian arms control and disarmament, their efforts now came to be the creation of a new legal standard, a nuclear weapons prohibition treaty. Their decision to work outside the NPT's strictures reflected a 'global impatience' (Meyer and Sauer 2018) with the status quo.

Towards the Treaty on the Prohibition of Nuclear Weapons

As noted in Chapter 3, non-nuclear states had been able to insert into the Final Document of the 2010 NPT Review Conference a statement of 'deep concern at the catastrophic humanitarian consequences of any use of nuclear weapons' (UN 2010). This was not welcomed by the nuclear weapon states; they seemed unable, however, to prevent this inclusion into the Final Document. This action was to have a significant impact on the way that subsequent multilateral gatherings on nuclear arms control and disarmament would be framed. ICAN had been formed a few years prior to this, had spread to dozens of other states, and was now primed to activate its message and coordination. From this point, certain states took the decision to explore and make widely available up-to-date information about the likely impacts of the use of nuclear weapons, from an explicitly humanitarian perspective.

In the months and years immediately after the 2010 NPT Review Conference, non-nuclear states, backed strongly by NGO actors, made a concerted effort to bring humanitarianism into multilateral discussions on nuclear weapons policy.[1] At various gatherings, notably at the 2012 and 2013 NPT Preparatory Committee meetings, and in the United Nations General Assembly's First Committee deliberations, statements were presented which stressed the inhumane nature of these weapons. Initially led by the government of Switzerland in 2012, these were soon backed by numerous states, and by the time of the 2013 UN General Assembly's First Committee meeting, a statement, led this time by New Zealand, was supported by 125 states, a significant increase from the numbers supporting such moves only a year earlier. At this time there was also a separate joint statement from a group of seventeen states, led by Australia, arguing that 'banning nuclear weapons by itself will not guarantee their elimination without engaging substantively and constructively those states with nuclear weapons, and recognising both the security and humanitarian dimensions of the nuclear weapons debate' (Woolcott 2013). This statement indicated early on that while there might be general support for the Humanitarian Initiative, not all non-nuclear states believed that this should lead to a prohibition treaty. Some allies of the United States, even those which might nominally (depending on the government of the day) be supporters of disarmament, who continued to rely on extended nuclear deterrence (or at least a perceived guarantee of extended nuclear deterrence, in the case of Australia) were still cautious about the pace of change.

Notwithstanding the Australian-led statement, and bolstered by the expression of humanitarian sentiments in the 2010 NPT RevCon Document, Norway, a NATO ally, seized the opportunity early to host what it called a 'Conference on the Humanitarian Impact of Nuclear Weapons' (HINW) in Oslo, in March 2013. Its aim was 'to provide an arena for a fact-based discussion of the humanitarian and developmental consequences associated with a nuclear weapon detonation'. All interested states, UN organizations, representatives of civil society, and other relevant stakeholders were invited to attend. The Norwegian Foreign Minister, Espen Barth Eide, invited all governments to send senior officials and experts (Eide 2012), drawing participation from 128 states (including two of the four non-NPT nuclear weapon states, India and Pakistan). A second Humanitarian Initiative conference was hosted by the Mexican government in February 2014, at Nayarit, this time with 146 governments attending. As the five NPT nuclear weapon states, the P5, had boycotted the earlier Oslo conference, there were concerted efforts to encourage their participation at Nayarit. Despite this, however, no officials from these states attended. A third conference was hosted by Austria in December 2014, but was also boycotted by the P5.

Several hundred civil society representatives participated in these conferences, drawn from a wide range of organizations around the globe, and including members of the ICRC, UN agencies, and from academia. The International Campaign to Abolish Nuclear Weapons, based on the ICBL model, was now the organization around which many hundreds of NGOs had coalesced. The Vienna Conference was opened by the Austrian Foreign Minister, Sebastian Kurz, and was addressed by UN Secretary General Ban Ki-moon, the President of the ICRC Peter Maurer, and Pope Francis, indicating the heightened level of attention which was now being given to what was seen as an urgent issue. As Helfand *et al.* (2016) observed, '68 years into the nuclear age, these were the first ever inter-governmental meetings dedicated to the humanitarian impacts of nuclear weapons'.

When the impasse at the May 2015 NPT RevCon indicated that no progress on disarmament was going to occur via that forum, and buoyed by the progress made at the Humanitarian Initiative conferences, the UN General Assembly in December 2015 passed a resolution to establish an Open Ended Working Group (OEWG) tasked with canvassing measures, legal provisions, and norms which could help attain a world without nuclear weapons.[2] The resolution explicitly noted 'the absence of concrete outcomes of multilateral nuclear disarmament negotiations within the United Nations framework for almost two decades' (UN 2015b). The OEWG released its report in 2016, recommending 'the negotiation of a legally binding instrument to prohibit nuclear weapons, leading towards their total elimination'. The First Committee of the General Assembly duly adopted a resolution to open negotiations for such an instrument the following year, a resolution which attracted 123 states. Two negotiating sessions in 2017 resulted in a final draft, and the Treaty on the Prohibition of Nuclear Weapons was adopted by a vote of 122 states in favour on 7 July 2017.

The creation of the TPNW was greeted with enthusiasm by the states and civil society actors engaged in bringing about this piece of legislation. The treaty, as it proclaims, is a 'legally binding prohibition of nuclear weapons' which 'constitutes an important contribution towards the achievement and maintenance of a world free of nuclear weapons' (UN 2017). The TPNW entered into force on 22 January 2021,[3] making the development, testing, production, stockpiling, stationing, transfer, use, or threat of use, of nuclear weapons explicitly prohibited under international law. Also prohibited is any assistance and encouragement of the prohibited activities by any state.

The treaty reflects very clearly the dissatisfaction felt by the non-nuclear states for decades. Its Preamble notes:

> the slow pace of nuclear disarmament, the continued reliance on nuclear weapons in military and security concepts, doctrines and policies, and the waste of economic and human resources on programmes for the production, maintenance and modernization of nuclear weapons. (UN 2017)

Various provisions of the TPNW are noteworthy and in some cases innovative:[4] unsurprisingly, the Preamble reflects concern about the catastrophic humanitarian consequences that would result in the use of nuclear weapons, and reiterates the view that any use would 'be abhorrent to the principles of humanity and the dictates of public conscience'. But the Preamble also acknowledges the 'unacceptable suffering of and harm caused to the victims of the use of nuclear weapons (Hibakusha), as well as of those affected by the testing of nuclear weapons', noting 'the disproportionate impact of nuclear-weapon activities on Indigenous peoples'. Importantly, and reflecting provisions in the landmines treaty, the TPNW calls for victim assistance to 'individuals affected by the use or testing of nuclear weapons'. It calls on states to 'take necessary and appropriate measure of environmental remediation in areas under its jurisdiction or control contaminated as a result of activities related to the testing or use of nuclear weapons'. Importantly, the treaty draws attention to the fact that the catastrophic consequences of nuclear weapons could never be adequately addressed, as they 'transcend national borders, pose grave implications for human survival, the environment, socioeconomic development, the global economy, food security and the health of current and future generations, and have a disproportionate impact on women and girls, including as a result of ionizing radiation'. Other gender matters were also highlighted: the treaty recognized 'that the equal, full and effective participation of both women and men is an essential factor for the promotion and attainment of sustainable peace and security', and urged 'supporting and strengthening the effective participation of women in nuclear disarmament' (UN 2017). The treaty also recognized 'the importance of peace and disarmament education in all its aspects and of raising awareness of the risks and consequences of nuclear weapons for current and future generations'.

The TPNW makes provision for any nuclear weapon state to join the treaty. While it is clear that the existing nuclear weapon states will not sign the treaty in the near future, Article IV of the treaty sets out the procedures for negotiating with any nuclear-armed state which might seek (at some point) to accede to the treaty. Negotiations will be conducted with a 'competent international authority', and will then include a time-bound plan for the verified and irreversible elimination of that state's nuclear weapons programme. Clearly then, the treaty leaves open the opportunity for nuclear weapon states to comply with international law and become full members.

Nuclear weapons fall under the new processes of arms control and disarmament

The implications of this treaty will be addressed more fully in the remaining chapters of this book. For now, it is useful to consider the practices that made this treaty possible, for two reasons: first, because they demonstrate a close affinity with those practices that enabled the banning of landmines in the mid-1990s, and thus represent a continuation of the tendency towards humanitarian arms control observed some years ago; and second, because they reveal a clear rejection of the elements of nuclearism which were discussed in Chapter 1.

The previous chapter outlined the broad interrelated practices and innovations that were applied to landmines and other weapons, and which came to constitute what is termed 'humanitarian arms control'. These practices and innovations – adopting new framings and using unconventional processes – can be seen very clearly in the achievement of the Treaty on the Prohibition of Nuclear Weapons.

Established arms control venues and processes were seen as unhelpful

One of the first points to note is that the Humanitarian Initiative, and ultimately the TPNW, were pursued precisely because the standard venues for addressing nuclear arms control and disarmament – the P5-dominated nuclear Non-Proliferation Treaty, its Preparatory Committee meetings, and its five-yearly Review Conferences – were seen as not able to deliver what was being sought. These traditional multilateral meetings had shown that nuclear disarmament could not be pursued effectively in these forums.

Discussions during NPT meetings were not only slow and cumbersome, but also ultimately ineffective when it came to promoting disarmament.

As with the initial attempt to ban landmines through the existing UN Convention on Certain Conventional Weapons (the CCW), so too had states sought to address nuclear dangers by adhering to the established and well-worn framework of the NPT, the mechanism created specifically to regulate nuclear weapons. But although the NPT was seen as one of the most successful treaties in international security, pivotal to the strength of the norm of nuclear non-proliferation, it was becoming evident, especially in the decades after 1995, that this mechanism could not advance the cause of a nuclear weapon free world. The NPT's three pillars were meant to be addressed equally, but in reality the pillar of disarmament was being ignored by the nuclear weapon states, whose focus was on retaining their own weapons and preventing other states from proliferating. As an institution, the NPT was simply not able to move forwards the processes needed for disarmament.

Nevertheless, it was becoming clear after 2010 that taking action outside the NPT could proceed, if a sufficient number of states wished to do so, and regardless of whether certain other states participated. Decision-making methods were important also: forums like the NPT and CD required unanimity or consensus if they were to produce statements for any action: this gave any state the capacity to veto any provisions. (Indeed on a number of occasions, the NPT Review Conferences have not been able to produce a Final Document, a result of one or more states disagreeing sharply with proposed statements.) Thus a new process, outside these institutions, rather than a process which allowed individual vetoes, was adopted.

Seventy-two years after the first use of nuclear weapons and with many thousands of nuclear weapons still in existence and being modernized, in 2017, 122 states concluded that the existing mechanism for disarmament could not, on its own, help to achieve what they sought. Instead, taking action *outside* the NPT was seen as the logical strategy, and the achievement of the TPNW in 2017 was a major milestone. (This is not to say that states supporting disarmament have renounced the NPT – indeed the leading advocates of the Humanitarian Initiative have all been, and continue to be, supporters of multilateral diplomacy in general and the Non-Proliferation Treaty in particular.)

The treaty proceeded without the great powers

Utilizing new venues and processes meant, as its corollary, that those seeking a ban were now willing to proceed without the P5 states. It goes without saying that in 2017 the TPNW was achieved – and could only have been achieved – without the engagement, approval, or membership of any of the great powers, the P5 states. Creating a new treaty was seen by non-nuclear states as the only way that a clear legal instrument outlawing these weapons could be achieved.

Stepping outside of the NPT meant stepping away from the institutional control that the P5 states had been able to exercise for so long. After decades of seeking to move to disarmament *with* the active involvement of the nuclear powers, engaging them in action plans, step-by-step processes, etc., it was apparent that the delegitimization of nuclear weapons could only be achieved *without* the nuclear weapon states. The Humanitarian Initiative was the catalyst for non-nuclear states to shift their focus away from a moribund and unproductive diplomatic arena, towards one which would be able to take decisions quickly and achieve a result that decades of campaigning at the NPT had not been able to do. In the end, non-nuclear states went ahead with their negotiations for a treaty because the nuclear-armed states simply did not have the power to stop them.

Related to this was the fact that since the ending of the Cold War, conditions for being involved in important security decisions had 'opened up' for many states. It enabled them to initiate and engage in arms control and disarmament processes in a way that was not possible during the Cold War. This allowed for a more inclusive process of negotiations, involving not just the large and powerful states but also small states and many that considered themselves activist 'middle powers' (Hynek 2007). As with the landmines convention, a process of 'self-selection' by states occurred, with the recognition that pro-ban states could act without the backing of the great powers. In the case of the TPNW, their message was clear: no longer would these smaller and middle-sized states seek to achieve their objective simply by appealing to the nuclear weapon states. As Acheson *et al.* observed, treating the nuclear-armed states as necessary participants in the negotiations on nuclear weapons would be to 'give them a decisive voice over the initiation, scope, pace, and the success or failure of such a process' (2014: 17). By 2017, it was clear that creating a treaty delegitimizing nuclear weapons under international law need not wait for the permission of the nuclear weapon states. Indeed, achieving such a treaty would be easier without these states. Taking action outside the NPT could proceed, if a sufficient number of states wished to do so, and regardless of whether certain other states participated. Had the nuclear weapon states participated in the creation of the treaty, negotiations would have invariably met the same fate that they did in the NPT.

In this sense, advocates of the treaty also understood that striving for universality, where all the nuclear states would at that point join, was not necessary. A prohibition treaty supported by the P5 states, while it would have been ideal, was clearly not going to happen. The Austrian Foreign Minister had noted ahead of the UN resolution in October 2016 that in any case 'no similar legally-binding instrument has started with universality' (Hajnoczi, cited in Reif 2016). What was more important than having every state 'on board' from the outset was to establish a clear legal prohibition. As with the landmines convention, it was felt that the treaty would exert moral force and gain membership over time. Achieving this legal step was essential, and it could only proceed if it was done without the great powers, the nuclear states, and their allies who supported them.

Civil society actors worked prominently and closely with states

A key factor that allowed for the TPNW process to be initiated and sustained was the continuous work of civil society actors, who engaged closely with non-nuclear states on this issue. In this sense, the Humanitarian Initiative came to be 'the big tent', under which a diverse range of states and civil society actors were able to work from a 'humanitarian impact' perspective (Williams *et al.* 2015: 10). While these actors, including the Hibakusha, had been involved in seeking the elimination of nuclear weapons for many decades, it was their expertise and commitment after 2010, once the humanitarian approach had been launched, that was instrumental in supporting the non-nuclear states at the various meetings and diplomatic forums. This civil society sector ranged from large membership NGOs, to smaller, professionally based organizations supportive of the idea of nuclear elimination. Numerous organizations around the globe – such as Chatham House, in London – held workshops with the aim of building knowledge and expertise on the humanitarian impacts of nuclear weapons (Williams *et al.* 2015). This combination of governments and specialists from universities, think tanks, scientific institutions, and other NGOs around the world, reinforced the momentum which was now clearly in place.

It was the interaction between civil society and various states that was so important here. It is only states, after all, which can sign treaties. In the landmines case, a single state, Canada, had formed the key partnership with the ICBL, but the nuclear ban campaign drew several enthusiastic backers. In the years from 2010 to 2017, Norway, Austria, and Mexico were essential champions, hosting conferences and commissioning research. (Norway had also been responsible for funding research on eliminating nuclear weapons for several years; despite this activism, as a NATO state it remains, for now, outside the TPNW.) Several other states were prominent too: South Africa, New Zealand, Costa Rica, Switzerland, and Ireland were notable both in terms of their support for the treaty and their partnership with networks of civil society members. States needed the support and the research provided by NGOs, while NGOs would not, on their own, have been able to create a treaty. In recognition of the work that ICAN did with states and other NGOs to raise awareness of nuclear dangers, and for its contribution to achieving the TPNW, it was awarded the Nobel Peace Prize in 2017, the first time that an Australian-born organization had been awarded this honour.

A sole focus on humanitarianism

As with the landmines campaign, the states and NGOs seeking a nuclear weapons prohibition treaty chose to focus solely on the humanitarian implications of nuclear weapons. The decision to 'cut to the chase', to transcend the preoccupation with 'national security', and to shift attention firmly onto the humanitarian dimension was appealing in its simplicity, and came to be the foundation of the TPNW. It removed the need to consider deterrence calculations, parity measures, and other factors debated by the nuclear-armed states which have in the past held up progress on a legal instrument banning nuclear weapons. John Borrie points to the functional similarities between, in particular, the cluster munition campaign and the application of humanitarian principles to nuclear arms: many states had used, or joined with their allies in using, cluster munitions, without much thought or knowledge about the effects of these weapons. He traces the process whereby these states were made aware of these effects, with many of them deciding eventually to abandon cluster munitions as illegitimate instruments of battle (Borrie 2014a: 625), notwithstanding the effect that this might have on their allies. So too were humanitarian considerations now brought to the fore regarding nuclear weapons.

The ICRC had heralded the opening up of a humanitarian discourse, ahead of the 2010 NPT Review Conference, and was also essential in activating follow-on events after the RevCon. The ICRC Council of Delegates in 2011 unequivocally urged the complete elimination of nuclear weapons, noting that it was difficult to see how any use of these weapons 'could be compatible with the rules of international humanitarian law, in particular the rules of distinction, precaution and proportionality' (ICRC 2011). The choice to focus simply on humanitarianism also went beyond the finger-pointing and the long-standing frustration with the slow pace of disarmament, and confronted instead the reality of the devastation that would be incurred in the event of a nuclear detonation, whether by accident, miscalculation, or design.

This is not to say that disarmament advocates had been unaware or dismissive of the security concerns of the nuclear weapon states; neither had they called for immediate or unfeasible elimination goals. As previous chapters have detailed, their calls had been for a series of steps towards the eventual elimination of nuclear arsenals, and a recognition of conventional weapon alternatives and diplomatic measures to assuage security fears among these states. But what they repeatedly saw was the failure to devalue the role of nuclear weapons in the doctrines of the nuclear states and the reluctance to abandon the destructive capacity of these weapons. Thus while the non-nuclear states acknowledged the complexity and dangers in international security, and had conceded that moving to disarmament would need to be a drawn-out and well-monitored process, they nevertheless had reached a stage where the well-worn, and often self-serving, arguments for 'security' were now put to one side. They would not disappear, but the sense was that these complications and risks were something that the nuclear states – who after all were responsible for these nuclear dangers – would have to address among themselves. For now, these arguments would be side-stepped in the determination to show that nuclear weapons were not an effective answer to global security challenges, but were, rather, a threat to humanity.

The landmines case had also shown that even if a weapon was considered to be militarily useful, humanitarian concerns could and should outweigh claims for military necessity. This was an important turning-point: it demonstrated the injunction made by the ICRC that, when it came to nuclear weapons, state prerogatives must give way to humanitarian considerations. This sentiment was reinforced by representatives of the Republic of the Marshall Islands, which had been the site of sixty-seven nuclear weapons tests between 1946 and 1958. This state launched a case in the ICJ in 2014 against all nine nuclear weapon states, arguing that their failure to 'live up to their disarmament obligations constitutes a flagrant denial of human justice'. They stated that a 'coherent and civilized legal system cannot tolerate unacceptable harm to humanity' and that a sustainable world order had to be 'predicated on a civilisation's right to survival rooted in … elementary considerations of humanity' (Republic of the Marshall Islands 2014: 3–4). Humanitarian priorities, rather than security calculations, were to prevail in 2017.

A simple ban

As with earlier achievements, the push for a nuclear weapons prohibition treaty was based on a simple objective: to further stigmatize and delegitimize these weapons by putting in place an outright ban, which would then contribute to the process of elimination. A clear ban, applying equally to all states, was sought. No attempt was made to include concessions for any states, and no consideration was given to particular circumstances in which it might be deemed permissible for these weapons to be held or used. As the landmines treaty showed, a simple ban did not require a timeline to be inserted (with the treaty entering into force, its legal standing outlawing nuclear weapons is automatically created). As with previous campaigns, there was no attempt made to include complex monitoring or verification measures. Instead, the treaty was an unambiguous and direct statement that the manufacture, possession, stockpiling, transfer, and use, and even threat of use, of nuclear weapons would violate international law.[5] As with other global prohibitionary regimes, the treaty seeks to ban outright, rather than to regulate, the weapon in question: in this sense it is useful to think of the NPT as a mechanism which sought to 'manage' or regulate these weapons (in an inequitable way), and the new treaty as one whose fundamental *raison d'être* is to make illegal these weapons in any and every case. Nick Ritchie (2016) has captured this issue well:

> [T]he problem is explicitly the weapon, not specific practices or specific actors. The threat to peace and security is … the existence of the weapons themselves irrespective of the possessor. Nuclear weapons in this framing are a collective international liability rather than an individual national asset. The underlying argument is that a stable and secure global society does not need nuclear scaffolding and that nuclear weapons constitute a continuing threat to global society rather than an inescapable structural necessity.

The TPNW was viewed as the necessary, initial, legal step on the road to a world without nuclear weapons. Seeking agreements which unequivocally prohibit unacceptable weapons has, as Ira Helfand reminds us, 'been the approach successfully used in relation to every other kind of indiscriminate, inhumane weapon' (Helfand *et al.* 2016: 91). The pattern that has become evident is that it is first necessary to stigmatize and delegitimize a weapon which is deemed to be unacceptable. Past experience has shown that weapons had been eliminated only *after* they had been banned.

That is, it was necessary to create a normative and legal prohibition before expecting a particular weapon to be eliminated. This had certainly been the case with biological and chemical weapons, and with landmines and cluster munitions also. The logic was persuasive: without a legal and normative framework in place, it is hard to condemn a weapon, especially one that is present in the arsenals of the great powers. And while there had always been a general sense that the use of these weapons would violate international humanitarian law, this had not been explicitly determined. A clear prohibition treaty provides this legal foundation. The humanitarian-driven search for a nuclear weapons prohibition treaty proceeded without the nuclear weapon states; it was seen as the necessary foundation stone upon which pressure can be placed for the nuclear states to move to disarmament.

Conclusion

The consequences of the Humanitarian Initiative and the negotiation of the treaty outlawing nuclear weapons on the basis of international humanitarian law signalled an important shift in the nuclear debate. In many ways, this has been a remarkable process: for over seventy years, seriously addressing the dangers attendant on nuclear weapons had been impossible. They have always been seen – and portrayed – as 'separate' somehow, as 'special', as too hard to tackle, and of course, as too closely related to the security practices of their possessor states to be truly challenged. As Chapter 1 outlined, at the same time that they have been seen as 'special' and 'untouchable', they have been presented as 'normal' elements of everyday life for the security needs of (a handful of) states, resistant to any calls for re-examination or resistance. By following the processes associated with humanitarian arms control, which had produced important results in banning landmines and cluster munitions, and in particular by practising actions that had not previously been taken within the established confines of the NPT, non-nuclear states were able to create a treaty which delegitimized nuclear weapons, for all states.

The decision in 2010, at the NPT Review Conference, to include reference to the catastrophic consequences of any use of nuclear weapons had clearly been a pivotal moment. It allowed the imposition of a qualitatively different kind of framework onto the debate about nuclear weapons, one that is unlikely now to be stopped, The 2010 NPT Review Conference was seen as only a partial success – it failed, for instance, to strengthen IAEA safeguards, to make any critical assessment of the US–India agreement to begin collaboration on nuclear materials and technology, or to secure further disarmament – but it marked the transition away from the emphasis on non-proliferation and towards a clear focus on the need for elimination, based on humanitarian assessments (Johnson 2011). It paved the way for the holding of three important conferences examining the humanitarian impacts of nuclear weapons, whose findings strengthened the hand of the non-nuclear states. These findings were then uppermost in the minds of diplomats at the 2015 NPT Review Conference, marking this occasion as a 'point of no return' (Sauer 2015b). And when the 2015 Review Conference broke down – as it was likely to do, given the inevitable resistance by the nuclear states to any strong language on disarmament – this freed the non-nuclear states to take their cause elsewhere. The 2015 Review Conference outcome was unsurprising, but it seemed to be the 'last straw', prompting non-nuclear states – many of them by now engaged closely with the Humanitarian Initiative – to switch their efforts to the alternative process of negotiating a nuclear weapons prohibition treaty. As ever, nuclear-armed states gave their reasons for not moving towards elimination, saying that the rest of the world must be patient, and that only when the 'right conditions' prevailed would it be sensible to move to a treaty. But this position was no longer supportable, and by 2017, a large majority of states were no longer willing to accept it.

It is important to reiterate that at this time there had been little progress towards disarmament. Had the P5 states made some convincing movement towards achieving even the limited step-by-step actions required of them, we might not have seen the breakdown at the 2015 Review Conference in New York. Instead, the feeling among non-nuclear states was that the world was further away from disarmament than it had been five or ten years earlier. There had been instances in the past where NPT Review Conferences had faltered in terms of reaching consensus, but the process had usually recovered and led to subsequent agreement to pursue negotiations, to preserve hope that a future conference would provide a more successful outcome. This was not the mood in 2015.

The result of this diplomatic fracture was that non-nuclear states soon took their cause elsewhere, frustrated that a negotiating process which they had tried to uphold for decades had been one where only the interests of a small but powerful minority had always prevailed, with no prospect of nuclear disarmament in sight, and with special rules reserved for this minority. Non-nuclear states subsequently considered themselves free to pursue the elimination of nuclear weapons in some other way. In one sense, the failure in 2015 liberated these states from continuing with a system that clearly was not working for their security needs. The push for the prohibition treaty gathered momentum very quickly, and negotiations were concluded in a relatively short period of time, with the innovative and unusual practices associated with humanitarian arms control now firmly in place.

Achieving this legal milestone was important, but so too are its implications for nuclearism. The transition away from a system dictated only by the nuclear states' preferred elements of nuclearism was put in place with the Humanitarian Initiative and the subsequent TPNW. From then, non-nuclear states have been able to place themselves in a position *outside* nuclearism, rejecting the practices which for decades had upheld and normalized nuclear weapons as providing security for a select group of states, but which threatened the security of all others. How the processes which led to the treaty, and the contents of the treaty itself, reflect a rejection of the elements of nuclearism is the subject of the next section of this book.

Notes

1 An extensive list of the various developments related to the Humanitarian Initiative is presented by Ritchie (2015).
2 An earlier OEWG had been established by the General Assembly in December 2012, but it was this second group, convened after the failure of the 2015 RevCon, which came to be most effective.
3 As of August 2021, eighty-six states had signed, and fifty-four states have ratified the TPNW.
4 Detailed works which examine the content and legal implications of the TPNW at length include Black-Branch (2021) and Casey-Maslen (2019). Other substantial works examining the road to the TPNW include Acheson (2021), Kmentt (2021), Sauer *et al.* (2020), Davis Gibbons (2018), Rietiker (2018), Camilleri *et al.* (2019), and Caughley and Mukhatzanova (2017).
5 The treaty prohibits the *threat* of using nuclear weapons, as not doing so could entrench the legitimacy of indefinite possession. Acheson *et al.* (2014: 15) note that a mere 'no-use' agreement would 'act merely as a restriction on nuclear weapons, rather than categorically rejecting them'.

Part III

Rejecting nuclearism

6

Rejecting nuclearism I: changing the discourse; bringing humanitarianism back; empowering new voices and actors; challenging material spending

As noted at the beginning of this book, nuclear weapons have been presented as essential for the security of the states which have them, as acceptable, even 'normal' elements of these states' military arsenals (even though there might be a taboo associated with them), and as essential, prized, and untouchable assets. To recap, the concept of nuclearism, developed by Lifton and Falk in the 1980s, consisted of the 'psychological, political, and military dependence' on these weapons, and the embrace of them as the 'solution' to (in)security (1982: ix). Chapter 1 of this book outlined five key elements which, I contend, helped nuclearism to be established, to flourish, and to be consolidated, to the point where an effective contestation of the nature or even the usefulness of these weapons has not been possible.

How might the TPNW affect this long-entrenched nuclearism? How might the processes used to achieve the treaty, its actual provisions, and its potential impacts, shake up dominant frameworks and reshape a global approach to nuclear weapons, one that is favourable to the goal of nuclear disarmament? I argue here that the various elements which have propped up nuclearism for so long are coming under unprecedented challenge; but this is a cautionary observation, because while nuclearism itself might be rejected, the TPNW is only the beginning of a long and uncertain process.

This chapter and the one that follows will outline how the elements of nuclearism discussed in Chapter 1 are being challenged and reshaped by the TPNW today. The elements of nuclearism identified were as follows: First was the language used to describe the role of nuclear weapons and the overall discourse that this created over several decades. Second, and closely related, was the avoidance of humanitarian concerns about nuclear weapons, and the presenting of these weapons as manageable, acceptable, and 'normal'. Third was the highly undemocratic nature of decision-making processes, an 'exclusivity' which enabled national security elites to plan for nuclear war largely free from public oversight. Fourth was the expenditure of vast material resources on nuclear projects, which served to elevate the status of these weapons almost beyond question. The fifth element identified was the way in which the P5 nuclear states have long used the nuclear NPT to ensure that the global nuclear order remains as it is, always favouring themselves as the guardians of this order.

Rejecting the discourse of security

An important result of the Humanitarian Initiative process and the subsequent treaty has been the ability of the non-nuclear states and civil society groups to shape, very deliberately, a new discourse surrounding nuclear weapons. This has been a primary development; it represents a significant shift in the way that nuclear politics is now being framed and addressed, even if the policies of the nuclear weapon states remain – for now – as immovable as ever. This discursive shift represents a notable evolution in the patterns of agency and influence in international security relations, and in the constitution of what is considered 'legitimate' regarding methods of warfare and specific weapons.

As Chapter 1 argued, for over seventy years, the traditional discourse surrounding nuclear weapons has been developed and refined by leaders and elites to reflect a strategic and often urgent national security perspective, portraying these weapons as prime defence assets, essential parts of the military programmes of the nuclear states. This was a discourse of security, strategy, and assumed 'rational' calculations, where weapons of immense destructive potential were normalized; as noted in Chapter 1, Mumford observed that the practices of acquiring, refining, targeting, and deploying these weapons came to be seen 'the normal motions of normal men, not the mass compulsions of people bent on total death' (1946: ix).

While many individuals and groups, and some states, over the past seventy-seven years have called for a more realistic description of nuclear arsenals, these weapons have prevailed as the defining element of military security for the states holding them, and these states continue to assert the strategic necessity of these arsenals for their security. The arguments for their retention have centred on the benefits of nuclear deterrence, even in a world where nuclear weapons do little to address post-Cold War security challenges, but they have also stretched, as programmes of modernization show, to the development of 'usable' nuclear weapons, to talk of possible 'first use' and 'limited' nuclear war. The speech defining nuclear weapons portrays them as providers of security, as essential elements in a world where their possession signalled – for some states only – a degree of power and prestige. This is so even though nuclear weapons have little, if any, military utility, that conventional weapon arsenals could substitute for deterring or responding to aggression, that nuclear deterrence is a risky strategy, and that any actual use of these weapons would run counter to prevailing notions about global peace and security. And with the formulation of nuclear policy reserved for what has been called an exclusive 'priesthood', the discourse on security and strategic stability has been very hard to dislodge. A sanitized language drew attention away from a focus on the likely consequences of nuclear use, with euphemisms and the competition for technological superiority driving the vertical proliferation of these weapons, as Moscow and Washington in particular celebrated their vast arsenals. Even as there were dissenting voices seeking to shift this 'normality', it was hard to reject or reformulate this entrenched framing of nuclear weapons. Nonetheless, this 'strategic' discourse is now facing its most serious challenge yet as a humanitarian focus begins to 'bite into' these traditional framings.

The rise of the Humanitarian Initiative and its attendant activities has arguably come to be the most successful attempt to portray nuclear weapons differently and to recast them in a different light. Again, it must be stressed here that while civil society actors had long argued for a humanitarian approach, the Humanitarian Initiative conferences were initiated and conducted by a large group of *states*, and that this new approach, undertaken as multilateral state-led diplomatic gatherings, informed and driven by scientific, economic, and climate-related reports, reflected a sharp move away from the usual NPT intergovernmental debates on nuclear weapons. It was as if, once the NPT RevCon's document in 2010 made explicit reference to grave humanitarian concerns, non-nuclear states felt themselves free to reframe – formally and collectively – the way that nuclear weapons *should* be discussed. In the same way that Canada had set the process for achieving a landmines ban onto a different and successful pathway, so too did Norway's, Mexico's, and Austria's convening of their Humanitarian Initiative conferences allow for non-nuclear states to develop a new discourse, to speak freely and canvass support for a legal prohibition against nuclear weapons.

The factors which have assisted in this process of shifting the discourse on nuclear weapons from one of 'security' to one focused on humanity include, undoubtedly, the changing structures of the post-Cold War era, which allowed for a greater number of states and even non-state actors to influence global politics, and the rise of human rights and humanitarian concerns more generally. This focus on protecting populations has clearly assisted the reframing of nuclear weapons as incompatible with international law.

But it is also important to remember that the nuclear states have until now managed to avoid having their nuclear arsenals associated with any such concerns. While they – especially the Western states in the P5 – might seek to identify with the values of international humanitarian law at a broad global level, they continue to maintain arsenals which promise destruction on combatants and civilians alike. It is the new, formal, identification of nuclear weapons with *in*humanity, with crimes that would shock the conscience of the world, that poses the most important challenge yet to those states insistent on retaining their nuclear arsenals.

The Humanitarian Initiative refocused attention on these weapons as instruments of destruction, by speaking of nuclear weapons as *the* quintessential weapon of mass destruction, posing a greater existential threat, and being far more lethal, than biological or chemical weapons. Changing the speech about nuclear weapons has made explicit the element of risk associated with them. Where the language surrounding nuclear weapons has been typically techno-strategic, focusing on military applications, the language used by the advocates of nuclear elimination, typically from civil society but now also firmly from states, has been focused on human concerns, the implications for the environment, for climate, for agriculture, for infrastructure, as well as on the impossibility of providing adequate medical treatment for survivors of a nuclear strike.

This discursive shift has been a deliberate strategy, designed to establish and strengthen the foundation for the stigmatization, prohibition, and eventual elimination of these weapons (Minor 2015). As John Borrie (2014a) has noted, particular weapons or methods of warfare come to be seen as illegitimate when there is a shift in perception that these are henceforth unacceptable. And shifts in perception are intimately tied to shifts in discourse. The previously restricted dialogues, which, in line with the nuclear weapon states' preferences had had a purely strategic focus, were now left behind at the NPT, and the newer humanitarian discourse would be the core of the campaign to achieve a legal prohibition of nuclear weapons. The reframing of nuclear weapons away from a 'political' issue and towards a 'humanitarian imperative' has also helped several mainstream, typically 'small-c' conservative groups to take up this cause. Rotary International, for instance, usually shy of taking a stance on 'political' and 'controversial' matters, now has a substantial number of members who support the TPNW and are calling for Rotary International to adopt the abolition of nuclear weapons as one of its chief humanitarian priorities.[1] Similarly, several faith-based groups are also making their voices heard in support of the elimination of nuclear weapons. These are remarkable achievements.

The successful application of a new discourse to landmines was important as a precursor, but imposing a new language onto nuclear weapons nevertheless remained a formidable task. We can see where the deliberate decision to change the prevailing discourse began: just before the 2010 NPT Review Conference, the President of the ICRC, Jacob Kellenberger, delivered a speech to the Geneva Diplomatic Corp, signalling a shift towards a much more activist ICRC stance against nuclear weapons. He proposed to realign the Red Cross very closely in opposition to these weapons. Asserting that 'the ICRC has a legitimate voice in this debate', he stated that:

> The existence of nuclear weapons poses some of the most profound questions about the point at which the rights of States must yield to the interests of humanity, the capacity of our species to master the technology it creates, the reach of international humanitarian law, and the extent of human suffering we are willing to inflict, or to permit, in warfare. (Kellenberger 2010)

This speech undoubtedly influenced the debate at the 2010 Review Conference. And once it was launched, this shift in language and the challenging of the 'rights' of states to possess these weapons gathered momentum. As Ray Acheson observed, the position taken by the ICRC is likely to have empowered states in favour of eliminating nuclear weapons to speak up, where their representatives might previously have been marginalized or intimidated by the traditional constraints of nuclear diplomacy (cited in Bolton and Minor 2016b: 385). As with the landmine, which had been (re) presented from being an element of protection to one which was seen as a threat to human security (Larrinaga and Sjolander 1998), nuclear weapons were now also redefined, no longer remaining as an indisputably 'legitimate' weapon in the arsenals of certain states.

Changing the discourse required the belief that these weapons have an unparalleled potential for destruction which outweighed any strategic utility (Acheson 2016: 405), and that they were unacceptable not only because of their direct effect on victims, but also because of their effects on humanity *as a whole*. This was a broader global view: as Nick Ritchie writes, the Humanitarian Initiative allowed for a framework which was based on a 'set of rules and norms for international society' rooted in concepts of common security and common humanity, 'rather than a realpolitik set of rules and norms rooted in [individual] state security and balances of military power' (Ritchie 2014c). Changing the discourse of nuclearism was necessary not just to protect individuals from an inhumane weapon; it was also necessary if we wish to avert an international catastrophe, and achieve global security without the threat of nuclear annihilation.

It was only by disrupting these dominant patterns of thought and belief, which had proved resistant to change for several decades, and classing them as abnormal, and as running counter to newer and preferred norms of political behaviour, that progress towards prohibiting nuclear weapons could be moved forwards. In essence, what was needed was for the long-held 'normal' nature of nuclear weapons' possession, what can be summed up as the discourse of security, to be recast as anomalous and fundamentally incompatible with notions of humanitarianism, human rights, and global responsibility.

Bringing humanitarianism (back) into the picture

The change of discourse noted above was, of course, manifested most clearly by the explicit emphasis on humanitarianism. The immediate result of the TPNW is that nuclear weapons language no longer exists in a humanitarian-free zone: where security elites have managed to avoid scrutiny of their policies on humanitarian grounds, this will change with the new treaty, which makes these weapons illegal for all states, on the basis of their incompatibility with international humanitarian law. The launch of the Humanitarian Initiative was the most obvious marker of an explicit shift away from previous framings and towards one which addresses the actual impact of these weapons on human beings, their environment, and on the entire planet. Various actors and processes were instrumental in enabling this shift.

That the ICRC and also the Vatican were strongly supportive of the Humanitarian Initiative was an important factor. This was because when it came to the question of nuclear weapons, the ICRC had for some decades preferred to retain a sense of what some have called 'neutral humanitarianism' (Rieffer-Flanagan 2009), not intervening directly on this issue because of its political nature. The ICRC had not been active in anti-nuclear programmes or condemned the practice of nuclear deterrence. By 2014, the Vatican, too, had come to adopt a much stronger position. In the 1980s, it had allowed what it called a 'strictly conditional moral acceptance of deterrence', but at the Vienna Conference and in line with the Vatican's ongoing studies into the issue, Pope Francis's clear message was that the practice of nuclear deterrence could no longer be accepted, that it was immoral and dangerous, and that it must cease (see Powers 2015; Welty 2016). In 2010, the Holy See's permanent observer to the United Nations had made a speech declaring that the ongoing retention of nuclear weapons and the modernization processes underway showed that nuclear weapons were 'no longer just for deterrence but have become entrenched in the military doctrines of the major powers' (cited in Powers 2015). At the Vienna Conference, the Vatican's representative to UN Agencies in Geneva delivered an extensive report, deemed 'the Vatican's most detailed treatment of nuclear weapons in many years' (Powers 2015). This document argued that while in the past the Church had expressed a provisional acceptance of deterrence, this was conditional on the nuclear states moving towards progressive disarmament. The report concluded that because this condition had not been fulfilled, 'the nuclear weapon establishment has lost much of its legitimacy' (cited in Powers 2015). These changing views on nuclear deterrence were significant: if deterrence was seen by the nuclear states as benign, safe, and even advantageous for security, this was now being challenged as immoral, unstable, and too risky to continue.

Where once nuclear weapons policy had been cordoned off from humanitarianism, applying humanitarian advocacy to these weapons reoriented the conversation. The conferences held under the Humanitarian Initiative were the venues for the delivery of numerous studies examining the humanitarian consequences of nuclear weapons, from professional and specialised individuals and organizations. These presentations focused on the impact that nuclear weapons' use would have on public health and prospects for assistance – the death and destruction that would occur, and the inability of agencies to respond effectively to such destruction and suffering – and also on the consequences of nuclear strikes on national and global economies, on development and food security, on environmental and climate change issues, and on the implications for inter-generational justice, where, it was noted, 'future generations will be robbed of their health, food, water and other vital resources' (Norway Ministry of Foreign Affairs 2013; see also Fihn 2013). Their research also addressed the impacts that nuclear weapons use would have on human infrastructure, where 'the electric grid, internet, banking, and public health systems, food distribution networks' (Helfand *et al.* 2016) would be severed. In noting the emergence of this humanitarian focus, Patricia Lewis (2013) stated that 'by any definition, nuclear weapons would be classed as inhumane. The fact that it has taken decades to discuss the problems they create ... demonstrates how adept our societies are at forgetting, disguising, and denying the overwhelming and the terrifying'. Some of these fears had been raised, in a somewhat loose way, since Hiroshima, but the ending of the Cold War meant that many people no longer feared the threat of nuclear annihilation. The three Humanitarian Initiative conferences channelled these concerns very effectively; they revitalized and refreshed them and brought the latest science, technology, and legal thinking to bear on these issues.

The findings of these conferences, widely disseminated and repeated in other forums, were crucial in convincing states to commit themselves to achieving a treaty prohibiting nuclear weapons, and are summarized briefly in the following sections.

Effects on humans and the environment

Unlike any other weapon invented, nuclear weapons have the capacity to destroy the planet and all life on it; their destructive capacity is unparalleled. Basing their modelling on a hypothetical scenario where only a small fraction of the world's existing nuclear weapons would be used – less than 1 per cent of existing weapons – the scientists presenting their findings concluded that, in addition to those dead from initial blast, burn and radiation causes, up to two billion people worldwide could starve as a result of climate change brought about by even a 'limited' nuclear war (Helfand 2013b). (More recent studies – Toon *et al.* 2019 – suggest that between 50 and 125 million people might die in the event of nuclear war between India and Pakistan.) Such a 'limited' use of these weapons would have catastrophic consequences: on human life, on health provision (where it is highly unlikely that states or other agencies will be able to provide effective medical assistance to survivors), on climate and the environment (where a nuclear winter resulting from even a small nuclear war would be likely to devastate vast areas of the planet), on food production (where widespread famine would ensue), on water and other resources (likely to be contaminated), and on other fundamental aspects of life (Helfand 2013a; Mills *et al.* 2014). These studies paint a picture of a dystopian world, from which human civilization might not recover.

The overall conclusions drawn from these reports and the conferences can be summarized as follows: first, that it would be 'unlikely that any state or international body could address the immediate humanitarian emergency' caused by a nuclear strike 'in an adequate manner' or 'provide sufficient assistance to those affected'; second, that the 'historical experience from the use and testing of nuclear weapons has demonstrated their devastating immediate and long-term effects'; and third, that the 'effects of a nuclear weapon detonation, irrespective of cause, will not be constrained by national borders', but rather, 'will affect states and people in significant ways, regionally as well as globally' (Eide 2013).

Two pieces of testimony are given below, reflecting the broad conclusions reached by scientists and doctors at the Humanitarian Initiative conferences. One of these scientists, Steven Starr, noted that if less than 1 per cent of existing US and Russian high-yield strategic nuclear weapons (many of which are on high-alert or launch on warning status, ready to launch within thirty seconds to three minutes) were used, not only would there be tens of millions of deaths, but also that,

> immense firestorms, produced by nuclear war fought with these weapons could lift 150 million tons of smoke into the stratosphere. There it rapidly would block 70% of sunlight from reaching the Northern Hemisphere and 35% of sunlight from reaching the Southern Hemisphere ... Average surface temperatures would become colder than those experienced 18,000 years ago at the height of the last Ice Age. (Starr 2009)

Starr assessed that because of these deadly changes to the climate, growing seasons would be mostly eliminated for a decade, causing human and large animal populations to die of starvation (Starr 2009). Later studies have further described the immediate effects on human beings caught in a nuclear strike. Princeton University's Program on Science and Global Security released data in 2019 showing how the use of even one tactical nuclear weapon could spark a nuclear war between the United States and Russia, which could kill thirty-four million people within five hours (Princeton University 2019). As observed by Helfand *et al.* (2016), even a limited nuclear war 'could kill many more people in an hour than were killed during the entire Second World War'.

Sue Wareham, a physician, former president of the Medical Association for the Prevention of War, Australia, and founding member of ICAN, addressed directly what would happen to people on the ground. A (necessarily) long excerpt from this follows:

> Initially there is an intense flash of light which can blind those who are looking towards it. Then follows a blast wave, causing tornado-force winds, collapse of buildings, and flying glass and other debris for up to tens of kilometres from the epicentre. The winds and intense heat would lead to firestorms which can also occur for many kilometres from the epicentre. At Hiroshima, ground temperatures reached 11,000 degrees F. Burning debris spreads the fires even further, the hazards being augmented by broken gas lines and fallen power cables. Dust and smoke would choke the city. For the victims – children, women and men – the injuries include any combination of burns, multiple fractures, blast injuries, rupture of internal organs, chest trauma, head injuries, and haemorrhage. Many would be trapped under building rubble. Underground shelters would probably be death traps as the firestorms consume all available oxygen. Health services tend to be located centrally in cities and many, probably most, would be destroyed. Those that did survive the attack would be totally overwhelmed. Any physicians and first responders who are not themselves victims would be unable to work in the totally devastated, radioactively contaminated wastelands that would extend for kilometres beyond ground zero. Health care depends on adequate communications, transport, electricity, sewerage and the other infrastructure that modern cities have. There is likely to be little water or even pain relief for most of the survivors, let alone meaningful medical assistance. After a variable period – hours, days or weeks, depending on the size of the dose – there is the onset of radiation sickness, the symptoms including bleeding, bruising, nausea, vomiting, diarrhoea, mouth and other gastrointestinal ulceration, fatigue, and loss of hair. Loss of white blood cells leads to the onset of fever and life-threatening infections. In the longer-term, radiation in the form of 'fallout' will occur downwind of a nuclear explosion. The fallout may then be inhaled by people and animals or ingested through contaminated food and water … In addition, epidemics of infectious disease and greatly increased potential for further war and civil conflict would follow. [W]hat's at stake [would be] unprecedented in human history. (Wareham 2016)

A further account, presented at the Vienna conference, was given by Hiroshima survivor, Setsuko Thurlow, who was a thirteen-year-old schoolgirl on 6 August 1945. After escaping from a collapsed and burning building, she saw the following:

> Streams of stunned people were slowly shuffling from the city centre toward nearby hills. They were naked or tattered, burned, blackened and swollen. Eyes were swollen shut and some had eyeballs hanging out of their sockets. They were bleeding, ghostly figures like a slow-motion image from an old silent movie. Many held their hands above the level of their hearts to lessen the throbbing pain of their burns. Strips of skin and flesh hung like ribbons from their bones. Often these ghostly figures would collapse in heaps never to rise again. (Thurlow 2014)

The words and phrases above contrast starkly with the kind of nukespeak and techno-strategic language used by nuclear policy elites noted in Chapter 1. These descriptions make the moral and ethical case against nuclear weapons very clear. And while it has long been known that nuclear strikes would have catastrophic effects, these recent findings ground the results in undeniably human terms. If anything, they show that the 'nuclear winter' theories of the 1980s, which were in any case either ignored or dismissed as fanciful, greatly underestimated the consequences of nuclear use and its impact on humanity and civilization. Scientific and technological advances since the 1980s have enabled us to see in much greater detail what would be the effects of a nuclear strike; in the words of Tilman Ruff (2016), 'the more we know, the worse it looks'. The studies have all presented a scenario more devastating than had been imagined before: they evoked images of 'unspeakable suffering' (Fihn 2013), of 'unparalleled catastrophe' (the term first articulated by Albert Einstein in May 1946), and the urgent need to 'prevent the unacceptable' (Fihn 2013). The research also suggested that the dangers posed by nuclear weapons represent a greater threat to the world than does climate change (Helfand 2016; Robinson 2019); climate change does and will continue to affect the planet, but its slower development would be eclipsed by the immediate and possibly irrevocable devastation brought about by an accidental or deliberate nuclear war. The findings of the three conferences examining the humanitarian impacts of these weapons only reinforced what many had already argued: the only way to prevent nuclear dangers was to eliminate all nuclear weapons.

Focusing on humanitarianism also allowed for a greater application of a gender lens to questions of nuclear weapons. As observers note, 'viewing nuclear weapons from different perspectives, including through a gender lens' (Borrie et al. 2016: 3) has contributed to the changed discourse.[2] A gender perspective allowed the debate to become diversified at the same time that it revealed the need to protect those likely to suffer most from nuclear weapons, children and women. Numerous recent works explore the role of gender in nuclear weapon debates;[3] they explore how a system of patriarchy – what some might describe as hyper-masculinity in the nuclear context – has coloured the issue of nuclear weapons and made it difficult to dislodge the status quo. While disarmament has often been perceived as a 'weak' or 'feminine' approach, and is contrasted against the strength and 'realism' that is accorded to nuclear security elites, this has added to the difficulty of mounting critiques of nuclear policy in the past. By addressing the impacts on women, and by giving women a strong voice in the Humanitarian Initiative processes, the debate has been made richer and fairer than ever before.

At a broader level, there have been some important legal developments regarding the impacts of nuclear weapons and these have been brought into the humanitarian approach. Within the fields of international law, some have claimed that the use of nuclear weapons would likely constitute a genocide, an act of ecocide, an omnicide, and would violate in the extreme the human rights of generations to come. The emerging body of law relating to ecocide, the precautionary principle and inter-generational justice gives further weight to the law prohibiting the threat and use of nuclear weapons (Ware 2016). These findings are summarized briefly below.

Nuclear weapons and genocide

For some time, various scholars have examined the threat of use of nuclear weapons, as part of deterrence policies, within the lens of genocide studies (see especially Lifton and Markusen 1990; Maguire 2007a; Markusen 2007; Evangelista 2010). The United Nations 1948 Convention on Genocide, in Article II, defines genocide as 'acts committed with intent to destroy, in whole or in part, a national, ethnical, racial or religious group' (UN 1948). In particular, it is the 'intent to destroy' that is relevant here: preparations for nuclear war, and indeed nuclear deterrence itself, would seem to demonstrate this intent (Avery 2013).

Robert Jay Lifton and Eric Markusen (1990) believed that 'the same psychological and social processes that enable people to plan and perpetrate genocide' can also 'facilitate the preparations for nuclear war' by creating 'a genocidal mentality – the willingness of governments and their citizens to engage in the mass killing of innocent human beings' (see also Markusen 2007: 361). These authors examined how factors such as 'the role of ideology, dehumanization, euphemistic language, professional socialization, [and] inter-organizational rivalries' were used to facilitate involvement in mass killing projects, those immediately recognized as 'typical' of genocides.

They argued that these same factors also characterized the planning for nuclear war. A special issue of the *Journal of Genocide Research* in 2007 explored the linking of nuclear weapons to genocide in a series of compelling articles (see especially Kuznick 2007; Maguire 2007a; Markusen 2007). As Markusen argued, the preparations and plans for using nuclear weapons 'entail the willingness to slaughter masses of defenceless human beings', with the nuclear war plans envisioning death tolls which would probably 'dwarf the largest genocides in modern history' (2007: 361). By way of example, he noted that the nuclear war plans of the United States in 1961 'were officially expected to kill between 360 and 425 million people. Presumably, Soviet nuclear weapons would have slaughtered as many or more' (Markusen 2007: 362). That nuclear weapons are coming to be seen as linked with genocidal policies is also evident in the decision taken by the organisers of Genocide Memorial Day, which listed as its theme for 2016, 'Nuclear Weapons, Genocidal Weapons of Mass Destruction' (Keating 2016).

The level of destruction wrought by nuclear weapons also lays open to question the role of the state. If nuclear weapons necessarily entail 'unjust risks and unjust harms' (Wigg-Stevenson 2015: 357), then their possession and the threat to use them (or to bring their use upon oneself, as mutually assured destruction would do) is fundamentally at odds with what we conceive as the necessary nature and purpose of the state (Robock and Toon 2012). At an individual human level also, living under nuclear deterrence has surely contributed to personal fear: fear that it might fail at any time, fear that its doctrines require the annihilation of millions of people, in one's own name and because of one's own quest for security.

Nuclear weapons and ecocide

Ecocide has been defined in a number of jurisdictions as the crime of 'extensive damage to, destruction of or loss of ecosystem(s) of a given territory, whether by human agency or by other causes, to such an extent that peaceful enjoyment by the inhabitants of that territory has been or will be severely diminished' (Higgins, cited in Jowit 2010). That nuclear weapons, if used, or detonated accidentally, would destroy extensive areas of land and affect the atmosphere, is a largely uncontested view. But the very recent developments in thinking about international law and the environment have significant consequences for nuclear weapons policy today. For decades, international humanitarian law had only outlawed destruction of the environment, or ecocide, in times of war. This thinking has undergone some change: in September 2016, the International Criminal Court announced that it could consider crimes committed 'by means of, or that result in, *inter alia*, the destruction of the environment, the exploitation of natural resources, and the illegal dispossession of land' (ICC 2016), suggesting that crimes which result in environmental destruction are now likely to be taken more seriously than they were in the past.

The term 'ecocide' had been developed in the 1950s by Arthur Galston, a scientist involved in identifying the chemicals required for making Agent Orange, who on learning of its destructive use in Vietnam, campaigned for the practice to cease. His use of the term resulted in its adoption by the landmark 1972 UN Conference on the Environment, held in Stockholm. Since then, various campaigners have sought to make ecocide an international crime (Falk 1973; Gray 1996; Franz 2002; Higgins 2010; Burroughs 2013; see also Zimmerer 2007, who has written of 'environmental genocide'), with advocates seeking to criminalize the destruction of ecosystems and to establish a legal duty of care for the environment, by holding people of 'superior responsibility' to account (Hall 2012).

Many of the studies which came to be associated with the Humanitarian Initiative focused extensively on the consequences of nuclear weapons for the environment (Toon *et al.* 2007a, 2007b, 2008), broadening concern to include not just the effects on humans, but also on other species, and on future generations. With attention now being given to environmental destruction as an international crime, the implications of any nuclear weapons' use – as well as that of nuclear weapons testing, and the storage of nuclear waste materials[4] – becomes increasingly problematic.

Nuclear weapons and omnicide

The word 'omnicide' was coined directly in response to the destructive potential of nuclear weapons. American philosopher John Somerville saw nuclear weapons as constituting, for the first time, the potential death of, literally, every living thing. He argued that the threat or use of nuclear weapons would constitute 'the ultimate crime against the future, omnicide, including the destruction of the human species' (Somerville 1986). For Somerville, the term 'war' in the nuclear age had become deceptive and redundant: with the advent of nuclear weapons, all life on the planet could be irreversibly exterminated as a result of the nuclear policies practised by the nuclear states.

The very real possibility that nuclear weapons could destroy not just human populations and civilization, but also much or all of the planet has bolstered fears of omnicide; for Krieger (2009) omnicide is 'the total negation and destruction of all life ... suicide for all. It is the genocide of humanity writ large'. Einstein had also described nuclear war as the destruction of the human world as a whole (cited in Somerville 1986). Writing on nuclear weapons, genocide, and omnicide, Berel Lang (1986: 122) observed that if genocide is the 'final solution', then 'omnicide would be a still more final solution'.

Such terms point to the inherent horror of nuclear weapons which motivates those seeking a nuclear-free world. As Joseph Cirincione (2016) points out, the drive to stigmatize, outlaw and then eliminate nuclear weapons has been fuelled 'less by ideology than by fear' of the enormous destruction that such weapons might bring. The Humanitarian Initiative was not a point-scoring exercise against the nuclear weapons states; it, and the decision to create a prohibitionary treaty, arose from frustration at the nuclear states' refusal to disarm, but also from the great sense of fear that nuclear annihilation can occur at any moment, and the concern that the nuclear weapon states are not acknowledging these dangers or acting to prevent them.

Nuclear weapons and the rights of future generations

A further argument that came out of the Humanitarian Initiative was that nuclear weapons' use would violate the human rights of future generations. There has been considerable development in the past two decades of trans-generational (or inter-generational) rights including the inter-generational application of international humanitarian law, and this is increasingly being related to the issue of nuclear weapons (Rendall 2007). The recognition of the need for inter-generational justice cannot now be ignored, argues Emilie Gaillard: using nuclear weapons would undoubtedly affect future generations, by having the potential to 'damage the future environment, food and marine ecosystems, and to cause genetic defects and illness in future generations' (Gaillard 2016). She observes that as the legal imperative to protect the environment is now inscribed in certain constitutions around the world, so too are trans-generational perspectives being applied to many elements of international peace and security.

Christopher Weeramantry (1996) had also affirmed that the rights of future generations have 'passed the stage when they were merely an embryonic right struggling for recognition'; they have by now 'woven themselves into international law through major treaties, through juristic opinion and through general principles of law recognised by civilised nations'. For Alyn Ware, this issue is of paramount importance:

> Even if there was some remaining possibility that a nuclear weapon could be used on military installations and personnel in a way that did not spread radiation to civilians, the offspring of surviving military personnel, and their subsequent generations, would be impacted by the radiation – both through long-lasting radionuclides and through inter-generational damage to genes. It is clearly illegal for the weapons to cause this damage to future generations. They may be offspring of military personnel, but they have their own human rights and are protected under international humanitarian law. (Ware 2016)

A further important effect of the application of humanitarianism to nuclear weapons is that these findings go beyond the somewhat indeterminate view expressed by the ICJ in its 1996 Advisory Opinion. While the ICJ noted that nuclear weapons would be 'generally' against the principles of the laws of war, the Court was unable to conclude definitively whether nuclear weapons' use, would be legal or not (ICJ 1996). For many, who would have preferred a more explicit ruling against nuclear weapons, this did not go far enough. Indeed this legal gap – where nuclear weapons were not explicitly prohibited by international law – was one of the major motivations for the states supporting the Humanitarian Initiative. But more than twenty years after the ICJ gave its Advisory Opinion, the new scientific research conducted on the impacts of nuclear weapons, together with the evolution of legal thought about issues such as the environment, inter-generational justice, etc., made it is possible to make a strong case for a clear legal prohibition. As Ware (2016) noted, since the 1996 ICJ decision, the developments in international law, such as those noted above, 'have removed any possible exceptions to the general illegality of the threat or use of nuclear weapons'. If there was uncertainty about the legality of a nuclear strike in 1996, two decades later it was argued that the new 'evidence-based understandings of what nuclear weapons actually do' (Helfand and Lederer 2016) renders any arguments for continued possession of these weapons invalid.

All of these arguments gave strength to those governments who believed that it was time to fill the legal gap regarding nuclear weapons with an unambiguously clear prohibition. As Michael Krepon (2016) observed:

> Medical, environmental, and humanitarian evidence about consequences has led to prohibiting and eliminating entire classes of weapons that are far less devastating in their effects than nuclear weapons. In the course of negotiating the treaties banning chemical and biological weapons, antipersonnel landmines, and cluster munitions, the security-based arguments for keeping them or delaying their elimination were raised and rejected.

So too, now, have been the arguments in favour of retention of nuclear weapons, at least by the many states which voted to negotiate the prohibition treaty. The impatience felt against the P5 states (IISS 2015) inevitably led non-nuclear states to adopt this clear humanitarian approach. The newly articulated thinking on the role, purpose, and implications of nuclear weapons emboldened non-nuclear states. In short, refocusing attention away from the P5's preferred discourse of 'security', and focusing strictly on a humanitarian approach, in just a few years, has provided the mechanism for states to delegitimize nuclear weapons, seen as an essential step in the process towards the eventual elimination of these weapons. This was something that, despite their best efforts over three decades, the non-nuclear states had been unable to achieve via the nuclear NPT.

Humanitarianism has been clearly incorporated into the TPNW, with its Preamble noting that states have acted to delegitimize nuclear weapons,

> Basing themselves on the principles and rules of international humanitarian law, in particular the principle that the right of parties to an armed conflict to choose methods or means of warfare is not unlimited, the rule of distinction, the prohibition against indiscriminate attacks, the rules on proportionality and precautions in attack, the prohibition on the use of weapons of a nature to cause superfluous injury or unnecessary suffering, and the rules for the protection of the natural environment. (UN 2017)

Bringing humanitarianism into the picture – in a clear and unequivocal way – represents a fundamental challenge to nuclearism. A forum and process outside the NPT, and vastly different to it, allowed the free exchange of ideas and principles which had not previously been able to find a home within traditional arms control diplomacy. This means that from now, nuclear weapon states, in their dealings with non-nuclear states, will not be able to call on arguments of security, military necessity, or nuclear deterrence without signatories to the prohibition treaty reminding them of the illegal nature of these weapons, and the fact that they have been declared, by the conscience of humanity, as immoral and unacceptable. Refuting previous discourses of nuclearism by adopting humanitarian arguments enables non-nuclear states to enter the debate, if they wish, on their own newly declared terms. These states accept that war might never be 'humanized', but inserting humanitarian considerations into methods of warfare and focusing on the adverse consequences of using particular weapons is increasingly seen as a global imperative.

Rejecting exclusivity: new voices in the nuclear debate

In the same way that a changed discourse, and its emphasis on humanitarianism, has come to challenge nuclearism, so too has the deliberate inclusion of new and previously unheard voices into the debate on nuclear weapons. Chapter 1 noted that it has typically been a small group of persons within politics – political leaders and select cohorts of national security elites – who have been given a privileged voice in the acquisition and development of nuclear weapons, and over nuclear policy planning more generally. Even as national security might require some restriction in the involvement of outsiders in defence and foreign policy planning, the exclusion of other voices in the specific realm of nuclear decision-making seems to be unparalleled. The chapter also noted that while this factor is undoubtedly a problem in non-democracies, it is perhaps not much better in the nuclear weapon states which are democracies. One could argue that the presence of an electoral system and other aspects of democracy allow for a civilian voice in foreign policy and defence issues, but the fact is that even in a multi-party democratic system, no effective rejection of the nuclear status quo has been possible.

In many Western states, the dominant political parties have all been captured, it would seem, by the practices of nuclearism, and even in those allied states where there has been a significant level of anti-nuclearism in politics – for example, Germany, Norway, Japan – public opposition to nuclear weapons has rarely led to a wholesale rejection of nuclear weapons (the exception have been New Zealand, and more recently Mongolia).[5] Once firmly enmeshed in the belief that nuclear weapons were needed as a guarantor of security, no party within the nuclear weapon states or their allies, even when in power, has been able to shake off the pervasive nature of the way that things simply *were*. And even where the governments of some of these countries sought to guide the nuclear weapon states towards disarmament – as we saw in the Canberra Commission, the Tokyo Forum, the Seven Nation Initiative, etc. – later governments have been less willing to sustain such challenges; the result is that ultimately, these reports have had no impact on the way that these weapons were seen by their possessors.

Essentially, the control of nuclear weapons policy has been closely guarded, helped by the formal discourse of security and strategy. Even if leaders have shown some inclination to move away from a reliance on nuclear weapons – as Reagan and Gorbachev did at Reykjavik in 1986, and Obama did at Prague in 2009 – these have not resulted in any serious challenge to nuclearism, whose powerful elements – including the decisions of security elites – have been able to wind back attempts to dislodge the existing state of affairs. Neither have the non-state voices been able to force a change in direction; proponents of disarmament from civil society have faced resistance and even discrediting. Keeping these voices at bay has helped to reinforce the view that nuclear weapons are essential for individual, national, and even global, security.

But the control over what nuclear weapons 'are' and what a nuclear attack would actually mean for human beings has now changed. By challenging the 'established pattern of power relations' (Borrie *et al.* 2016: 30), the focus on humanitarianism opened a space for numerous voices which had not been heard, or heard clearly, before. All of these voices contributed to the reframing of the nuclear issue firmly within an explicit and hard to refute logic of humanitarianism, and they were all instrumental in the move to negotiate the prohibition treaty. The testimony by victims and survivors was crucially important. By becoming incorporated into the debate, this testimony ensured that the Humanitarian Initiative process, as Tom Sauer (2015a) notes, 'has gone back to the basics: it focuses on the effects of the use of nuclear weapons on people instead of the "security" effects of their non-use'. In this sense, the Humanitarian Initiative can be cast as 'the first narrative that fundamentally challenges the nuclear deterrence paradigm' (Sauer 2015a). This approach, as Ritchie (2016: 53–54) argues, was 'rooted in a collective moral revulsion and rejection of specific categories of violence, especially massive, inhumane and indiscriminate forms of violence'.

The new voices included NGOs from various fields,[6] but also smaller states which had not had a strong role in formulating international security policy previously. This has been a valuable symbiotic process: at the same time that particular states welcomed civil society expertise, this participation of civil society actors may have spurred some states to affirm views that they may not have felt able to express earlier or in different forums. It was this partnership between NGOs and like-minded states which allowed for success in establishing a global prohibitionary treaty, which years of diplomatic wrangling had not been able to achieve.

The innovative nature of this kind of diplomacy should not be ignored: in the past, if NGOs had been involved in policy decisions, this was likely to have been in areas such as social policy, human rights, and perhaps development policy. Security issues have been seen as 'high politics', and have been 'particularly resistant to pressures exerted by nongovernmental actors' (McFarlane 2000: x; see also Price 1998). That NGOs would come to play a role in one of the highest of 'high-politics' issues – international nuclear weapons policy – was remarkable because their involvement in affairs considered central to national security and defence policy has historically been very limited (Knopf 2012). Now, NGOs have been able to initiate and influence state policy directly over issues which lie at the heart of state sovereignty, namely, defence, national security, and the weapons that would henceforth be considered legitimate to use in warfare. Richard Price, writing on the landmines ban, noted the significance of the role of transnational non-state actors 'working through issue networks to affect how states prepare for and wage war', typically one of the 'hard cases' for direct citizen involvement (Price 1998: 613). This was therefore a significant shift, where 'outsiders' were intruding into a field of policy normally reserved for political elites, or 'insiders'.

The scale and nature of this civil society engagement was crucially important in driving the nuclear ban: during the various conferences leading up to negotiation of the TPNW, there was an intensive and closely directed set of activities carried out by specialized advocacy groups. Civil society actors were drawn from the medical, legal, and scientific professions, but they also included environmental groups, religious organizations, women's groups, celebrities, and others. Determined and influential professional groups of NGOs, well-educated on the particular subject and often with first-hand experience in the field, have for some time been forging new pathways in the area of advocating for change, taking their specialized skills and experience directly to political and diplomatic forums (Rutherford and Brem 2003; Randin 2006; Knopf 2012).

In particular, the role of health professionals has been important in the nuclear debate; a pivotal article in the *World Medical Journal* recounted the extensive interaction that medical practitioners have had with nuclear issues, from the earliest activity in Hiroshima (Helfand *et al.* 2016). In this sense, health workers, demonstrating their responsibility to uphold health and to prevent harm, can be seen to have 'earned' a central role in advocating for the elimination of nuclear weapons. The group, International Physicians for the Prevention of Nuclear War (IPPNW), and the Medical Association for the Prevention of War (MAPW) had been important in fostering ICAN in Australia in 2007; ICAN subsequently grew into a global coalition of 570 partner organizations, and by 2017, when the new treaty was being negotiated, was operating in ninety-eight states, making it the most prominent civil society group involved in coordinating campaigns, raising awareness, and supporting non-nuclear state advocacy. Additionally, a group of almost 4,000 scientists signed a letter of support to states negotiating the TPNW at the United Nations, avowing that 'scientists bear a special responsibility for nuclear weapons, since it was scientists who invented them'.[7] As Borrie *et al.* (2009) had earlier noted, the involvement of practitioners such as health professionals, and those affected by the weapons themselves, such as the Hibakusha and groups from testing sites, added greatly to the legitimacy of such deliberations.

NGOs were active not only in drawing attention to the impacts of nuclear weapons, but they also came to be important interlocutors in the creation of the treaty. The shift away from reliance on the NPT process, run by states and along traditional lines, to the Humanitarian Initiative conferences, where self-selecting pro-ban states, propelled along by NGOs, occupied centre-stage, was a crucial turning-point. It was the participation of NGOs in Oslo, Vienna, and Nayarit, and in individual states where NGOs conducted domestic campaigns, which was an essential factor in driving negotiations for the prohibition treaty. Their call for an unequivocal ban, their intense lobbying of government delegations, and their highly coordinated country campaigns, were important in the lead-up to the TPNW. Their activities, reports, and studies enabled non-nuclear states to work on the deliberate recasting of nuclear weapons, which took the debate away from the prevailing political framework which had never been able to move beyond the discourses of deterrence, parity, yields, delivery systems, etc., and where a step-by-step approach – or at least the *promise* of a step-by-step approach – to disarmament was the only one that nuclear weapons states would consider. Instead, these new voices lifted this issue onto a new platform, cutting through the reasons and delays which had long been made by the nuclear-armed states, and reframed the debate squarely within a humanitarian and global justice framework.

In terms of civil society involvement, from a sceptical point of view, it can be argued, of course, that we are not seeing the type of mass public demonstrations against nuclear weapons that were evident at various times during the Cold War, and that this might signify a lack of interest in this issue. But we must note the significant change in the *way* that non-state actors have sought to influence governments on security issues. Especially in the 1960s, 1970s, and the early 1980s, there was much more overt public support than there is today for 'banning the bomb', with street marches and other campaigns visibly dedicated to exposing the perils of nuclear warfare. Some might argue that without such protests today – what we might term a prominent 'disarmament movement' like the ones seen in previous decades – the nuclear elimination cause is unlikely to succeed. But the absence of hundreds of thousands of protesters does not necessarily mean that the cause is lost.

First, this kind of mass protest has been in decline in many countries. The anti-Vietnam war, civil rights, and anti-nuclear movements are memorable for their huge gatherings and as events that continued for several years. And the late 1980s saw large public demonstrations in the Soviet bloc arguing for human and political rights. But this kind of civil society activity – mass demonstrations – is not often seen today, or at least, if it is seen, it has tended to coalesce around the most visible global issue of our times, namely climate change, and more recently, around anti-racism movements. Second, it is important to remember that the threat of nuclear annihilation is no longer widely present in the public consciousness. If the average person thinks about nuclear weapons today, it is usually within the context of headline news announcing that 'rogue states' like North Korea or Iran had acquired, or were suspected of acquiring, these weapons (Sauer and Pretorius 2014). No other 'news' about nuclear weapons filters through, and certainly little to suggest the danger the world faces every day with the existence of many thousands of nuclear weapons. The end of the superpower confrontation in 1991, which in any case happened relatively amicably, was presumed to have swept away the dangers that had hung over vulnerable populations for decades. Those with little information about the reality of nuclear weapons today would be inclined to feel that there was no nuclear threat. This helps to explain the lack of massive street demonstrations today focused on eliminating nuclear weapons.

But another dimension of the civil society story is important to note: while there may not be huge numbers of people marching in the streets, those groups active in this field are invariably highly motivated, focused, and well-educated about the problem at hand. As noted above, their numbers include professionals drawn from around the globe, and their activities tend to be sharply concentrated on the nuclear weapons debate as a single-issue focus. As with the landmines campaigns, they have brought to bear their considerable experience and training to address the real-life consequences of the impacts of these weapons. Steadfast and highly committed, these civil society actors make up for the absence of the larger but more diffuse groups of protestors seen in the past. And it has been much harder for governments to reject the work of these NGOs; their particular expertise – whether it be science, medicine, or the law – cannot be as easily dismissed as were the protestors carrying placards in previous decades. While less visible than those mass movements, the members of these newer kinds of NGO work over prolonged periods of time to sustain the cause they support.

It is certain that these civil society actors will continue to maintain their activities by placing pressure on governments to sign and to comply with the treaty's provisions, and that they will mobilize further support in favour of the elimination of nuclear weapons.[8] This combination – of highly active, committed, and professional NGOs, together with a substantial mass of states acting with them – has been important in achieving a legal prohibition against nuclear weapons. Where large states once negotiated arms control strictly within a security-focused framework, civil society groups have harnessed a humanitarian imperative, worked with smaller, like-minded states, and helped to forge a ban-treaty regardless of the wishes or preferences of the great powers. Clearly, the end of the Cold War allowed the 'opening up' of many aspects of foreign policy, resulting in what John English (1998: 131) has called 'a new texture' in international relations, 'where negotiating tables have new players and shapes, where linkages and networks transcend state limits' and certainly where moral issues have intruded. It signifies the emergence of an important new advocacy voice in security debates.

The introduction of these new voices has reframed the 'normal' picture of nuclear weapons. Kennette Benedict (2012) suggests that 'if nuclear war planning robbed us of our democratic rights as humanitarian agents, then disarmament affords us the opportunity to regain these' rights. At the very least, achieving a ban on these weapons, as a step towards eliminating them, has helped to reshape thinking about the legitimacy of a world in which a few people possess the capacity to launch unparalleled catastrophe onto others (Acheson 2015: 406): that civil society actors are driving decisions about how military power can be waged represents a potential return to a more democratic deliberation about security.

The larger picture here is important: the efforts to restrict or ban nuclear weapons in the past few decades have been driven not by the most powerful states in the international system, but rather by groups of relatively inconsequential actors. Arms control and disarmament diplomacy has become increasingly multilateral, involving small and middle-sized states, as well as non-governmental groups. If nuclear weapon policies since 1945 were effectively imposed on national populations and on the international system as a whole – a thoroughly 'top-down' process allowing no real, effective challenge from below – the processes we have seen recently are building from the bottom upwards, constructing new conversations and launching a prohibitionary regime without the great powers.

We can understand this development as a natural reaction to the possibility of nuclear catastrophe. Echoing Jacob Kellenberger, Ramesh Thakur has argued that 'if the consequences of a nuclear war are systemic, then decisions on arsenals, doctrines and use cannot be solely a matter of sovereign privilege' (Thakur 2016b). All states and individuals have the right to be heard if they are likely to be negatively affected by the decisions of a handful of states. As Thakur (2016b) and others encapsulate it, there should be 'no incineration without representation'.

The TPNW, based on the unacceptable humanitarian impacts of nuclear weapons, pushed formally by a collection of middle-sized and small non-nuclear states, poses a challenge to traditional interpretations of international politics which argue that military capabilities in an anarchical international system essentially limit the effect that such actors can wield. As Bolton and Minor (2016a) write, decisions on nuclear arsenals have typically been 'the preserve of presidents, premiers and generals of the world's great powers', and not that of 'underfunded activists, feminist campaigners, radical nuns or even diplomats of small states'. And yet, it is precisely these latter actors who have achieved the legal prohibition of nuclear weapons. Smaller states like Austria, New Zealand, Mexico, South Africa, Mongolia, and Costa Rica, which have strongly supported the prohibition treaty, do not usually feature prominently in international security. Yet their governments' activities with other like-minded states have been able to create a standard which can have an important cumulative effect. Nick Ritchie (2016: 56) has expressed the importance of this new agency:

> Emphasising the illegitimacy of nuclear weapons shifts the direction of disarmament diplomacy away from an exclusive focus on trying to change the policies of the nuclear-armed states. It moves it towards changing the normative international environment in which nuclear weapons and nuclear-armed states are embedded. It shifts the centre of power in disarmament diplomacy

away from the agency of those that have nuclear weapons, their relationships with each other, and their nuclear weapons programmes. Instead, it empowers a much broader community of States to change the international social structure of nuclear legitimacy and illegitimacy.

The Humanitarian Initiative enabled these new voices to be heard, and they spoke a new language, one that did not come from the ranks of national security elites and arms controllers, or from a focus on strategic studies (Minor 2015). It was the voices of victims of nuclear tests and the survivors of the Japanese bombings, together with the expert testimony of scientists, doctors, climate specialists, and others, which brought to the fore issues that had always been present but which had invariably been unspoken by the nuclear weapon states and their allies. They rejected the view that the high politics of defence and security should be limited to those insiders who for decades remained unaccountable to the broader global community.

Rejecting nuclear budgets: challenging material spending

Given their success in framing arms control questions within a humanitarian lens, civil society actors and like-minded states are likely to increase, rather than decrease, their ongoing involvement in nuclear weapons decisions. Within certain nuclear weapon states at least, this suggests that the allocation of material resources to nuclear weapon programmes will become a much more contested issue in light of the new treaty. After decades of these budgets being almost sacrosanct, the treaty enables citizens to question more effectively the costs associated with the acquisition, retention, and modernization of nuclear weapons. Public bodies are increasingly watching over military budget processes, especially when it is clear that governments have been engaged in cuts to health, education, and welfare programmes, when the opportunity costs of nuclear weapon spending are exposed (Pifer 2020), and when the effects of the COVID-19 pandemic has led to calls for reining in military spending.[9] At the height of this catastrophic pandemic, ICAN released its report on global spending on nuclear weapons, arguing that the US$79.2 billion spent on nuclear weapons in 2019 (an increase of over US$7 billion from the previous year) was an unconscionable 'choice' made by the nuclear states.

Most importantly perhaps, the prohibition treaty is likely to have an effect on financing, boycotts, and divestment policies. Article 1(e) of the treaty expressly forbids assisting, encouraging, or inducing any state to engage in any activity prohibited by the treaty. One such form of assistance is argued to be financial investment in, and material support of, nuclear weapon programmes. We have seen, especially since 2010, an increasing scrutiny of the funding of these programmes. Many financial institutions have changed their policies in light of international treaties banning specific weapons, including landmines and cluster munitions. A landmark report completed by PAX (formerly Pax Christi), *Don't Bank on the Bomb: a Global Report on the Financing of Nuclear Weapons Producers*, originally appeared in 2013 and named those national and global financial institutions which were shown to be investing in companies whose activities included manufacturing nuclear weapons. Subsequent editions have recognized and applauded those financial institutions which had divested themselves in previous years from companies involved with research or manufacturing of nuclear weapons. A 2018 edition identified 329 banks, insurance companies, pension funds, and asset managers from twenty-four countries, which continue to invest significantly in these corporations, all of which have a vested interest in high nuclear weapons budgets, especially in the United States and Europe (PAX 2018). Nevertheless, the 2019 report, *Producing Mass Destruction: Private Companies and the Nuclear Weapon Industry* (PAX 2019) identified an ongoing tally of twenty-eight major nuclear weapon producing companies.

Civil society is particularly active in this field, monitoring and reporting on the activities of financial institutions, with the aim of persuading them to invest ethically and to boycott companies profiting from the weapons industry (IBP/PNND/WFC 2016; PAX 2017; PNND 2017). This kind of pressure on corporations to invest ethically is being conducted in other spheres of interest too, especially in the fields of protecting the environment and preventing child labour exploitation practices. As the group Article 36 (2013) notes, for individuals, states, and even corporations, 'stigma shapes how certain weapons are recognised as unacceptable and incompatible with the identities we wish to hold in the world'. With the clear delegitimization of nuclear weapons that the prohibition treaty brings, it is likely that banks and other financial bodies will become more sensitive to their public images and reputations, and will invest accordingly. The treaty thus reduces what Acheson *et al.* (2014: 12) call the 'incentives' for private companies to accept any work related to nuclear weapons. Ritchie (2010) has also explored how commercial factors have influenced the promotion of a nuclear weapons culture and enabled states to cling to their arsenals, pointing to the importance of identities and networks; all of these are likely to come under increased scrutiny with the new treaty, as thousands of supporters challenge their banks and superannuation funds to divest or to face customers willing to move their money elsewhere. As *Don't Bank on the Bomb* and other reports show, there is already evidence of several financial institutions, once challenged about their investments, shunning the producers of nuclear weapons. The work conducted by PAX and others in this field is impressive in its depth and intrusiveness, and should not be underestimated as an important element reinforcing the need for 'humane' investment choices.[10]

Given the extensive plans by all the nuclear weapon states to modernize their arsenals, a sustained scrutiny of the institutions funding these activities can be bolstered by the treaty which clearly confirms the illegality of these weapons. This could have substantial implications for these modernization programmes. As NGOs note:

> the divestment campaign accompanying the treaty banning cluster munitions has been successful in affecting the financial interests of corporations producing these weapon systems … Some governments have already begun divesting from nuclear weapons producers … As more pension funds, banks, and public investments are removed from nuclear weapons producers, the political effects will increase. (Acheson *et al.* 2014: 28)

This will be particularly important in those states where defence contractors and supplier corporations operate and perpetuate a 'normal' nuclear weapons culture. The new treaty will be useful to politicians favourable towards disarmament, but who presently face significant pressures from commercial interests heavily invested in the manufacture of nuclear weapons (Acheson *et al.* 2014: 16). In a working paper submitted to the OEWG in March 2017, a gathering of parliamentary representatives and civil society organizations explicitly asked that the nuclear prohibition treaty should prohibit the financing of nuclear weapons (PNND 2017; see also IPB/PNND/WFC 2016); while the treaty makes no mention explicitly of 'financing', it does, as noted, prohibit the assisting, encouraging, or inducing of any others to develop nuclear weapons. The treaty is likely to stimulate further the scrutiny and shaming of banks and other institutions involved in the financing of nuclear weapons, making it more costly and less 'normal' for them to continue in defiance of global public opinion and international law.

Conclusion

The points explored in this chapter suggest that many of the elements sustaining nuclearism are now coming under pressure. After more than two decades of seeking to work *with* the nuclear weapon states through the NPT, non-nuclear states and a wide range of civil society actors have generated a legal prohibition without them. The way that they have done this, and the provisions of the treaty itself, represent a key challenge to those elements which have enabled nuclearism to prevail for so many decades.

That the nuclear weapon states have been able to maintain their position for so long makes this shift – towards seeing nuclear weapons as unacceptable to the conscience of humanity – all the more notable. If military policy can be regarded as the legitimate planning for violence by the state, and essentially the preserve of a government and its national security elite, then planning for nuclear war can be said to represent the zenith of a state's capacity for destruction. But such policies and planning have implications not only for those states and populations directly targeted or targeting: their impact cannot be confined in geographical space or in time. Nuclear weapons affect national, regional, and international security, and represent, as John Somerville perceived it, a potential 'omnicide', an impact on life altogether.

This embodiment – *par excellence* – of concentrated state power has now been subjected to a discursive, moral, and financial scrutiny via the application of a humanitarian lens. If traditional arms control processes were conducted by the great powers, between themselves, the application of a 'humanitarian disarmament' framework to nuclear weapons recognizes that 'everyone has the right and responsibility to take steps to prevent the use of nuclear weapons' (Johnson 2012). This achievement is all the more notable for the fact that nuclear weapons policy has been hitherto the most unassailable element within the already heavily fortified domain of national security.

The achievement of the new treaty, the discourse surrounding it, the incorporation of new actors and new voices challenging nuclear policies and nuclear spending all represent a rejection of many of the fundamental elements of nuclearism. But it is perhaps the final element of nuclearism explored in Chapter 1 – the control over a global nuclear order, utilizing especially the nuclear NPT – which will pose the most substantial disruption to the nuclear weapon states. The next chapter addresses this claim.

Notes

1 See, in particular the Rotary Action Group for Peace Subcommittee on Nuclear Weapons Education and its ancillary activities.
2 For an assessment of how nuclear weapons have an impact on women which is different to that on men, see Borrie *et al.* (2016).
3 These include works by Acheson (2015, 2021), Cohn *et al.* (2005), and Duncanson and Eschle (2008). See also the special issue on Women and Nuclear Weapons Policy in the *Bulletin of the Atomic Scientists* (2014). A Women's International League for Peace and Freedom Report (WILPF) of 2021 noted that WILPF has been articulating 'the links between militarism and gender norms such as violent masculinities' (RCW 2021); the report contains a wide database of works on gender and disarmament.

4 Maguire (2007b) reminds us that nuclear testing and its catastrophic effects have invariably been inflicted on lands and people far removed from possessors of the bomb, and terms this a 'cultural assault'.
5 It had been evident by 1984 that that an anti-nuclear stance was favoured by the New Zealand populace; as a result, the Labour Party swept to power on an explicit anti-nuclear campaign. The country was subsequently suspended from the ANZUS treaty. In 1987 New Zealand passed the 'Nuclear Free Zone, Disarmament and Arms Control Act'. This non-nuclear norm has become so entrenched in New Zealand politics and society that it is now upheld by all the major parties. The state of Mongolia also declared its entire territory to be nuclear free, in 1992.
6 Non-state actors have long been active in protesting against nuclear weapons, especially in certain periods in the 1960s, 1970s, and 1980s; in this sense, NGO activity in arms control and disarmament is a not an entirely new phenomenon. What was new from around 2010 was the collaboration between these groups and various like-minded state governments.
7 This was the 'Open letter from scientists in support of the UN nuclear weapons negotiations' submitted via the Future of Life Institute, 2017.
8 A small selection of these activities include ICAN's launch of the Cities Appeal in October 2018, which has resulted in hundreds of city council governments around the world pledging to place upward pressure on national legislatures to comply with the TPNW; the establishment in numerous countries of bipartisan 'Parliamentary Friends of the TPNW' groups, with cross-party politicians urging national legislatures to uphold the TPNW; the commissioning and dissemination of research reports; holding workshops on divestment strategies for the general public; working with Indigenous groups; regular interaction with media; and seeking opposition groups' commitments to joining the TPNW in those states not yet members.
9 Numerous short works have appeared on this issue. For a selection see Monbiot (2020) (who facetiously said 'Let's nuke the virus'), Wareham (2020), Helfand *et al.* (2020), and Hanson (2020).
10 Two examples illustrate this growing trend: the PAX website notes that KBC, a Belgian financial institution, has responded to the positioning it was given in the 2016 update of *Don't Bank on the Bomb*. The organization, keen to assert its humanitarian credentials, noted that it had amended its policies in the period since the PAX research was conducted. Noting the divestments that it had made, the company stated that 'KBC is aware of its role in society, and takes its responsibilities in that regard very seriously ... These new polices include further tightening of our policy on arms-related activities'. In Norway, there has been for some time a sense of obligation about ethical investment practices. In 2004, the Norwegian Government Pension Fund adopted ethical guidelines which exclude from investment companies that produce nuclear weapons components, on the basis that they violate fundamental humanitarian principles.

7

Rejecting nuclearism II: disrupting the nuclear order

The previous chapter addressed how four elements of nuclearism – a specialized strategic discourse, a neglect of humanitarian issues, the limited voices in nuclear politics, and the spending of vast resources on nuclear weapons – have all come to be challenged by the processes of the Humanitarian Initiative and the provisions of the Treaty on the Prohibition of Nuclear Weapons. The fifth broad element supporting nuclearism detailed in Chapter 1 of this book was the domination of the global nuclear weapons debate and the construction of a global nuclear order by the P5 nuclear weapon states, who have exploited the nuclear Non-Proliferation Treaty to produce outcomes favourable to themselves. This powerful element is now far less secure than it was, and the prohibition treaty is the reason for this disruption.

The global nuclear order, broadly viewed, was created on the basis of a particular set of ideas about nuclear weapons and the 'legitimate' possession of nuclear arsenals, and it has allowed the nuclear weapon states to deploy these weapons against their enemies, and also against humanity as a whole. The nuclear order that these ideas and practices have created, and which is embedded into the specific institution of the Non-Proliferation Treaty, has entrenched the two-tier nature of nuclear politics, limited formal multilateral debates on nuclear disarmament to that particular instrument, and enabled the ongoing possession of nuclear weapons by the P5 states with impunity. The structures of power mandated in the NPT have established a hegemony over non-nuclear states, and allowed the P5 to shape a global nuclear order strategically favourable to themselves.[1]

The NPT has served the P5 states well in terms of their non-proliferation goals, but these same states prevent the use of this institution as a means of furthering disarmament. As the only framework to reduce the prospect of nuclear weapons being used – at least until the TPNW came into effect – the NPT, together with its Preparatory Committee meetings and five-yearly Review Conferences, has always benefited the nuclear weapon states (Acheson *et al.* 2014: 6). Even though it was through the NPT that non-nuclear states were able to push for the 'strengthened review processes' (in 1995), the '13 Practical Steps on Nonproliferation and Disarmament' (in 2000), and the '64-point Action Plan' (in 2010), all designed to reduce nuclear dangers and to further disarmament, these conditions have remained unfulfilled by the P5 states who continue to determine what will and will not happen to their arsenals, regardless of their obligations under the treaty. For the P5 states, instead of accepting the argument that reducing and ultimately eliminating nuclear arsenals via the NPT is a necessary step towards preventing catastrophe, it has been the idea of non-proliferation, of denial to others, which has trumped other considerations, and which has left intact their own self-arrogated position of dominance in the nuclear order. The evolution of the NPT has become for the P5 states the institutionalization of *their* global nuclear order.

By contrast, the TPNW and the processes used to achieve it constitute a deliberate reshaping of this order, one that rejects the unequal nature of the NPT and the projected assumption that it is the nuclear weapon states which could and should control how nuclear weapons are viewed and held. Previously unable to shape the contours of this order in any significant way, non-nuclear states have now exercised a degree of power (Johnson and Varano 2015; Hanson 2022) and agency by delegitimizing nuclear weapons, for all states, equally. The new treaty roundly rejects the notion that any special class of states should be permitted to hold these weapons or that the global nuclear order should continue to be determined by these states.

The NPT: stretched to its limits

The NPT, argues Lennane (2016), has provided 'legal cover for the P5 states', at the same time that it also 'handily protects their interests by conflating them' with those of the non-nuclear states, who also clearly benefit from non-proliferation within their own ranks. But for these latter states, the fact that a bargain had been made was always important: especially for those drawn from the Non-Aligned Movement, participation and ongoing compliance was contingent on progress being made on disarmament; this was especially the case after the indefinite extension of the treaty in 1995. But their inability to shift the dynamics of the global nuclear order using the established methods of diplomacy via the NPT has alienated many of these states who now believe that that treaty offers little hope for resolving their disarmament concerns. As Australian Canberra Commissioner Robert O'Neill (2007) observed, 'the double standard built into the NPT is likely to prove fatal'.

And so it appears to be the case, with numerous states losing hope that the NPT could address their own security concerns. By the time of the 2015 Review Conference, there was deep resentment felt by Egypt and the NAM states at what they saw as a clear indifference to their long-standing wishes for a treaty which was universal and which did not perpetuate a set of double standards placing them at a permanent disadvantage against their nuclear neighbour, the state of Israel. The Egyptian head of delegation announced in 2015 that the world community was witnessing 'the fallacy of the 1995 process' (cited in UN 2015); while the South African head of delegation spoke for many when she claimed at the conclusion of the Conference that, 'there was a sense that the NPT had degenerated into minority rule – as in apartheid-era South Africa – where the will of the few reigned supreme over the majority' (cited in UN 2015). What might have been seen in 1970 as a promising 'compact' between states both to restrict and eliminate nuclear weapons (Butler 1996) was now perceived as a one-sided mechanism used only for non-proliferation, leaving the status of the great powers intact. Far from being an instrument used to pursue a global public good, the NPT can be characterized instead as a 'nuclear control order' (Ritchie 2019) where the position of its nuclear-armed states remained intact. Non-proliferation was instituted as 'an indisputable public good', but views which sought disarmament, or even reducing nuclear dangers (Craig and Ruzicka 2013) were never able to gain traction in the NPT.

This hegemony has been likened to what Gusterson (2006) has called a 'nuclear colonialism', a global hierarchy between dominant states in the West and states in the developing world.[2] In a similar vein, Johnson and Varano (2015) contend that non-proliferation and disarmament have been subject to a form of 'diplomatic colonialism', in that 'the self-important militarist interests of a few states' have prevailed over that of others. Such critics have pointed to the contrast created by the powerful and established nuclear weapon states who argue that what they practise is a 'safe' and 'responsible' possession of nuclear weapons, for the purpose of deterrence, but who at the same time decry as 'dangerous' and 'threatening' the nuclear weapons sought by others. A state suspected of wanting to acquire nuclear arms is seen as doing so because it intends to threaten the free world, rather than for any such 'legitimate' purpose as deterrence against its adversaries. Under this thinking, it is not nuclear weapons that kill people; it is 'other' people who kill people (Price 2007). And those 'other' people are bound to be untrustworthy 'rogue' regimes. Within this formulation, nuclear weapons – especially for US governments – are not the problem: 'bad guys' are the problem, and preventing them from acquiring nuclear weapons, while retaining one's own 'necessary' arsenal, is legitimate (Crossette and Perkovich 2009: 131).

That nuclear politics practised especially by the great powers, the United States, Russia, Britain, France, and China, reflected elements of oppression, where legitimacy was based on their testing of these weapons prior to 1967, but where aspirations to nuclear status after this date attracted opprobrium, was not lost on states such as India which had long railed against this inconsistency. But the notion of colonialism can be extended also to the system which allowed the nuclear states a self-appointed legitimacy and authority to dismiss critics of nuclear weapons as unrealistic and destabilizing. Anti-nuclear voices have long been marginalized as unrealistic, and calls for disarmament have been dismissed as utopian and strategically unsound. As Ray Acheson has observed, nuclear politics played out within a specific discourse of rationality, in which the 'reasonable, realistic, pragmatic' status quo powers denied the claims of the 'weak, irrational and irresponsible' advocates of disarmament (cited in Bolton and Minor 2016a).

As part of their dominance, Western nuclear states have focused on imposing nuclear safeguards, nuclear security, and nuclear export control measures on non-nuclear states, measures which have been progressively strengthened and which have become more taxing on the non-nuclear states, including through the selective use of UN Security Council resolutions (Rauf 2016: 236). In particular, the United States and its allies have kept up the pressure for these measures, while deflecting attention away from their own lack of implementation of disarmament steps. This emphasis on non-proliferation has been largely accepted as a fundamental pillar of international security. It has enabled, for instance, a widely held view that Iran's suspicious nuclear activities had to be addressed, and that this state, together with a known proliferator, North Korea, were potential threats to regional and global security. But the other side of the non-proliferation coin – disarmament – remained as elusive as ever.

As early as the 1970s, Hedley Bull had noted that non-nuclear weapon states had begun to view the NPT not as a promise to disarm, but as an 'instrument of superpower hegemony designed to freeze in place a two-tier nuclear world' (cited in O'Neill and Schwartz 1987: 220). Non-nuclear states had been willing to accept this inferior status because the NPT also clearly brought benefits of non-proliferation to them. But it was evident that the P5 states were failing to accept and implement their particular responsibilities under Article VI: they were intent on a dangerous arms race, and they were not managing their strategic relationships effectively, thereby increasing the risk of nuclear war. Bull argued that the P5 states could not justify a claim to be 'nuclear trustees for mankind'; ultimately, he believed, these states could come to be seen as 'the great irresponsibles' (Bull 1980). He had warned more broadly that unless the dominant powers took seriously the security concerns of other states in the world, and not just their own narrow security interests, it would be difficult to sustain the mechanisms and rules that regulated nuclear non-proliferation and other policies favourable to themselves (Bull 1976).

Moreover, and as noted in Chapter 1, since the late 1990s, the United States and Britain have adopted a managerial approach to the issue of nuclear weapons, wanting to deny them to suspected proliferators (notwithstanding how difficult it is to sustain indefinitely a position where one can claim the alleged security benefits of nuclear weapons for oneself while at the same time refusing these benefits to other states on the basis that they did not need them). The United States and Britain have taken it upon themselves to launch military action against adversaries suspected of violating the non-proliferation norm, and this has only compounded the initial inequality in the NPT. In his analysis of the global nuclear order, William Walker observed that tensions in this order occurred most discernibly under successive governments in the United States from 1998, when President Clinton (with UK Prime Minister Blair), impatient with diplomatic processes, and without UN authorization, initiated the bombing of alleged WMD sites in Iraq, 'ostensibly in response to the failure of cooperative disarmament' (Walker 2004: 51). Thus by the late 1990s, and even as the NPT had been extended indefinitely a few years earlier, confidence in the nuclear order was already eroding.

What was frustrating was that the NPT had made important strides, but these were only in those areas favoured by the nuclear weapon states. The treaty is, as Thakur argued, 'the most brilliant half successful arms control agreement in history' (2015: 191). But it may be that the NPT has now 'come as far as it can ... and to a plateau' (Dhanapala and Rauf 2016). It is also worth remembering that even where there were reductions between the United States and Russia after the Cold War, it was not the NPT which was responsible for this. Despite their own adherence to the treaty's non-proliferation strictures, non-nuclear states have not been able to persuade the P5 to comply with Article VI, or with the promises they have repeatedly given.

By the time of the 2015 Review Conference, this had become a very serious problem: the Humanitarian Initiative was by this time well under way, with three conferences concluded, but as it was looking likely that the RevCon was not going to be productive, it was clear that non-nuclear states would now look outside the NPT. Even when the 2015 RevCon failed, US officials continued to insist that all states must stick to the NPT and its processes. They released a memo urging NATO allies not to vote in favour of the subsequently proposed nuclear prohibition treaty, arguing that disarmament advocates wanted to shift the focus away from what Washington claimed was 'the proven step-by-step approach to nuclear disarmament' (US Mission to NATO 2016). The US reiterated its faith in nuclear deterrence, and claimed that a prohibition treaty would 'undermine the strategic stability that has underpinned the international security structure since the end of World War II', and that the step-by-step process was 'the only pathway to eventual nuclear disarmament'.

From the early days of the Humanitarian Initiative, the P5 states made it clear that they believed that such a focus 'will divert discussion away from practical steps to create conditions for further nuclear reductions' (Burt 2013). The conferences were said to be 'distractions' from the ongoing work being conducted by the P5 (United Nations 2013a, 2013b). Russia stated that it already understood the consequences of nuclear detonation and its ambassador concluded that 'the catastrophic character and unacceptability of any use of nuclear weapons is self-evident and requires no further discussions' (Borodavkin 2014). Moscow's statement to the UNGA First Committee in 2013 had suggested that the world should not 'waste time on such useless topics' as the Humanitarian Initiative, and that anyone seeking to achieve nuclear disarmament outside the agreed framework – that is, the NPT – was a 'radical dreamer' who had 'shot off to some other planet or outer space' (cited in Acheson 2013: 3). There was, therefore, no view among the P5 nuclear weapon states that they should engage with this process. They chose largely to boycott the conferences, arguing that these were not the 'real business' of arms control and disarmament. Ultimately however, these 'distractions' and 'useless topics' have prevailed, and have led to a treaty which categorically rejects the preferences of the nuclear states.

Building a global nuclear order beyond the NPT

It is unsurprising that non-nuclear states, by voting for adoption of the Treaty on the Prohibition of Nuclear Weapons, have rejected the global order which favoured the P5. And it is precisely this which cuts most deeply against the dominance of the nuclear weapon states: their established order, enabled by the structures of the NPT, is likely to be challenged by several interrelated developments, discussed below.

Unlike the NPT, the prohibition treaty crystallizes the legal proscription of nuclear weapons for all states

First, the TPNW brings with it a categorical rejection of nuclear weapons for any and all states, under any circumstances. For the first time, non-nuclear states have created their own vehicle, one which allows them to declare formally and unambiguously the illegality of nuclear weapons. Stating that the manufacturing, possession, deployment, use, and even threat of use of nuclear weapons is illegal represents a significant overhaul of earlier views.

As noted, even the 1996 ICJ Advisory Opinion was not able to offer this clear and uncompromising judgment.

This ambiguity has been resolved: the evolution of international law in the two decades since the ICJ Opinion, together with the research on the humanitarian impacts of nuclear weapons, are now reflected in a treaty which sees these weapons as illegitimate in all cases and for everyone. Immediately, the two-tiered nature and the weak wording of the Non-Proliferation Treaty have been surpassed by a legal proscription which has global application. Even as the nuclear states have not signed the TPNW, and argue that it is not, therefore, binding on them, the treaty has nevertheless provided a formal picture of these weapons as inhumane and illegitimate; even if the nuclear states continue to vaunt them, this new treaty deems these weapons as unacceptable to be held by any state.[3]

The TPNW refutes the claims made by those in the nuclear-armed states that they have a 'right' to nuclear weapons, that the NPT 'allows' them to retain their arsenals because it does not specify a timeframe for the implementation of Article VI, or that their possession of nuclear arms is permitted because there is no express international law that disbars possession. Without the new prohibition treaty, these claims, while disingenuous, might technically be true. With the treaty now in force, any claims by states that they are entitled to possession of these weapons can be contested and invalidated on moral grounds. So too can the 'geopolitical rationalizations of the nuclear status quo' (Falk 2017). As Acheson *et al.* (2014: 25) point out, from now, any assertions made by a state that it can possess these weapons can only be made on the basis that that state recognizes that it has 'refused to join the international legal framework on this issue', and not because it has, under the NPT, or because of any good fortune, any special or deserving status.

A notable aspect of the TPNW is that it outlaws even the *threat* of using nuclear weapons, making the very practice of possessing nuclear weapons and policies of nuclear deterrence illegitimate. As discussed in earlier chapters, one of the difficulties in dislodging the idea of relying on nuclear deterrence is the fact that the nuclear weapon states have invariably justified their programmes as being essentially defensive in nature, stating that these weapons are not intended to be *used*, and that therefore, the possession of them is a benign and uncontroversial practice.[4] Putting aside for now the statements where these countries have said that they *do* intend to use these weapons, even in a first strike, this reasoning – that these are weapons for deterrence purposes only, as evidenced by the long history of non-use – has helped these states to avoid, until now, widespread and direct opposition to nuclear weapons from the public at large.

Nuclear deterrence (and extended nuclear deterrence) do not merely imply, but actually promise, the use of nuclear weapons to inflict massive destruction on civilians, cities, and environments. Prohibiting the threat of use therefore has implications for policies of nuclear deterrence currently practised by states. The pressure of this legal clarity means that nuclear states will now need to explain 'why they will not accept the illegality of weapons of mass destruction that threaten the gravest humanitarian consequences' (Article 36 2013b: 2).

The rejection of nuclear weapons in any and all circumstances strengthens the existing stigma against these weapons. Clearly, a norm of non-use has developed in the past seventy-five years, suggesting that these weapons have not been launched because their use carries a stigma which no nuclear weapon state has been willing – so far – to disturb deliberately. The legal prohibition adds to this norm and reinforces existing views of the unacceptability of this particular kind of weapon. Moreover, the treaty underscores the point that the extensive modernization and expansion programmes underway in the nuclear states are inconsistent not just with the prohibition treaty, but also with their NPT commitments; the treaty is thus an effective tool in the condemnation of these processes (Johnson 2013; Carlson 2016).

The prohibition treaty has implications for both disarmament and non-proliferation; as such, it will complicate non-proliferation campaigns driven by the nuclear weapon states

The Humanitarian Initiative and the prohibition treaty have direct relevance and importance to the causes of both disarmament *and* non-proliferation; the treaty reaffirms both norms (APLN 2016). This is generally a good development, in that states now have a clear legal framework against proliferation and possession of nuclear weapons by all and any states, without distinction. But by doing this, it challenges and complicates the non-proliferation and counter-proliferation efforts made by states like the United States and its allies.

It will be harder for these states to pursue non-proliferation efforts than in the past; should they not show some willingness to disarm, it will be more difficult for them to hold states like Iran accountable to standards which they themselves reject. Israel too, which has a stake in preventing the spread of nuclear weapons in its region, will inevitably be faced with having to justify its own nuclear arsenal against the illegality of nuclear weapons. Pushing a norm – in this case non-proliferation – will not be easy when those states preoccupied with imposing this norm are themselves seen to be violating related global norms and principles. The NAM states in particular are likely to be vigilant in exposing the double standards evident in the status quo, especially given their rancour over the failure to establish a Middle East zone free of weapons of mass destruction. This could become the clearest example of the prediction that unless the great powers are willing to consider not just their own security concerns, but also those of the smaller and less powerful states in the international system, they will face rising impatience and a backlash against their own principles (Bull 1961). The TPNW will work against the preferences of the nuclear weapon states, and these states are likely to lose the upper hand they currently hold (Sauer 2015b), as the non-nuclear states engage in a process of 'revolt' and resistance (Acheson 2016) against the status quo.

The prohibition treaty will force nuclear states to justify their military choices

As with the landmines issue, the TPNW will allow non-nuclear states and civil society to 'shift the burden of proof' from weapon opponents onto weapon proponents. Price noted that in the context of the Ottawa treaty, proponents 'must make the case that land mines are not only marginally useful but also irreplaceable or even decisive' (Price 1998: 633). Similarly, those continuing to rely on nuclear deterrence will need to make the case for the allegedly unique, beneficial nature and the irreplaceable value of nuclear weapons. They will need to show why they believe that conventional weapons' deterrence cannot achieve at least the same level of security. At the very least, arguments for military utility and military necessity regarding these weapons will now have to be made transparently and convincingly. The nuclear states have not, until now, had to identify or defend their calculation of military utility and humanitarian consequences with regard to these weapons.

As earlier chapters have shown, nuclearism allowed for an illogical build-up of nuclear arsenals, regardless of their actual utility, out of proportion to military requirements, persisting long after the Cold War ended, and always beyond the reach of effective scrutiny. Lynn Eden's (2006, 2011) observations, that it was the almost untrammelled development of nuclear calculations and plans, fuelled by inter-agency rivalries, which determined threats to the United States, rather than the other way round, illustrates this issue well. With the prohibition treaty, clear and public justifications, including why a *nuclear*, rather than any other kind of, weapon is necessary for a particular military objective, will now be required. Neil McFarlane (2000: xii) has made a similar argument, noting the importance of 'pressure and persuasion' in the landmines ban process. He noted that advocacy for a particular outcome 'involves efforts to alter politicians' views of cost and benefit' of a particular practice, and that over time, views on these military calculations are likely to change once international accountability begins to be applied. This has relevance today, where the recasting of nuclear weapons as contrary to international humanitarian law and the civilized opinion of many of the world's states has been established. With the military utility of nuclear weapons being in any case low, any assertion that they are vital for a particular state, and that they thus need to be retained, will be increasingly hard to demonstrate.

The existence of the treaty will affect national discussions on nuclear weapons within the nuclear-armed states. Pointing to the question of the United Kingdom's renewal of its Trident submarines as an example, Acheson *et al.* (2014) note that henceforth, any such debates will be conducted against the backdrop of the illegality of these weapons: as they note, the TPNW provides 'a strong entry point for critiquing the wisdom and legitimacy' of investing public money in weapons which international law considers now to be immoral and unacceptable. Politicians in nuclear-armed states will find it harder than in the past to dismiss domestic calls for these weapons to be removed from their national security doctrines and from their territory (Acheson *et al.* 2014: 21). Crucially, in these debates, it will be the nuclear weapon states which will have a difficult case to make (Sauer 2015b), facing pressure to explain and justify their decisions.

The question of whether to join the prohibition treaty will be made all the more difficult for those states which claim strong allegiance to the NPT (as the P5 states do). This is because the NPT commits *all* state parties, not just the nuclear weapon states, to 'pursue negotiations in good faith on effective measures relating to cessation of the nuclear arms race at an early date and to nuclear disarmament' (UNODA 1968). More recently, the implication has been that all states should pursue these goals not just by complying with Article VI, but also by taking additional legal measures where necessary; nuclear disarmament is thus seen as a shared responsibility (Sagan 2009b). Those states arguing that they prefer to pursue disarmament via the stalled NPT process will be confronted with the fact that membership of the prohibition treaty is compatible with advancing the principles and ideals set out in the NPT.

The prohibition treaty provides a new diplomatic forum, under the control of the non-nuclear states, and can build a culture of compliance

The possibility that the TPNW might come to surpass the NPT in time as the key forum for nuclear matters will be a disquieting one for the nuclear weapon states. The treaty includes follow-up mechanisms: Meetings of States Parties, and Review Conferences, constituting forums which will be 'under the control of those *without* the weapons – in contrast to forums [like the NPT] that serve only the interests of those who retain' them (Lennane 2016). These forums will be used to develop a culture of compliance, placing pressure on states outside the treaty. This 'moral authority' will arguably make it harder for states to defy anti-nuclear sentiment. Having a clearly established strong standard helps 'pull others up towards it' (Article 36 2013b: 4) especially if that standard is supported by a growing number of states.

This is not a new idea: it has been long recognized that institutionalizing specific prohibitions – whether they be against slavery, piracy, or inhumane weapons – has the enduring effect of pressuring non-adherents to justify their ongoing practices or to abandon these practices and join the prohibition. The clear prohibition encased within the TPNW will provide leverage for non-nuclear states and civil society, as the illegality of nuclear weapons becomes an established reference point in international relations. As Acheson *et al.* (2014) point out, a treaty enables groups in the domestic sphere to ask the question of their governments directly: are you in favour of making nuclear weapons illegal? Until now, it has not been easy or straightforward to interrogate a government directly about its nuclear-related intentions; with the new treaty, this becomes an easier practice.

Review processes will not be restricted to state-based follow up conferences. Civil society groups are already active in monitoring the global impact of the new treaty. In 2018, just months after the creation of the TPNW, the first *Nuclear Weapons Ban Monitor* was published, financed in part by the Norwegian government. The monitor will act as a 'watchdog', whose purpose is to measure progress towards a world free of nuclear weapons. With dedicated staff drawn from the fields of law, health, and government, its annual report will evaluate 'the extent to which the policies and practices of all states comply with the prohibitions in the TPNW, regardless of whether they have joined the Treaty' (Nuclear Weapons Ban Monitor 2018).

The legal reinforcement of an existing stigmatization – which is what the new treaty amounts to – can be important in shaping attitudes against the weapon deemed unacceptable, and in building compliance with the objectives being sought. The history of the chemical and biological weapons conventions is a case in point: the early twentieth-century stigmatizing of these weapons marked an important stage from which states and populations would come to see these as unacceptable weapons, but the establishment of formal legal conventions (in 1972 and 1993 respectively) allowed for a much firmer stance against offending states. These weapons are now rarely used, and when they have been, international opprobrium has been swift.

The illegitimacy that comes with a ban means that violating states can be upbraided; the immorality attached to particular practices or weapons suggests that states which choose to violate such norms work from a default position of a pariah nation, an outsider to the community of nations which has outlawed these weapons. Aware of the stigma and likely condemnation, even if they do engage in the prohibited practice, such states are not likely publicly to endorse this behaviour. Richard Price, when writing on the landmines ban process, noted that, 'the more states that tipped toward the ban, the more normal ban support became, and the more powerful was the ICBL's resort to the technique of shaming to induce norm adoption' (Price 1998: 635; see also Price's 1995 examination of the chemical weapons taboo). As with the landmines process, the dynamic of states emulating the behaviour of others will be important.

At a practical level, the prohibition treaty establishes a framework within which both civil society and state diplomatic efforts to strengthen the treaty will grow. It may well be, as Sauer and Pretorius (2014: 248) observe, that the broader public is more likely to become interested in nuclear weapons under a humanitarian dimension than they have been under a traditional arms control approach, restricted as these have been to selected decision-makers with their specialized jargon and their focus on somewhat abstract notions of nuclear strategy. Campaigning for adherence to the treaty will be facilitated by dedicated groups tasked with applying pressure on states, including like-minded states, international organizations, NGOs, and academics (Acheson *et al.* 2014). Civil society actors are likely to focus on concrete objectives such as the extension of nuclear weapon free zones, the provision of assistance and legal guidance to assist allies to negotiate their extraction from a nuclear umbrella, and efforts to diminish further the role of nuclear weapons in global security (Article 36 2013b). Such practical assistance might, over time, also include programmes to strengthen security among nuclear-armed states, especially in a regional context, by developing confidence-building mechanisms, monitoring and verification of dismantlement exercises, and processes of collaboration and trust-building between nuclear weapon states. This latter issue has already produced some excellent academic literature and policy engagement (see for example Booth and Wheeler 2008; Wheeler 2010; Wheeler and Ruzicka 2010, and the programme at the University of Birmingham on 'Trust Building in Nuclear Worlds').

The prohibition treaty forces states to declare their position on humanitarian law

The presence of the prohibition treaty puts the nuclear issue into sharp focus, because the decision that a state makes to join or reject a treaty will bring its own dynamics and consequences. For a start, leaders of all states will be faced directly with the option of joining or not joining the new treaty, and the choice that they make will become an important public and global declaration of their acceptance or rejection of a newly delineated international norm. The onus will be on those states which reject the treaty to justify their decisions to their domestic audience.

In the same way that this question will make uncomfortable the leaders of the nuclear-armed states, so too will it provide a useful opportunity for any state wishing to demonstrate its humanitarian credentials and willingness to 'champion' this new initiative. The TPNW brings every state into a process of determining what is and is not acceptable in warfare. The treaty is an important accomplishment, achieved despite strong resistance from the major powers and despite the entrenched nature of nuclearism. Once well underway, this movement can attract the support and backing of states keen to exercise and demonstrate their agency in this process. This is not likely to occur initially among prominent states allied to the United States, but over time they too might declare their identification with a process which denounces nuclear weapons.

This suggests that elements of identity politics and reputation will be important in the long-term process of moving to a nuclear-free world, and that the emergence, reinforcement, and 'cascade' of the norm defining nuclear weapons as abhorrent will place pressure on all states. Richard Price observed that 'the role of moral persuasion and the social pressure arising from identity politics and emulation are particularly crucial' (Price 1998: 616).

The prohibition treaty poses a sharp dilemma for any opponents normally committed to a rules-based order, multilateralism, and human rights

Related to the points above, the treaty will make uncomfortable those nuclear weapon and nuclear allied states which value their reputations as promoters of a multilateral, rules-based international order built on principles of liberalism, democracy, good governance, and human rights. North America, the European Union, and US allies in East Asia and Australia have long defined themselves as upholders of an international order based on particular values (even if these values have sometimes been breached). With the prohibition treaty now in force, the nuclear positions of many of these states will not be seen as aligning with their professed norms, and not consistent with their attempts to foster respect for multilateralism, the UN, and the rule of law.

This dilemma is going to be felt most keenly by states within the European Union. The EU is often seen as a body acting on the side of humanitarianism, supportive of international law, and a rules-based global order, and as providing a more moderate global alternative to the sometimes divisive foreign policies of the United States. In particular, the EU has been instrumental in supporting the landmines ban, the cluster munitions convention, the Arms Trade Treaty, the International Criminal Court, and numerous other multilateral endeavours. Writing just after the success of the landmines treaty, Hubert (2000: 69) noted the enthusiasm of several Western states 'to be at the forefront of … humanitarian campaigns' (Hubert 2000: 69). However, the EU has never had a common policy on nuclear weapons' possession and use. It has a robust nuclear non-proliferation strategy, but there has been no common disarmament position other than a general, albeit vague, commitment to the pursuit of nuclear disarmament. Pullinger and Quille (2003) have argued that nuclear disarmament issues within the EU are 'neglected, presumably to avoid confrontations with the UK [at least until 2020] and France' and to allow other agenda items to move smoothly. But an ongoing failure to support a legal move towards disarmament will have an impact on that organization's reputation, even to the point where, as Portela notes, the EU would add to 'the perception of Western "nuclear hypocrisy" among Third World countries' (Portela 2003).

This fact – that European Union states have managed to avoid a clear commitment to nuclear disarmament until now – is something that will have to be addressed: with a clear prohibition treaty, the EU faces a situation where it will be difficult 'to remain silent' (Berghofer 2016) or ambivalent. Especially for states like Germany, Belgium, Denmark, and the Netherlands, remaining outside the new treaty will become a political position increasingly difficult to justify to their constituents. They may not wish to continue to be associated with a discourse that frames nuclear weapons as inhumane and condemned by law. Even if there is a reasonably supportive domestic commitment by some to nuclear weapons, there will be substantial numbers of other citizens unhappy about a continuing nuclear programme, and these latter groups will now have a treaty to support their challenges to their respective governments. Other US allies – Canada, Japan, and Australia – which have invariably positioned themselves as good international citizens, supportive of international law, human security, and the rules-based international order more generally, and who have put forward their own studies calling for nuclear disarmament – will be caught in the same conundrum.

This point is important: by appealing to states on the basis of their avowed commitment to multilateralism, the rule of law, and to their reputation as 'civilized' states, the advocates of a treaty recognize that reputations matter at the international level, and that more and more states for whom humanitarianism is important – and this is the case with the EU as a political body – might eventually come to support the treaty. One strategy will be moral persuasion: as Borrie notes, showing those in power that changing prevailing practices will be 'more consistent with other "responsible" norms of behaviour' to which they evidently aspire, can prove to be an effective process (Borrie 2014b).

The irony – that the very states which claim a reputation as responsible and law-abiding members of international society, and who were themselves the initiators of international humanitarian law, are the ones whose governments are resisting the treaty – will not be lost on the treaty's supporters. If we look at the 122 states which voted in favour of negotiating the treaty, we can see them as 'a relatively disempowered non-nuclear many' (Ritchie 2017) who have nonetheless succeeded in establishing a regime which lays bare the double standards of the nuclear 'few'. Their support of the treaty marks them as significant agents of change on an issue which has been controlled almost completely by the large and powerful states, but it also positions them as upholders of a rules-based international system and as champions for a more humane, non-nuclear approach to global security.

The prohibition treaty can, in time, have an impact on allies' relationships with the United States

The EU's dilemma is compounded by the fact that there is a growing overlap between the EU and the North American Treaty Organization, where allies of the US are under an extended nuclear deterrence arrangement (END). This makes it difficult for the EU as a whole to affirm the humanitarian principles in the TPNW, because of a process of what some have called the 'NATO-ization of the European Union' (Marin-Bosch 1998: 35). In 2003, the EU had eleven states which were NATO members; in 2022, the EU has twenty-one (out of twenty-seven) member states which are also NATO members. NATO's 2010 Strategic Concept has stated that its members are committed to a goal of a nuclear weapons-free world, but the expansion of both the EU and NATO has resulted in more states within the EU that are, at best, 'guarded supporters' (Neilson and Hanson 2014) of disarmament, but mindful of the alliance and not likely to support the TPNW readily.

Yet the existence of the TPNW might nevertheless come to challenge the relationships between the nuclear weapon states and their allies, affecting especially the United States' allies in NATO. None of these allies voted in favour of the prohibition treaty in 2017, and the United States exerted considerable pressure on them not to do so. But these positions are not set in stone. It is possible that individual states allied to the United States will, over time, review their position and sign the new treaty. The states most likely to reconsider alliance solidarity will be those states within NATO which have already shown that they are sympathetic to the Humanitarian Initiative, such as Norway, Germany, Denmark, Iceland, Belgium, and the Netherlands, as well as those whose governments might not have been closely involved in the Humanitarian Initiative, but whose civil society sector flourishes, such as in the United Kingdom.

The United States is likely to continue to place pressure on its allies not to support the new treaty. The memo from the US Mission to NATO in 2016 warned that the effects of the treaty 'could be wide-ranging and degrade enduring security relationships' and that NATO allies 'should not underestimate the breadth of potential impacts across security relationships' (US Mission to NATO 2016). Washington urged that it was 'important for us to avoid introducing any doubt regarding Alliance unity' (US Mission to NATO 2016). US allies might find that they face threats of political and economic repercussions should they support the new treaty, including the disruption of defence and security cooperation (Acheson *et al.* 2014: 18). But they might not. It could be that the United States will need its allies more than they need the United States, especially when it comes to collaboration on other issues such as counter-terrorism and non-proliferation.

In any case, differences within NATO over the new treaty need not mean the disintegration of the alliance. It is important to remember that the prohibition treaty does not seek to sever existing alliance relationships; it intends only to delegitimize the role of nuclear weapons (Ritchie 2017). And there are already signs that some NATO states are weighing their options carefully. The Netherlands, contrary to US requests, deliberately abstained from (rather than went against) the 2016 vote on negotiating a new treaty, and there are other developments which suggest that the United States might not be able to force its NATO allies as it expects. Some NATO states have consistently voted in favour of humanitarian resolutions, and in particular, Norway's commitment to disarmament, including its high level of financial support for NGOs and academics working in this field, and its hosting of the first Humanitarian Initiative conference remains a powerful reference point, as does Norway's reputation for supporting the elimination of landmines and cluster munitions, and its exceptional provision of humanitarian assistance in general. In a move bound to irritate Washington, Norway and Germany have announced that they will attend the first Meeting of States Parties to the TPNW in August 2022, as observers.

Those NATO states which still host US tactical nuclear weapons on their territory – Germany, Italy, Belgium, the Netherlands, and Turkey – are likely to consider these issue very cautiously. In January 2020, a vote in Belgium's Parliament on removing nuclear weapons from Belgian soil and joining the TPNW was close, but was ultimately lost after pressure from the American ambassador.[5] In 2016, the Dutch Parliament adopted by a large majority a resolution urging the government to call for negotiations for a nuclear weapons ban. The debate preceding the resolution had been forced by the actions of civil society groups, including the presentation to

Parliament of a petition containing 45,000 signatures. A Dutch civil society advocate, Freek Landmeter, argued that 'Parliament wants a global ban, a majority of the Dutch public wants to be rid of nuclear weapons', and that the Netherlands government has always 'voiced its support for a nuclear-weapons-free world' (cited in PAX 2016b). Germany too is likely to face domestic challenges to its reluctance to join the new treaty. A study commissioned in 2016 by IPPNW and ICAN showed that 93 per cent of Germans supported a prohibition of nuclear weapons (cited in Hoffmann-Axthelm 2016). One civil society member noted that German people 'presume that they have a broad societal consensus against nuclear weapons – and are unaware of the fact that their government is undermining their position' (Hoffmann-Axthelm 2016), signalling trouble to come when these people are made more fully aware of their government's apparent support for nuclear weapons.

Studies have emerged which assess the compatibility of membership of the new treaty with continued NATO membership. Among these are the Clingendael Report (Guven and Van der Meer 2015), the International Law and Policy Institute (ILPI) Reports (Lothe-Eide 2014; Pax 2016c), and the Harvard Human Rights Clinic Report (IHRC 2018). These have all concluded that there need not be any incompatibility. Although there is currently a NATO policy on nuclear weapons at the intergovernmental level, this has not always been the case. Historically, there has always been room within NATO for variations in member state policies on arms control and disarmament, and members have been able to determine their own national policy towards nuclear weapons (Guven and Van der Meer 2015; Pax 2016c). Several examples demonstrate this pluralistic approach: Denmark, Norway, and Spain, for instance, prohibit the deployment of nuclear weapons on their territory in peacetime, while Iceland and Lithuania do not allow deployment at any time (Lothe-Eide 2014). An ILPI report concludes that, 'as a matter of international law, there is no barrier to member states' adherence' to a prohibition treaty (Lothe-Eide 2014). As with the Clingendael study, it finds no contradiction and also suggests some possible benefits: 'concerns about the political implications for NATO ignore historical variations in member state military policy' and there is 'value in a ban on nuclear weapons for promoting NATO's ultimate aim: the security of its member states' (Lothe-Eide 2014).

Interoperability with the nuclear members of NATO – the United States, Britain, and France – will be problematic for a NATO state which chooses to sign the TPNW: incompatibilities will arise within the sphere of NATO's nuclear policies and activities. As the new treaty prohibits any encouragement of or assistance with nuclear use, it logically outlaws practices of hosting US NATO nuclear weapons and participation in war-planning or exercises involving nuclear weapons. It would also prohibit any communication of a willingness to use nuclear weapons. Should a NATO state wish to remove itself from the nuclear umbrella, there would undoubtedly be some upheaval, and any such move is bound to be discouraged by the United States. But this does not mean that it is impossible.

The Atlantic Charter, which established NATO in April 1949, makes no mention of nuclear weapons, and neither do many of the organization's earlier Strategic Concepts. NATO did not begin as an explicitly nuclear alliance, even if it is widely perceived to be such at the moment. Egeland (2017) suggests that NATO would probably survive denuclearization: 'this would actually just take NATO back to its original shape'. Certainly, if members wished to exit the nuclear umbrella but also remain in NATO, then the organization's Strategic Concept (NATO 2010), which expressly states that NATO is 'a nuclear alliance', would have to be amended. As long as NATO continues to base its deterrence capabilities upon a mix of conventional and nuclear weapons – which is the current doctrinal position – then membership of the prohibition treaty would not permit NATO membership (Guven and Van der Meer 2015). But changing these doctrinal statements would not be impossible for NATO states to do (Pax 2016c; Egeland 2017) and there may be benefits to be gained by doing so. Member states are more likely to want a continued European military alliance, even one without an express reliance on nuclear weapons, than an organization which loses membership or is deeply fractured by dissenting views.

Recently, NATO statements on the prohibition treaty have softened somewhat, and there appear to be glimpses of disunity among its members. In September 2020, the Belgian government indicated that it would play a proactive role at the Tenth NPT Review Conference, including examining 'how the UN Treaty on the Prohibition of Nuclear Weapons can give new impetus to multilateral nuclear disarmament' (cited in Sauer and Nardon 2020). Canada and other states have also moderated their language, which initially had been hostile towards the TPNW. And ahead of the treaty's entry into force date, fifty-six former leaders, foreign ministers, and defence ministers drawn from US allied states put forward an 'Open Letter in Support of the Treaty on the Prohibition of Nuclear Weapons' (TPNW 2020).

In sum, there may not be a great deal to stop a NATO state which joins the nuclear prohibition treaty from continuing to be a member of the organization, as long as they do not claim the putative benefits of remaining under the nuclear umbrella. All of the proposals for eliminating nuclear weapons have in any case called for the salience of nuclear weapons to be reduced and for the nuclear weapon states to move to minimize the role of nuclear weapons in their security doctrines. Rewording NATO's next Strategic Concept, due in 2022, could serve as a useful confidence-building measure between the alliance and Russia, and may prompt Moscow to make concessions of its own. NATO states can have an important role to play in contributing to the debate on whether reliance on nuclear weapons is desirable (Guven and Van der Meer 2015: 12). Should any NATO members join the treaty, this would present an opportunity for NATO to shift its deterrent focus onto its (considerable) conventional weapons' capability.

Similarly, US allies in the Pacific will be faced with choosing between the TPNW and the status quo of their relationship with Washington. Japan, South Korea, and Australia are all, for the moment, non-signatories of the TPNW.[6] As with NATO states, this might change. The Opposition Labor Party in Australia, for example, pledged in its 2018 national conference that, once in government, it would sign and ratify the prohibition treaty.[7]

The prohibition treaty challenges the primacy of the NPT

There is at least one further point to consider within the context of changes to the global nuclear order. Some scholars suggest that there ought now to be a mass defection from the Non-Proliferation Treaty, a collective withdrawal by all those states which adopt the new prohibition treaty (Joyner 2015, 2016b; Pretorius and Sauer 2021). They argue that this would serve to strengthen the TPNW's norm, representing an opportunity to solidify further the delegitimization of nuclear weapons. A collective withdrawal, Joyner argues, could be conducted, 'thus marking the institution of a new normative standard, unmixed with the baser matter of the NPT'. His belief is that unless this happens, the TPNW will simply be 'marginalized' by the nuclear states, who would continue to assert that it is the NPT which remains the 'cornerstone' and only 'treaty on nuclear weapons possession, proliferation and disarmament'. If non-nuclear states assert the TPNW as a replacement of the NPT, the positive effects of the TPNW will be maximized (Joyner 2016b).

This remains a controversial suggestion, and it seems unlikely that large numbers of non-nuclear states will abandon the NPT, at least in the near future. But it could be argued also that the NPT has by now served its purpose by developing a strong non-proliferation norm, and that that norm is now reasonably viable even without the instrument which fostered it and gave it potency. Supporters of defection might claim that the TPNW's norm is a stronger condemnation of the possession, use, and threat of use, of nuclear weapons than the NPT is. Because it applies equally to disarmament and non-proliferation, the argument might be made that the NPT is redundant. Should there be a mass defection from the NPT, this would constitute a dramatic and physical reorientation of the global nuclear order, a severance from the structures of nuclear governance that have dominated world politics for several decades.

The fact that the nuclear states have disregarded Article VI for so long could result in the NPT no longer seen as legitimate. If the largest group of states in the NPT comply with its provisions, but the P5 do not, then that treaty's 'legitimacy and ultimately its survival' might be called into question (Pretorius and Sauer 2021). Again, the P5's failure to take even modest steps towards disarmament, their deep entrenchment of nuclearism, and their dismissal of the needs of other states, could mean, in time, the end of the NPT. These states have underestimated the importance of Article VI to non-nuclear states: some non-nuclear states might not have joined the NPT in the first place if Article VI had not been present and if they did not have confidence in the promises of the P5. The 1995 indefinite extension of the NPT still rankles with many states: as noted in earlier chapters, that event removed what leverage the non-nuclear states had to influence nuclear politics. Indefinite extension freed the P5 states of any firm obligation to disarm. That event has probably only emboldened the nuclear states to disregard Article VI, 'with impunity' (Pretorius and Sauer 2021).

Mass defection from the NPT was raised even before the Humanitarian Initiative and plans for a prohibition treaty were established. Doyle (2009: 8) has argued that the failure of the P5 states to disarm 'counts as a political failure to meet expectations of a large segment of the non-nuclear-weapon states' and that the P5 states have 'injured the NPT regime more severely' than have weaker states like Iran, that they have possibly 'even subverted it' (Doyle 2009: 2). Given the frustration with the nuclear states who behave as the exclusive 'guardians of the current international power-sharing arrangement', mass defection from the NPT might be legally and politically necessary; indeed, as some argue, it might be the ethical and 'responsible' course of action to undertake (Doyle 2009: 2).[8]

Thus both before and after the negotiation of the TPNW, various analysts have considered abandoning the mechanism with which they have worked for over fifty years. Describing these developments, Ramesh Thakur suggests that an analogous situation is with membership of a club whose rules one disagreed with: one can stay as member and even 'try and change the … rules from the inside'. But if numerous efforts to bring about change fail, then one has to decide whether to leave or to 'become morally compromised with respect to one's own ethical code' (Thakur 2016b).

It is too early to determine whether some non-nuclear states will embark on a collective withdrawal from the NPT,[9] but it is telling that arguments for leaving were made even prior to the TPNW, as a way of 'shocking' the nuclear-armed states into fulfilling their obligations, as well as after it was achieved, where collective withdrawal would place more emphasis on the new instrument. Either way, this would represent a major blow to the P5-dominated global nuclear order.[10]

Ultimately, however, the emergence of the TPNW does not require states to 'walk away' from the NPT. Some have argued that it endangers the NPT, that it is indeed 'a barely concealed assault on the entire fabric of the NPT' (Ruhle 2017). But this is a somewhat spurious argument. The TPNW enacts and complements one of the key objectives of the NPT, namely that of seeking an end to the nuclear arms race, and achieving a world free of nuclear weapons. As Egeland *et al.* (2018) have observed, 'not only may the TPNW be reconciled with existing legal instruments, the new Treaty supports and reinforces key norms and institutions on which the nuclear non-proliferation and disarmament regime is based'. When contrasted with the intransigence of the P5 states, it seems unlikely that any weakening of the NPT will occur as a result of the actions of those in favour of the prohibition treaty. Continuing arguments that the TPNW is incompatible with the NPT carry little weight; the TPNW's Preamble specifically notes the 'vital role' of the NPT (UN 2017). And most observers seem to wish the NPT to continue. It is a rare example of established multilateralism addressing a key existential threat, at a time when global cooperation on security and other issues is rather thin on the ground (Shetty 2022).

Nevertheless, we should not count on the NPT existing in its current form indefinitely.[11] The NPT, while it was successful in limiting proliferation, is no longer seen by many states as fit for purpose – or at least for the purpose of disarmament. Increasingly dysfunctional, the NPT's Review Conferences have been overtaken by states in favour of a more direct method of achieving a prohibition treaty; the depth of frustration felt by the non-nuclear states has very possibly been underestimated by the P5 states (Green 2013). The NPT is likely to continue, at least for some time, but substantive discussions may shift to the Meetings of States-Parties of the TPNW, just as they did with the specially convened meetings and conferences outside the NPT, in Oslo, Nayarit, and Vienna, and from there to the Open-Ended Working Groups within the United Nations. Even as the NPT is likely to survive in some form, its primacy can no longer be guaranteed.

The prohibition treaty alters the nature of action and status in nuclear debates

All the above points suggest an evolution in the way that security and issues of agency are being conceived. What we have seen in this case, as we saw with the landmines and cluster munition bans, is a group of actors – essentially those we would characterize as being materially weak actors in the international system, with little or no compelling means of influence – coming to have an impact, even if this is only a symbolic impact at the moment, on the great powers and their possession of these weapons. In particular, if we contrast the financial and political influence wielded by nuclear weapon states and their defence contractors with the limited resources of small states and the very small amount of funding available to civil society organizations, this achievement becomes all the more notable. Being able to counter the great powers and the lobbying weight of corporations involved in the manufacture of nuclear weapons with the power of ideas and norms demonstrates an evolution in how we might think about the nature of international security politics, and in turn about the contours of the nuclear order. Effectively, the actions of small and middle sized sates and NGOs has challenged all aspects of nuclearism, and moved the spotlight of reproach onto the nuclear weapon states, as long as these states choose to remain opposed to the banning of these weapons.

We saw, from the mid-1990s onwards, that the assent of the large and powerful states in the international system was not necessary to achieving the legal prohibition of a particular weapon. International law and restrictions on the way that warfare can be waged, and what is considered to be a legitimate or illegitimate weapon, does not depend on the acquiescence of the dominant states in the international system. Not only is this acquiescence not needed; the new treaty clearly contradicts and makes illegitimate the everyday doctrines of these dominant states. In this sense, the TPNW is a key example of a prohibition regime coming into existence without the support of the great powers in the international system.

In his notable 1990 essay, Ethan Nadelmann provided an institutional analysis of how global prohibition regimes arise. He pointed to the fact that 'just as few people during the 18th century could have imagined the emergence of a global antislavery regime ... few in this century can imagine that activities which are entirely legitimate today may evolve into targets of global prohibition regimes' (1990: 523). He suggested that norms which question prevailing beliefs and practices 'emerge and are promoted because they reflect not only the economic and security interests of the dominant members of international society, but also their moral interest and emotional disposition' (1990: 524), arguing that it is the large and powerful states in the international system which are the key drivers of change: those norms which evolve into global prohibition regimes typically reflect the 'laws of states that have dominated international society to date', namely the European nations and the United States.

And yet, with the TPNW, we have the seen the very opposite of this happening: while the large and powerful states have been successful until now in holding off any challenge to their nuclear policies and to nuclearism in general, the creation of a prohibition regime has been due to the actions of smaller, less significant actors, both state and non-state. Moreover, the targets of their actions are the materially powerful states of the world, and the framework they have constructed explicitly rejects the practices these states have upheld for so long. A prohibition regime might in the past have required great power propulsion, but as we have seen with the landmines and cluster munitions debates, and now with the nuclear prohibition treaty, the drivers of change in determining what is considered legitimate behaviour can be very different.

The achievement of the TPNW, as a clear defiance of the wishes and interests of the major powerful states would seem to be inimical to the received wisdom about how international politics operates: traditional realist understandings of international relations focus on the power capabilities of states in an anarchical world, leaving little scope for small or medium-sized states, those with little military 'clout', or for other kinds of actors, to initiate or drive key security decisions. These states, and their NGO partners, have typically been seen as 'hapless bystanders' and 'have-nots' (Mueller and Wunderlich 2020) when it comes to nuclear weapons policy. The agency of small states and civil society actors has typically been discounted as negligible, but this is no longer the case. The new approach has explicitly challenged the prevailing global nuclear order, creating a new framework within which nuclear weapons will be viewed and within which newly empowered agents will work to effect change.

Conclusion: rejecting nuclearism by challenging the dynamics of the global nuclear order

Where the NPT seems to have frozen in place a special status for the nuclear weapon states and a subservient position for all others, the prohibition treaty allows for the empowerment of non-nuclear states in a way that the NPT has never been able to do. Even as the NPT has required that all states parties have a responsibility to advance the process of nuclear disarmament, its limits have meant that efforts made by the non-nuclear states to do this have always been subjected to the overriding preferences of the P5 nuclear states.

Non-nuclear states sought to work with the nuclear states for several decades in a bid to move towards disarmament. Within the structures of the established nuclear order, they have asked for compliance with the NPT. Numerous proposals were put forward to bridge the growing gap between nuclear and non-nuclear states, so that the rancour of the non-nuclear states might be curbed, and common ground be found. The New Agenda Coalition worked hard within the NPT to put forward suggestions acceptable to the P5; numerous proposals exist for bringing together nuclear and non-nuclear states to engage in constructive discussions (Rauf 2017) which might ameliorate the growing polarization between these two groups; and concepts such as 'responsible nuclear sovereignty' (Walker 2010; Brixey-Williams and Ingram 2017) have been put forward as a way of respecting nuclear realities while also politely encouraging the nuclear states to show progress on disarmament. The United States launched a new initiative in 2018, 'Creating an Environment for Nuclear Disarmament' (CEND), designed to assuage the hostility of the non-nuclear states ahead of the 2020 RevCon, but it too simply perpetuates the status quo. As a US official declared, 'disarmament can and will move forward only to the degree that the international community is able to address the security issues that underlie states' rationales for retaining nuclear weapons' (Ford, cited in Bugos 2020). Critics of CEND argue that it continues to postulate 'mythical prerequisites for the implementation of nuclear disarmament' (Pretorius and Sauer 2021). The 'Stockholm Initiative' was launched in mid-2019 by Sweden and the foreign ministers of sixteen states, with the aim of progressing disarmament via a 'Stepping Stones Approach' (SSA). None of these initiatives has worked; they have all left the prevailing nuclear order intact and have failed to move the nuclear weapon states to take disarmament seriously.

With the TPNW, non-nuclear states are able to take their own action to advance the long-term goal of the elimination of nuclear weapons. As Sauer and Pretorius (2014) point out, the significance of the treaty is that 'it starts by harnessing the agency of non-nuclear weapon states', where a large number of countries, motivated by the unacceptable consequences of nuclear weapons, has decided to move ahead to prohibit them, no longer constrained by nuclearism, the nuclear weapon states or their allies. The treaty is even being seen by some as a 'game changer, draining power and status' from the nuclear weapon states and 'increasing the imperative for concerted nuclear disarmament rather than perpetual proliferation' and modernization (Johnson 2012). Still others claim that the Humanitarian Initiative and the prohibition treaty have been important in 'dismantling the arguments [of the nuclear states], disrupting their narratives, and ultimately standing up to their projection of power' (Acheson 2018: 245).

If the P5 nuclear states have succeeded in imposing their own framework of order onto the world, including by particular kinds of diplomacy which deprived non-nuclear states of any real agency, by exploiting the unequal structures of the NPT, and by insisting that states must work for change within this framework only, then these circumstances have been altered. Non-nuclear states have created their own framework which redefines nuclear weapons, allows for new processes of diplomacy and norm-building, and places the policies of nuclear states squarely outside the realm of 'legitimate behaviour'. This way of addressing nuclear weapons is more than just 'naming and shaming'; it fundamentally redefines the activities (Borrie 2014a: 642) and the status of various countries in the international system. Rather than continuing to seek to change the policies of the states holding nuclear weapons, a practice which has in any case been largely futile, advocates of the treaty have instead changed the 'environment in which nuclear weapons and nuclear-armed states are embedded' (Ritchie 2016: 56). This will affect the broader international context within which nuclear weapons are henceforth discussed; it shifts normative power away from the nuclear states and 'empowers a much broader community of States to change the international social structure of nuclear legitimacy and illegitimacy' (Ritchie 2016: 56). The nuclear weapons prohibition treaty is important precisely because it is targeted at nuclearism, at the long-held norms, policies, and practices of the nuclear weapon states, and especially those of the great powers, the P5, essentially challenging them where they have been, until now, most insulated from external interference – interference by their own citizens opposed to nuclear weapons, and interference by a global community which has long been subjected to an unequal nuclear order enshrined in the NPT. Richard Falk, one of the originators of the term nuclearism, argues that the new treaty represents a 'distrust of the elaborate geopolitical rationalizations of the nuclear status quo' (Falk 2017). In delegitimizing nuclear weapons, the TPNW has also delegitimized the existing global nuclear order.

This may seem exaggerated, but changing the legal context alters the dynamics of the nuclear order. A ban on nuclear weapons effectively 'turns the tables', with the burden of justifying their policies now shifting to the nuclear-armed states (Sauer and Pretorius 2014). Nuclear states will now have to defend publicly what previously had required no explicit justification (see Price 1998: 632 on this dynamic in the landmines ban). The unproductive approach preferred by the nuclear states in the NPT has thus been, if not replaced, then overshadowed by a new, 'principled approach' (Sauer and Pretorius 2014). For advocates of disarmament, the treaty finally allows nuclear weapons to be seen as 'weapons of terror, instability and insecurity' (Acheson and Fihn 2013: 9) affecting the entire world, rather than as (perceived) guarantors of a tenuous security for a select few. If nuclearism can be seen as the collective ideas and practices which have created the nuclear status quo, that status quo has in turn been used as a justification for why things can never change. Nuclearism's self-reinforcing tenets have upheld the position of the NPT as the 'natural' order of things. But by creating a prohibition treaty outside of the usual structures and processes which have prevailed for decades, nuclearism is now rejected as a justification for continuing policies.

Notes

1 The initial construction of the NPT in the 1960s involved, of the P5, only the United States, the USSR, and Britain. China and France did not accede to the NPT until 1992. Thus much of the groundwork laid for the nuclear order was a product of the two superpowers and Britain. Nonetheless, all five of the NPT nuclear states have continued to benefit from its provisions; none of them has shown a serious willingness to disrupt the privileges that the NPT endows on them.
2 The possession of nuclear weapons is not by Western states only of course. But it has been the case that the American, British, and (sometimes) French states have determined who can 'responsibly' have nuclear weapons and who cannot. Of course the US decision to assist India and single it out as a 'responsible' nuclear state in 2005 has complicated this distinction between 'responsible' nuclear states and the 'irresponsible' proliferators. Favouring India as a nuclear state, with which the United States could 'do business', in violation of NPT rules, has further eroded the legitimacy of the NPT.
3 For a dissenting, but minority, opinion which argues that the new treaty does not establish new legal norms, see Highsmith and Stewart (2018).
4 A claimed benign – or deterrence-only – possession of these weapons is problematic. As Michael Krepon (2016) notes, even without actually detonating them, possessor states 'use' their nuclear weapons 'all the time to project national power and bully the rest of the world'.
5 In September 2019, 152 Belgian mayors had signed an open letter urging the government to join the new treaty; the eventual parliamentary vote was seventy-seven against and sixty-six in favour (Stone 2020). By January 2020, this had changed to seventy-four rejections.
6 Australia is not under an explicit nuclear umbrella; its ANZUS alliance with the United States only commits the two members to consult in the event of an attack against either of them. Nonetheless, and sometimes to the bewilderment of US officials, Australian leaders have claimed such a nuclear assurance. Since 1994, this perception has been firmly incorporated into Australian Defence White Papers.
7 The Opposition Labor Party's Leader reaffirmed that 'Labor in government will sign and ratify the UN Treaty on the Prohibition of Nuclear Weapons'. He noted that 'I am a very strong supporter of our alliance with the United States … [but] the fact is that we can disagree with our friends in the short term, while maintaining those relations' (Albanese 2018).
8 Doyle concludes that if this were to happen, and the NPT were to unravel, 'the nuclear-armed states would then deserve the insecurity whirlwind that they helped to sow' (Doyle 2009: 2).
9 The postponement of the 2020 NPT RevCon until 2022 (or later) due to the COVID-19 crisis has, for the moment at least, held at bay the dissension between the nuclear haves and have-nots which is likely to be revealed when that conference is reconvened. For an assessment of the NPT's current prospects, see Rublee and Wunderlich (2022).

10 When it was evident, after the failure of the 2015 NPT RevCon, that non-nuclear states would pursue disarmament elsewhere, the P5 produced joint statements urging a turn back to the NPT. At the 2016 P5 Conference in Washington, they reaffirmed collectively and strongly that 'the NPT remains the cornerstone' for pursuing non-proliferation, for the peaceful uses of nuclear energy, and 'for the collective pursuit of nuclear disarmament'. They stated that 'the preservation of the integrity of the NPT' was essential to international peace and security' and expressed their 'deep concern with efforts to pursue approaches to nuclear disarmament that disregard the global strategic context'. They claimed that such efforts 'threaten the consensus-based approach that has served for decades to strengthen the NPT regime'. They reiterated that their step-by-step approach is the only 'realistic way to achieve a world without nuclear weapons' (US Department of State 2016).

11 One possibility is that non-nuclear states at the next NPT Review Conference – whether this is held in 2022 or later – will ask the nuclear states for a time-bound commitment to disarm. Giving notice that unless disarmament occurs by a prescribed date, these states could leave the NPT *en masse* (which some are already considering) might provide a sense of urgency and pressure not previously present in the NPT.

Part IV

Ending nuclearism?

8

Challenges to and likely impacts of the Treaty on the Prohibition of Nuclear Weapons

When the Treaty on the Prohibition of Nuclear Weapons was adopted by 122 states at the United Nations on 7 July 2017, there was celebration among the states and organizations which had campaigned for such an outcome. Yet in the five years since then, we have seen not a respect for its provisions, but instead, a continued reliance on nuclear weapons in the speeches and practices of leaders in the nuclear weapon states. They have illustrated this amply: in 2018, the US Nuclear Posture Review appeared to lower the threshold for using nuclear weapons, widening the circumstances under which a first strike will be considered (Reif 2018b). The United States and Russia withdrew from the Intermediate Nuclear Forces Treaty in 2019, and the Open Skies Treaty, a vital confidence-building measure, in 2020, and the United States called for large increases in the US nuclear weapons budget (Reif 2019). In 2021, President Biden, despite his campaign promises to lower the salience of nuclear weapons in security and to end wasteful spending on new nuclear weapons, has committed to upholding the contentious programmes of the Trump era. Russia's President Putin has boasted of the lethal capabilities of his nuclear arsenal and the development of new nuclear cruise missiles designed to evade US missile defences, in what one analyst described as 'an escalated level of martial rhetoric even by his pugnacious standards' (Troianovski 2018). Russia has also made 'occasional explicit nuclear threats against other countries' (Kristensen and Korda 2020) and in June 2020 endorsed a nuclear policy allowing for a nuclear response even in the event of a conventional attack against itself (Isachenkov 2020). This was raised again in the context of Ukraine's invasion in 2022. Even the United Kingdom, seen by many as more circumspect in nuclear issues and more attuned to the need for disarmament, has announced that it will increase its nuclear stockpile, expand its options for the use of nuclear weapons, and move towards a policy of greater ambiguity in nuclear decision-making (UK 2021).

In light of all this, it is not unreasonable to ask what the impact will be of the Treaty on the Prohibition of Nuclear Weapons. Sceptics might conclude that the treaty will have no value, given that it is not signed by the nuclear weapon states or their allies, and will not have any enforcement capabilities. They claim that the treaty presently does nothing to reduce the number of nuclear weapons, and that as long as the nuclear weapon states continue to privilege their arsenals over calls for disarmament and respect for humanitarian law, the achievement of this legal prohibition is not especially significant. Understanding the nature of the treaty, and its limitations, is thus an important requirement in any debate on the governance of nuclear weapons, and this chapter offers some initial observations on these questions.

Problems facing the TPNW

The treaty will face several challenges which, initially at least, might indicate a limited impact. A number of interrelated issues suggest that we have to treat with caution any claims that the TPNW provides an easy road to disarmament.

The nuclear weapon states refuse to sign the treaty

First, it is clear that the treaty has not been signed or supported by the nuclear weapon states; nor is this likely to happen in the near future (US Mission to the UN 2017). Even negotiations for the treaty were boycotted by these states, and they have overwhelmingly resisted its development (Falk 2017). Critics argue that as long as the nuclear weapon states refuse to be a part of the prohibition regime, a ban will not make any difference (Izewicz 2016; Harries 2017a; Ruhle 2017). For them, the treaty will be only a symbolic statement, and not something that has any real effect on policy. And indeed, judging by the continuing rhetoric of nuclear threats and ongoing modernization programmes, the TPNW seems to such critics little more than a blip on their radar of international developments.

This is indeed a problem: arguably, no other major treaty has had to face the collective hostility of so many powerful states. And while a prohibitionary treaty is an aspirational achievement, meaning that it is expected that over time it can come to have a persuasive effect on all states, the level of antipathy shown by the nuclear states towards the TPNW has been remarkable. But the fact that a proposal is opposed by certain states does not mean that that proposal should not be made. Many established humanitarian principles – against slavery, the death penalty, torture, etc. – have initially been strongly opposed by parties who could not conceive of having to change their practices. Those negotiating the TPNW understood that it was not likely to attract signatories from among the nuclear states in the near future. Still, the extent of opposition towards the treaty suggests that disarmament remains a distant prospect.

The TPNW is not legally enforceable on those states which do not sign it

Second, the TPNW cannot impose legal obligations on any non-party. While the treaty does constitute binding international law, as with other treaties it has no material authority over any state which refuses to sign it. The rights of sovereign nations to consider themselves free from any binding obligations in a treaty to which they have not expressly consented, remain strong. In this sense, the nuclear weapon states cannot be considered to be bound by the TPNW's provisions. We might argue that they *should* be affected by this norm, at least over time, and consent to be bound by this aspirational principle. But it is not likely that the TPNW will evolve in the near future into even a process of customary international law, where those parties non-signatory to a particular treaty can be held accountable against that agreement. As legal observers note, customary international law can be argued when a long-standing and widespread pattern of concordant state behaviour is evident and where there prevails a strong sense of a legal obligation among the community of states as to the virtue of any particular treaty (Ifft and Koplow 2021). The TPNW will not be considered to have achieved the status of customary international law for many years, especially if none of the major powers – especially the United States, Russia, China, France, and the United Kingdom – do not accede to the treaty. This fact dampens somewhat the claims made earlier in this book about the fact that non-nuclear states have created a treaty without the blessing or involvement of the great powers. That still stands as an important achievement, and no doubt if things had been left to the P5 states, no progress on a prohibition treaty or on disarmament more generally would have occurred. The stark reality, however, is that although the treaty is now clearly part of international law, it has no enforceable status on those countries which choose not to sign it. The treaty's advocates will use the TPNW and the norms it enshrines to exert influence on the nuclear weapon states, and in time it could come to constitute customary law, or at the very least a strong moral barrier to the use of nuclear weapons, but punitive action against non-signatory states will not be possible.

Major allies of the United States have not (yet) signed the treaty

Third, it is also the case that major allies of the United States have yet to affirm the treaty.[1] As noted in the last chapter, pressure will be placed particularly onto liberal democratic states normally in favour of humanitarianism and international law to join the TPNW; however, this has not yet translated into definitive support for the treaty. Even though some NATO allies have been demonstrably in favour of reducing the salience of nuclear weapons in security doctrines, of issuing no-first-use statements, of eliminating the remaining tactical nuclear weapons that remain on European soil, and even of nuclear disarmament, the reality is that none of them have yet signed the TPNW. Even though Norway, Germany, Belgium, and the Netherlands, for instance, had been involved in the Humanitarian Initiative from the beginning, none of these states has yet shaken off the pressures placed on them by Washington. Some NATO states seem genuinely troubled by the presence of nuclear dangers. But their views have not been strong enough to jeopardize their relationship with the United States, or with Britain and France, the other two nuclear states within NATO. Norway, Germany, Belgium, and the Netherlands have been 'guarded supporters' of the Humanitarian Initiative, but they are not (so far) what might be called the 'drivers of disarmament' (Nielsen and Hanson 2014).

The NATO dimension continues to prevent the EU from endorsing the prohibition treaty. Even though the EU is typically seen as a block of liberal states which respect to the rule of law and humanitarianism, it is unlikely in the near future to declare a collective pledge of support for the treaty. Important foreign and security policy decisions are still taken by EU members at the national level, although the EU does attempt to put forward a common foreign and security front as far as possible, within the limits of its intergovernmental framework. As such, it was possible to see a collective 'EU position' on many international issues, including on some key arms control agreements. When it comes to nuclear weapons, however, these same Western states are still reluctant to translate their support for humanitarianism into explicit affirmation of a treaty prohibiting nuclear weapons (Nielsen and Hanson 2014; Cronberg 2015; Berghofer 2016). Put simply, it will not be possible for the EU to champion nuclear disarmament in the way that the organization did for other cases, precisely because it will require the twenty-one EU states which are also members of NATO to renounce nuclear weapons, and for those that host nuclear weapons on their territory to put in place significant changes to their existing policies and practices. The NATO-ization of the European Union has made the EU's reluctance to push disarmament even more pronounced in the past two decades (Smetana 2016): expanding the EU eastwards brought a large number of former Soviet-bloc states – now also NATO members – into its fold, and these states claim the United States' nuclear umbrella more than many of NATO's older members might do. Expanding the European Union has come to mean – if unintentionally – embracing NATO's nuclear posture in a way that was not so prominent until relatively recently in the EU's history. For all these reasons, it is clear that the EU cannot be relied upon, at least not in the immediate future, to give support to the prohibition treaty. EU backing for the TPNW would be an exceptionally useful endorsement, but for now, at least, the EU will not be able to give such an endorsement, precisely because it incorporates France, a nuclear weapon state, and many others who are both EU and NATO members.

As with NATO allies, so too have Japan, South Korea, and Australia been reluctant to support the new treaty. For now at least, they have not wished to antagonize their major ally. And for Japan and South Korea, the proximity of North Korea and its provocative nuclear and missile practices is of great concern. For the most part, these governments remain supporters of extended nuclear deterrence, even though the sophisticated conventional weapons capabilities of the United States are likely to be able to deter or respond to an attack on these states, and especially given the credibility concerns associated with extended nuclear deterrence. As noted in the previous chapter, there is always the possibility that new governments in these countries, spurred by their populations, might come to support the treaty. Nonetheless, as of 2022, no ally formally under the US nuclear umbrella has lent the treaty its support.

The treaty has yet to attract widespread ratification

Third, and related to the above points, so far only a relatively small number of states, and, arguably, only states of limited consequence, have signed and ratified the treaty. Critics of the TPNW have been quick to point out that even though 122 states voted in 2017 to adopt the treaty, as of early 2022, only eighty-six states have signed, and only fifty-nine have so far ratified the treaty. Those states which have ratified tend to be small states, drawn mostly from the developing world, together with a few of the smaller/middle-sized states such as Austria, South Africa, Ireland, and New Zealand. It cannot be denied that currently, the treaty has neither the support of 'a critical mass of states', or 'a mass of critical states', that is, states with significant material and persuasive standing in the world (Vilmer 2020). In other words, we are not seeing the 'heavy hitters' of world politics take up this cause. Again, it is possible that some of the 122 states which were supportive of the treaty in 2017 but who have not yet signed will come to do so as their domestic governments change; domestic pressure will certainly be placed on many of them to do so. For now, however, the treaty has no large and materially powerful states as members.

Nuclear weapons remain firmly entrenched in security doctrines

A fourth problem facing the treaty is that unlike landmines and other 'inhumane' weapons which have been successfully eliminated or at least greatly reduced, nuclear weapons are firmly entrenched in the security doctrines of those states that hold them. Eliminating nuclear weapons will be considerably harder than eliminating landmines and cluster munitions, and will face obstacles which were overcome much more easily in earlier efforts to prohibit weapons considered inhumane. Landmines and cluster munitions, chemical and biological weapons, were easier to ban, and easier for states to give up, because they were not deeply, and centrally, ingrained into the security policies of their possessors. As Matthew Harries observes, 'nuclear weapons have to be reckoned with as important instruments of state power' (Harries 2017a). These states are deeply wedded to their nuclear weapons, however irrational we might think this is. The centrality of nuclear weapons in their security policies is clearly evident, in contrast to the much less entrenched role that landmines or cluster munitions played for these states. And as noted, this role seems to have become revived in recent years.

It might be that sudden shifts in the dynamics between the nuclear weapon states will occur and this will encourage a return to arms control and disarmament imperatives. The years 2016–22 were particularly bad for arms control, with the withering of several treaties and the growth of bellicose relations between the major powers. There have been some positive moves, with President Biden renewing the NewSTART treaty in February 2021, but for the most part, and despite substantial lobbying from the advocates of nuclear elimination, doctrines and policies remain as rigid as ever and nuclear weapons are firmly entrenched as central elements of national security.

Nor is it likely that the 'soft compliance' effect that the landmine and cluster munitions treaties created can occur. A key achievement of those campaigns is that even the large and powerful states which did not sign these treaties have in fact come to comply with their provisions, (to varying degrees). For instance, the United States no longer uses landmines or cluster munitions, even as Washington refuses to sign the respective treaties. Russia and China act similarly.[2] These treaties were not only successful in enlisting signatories who renounced the use of these weapons; they also came to have an impact on non-signatory states. The norms enshrined in them, in other words, created the remarkable situation where for the most part, even the great powers do not use these weapons. But this phenomenon – of inwardly complying with the rules while outwardly ignoring them – is not feasible in the case of nuclear weapons. For one thing, any 'soft compliance' with nuclear disarmament is physically impossible, because nuclear disarmament actively requires both declaratory and operational processes, the commitment and the actual dismantlement of existing stocks. Only the physical destruction of stocks and a commitment to a nuclear-free world will count. The deeply embedded nature of nuclearism suggests that change, if it happens, will be slow.

Securing domestic support for nuclear disarmament might be harder than it was during other campaigns

Third, securing domestic support for the prohibition treaty is likely to be more complex, and arguably harder, than it was for previous disarmament campaigns. The call to eliminate nuclear weapons is hampered by the (fortunate) fact that these weapons have not been used in war since 1945, that they are not being used on a daily basis, and that there are few 'victims' presently suffering from the devastation of a nuclear strike. The landmines campaign was particularly effective in bringing the plight of children and other civilians to the world by the wide dissemination of graphic photographs and testaments of the everyday casualties of these weapons. The ICBL was able to reach the hearts and minds of millions of people very quickly, and it used these visual tools effectively. Medical personnel spoke directly about things like suffering, amputations, and the need for prosthetics, in a way that caught the public's sympathy and support. In an age where confronting images are likely to be important in galvanizing public support, there is relatively little 'material' to utilize when seeking the elimination of nuclear weapons.

We do have, importantly, the testimony of many of the Hibakusha, the Japanese survivors from Hiroshima and Nagasaki (see, for example, Thurlow 2014, 2020; Southard 2015; Sullivan 2016). Some of these survivors spoke at the conferences on the Humanitarian Impact of Nuclear Weapons and were especially active during the seventy-fifth commemoration of the bombing of their cities. Their narratives are important as firsthand testimony of what nuclear strikes were like. But the Hibakusha are by now in their 80s and 90s, and the direct links with the reality of nuclear war that they represent will soon be gone.

We also have evidence of the impact of nuclear weapons tests, and the stories of those affected by the nuclear tests conducted between 1945 and 1996.[3] There are growing calls for compensation and restitution from groups in Australia, the South Pacific, and elsewhere, whose health and environments were calamitously affected by nuclear tests. Even so, these stories and images will not represent the impact of the actual use of nuclear weapons in a conflict. The Humanitarian Initiative conferences have publicized these likely effects in various reports, but this is not the same as presenting real evidence of actual 'attacks'.

As such, this issue is not prominently in the public eye. If the general public thinks about nuclear weapons – which they tend not to do often – they invariably are of the view that the real dangers have passed. The end of the Cold War brought an end to the fear of mass annihilation. As James Doyle

(2013: 27) reminds us, nuclear non-use has meant that many people have become complacent: they have used the taboo 'as a reason to believe that the risk of nuclear war is overblown'.

There is evidence that public support can be enlisted, and when asked specifically whether these weapons should be banned, significant majorities tend to support disarmament.[4] The campaign has also gathered support from groups across society, including medical professionals, faith leaders, unions, youth groups, and local governments.[5] But it will be more difficult than it was in the landmines case to channel this support into direct action and elimination, especially given the entrenched nature of nuclear weapons.

Securing civil society support in non-democracies will be difficult

Some argue that precisely because the treaty enables and validates anti-nuclear civil society actors, it is an unwise development, giving the non-democratic nuclear weapon states – which presumably would face far less domestic pressure – an advantage (Roberts 2015; Harries 2017b; Ruhle 2017). For these critics, supporting the treaty automatically advantages authoritarian states like China, Russia, and North Korea, and also, arguably, India and Pakistan. Matthew Harries argues, with some hyperbole, that the creation of the new treaty is nothing less than an 'attack on the nuclear-armed democracies – the United States, in particular – and their allies to the near-exclusive benefit of Russia and China' (Harries 2017b). As non-democratic states are not likely to feel domestic pressure, they will be less compelled to join the treaty; critics argue that it would therefore be folly for the democratic nuclear-armed states to agree to such a treaty.

It must be acknowledged that while the element of civil society activism found in NATO states, Japan, South Korea, and Australia, will work to strengthen domestic support for the nuclear prohibition treaty, these activities cannot be replicated in the same way for all nuclear weapon states. Domestic pressure will be a far less influential factor in the states where authoritarian leaders retain a firm hold over policy. Additionally, China, India, Pakistan, and North Korea have long noted the discrepancy between the massive arsenals of the United States and Russia, compared to their own, substantially lower, numbers, and point to continued intransigence on the part of these states as reasons for why they will not reduce their numbers.

This does not mean, however, that non-democratic states would be exempt from pressure altogether (Ritchie 2017). If the United States took the lead and urged Russia towards much lower bilaterally agreed numbers than they hold presently, the other nuclear states – even the non-democratic ones – are likely also to evaluate their positions. In any case, as Sauer (2015a) reminds us, even non-democracies can change their policies; he points to the fact that the four states which gave up their nuclear weapons in the early 1990s – South Africa, Kazakhstan, Ukraine, and Belarus – were not democracies at the time they reversed their nuclear status. A lack of domestic pressure therefore, while possibly being advantageous for non-democratic leaders, may well see even greater pressure applied from outside.[6] Nonetheless, even the prospect of an unequally applied pressure to disarm will be used by opponents to resist the TPNW.

Verification provisions in the treaty remain underdeveloped

A further difficulty is that some observers believe that the treaty is flawed because it lacks appropriate verification and safeguards provisions (Carlson 2017; Vilmer 2020). There are two related but contentious issues here: first is the ability and authority of the TPNW to verify dismantlement of warheads during a process of disarmament in a nuclear weapons state wishing to join the treaty; second is the safeguards standards required of states parties to the TPNW, both non-nuclear states and any nuclear weapon state wishing to join. In the case of the first issue, it should be noted that the prohibition treaty was not designed to regulate the actual dismantlement of nuclear arsenals and provide the monitoring and verification procedures, including on-site inspections, etc., that would be required as this process is happening. The treaty allows for a nuclear weapon state to join, through a 'destroy [the nuclear weapons] and then join' process, or through a 'join and then destroy' process. The treaty notes that its States Parties 'shall designate a competent international authority or authorities to negotiate and verify the irreversible elimination of nuclear-weapons programmes' in any nuclear weapon state which seeks to join the treaty, but it has been criticized for the vagueness of this wording, and for its deferment of the details of full verification procedures.

As with some other treaties, those negotiating the TPNW determined to leave these decisions to other authorities, and to restrict the treaty to its basic principle: the illegality of nuclear weapons under international humanitarian law. As Giorgou (2018) notes, 'the TPNW is not, and was never meant to be, a Comprehensive Nuclear Weapons Convention. What principally distinguishes the former from the latter model is the existence of provisions, including obligations, related to the verification of the complete and irreversible elimination of nuclear weapons'. While these elements will certainly be needed if we are to achieve and maintain a world free of nuclear weapons, this was not the role specifically envisaged for the TPNW (Giorgou 2018).

Related to this point about monitoring and verification, there is a perennial, but overstated, fear that even if states do agree to disarm, we might never know for sure whether they have really dismantled their weapons.

This is frequently raised as an argument for why the nuclear states cannot, apparently, move to a nuclear-free world. In reality, significant resources and attention have been paid to this issue in the past few decades, and we can be reasonably confident that once states agree to dismantlement, we do possess the scientific and technical processes needed to verify that this has been done successfully. Two nuclear weapon states, Britain and the United States, have worked collaboratively since the 1990s on several cooperative verification projects. At a multilateral level, the International Partnership for Nuclear Disarmament Verification (IPNDV) was formed by the United States in 2014. The IPNDV is a collaboration between a diverse group of states who work on the technical requirements for monitoring and verification; a non-governmental organization, the Verification Research, Training, and Information Centre (VERTIC) has operated since the 1980s. Several analysts have explored the complexities of monitoring and verification, as well as how we might respond to any instances of 'breakout', where a state might covertly develop a nuclear weapon, after other states have disarmed. While there are undoubtedly challenges ahead, the prospects for successful detection and management of these processes are better than many laypeople might think (Mack 1997; Caughley 2016; Erasto *et al.* 2019).

The important point here is that it was never the responsibility of the TPNW itself to specify in detail or to conduct processes of monitoring and verification: there are existing mechanisms for this. The TPNW's role is expressly to make nuclear weapons illegitimate and illegal for all states. Ritchie and Egeland (2018: 136) point out that the purpose of the ban-treaty has not been 'to regulate the destruction of nuclear stockpiles'. This is a process that the nuclear weapon states will likely have to conduct among themselves, via a new Convention, or under the authority of a (yet to be established) 'competent international authority' after they agree to embark on a managed system of elimination. The ban-treaty is less a typical arms control treaty than it is a statement of international humanitarian law; its purpose is to strengthen the normative shift rather than to oversee the actual destruction of these weapons (Egeland 2018). On the second issue noted by some critics, regarding the safeguards standards required of states signing the TPNW, the argument is that more stringent IAEA requirements should have been demanded. A few critics have argued that requiring only a Comprehensive Safeguards Agreement (CSA) with the IAEA was a lost opportunity, and that the IAEA's Additional Protocol (AP) should have been made mandatory for any state wishing to join the treaty. However, even the nuclear Non-Proliferation Treaty only requires the conclusion of a CSA, and does not require States Parties to have agreed an AP; this is an optional measure, although it is encouraged. Rather than imposing a more stringent requirement, the prohibition treaty's text requests that a state which already has an AP in place is legally required to retain this as a State Party to the TPNW, but for states that do not, only the CSA is required, although, as with the NPT, all States Parties are encouraged to adopt the AP. Nonetheless, some critics believe that the failure to insist that all treaty signatories must have signed the IAEA's Additional Protocol is a significant flaw. Carlson (2017) argues that the failure to do so 'undermines the requirement unanimously endorsed by NPT Review Conferences, for the highest safeguards standard' to apply to all countries (2017). This criticism seems overdrawn, and is refuted by some observers (Giorgou 2018; ICRC 2018).

The safeguards provisions in the TPNW are indeed underdeveloped, but this was a deliberate policy: negotiators working within a limited timeframe and seeking to accommodate diverging views chose to complete a straightforward prohibition treaty, leaving monitoring and verification processes for other bodies in the future. Nonetheless, this perceived weakness adds to the objections against the treaty, and might further hamper widespread adherence.

The points above all suggest that we cannot expect a nuclear ban-treaty to have the same kind of ready support that we saw for previous disarmament campaigns. Without much in the way of evidence that nuclear weapons are creating direct disasters today, it will be harder to generate strong support for elimination.

Limitations and difficulties still allow for a treaty of consequence

None of the above points mean, however, that the TPNW is without consequence. It is vital to note that supporters of the treaty do not see it as an easy road to disarmament. The treaty itself cannot predict the pace and success (or otherwise) of the elimination of nuclear weapons. Once non-nuclear states were determined to act, the treaty was achieved relatively quickly. But it is the actions that will follow the treaty, over the next ten, twenty, or more years, which will be crucial in determining the path of disarmament. The hard work facing disarmament advocates lies in the future.

On the face of it, a nuclear prohibition treaty might seem to hold few chances of success. While it might seem, at first glance, 'preposterous' (Lennane 2016) that non-nuclear states have negotiated this treaty, the TPNW and the processes that preceded and will follow it, will increasingly reject the ideas, practices, and justifications that make up nuclearism. It seems counter-intuitive to think that a treaty unsigned by the nuclear states can have any impact:

> Nations that do not have nuclear weapons – nations already prohibited from possessing such weapons – negotiate a treaty among themselves outlawing the

weapons they do not have. Nations that actually possess the weapons remain outside the treaty. How could this possibly affect prospects for nuclear disarmament? (Lennane 2016)

This is a fair question (although in this case it was posed rhetorically by an advocate of disarmament). But any assessment which holds that a treaty cannot be successful unless the nuclear-armed states sign it suggests an incomplete understanding of the place and potential of prohibitionary regimes in global politics. Change is always possible: with sustained and principled leadership, virtuous circles can be achieved. As one observer notes, 'it is only through the strength of principled examples and ambitious diplomacy that responsible nations can hope to make the legacy of Trinity and the nuclear threat to civilisation a thing of the past' (Stoltz 2020).

Again, it is important to remember that the elimination of a particular weapon has occurred only after that weapon has been stigmatized, and then legally prohibited. The cases of weapons addressed in the late nineteenth and early twentieth centuries, together with the later conventions against biological and chemical weapons, landmines and cluster munitions, all showed that the sequence has been first to stigmatize and then to prohibit legally; it is only after these stages that elimination (or almost complete elimination[7]) has occurred. The value of a prohibitionary, or ban, treaty lies in its message: it makes explicit the wishes and moral priorities of those who sign it, and it signals an expectation of behaviour by others. It should be seen as a stigmatizing and delegitimizing treaty. The nature of a prohibitionary treaty means that it operates in a different way to most contractual arrangements between various parties where obligations are codified and enforced, essentially signifying that agreement has already been reached, and where legal documents are a mechanism for verifying compliance. The prohibition treaty, by contrast, sets out the standard for desired behaviour, inviting states to accede to this code of conduct. It does not need the nuclear weapon states to sign it now for it to have a persuasive and normative power. Lennane has captured the potential of the treaty well:

> Nobody is under any illusion that nuclear-armed states will simply join a ban treaty and start disarming. Rather, the value of a ban treaty lies in its potential as a political tool for disrupting the status quo. A ban treaty will break up the crusty rhetorical accretions that have accumulated over decades of ambiguity, delay, obfuscation, and attempts to obstruct disarmament. A treaty will clear away hypocrisy, shine a revealing light on the motives and behavior of nuclear-armed states, and reshape the disarmament landscape so that work may begin anew on more stable foundations. Obviously, it is nuclear-armed countries that will have to do the actual disarming. But before this can begin, a number of obstacles must be cleared away. Nations without nuclear weapons, by pursuing a ban treaty, can start to clear them. (Lennane 2016)

Thus, while it is important to understand and acknowledge the challenges facing the treaty, there are some grounds for thinking that it might come to have a cumulative impact on the calculations of the nuclear weapon states and their allies. It would be wrong to dismiss the prohibition treaty on the grounds that the nuclear states have not signed it; there are numerous ways in which the very act of creating a nuclear weapons prohibition treaty alters the political landscape of nuclear politics. By establishing a firm denunciation of nuclear weapons, despite the efforts of the great powers who for decades have sought to prevent anything like this from occurring, by taking this process out of the NPT and determining to proceed anyway, without the nuclear states, the non-nuclear states have overcome a significant obstacle in the path to de-nuclearization. The normative appeal of the new treaty is likely, over time, to lead more states to join, and to make those states which remain outside the treaty and which retain nuclear weapons, increasingly isolated, holding weapons that have been clearly denounced by the rest of the world. The claim by the nuclear weapon states that, because they have not signed it, the TPNW is not legally binding on them might be technically true, but these states cannot escape from the fact that they will now be seen – more than ever – to be acting in defiance of international law.

Conclusion

In this sense, the normative arguments marshalled by the non-nuclear states – traditionally weak participants in international relations – are building a new construction of what it means to be a nuclear weapon state, with the attendant moral censure that this will bring. The process has empowered non-nuclear states and placed the obligation on nuclear states to justify their defiance of a law based on 'the principles of humanity and the dictates of public conscience'. As it erects further moral and legal barriers against nuclear weapons, even without universal support, the treaty's normative power is likely to be significant. It brings obligations and a scrutiny that could not previously be applied to the nuclear weapon states. At the very least, the delegitimizing effect of the prohibition treaty ensures that nuclear weapons are seen clearly as inhumane, a factor which in itself will reinforce the practice of non-use, if nothing else. And even if the nuclear weapon states do not contribute to the ban itself, the global landscape can be redefined in a way that various practices might evolve away from prevailing patterns (PAX 2016d). The TPNW is already affecting the way that we think about change and patterns of agency in the nuclear weapons debate. Its cumulative impact increases 'the political cost for those keeping such weapons' and reduces 'the political incentives for others to acquire them'

(Acheson *et al.* 2014: 25).[8] Supporters of the treaty do not see it as an easy road to disarmament; in many ways, it is what comes after the treaty which will be important. The actions that will follow the treaty, over the next several years, will be crucial in determining the elimination of nuclear weapons. The treaty itself cannot predict the pace and success (or otherwise) of the nuclear disarmament project. Shifting hardened attitudes will be difficult, even if these weapons have extremely limited utility. As such, the calls for eliminating nuclear weapons, even after the prohibition treaty enters into force, will need to be made in a sustained way, and possibly for many decades.

Notes

1. Some Western allies have signed the treaty, but none of these consider themselves to be under a formal US extended nuclear deterrence agreement. Over sixty countries worldwide have some kind of defence pact with the United States (Beckley 2015), especially via the Organization of American States. Some of these loosely defined allies include Brazil, Chile, Mexico, the Philippines, and New Zealand, all of whom have signed the TPNW.
2. The United States has not used cluster munitions since 2003 (with one exception in 2009). Russian use of cluster munitions has continued, but overall, even this use has diminished.
3. In particular, the Marshall Islanders have been active in bringing their experiences to the rest of the world. Stories are emerging from many First Nation peoples, whose land was affected by nuclear testing, and who were often passed from one site to another, on the orders of the testing state.
4. Where the public has been consulted about this issue, polls show that there is a majority view that nuclear weapons make the world a more dangerous place, and that a process of phased, balanced, and monitored disarmament is generally favoured. Evans *et al.* (2015) have included a number of survey results in their 2015 book which suggest a significant level of support for elimination: the Global Attitudes Survey, for example, canvassed the responses of 48,643 people in forty-four different countries; the survey by World Public Opinion.org on 9 December 2008 involved 19,000 respondents. A 2007 Global Public Opinion on Nuclear Weapons found that 79 per cent of the 6,000 adults surveyed in six states believed that nuclear weapons made the world a more dangerous place (cited in Evans *et al.* 2015: 81).
5. The Cities Appeal has seen over 400 cities around the world endorse the TPNW and call on their national governments to join the treaty.
6. The non-democratic nuclear states have indicated at NPT forums and elsewhere that they will move to disarmament once the major powers have lowered their numbers significantly. This is not to say that any such promises should be taken at face value, any more than the promises of the major powers should

be believed. But the essential point – that once underway, real moves to disarmament can occur among all nine nuclear weapon states within a phased and monitored process and with security guarantees given – should not be dismissed.
7 While disarmament conventions have resulted in the destruction of stocks of these various weapons, there are some remnants of their possession, and even use, among a very few states. But as any use of landmines or chemical weapons shows today, these are increasingly denounced as methods of warfare.
8 Acheson *et al.* (2014: 26) point out that over time, 'states' non-adherence to a legal regime can evolve … so that initial strong rejection of a norm can soften to policy and practice that is consistent with the norm'. A treaty framework which outlaws nuclear weapons might also serve in time as a potential face-saving option for any nuclear weapon state which decided to move seriously towards the elimination of its arsenal.

Conclusion

We have been fortunate that nuclear weapons have not been used since 1945, but the chance of them being launched, accidentally or intentionally, is still too high to warrant complacency. The Bulletin of the Atomic Scientists in January 2020 moved the 'Doomsday Clock' to 100 seconds before midnight, the closest it has been to disaster in its history (Spinnaze 2020). This remained the case in 2021 and 2022 (Mecklin 2022). Speaking in January 2019, former US Secretary of Defense, William Perry (cited in DeRensis 2019) expressed his belief that 'the danger today of a nuclear catastrophe is greater than it was during the darkest years of the Cold War'. He added that in addition to the long-standing possibilities of nuclear war by accident due to a false alarm, and nuclear war due to miscalculation, we also have new challenges not faced during the Cold War: the risk of nuclear terrorism, and the threat of a nuclear regional war (specifically in South Asia). Perry observed that he himself had witnessed a number of false alarms, where by sheer luck, nuclear disaster was averted (Perry 2015).

This is troubling enough, and yet, current policies do not reflect these dangers (Perry and Collina 2020). There has been little recognition of these hazards, and no progress in achieving the risk-reduction strategies needed to help us avert a nuclear disaster. Former Russian Foreign Minister Igor Ivanov has added his assessment: 'The risk of confrontation with the use of nuclear weapons in Europe is higher than in the 1980s' (cited in Emmott 2016), and the war in Ukraine raises these stakes significantly. It is useful to keep these sobering assessments in mind as we contemplate the role of the TPNW.

The ending of the Cold War was an ideal time to take stock of nuclear dangers and move collectively to the elimination of these weapons. One of the key failures of political leaders in the nuclear weapon states in the aftermath of the Cold War was their unwillingness to reassess and revise their nuclear doctrines in light of the dramatically changed – and vastly improved – political landscape of the early to mid 1990s. There was a failure to consolidate the peace between the great powers which the end of the Cold War had provided, by shaping the world and its international security architecture in a more inclusive, equitable, and sustainable fashion. Continuing to retain high levels of nuclear weapons was a dangerous practice. The window of opportunity was open for some years and it represented a chance to steer the world away from further nuclear proliferation and the risk of nuclear catastrophe via a process of phased and balanced reductions, a switch to conventional deterrence, and an emphasis on common security concerns.

Outlawing and eliminating nuclear weapons was the best way of reversing what Richard Butler (1996) had called 'history's greatest accident'. Yet the extent to which nuclearism had become embedded in national and international policies was overwhelming, and suggestions that doctrines should be looked at anew were not heeded. General Lee Butler, former head of US Strategic Air Command, admitted that, by 1998, he was 'seized by a sense of profound dismay, of opportunity lost, of danger prolonged', and disappointed by 'how badly the handful of nuclear weapons states have faltered in their responsibilities to reduce the saliency of their arsenals' (Butler 1999).

All nine nuclear weapon states have a profound responsibility to avert a nuclear war. This responsibility applied from the earliest days of the nuclear arms race. The nuclear age has always been marked by dangerous rivalry and the threat of catastrophe, and the global nuclear order has been characterized by inequalities and inconsistencies. These problems have become even more pronounced today: although numbers have dropped, the lethality of many nuclear weapons has grown, as has the sabre-rattling between the United States and Russia, the United States and China, the United States and North Korea, and between India and Pakistan. And non-nuclear states have shown increasing anger at the refusal of the nuclear states to take their responsibilities seriously. The P5 keeping their nuclear weapons during the Cold War might have been an acceptable (albeit unpalatable) position, but the expectations now are that changes must occur, that entrenched nuclearism has to be challenged, as a key step towards a nuclear-free world.

The NPT nuclear weapon states, the P5, and especially the United States and Russia – whose arsenals constitute the bulk of the world's nuclear weapons – have a special obligation to create a safer and more equitable security order. As permanent members of the UN Security Council, they have what can be termed 'special responsibilities' to lead the way in the ending of nuclear arms races and towards disarmament (even as their membership of the Security Council was never granted on the basis of their nuclear status). These responsibilities are assigned to those states which have the capabilities to alleviate global dangers, especially where it is their own actions which make the rest of the world vulnerable to risk (Bukovansky *et al.* 2012: 222). In other words, the nuclear weapon states, and especially the United States and Russia, have an obligation to change geopolitical circumstances by reducing and eliminating nuclear dangers which threaten entire regions and, potentially, the whole world. As Dunworth (2015) observes, for these states, taking effective measures for nuclear disarmament is not merely a 'foreign policy option', but an urgent moral requirement.

Yet still these measures are not being taken. Nuclearism has prevailed for over seventy years, and we can rightly characterize it as entrenched, self-serving (for the nuclear states), and ultimately illogical. Indeed we must remember the context of inconsistency and double-speak which has characterized the entire nuclear weapon endeavour. Lennane reminds us that this has been a 'surreal, looking-glass world', where

> doublethink and delusion rule – where nuclear weapons are simultaneously treasured and reviled by those who possess them, where the modernization of nuclear arsenals is presented as a step toward disarmament, and where disarmament strategies that have delivered essentially nothing but deadlock and failure for more than 40 years are earnestly advocated as practical, sustainable, and realistic approaches. (Lennane 2016)

The nuclear weapon states claim to seek the conditions for a world free of nuclear weapons, but maintain that they need these weapons for 'stability', and that the time is not right for eliminating them. Those advocating disarmament, or even cuts to the bloated nuclear arsenals, are branded 'nuclear Utopians', with their 'eccentric explanations', while 'nuclear realists' (Payne 2015) 'understand' that the nuclear states cannot do without nuclear weapons. Proponents of nuclear weapons characterize disarmament as a 'dream' that 'seduces' (Tellis 2013), and urge that instead of succumbing to this alluring dream, everyone must instead accept the 'enduring reality' of nuclear weapons. But even as nuclear proponents attempt to justify the continuation of deterrence policies they cannot provide satisfying answers to the following questions, 'If nuclear deterrence is so essential to security, why cannot *every* state be allowed to possess nuclear weapons?' and 'How can we ensure that a catastrophic mistake will never happen?' Nor do they seem to give much consideration to the fact that conventional weapon capabilities are more useful militarily and can serve as more credible deterrents to aggression.

At a more fundamental level, there are those who argue that the material characteristics of nuclear weapons render any rethinking or devaluing of them impossible, that their value is immutable and unchangeable, regardless of how people seek to reconceptualize them (Martin 2013). Under this view, it is useless to try to reorient beliefs and policies towards disarmament, because a de-nuclearized world is, simply, 'an impossible goal' (Martin 2013). This insistence in persisting with nuclear weapons reflects what Ungar has called the 'paradox of indispensability', where nuclear weapons, 'as instruments of mass extinction … paralyse their owners from being able to use them', but are nonetheless viewed as vital and able to 'provide a magical sense of impossible omnipotence that can overcome the paralysis'. It is, Ungar concludes, 'a case of the virtually use-less being regarded as utterly vital' (Ungar 1992: 85). If these weapons are of little or no use today, and if their retention might lead to further proliferation, possible terrorist acquisition, mistaken or deliberate use, and if today's security requirements call for dramatically different approaches, then there seems little need to maintain costly, imprecise, clumsy (in terms of military utility), dangerous, and manifestly inhumane nuclear weapons. As Taylor (2007: 667) has summed up, nuclear weapons 'continue to pose significant risk in the absence of compelling security needs'.

Critics opposed to the negotiation of the nuclear weapons prohibition treaty invariably pointed to various arguments for why this would be an undesirable outcome. Their overriding and often unexamined mantra is that proponents of nuclear disarmament need to live in the 'real world' where strategic calculations have to be made in the interests of national security. The chapters above have sought to refute these claims, but it is also worth noting here the comments made by Patricia Lewis, in response to claims that a treaty is not appropriate at the present time, and that its proponents do not live in the 'real world':

> The real world is one in which the US-Russia bilateral process has ground to a halt ... I think we all know what genuine commitment to progress looks like and smells like, and we all know that that is not happening at the moment in the NPT. The real world is also what is providing the urgency and impetus for those who are trying new approaches. They are very worried about the future – that is really what it comes down to. Leadership comes in many forms and we are not seeing it from those who possess nuclear weapons. (Lewis 2015)

Embarking seriously on a process of phased, balanced, and verified reductions, leading to the eventual elimination of nuclear weapons, is a desirable goal. It will bring some risks, but not moving in this direction is likely to be worse. A world without nuclear weapons will not be risk-free, but maintaining the present system looks increasingly untenable. The numerous 'close calls' which have come to light, the precarious levels of nuclear safety and security in all the nuclear weapon states, the risks of deterrence failing, together with the deteriorating relationships between a number of nuclear-armed states all suggest a level of danger that is deeply troubling. As Perry (2016) has noted 'our system – with all of its safety features – was still vulnerable to a single person erring and bringing about the end of civilization'. It is important to keep this in mind as a useful corrective to arguments that disarmament will be 'too hard'. Inertia could be costly, and unlike some other political issues, being wise after the fact will not bring any comfort. Experience and wisdom gained from hindsight are valuable tools in the conduct of international relations and in life more generally, but with any nuclear weapons' use, the cost is likely to be tragic and enormous, and the luxury of careful reflection once a catastrophe has occurred could be meaningless.

The main arguments presented in this book are that decades of seeing nuclear weapons as 'normal' elements of international security, enabled by the processes of nuclearism, allowed for a risk of widespread destruction, which was nevertheless detached from the realities that the actual use of nuclear weapons would bring. Nuclearism – what I determined as a peculiar strategic discourse, the lack of a humanitarian perspective on the real impact of nuclear weapons, the exclusion of any meaningful public debate about these weapons, the vast resources dedicated to ensuring this level of overkill, and strict control of the global nuclear order – have allowed for an abnormality in international relations, which has been resilient to any challenge or change. Nuclearism was supported and driven by a small group of individuals, within a small group of states in the international system, who wielded extraordinary levels of power and authority over millions of people and over the planet as a whole. The belief that nuclear weapons are essential for the security of their holders has prevailed for so long that it is presented as unquestionable 'fact'.

This state of affairs which dominated thinking for so long, and which still persists in many circles within the nuclear-armed states and their allies, has now come to be rejected as illegitimate by a substantial group of non-nuclear states and civil society organizations. The Humanitarian Initiative came to be the key development for refuting nuclearism. It recast the debate in a way which was tangibly different to anything that had been attempted in the past, and presaged the move to draw up a legal proscription of nuclear weapons. Nuclearism ensured that there had never been a nuclear prohibition treaty in the same way that there existed treaties banning the possession and use of chemical and biological weapons, the other two kinds of weapons of mass destruction. The TPNW is important as the first unambiguous ruling against nuclear weapons, but also as an important development in the broader context of global processes to eliminate weapons of mass destruction. As noted, another significant aspect of the Humanitarian Initiative was the fact that it was pursued by *states*. Various individuals and NGOs have long argued against nuclear weapons, but it was only after 2010 that this same approach came to be taken up overtly and collectively by a large grouping of independent sovereign states. This process, reinforced by civil society pressure, then developed rapidly; once momentum was underway, a treaty seemed inevitable.

This push for a humanitarian framework has challenged each of the elements of nuclearism outlined in this book. The absence for so long of humanitarian considerations, the persistence of strategic calculations quarantined from any meaningful democratic oversight, and the allocation of vast sums of money in the name of national security, allowed the 'normality' of nuclear weapons to flourish, with little serious risk of being dislodged.

This history of normality has masked what is better defined as an entrenched abnormality in human and international relations, one that tolerates the possibility of widespread human suffering and even destruction of parts or whole of the planet, in return for a promise of alleged security against others. And the nuclear Non-Proliferation Treaty, or rather the subverting of the Non-Proliferation Treaty by the P5 states, has helped to entrench this situation. As illogical and undemocratic processes, costs, and strategies continued, exasperated non-nuclear states and civil society organizations made little headway, suggesting that we might have to face a future of 'nuclearism forever'.

The nuclear-armed states, together with many of their allies, view the humanitarian approach with hostility and as a diversion from NPT efforts to address disarmament. Early on, they dismissed the credibility of the Humanitarian Initiative, and refused to accept that new data shown by this process was useful. They also disregard informed views that their arsenals face risks of accidental detonation. Essentially, they remain 'wedded' to the process they preferred, the NPT's step-by-step approach, based on their own assessments of what they see as strategic stability (Rauf 2015), and bluntly refuse to consider the need for fundamental change.

The elimination of nuclear weapons is feasible, and with genuine commitment on the part of the nuclear states, can be done while protecting their security. As Shultz *et al.* (2008) have observed, there is good reason to believe that we can embark on building an international consensus on the ways to deter or respond to any attempt to break-out of a world with zero nuclear weapons. Technical processes of monitoring and verification improve with each passing year. And while there might be some strategists who will not re-examine many of their long-held assumptions, there are also many respected analysts who believe that a closely monitored and phased program of mutual and balanced reductions between the nine nuclear-armed states can succeed. There is also no reason to demand that the process of elimination has to be done quickly (although the patience of non-nuclear states will not last indefinitely). As various studies and reports have noted, a measured process involving all of the nuclear weapon states and buttressed by security assurances over an extended period of time will be required.[1] In any case, there are many fairly straightforward and cost-free measures that can be taken immediately to lessen the risks of accidental use.

Moreover, to believe that things cannot change is not rational or supportable; it neglects the importance of human agency and the history of substantial shifts, also based on humanitarian grounds, which have already taken place in global politics. The elimination of nuclear weapons does not require that these weapons be 'un-invented'; rather, it affirms that their possession and use can be managed by strong norms and institutions. Moving to a nuclear-free world requires us to take a leap of faith, but not doing so is likely to be far riskier in due course. Nuclear weapons and the promise of massive destruction might have become 'normalized' over the decades, but continuing with the status quo is simply too dangerous. Living under the indefinite threat of nuclear obliteration is an undesirable condition, an inevitable resignation to a doomed future. Leslie Paul Thiele, in his essay on the growth of civil society involvement in international politics, noted that 'nuclear deterrence (even with reduced arsenals) constitutes a peace founded on fear, or better said, an attempt to ground security in terror'. It is far better, he argued, to seek to transcend the politics of fear, to show a 'refusal to live in a Hobbesian world, a refusal to suffer the consequences of a politics founded on fear, which, by definition, is a politics not of participation, but of resignation' (Thiele 1993: 275).

Will rejecting nuclearism be enough?

Will merely rejecting nuclearism – which is essentially what the treaty, and the processes behind it, have done – make any real difference to the prospects for disarmament? It is true that the realities of hard power and the continuing reliance on nuclear weapons by certain states cannot easily be discounted. The outlawing of nuclear weapons represents a substantial, if still symbolic, challenge to the military doctrines and preferences of the dominant states. The new treaty may well constitute a key moment in redefining the global nuclear order, and as such, could become one of the most significant developments in international security since 1945, at least on a normative and declaratory level. It represents, as Nick Ritchie has observed, 'a withdrawal of consent by signatory governments for current practices that tacitly legitimise nuclear weapons' (Ritchie 2016: 55). The TPNW dispels any lingering view that a state possesses *carte blanche* sovereign 'rights' to do whatever it likes in the name of national security, regardless of the cost to others. Yet the treaty has no material means of compelling the nuclear weapon states to disarm. It does not signal any guarantee that these weapons will in fact be eliminated, or that they will never be used. It is entirely possible that even as the treaty dislodges the notion of nuclearism, the nuclear states may still do nothing to alter their possession of these weapons of massive destruction. While the TPNW has the potential to shift – and indeed already is shifting – the long-standing elements of nuclearism, this does not necessarily mean that this shift will result in disarmament.

Ultimately, the decision to change lies in the hands of the nuclear states. Rejecting nuclearism has been an essential process in signalling to these states that their behaviour will no longer be seen as acceptable. The 'business as usual' statements and policies of the nuclear states will now be subjected to unprecedented scrutiny, and nuclear arms control and disarmament discussions – at least at the multilateral level – will no longer be able to proceed in the way they did prior to the prohibition-treaty. Together with the processes which preceded it and which will follow it, the treaty might come to be the only possible way to change the view of nuclear weapons which has prevailed for decades: as a currency of power (Harrington de Santana 2009; Tannenwald 2019).

The ideas and practices of nuclearism, where absolute authority, hegemony, and exclusivity combined with the command of unparalleled destructive force, have been sharply contested. The TPNW has challenged and disrupted – if not yet replaced – the hegemonic discourse, the undemocratic nature of nuclear decision-making, the 'sacred cow' of nuclear weapon budgets, and the control of a nuclear order unassailable for decades. By generating voices and pressure from a widespread array of actors, the Humanitarian Initiative and its product, the Treaty on the Prohibition of Nuclear Weapons, have reshaped the contours of the nuclear weapon debate. The result has been the loss of legitimacy for nuclearism.

Indeed the treaty has forced the issue of the legitimacy of nuclear weapons directly into the open in a way that previous efforts have not been able to do. It has not required the consent of the nuclear weapon states; nor does it have to make any special concession towards these states based on their possession of nuclear weapons prior to 1967, as the NPT does. The new treaty is an essential step in the transformation towards a more rational, democratic, and humane approach to the problems that nuclear weapons pose. It has the capacity to move the world out of the status quo nuclear regime and into a potentially transformative regime. The norm enshrined in the treaty can have an important restraining effect, which should be recognized and celebrated. Still, this might not be enough to force a change in actual behaviour.

In this sense, we are only at the second stage of the three-stage disarmament process identified earlier in this book. Nuclear weapons have been stigmatized, and now delegitimized. This delegitimization is a norm which is likely to cascade as more states join the treaty, and especially if it comes to attract key state supporters. But the third part of the process, the elimination of the weapon in question, will only occur when the nuclear weapon states internalize this norm sufficiently and act to comply with it. The TPNW constitutes a clear legal effect, but it will also require a political decision to be taken by those states possessing nuclear weapons to move towards change. There is good reason to believe that such political decisions *can* be taken; in the same way that states have affected change in the international system earlier, determining particular practices and standards of behaviour, so too is it feasible that these states can create a viable non-nuclear future.

It must be remembered that nothing previously has been able to challenge nuclearism directly. Not even the numerous authoritative studies and reports which outlined the dangers and provided pathways to move to a process of phased, balanced, and verified reductions have been able to dislodge the habituated nature of nuclear weapons, nuclear deterrence, and nuclearism more generally. None of the Review Conferences of the NPT held since the Cold War ended has been able to exert pressure on the wizards of Armageddon. It has not been possible to persuade these states to implement even the relatively cost-free measures of reducing the prominence and value of nuclear weapons in their security doctrines, taking warheads off dangerous, high-alert levels, and providing guarantees to non-nuclear states that nuclear weapons would not be used against them.

Nuclearism will be discredited, but such a discrediting alone might not serve to force policy changes in the nuclear weapon states. We must be careful to differentiate between discrediting nuclearism – something that I believe the TPNW has done and will continue to do – and suggesting that nuclear states will inevitably accept this new casting and disarm. Nonetheless, it seems that without this discrediting, it will never be possible to persuade the nuclear states to alter their policies. Critics may be right in saying that regardless of any treaty – even one directed so clearly at the practices of the great powers – these states will always act as they choose, with little regard for moral or reputational consequences. This will not be the first time that large and powerful states in the international system have shown an indifference to emerging global norms. There is no guarantee that nuclear-armed states will listen to the rest of the world in this project, and it is entirely possible that we will end up living indefinitely within the precarious architecture constituted by these weapons. They might even be used in the near future. It might be that nuclear weapons will remain the most illogical, useless, expensive, undemocratic, and destructive project that humans have undertaken.

The Treaty on the Prohibition of Nuclear Weapons is no small achievement: it provides the explicit outlawing of a weapon which previously had not been unambiguously banned, a legal clarity which was lacking in the international system. And at the very least, it can represent one more hoped-for obstacle in the way of nuclear catastrophe. Shifting course away from such an event is precisely what the non-nuclear states and civil society actors have sought to do; by creating a treaty which further stigmatizes and firmly outlaws nuclear weapons, these agents of change are reclaiming fundamental rights which have long been obscured by the clouds of great power control and the normalization of a nuclearism which has, until now, defied serious challenge. Rejecting the normalization of nuclear weapons might not prevent an individual intent on launching these weapons, but by ensuring, now, that this normalization can no longer proceed without being challenged, it is probably the best mechanism we possess in the search for a nuclear weapon free world.

The stark reality is that if the new treaty and the clear refusal to give any legitimacy to nuclear weapons cannot ultimately change the position of those who hold these weapons, then there is probably little else that can do so either. The Humanitarian Initiative and the TPNW have provided the most compelling challenge ever to be mounted against nuclearism. But continued intransigence on the part of these states and an obstinate faith in the infallibility of deterrence means that nuclear catastrophe, by accident or by design, is likely to happen sooner or later. And if that does happen, its ramifications and its tragedy will diminish all of us.

Note

1 Many of the studies and commissions explored in earlier chapters have explored the technical and political aspects of moving to a nuclear weapon free world. An additional and excellent source is by Bruce Larkin (2008), which comprehensively lists problems, commonly held views (and myths) and proceeds to supply persuasive and informed responses to these.

References

Acheson, Ray. 2021. *Banning the Bomb: Smashing the Patriarchy!* Lanham: Rowman & Littlefield.
Acheson, Ray. 2018. 'Impacts of the Nuclear Ban: How Outlawing Nuclear Weapons is Changing the World', *Global Change, Peace and Security*, 30(2).
Acheson, Ray. 2016. 'Foregrounding Justice in Nuclear Disarmament: A Practitioner Commentary', *Global Policy*, 7(3).
Acheson, Ray. 2015. *Sex, Gender and Nuclear Weapons*. Reaching Critical Will/ International Campaign to Abolish Nuclear Weapons (ICAN).
Acheson, Ray. 2013. 'Editorial: Overcoming Obfuscation', *First Committee Monitor*, Number 4. Reaching Critical Will, 28 October. www.reachingcriticalwill.org/images/documents/Disarmament-fora/1com/FCM13/FCM-2013-4.pdf (accessed 17 January 2022).
Acheson, Ray, and Beatrice Fihn. 2013. 'Preventing Collapse: The NPT and a Ban on Nuclear Weapons', *Reaching Critical Will*, October. www.reachingcriticalwill.org/images/documents/Publications/npt-ban.pdf (accessed 17 January 2022).
Acheson, Ray, Thomas Nash, and Richard Moyes. 2014. *A Treaty Banning Nuclear Weapons: Developing a Legal Framework for the Prohibition and Elimination of Nuclear Weapons*. London: Article 36 and Reaching Critical Will. www.reachingcriticalwill.org/images/documents/Publications/a-treaty-banning-nuclear-weapons.pdf (accessed 17 January 2022).
Acheson, Ray, John Ainslie, Merav Datan, Hans Kristensen, Greg Mello, Zia Mian, Pavel Podvig, M. V. Ramana, and Hui Zhang. 2017. *Assuring Destruction Forever: 2017 Edition*. Reaching Critical Will, April. www.reachingcriticalwill.org/images/documents/Publications/modernization/assuring-destruction-forever-2017.pdf (accessed 17 January 2022).
Acronym Institute. 1998. *Reviewing the Non-Proliferation Treaty: Preparing for the Future: Information, Ideas and Documents on the Strengthened Review Process of the NPT for Participants to the Second PrepCom, Geneva, 27 April to 8 May, 1998*, Acronym Report No. 11 – April 1998. www.acronym.org.uk/old/archive/acro11.htm (accessed 17 January 2022).
Albanese, Anthony. 2018. 'Speech to the 48th National Conference of the Labor Party of Australia – Moving Support for the Nuclear Weapon Ban-Treaty', Adelaide, 18 December. https://anthonyalbanese.com.au/speech-moving-support-for-the-nuclear-weapon-ban-treaty-tuesday-18-december-2018 (accessed 17 January 2022).

References

Alcalde, Javier. 2014. 'Human Security and Disarmament Treaties: The Role of International Campaigns', *Global Policy* 5(2).

Aldrich, George H. 1994. 'From the St Petersburg Declaration to the Modern Law of War', in Nicholas Borsinger, ed., *125th Anniversary of the 1868 St Petersburg Declaration: International Symposium on the Law of War 1–2 December 1993, Summary of Proceedings*. Geneva: ICRC, 50–51.

Allan, Stuart. 1992. 'No Truth, No Apocalypse: Dismantling the Cultural Dynamics of Nuclearism in Official and News Discourse', PhD thesis, Carleton University. https://curve.carleton.ca/system/files/etd/ffbc64e6–5910–44b3–9422-a60d79838 ec8/etd_pdf/80acb8a6a3396928e11973d566fa4101/allan-otruthnoapocalypsedis mantlingtheculturaldynamics.pdf (accessed 17 January 2022).

Allen, Daniel R. 2015. 'The Only Way to Win: The Enduring Problem of Nuclear Deterrence', *Christian Scholars' Review*, 44(4).

Alliance for Nuclear Accountability. 2016. *Trillion Dollar Trainwreck: Out-of-Control US Nuclear Weapons Programs Accelerate Spending, Proliferation, Health and Safety Risks*, Report from the Weapons Communities of the Alliance for Nuclear Accountability, April. http://static1.squarespace.com/static/52311 edfe4b0830625de8366/t/570e52ce9f7266ca3cf4fd6d/1460556499601/trillion_ dollar_trainwreck.pdf (accessed 17 January 2022).

Alperovitz, Gar. 1996. *The Decision to Use the Atomic Bomb*. New York: Vintage.

Anderson, J. 2016. *Applying Jus In Bello to the Nuclear Deterrent*, Arms Control Wonk. www.armscontrolwonk.com/archive/1201208/applying-jus-in-bello-to-the-nuclear-deterrent/ (accessed 17 January 2022).

APLN. 2016. *APLN Statement on the Fifth Nuclear Test by the DPRK*, 10 September. www.a-pln.org/statements/statements_view/APLN_Statement_on_ the_5th_Nuclear_Test_by_the_D.P.R.K (accessed 17 January 2022).

Arbatov, Alexei G., and Vladimir Dvorkin. 2006. *Beyond Nuclear Deterrence: Transforming the US–Russian Equation*, Carnegie Endowment for International Peace.

Archer, Colin *et al.* 2016. *Move the Nuclear Weapons Money*, International Peace Bureau/Parliamentarians for Nuclear Nonproliferation and Disarmament/World Future Council.

Arkin, William. 2002. 'Secret Plan Outlines the Unthinkable', *Los Angeles Times*, 10 March. http://web.archive.org/web/20020315070751/ www.latimes.com/news/ opinion/la-op-arkinmar10.story (accessed 17 January 2022).

Arkin, William, and Hans Kristensen. 2020. 'US Deploys New Low-Yield Nuclear Submarine Warhead', Federation of American Scientists, 29 January. https://fas. org/blogs/security/2020/01/w76–2deployed/ (accessed 17 January 2022).

Arms Control Association. 2022. *Nuclear Weapons: Who Has What at a Glance*, January. www.armscontrol.org/factsheets/Nuclearweaponswhohaswhat (accessed 11 January 2022).

Arms Control Association. 2020. *The Nuclear Testing Tally*, Arms Control Association Fact Sheets and Briefs. www.armscontrol.org/factsheets/nucleartest-tally (accessed 17 January 2022).

Article 36. 2013a. *Humanitarian Impacts from a Single Nuclear Weapon Detonation on Manchester*. https://article36.org/wp-content/uploads/2013/02/ ManchesterDetonation.pdf (accessed 17 January 2022).

Article 36. 2013b. *Banning Nuclear Weapons Without the Nuclear Armed States*, Briefing Paper, October. www.article36.org/wp-content/uploads/2013/10/Banning-without.pdf (accessed 17 January 2022).

Australian Government, Department of Foreign Affairs and Trade. 1996. *Report of the Canberra Commission on the Elimination of Nuclear Weapons*, 13 August. http://dfat.gov.au/about-us/publications/international-relations/Pages/the-canberra-commission-on-the-elimination-of-nuclear-weapons.aspx (accessed 17 January 2022).

Avery, John Scales. 2013. *Nuclear Warfare as Genocide*, Nuclear Age Peace Foundation, 27 December. www.wagingpeace.org/nuclear-warfare-as-genocide/ (accessed 17 January 2022).

Barnett, Michael. 2005. 'Humanitarianism Transformed', *Perspectives on Politics*, 3(4).

Barnett, Michael, and Thomas Weiss, eds. 2008. *Humanitarianism in Question: Politics, Power, and Ethics*. Ithaca, NY: Cornell University Press.

Becker, Una, Harald Muller, and Simone Wisotzki. 2008. 'Democracy and Nuclear Arms Control: Destiny or Ambiguity?', *Security Studies*, 17(4).

Beckley, Michael. 2015. 'The Myth of Entangling Alliances: Reassessing the Security Risks of US Defense Pacts', *International Security*, 39(4).

Bederman, David J. 2009. 'International Law in the Ancient World', in David Armstrong, ed., *Routledge Handbook of International Law*. London: Routledge.

Benedict, Kennette. 2012. 'Democracy and the Bomb', *Bulletin of the Atomic Scientists*, 15 November.

Benedict, Kennette. 2011. 'A Democratic Theory of Disarmament', *Bulletin of the Atomic Scientists*, 19 November.

Berghofer, Julia. 2016. *The European Union and Nuclear Disarmament: A Sensitive Question*, Heinrich Boll Stiftung, 25 May. https://eu.boell.org/en/2016/05/25/european-union-and-nuclear-disarmament-sensitive-question (accessed 17 January 2022).

Berry, Ken et al. 2010. *Delegitimizing Nuclear Weapons. Examining the Validity of Nuclear Deterrence*. Monterey: Center for Nonproliferation Studies. www.files.ethz.ch/isn/116230/2010-05-delegitimizing_nuclear_weapons_may_2010.pdf (accessed 17 January 2022).

Best, Geoffrey. 1983. *Humanity in Warfare: Modern History of the International Law of Armed Conflicts*. New York: Columbia University Press.

Birch, Douglas. 2014. 'Nuclear Weapons Lab Employee Fired After Publishing Scathing Critique of the Arms Race'. https://publicintegrity.org/national-security/nuclear-weapons-lab-employee-fired-after-publishing-scathing-critique-of-the-arms-race/ (accessed 17 January 2022).

Biswas, Shampa. 2014. *Nuclear Desire: Power and the Postcolonial Nuclear Order*. Minneapolis: University of Minnesota Press.

Biswas, Shampa. 2001. 'Nuclear Apartheid as Political Position: Race as a Postcolonial Resource?', *Alternatives*, 26.

Black-Branch, Jonathan. 2021. *The Treaty on the Prohibition of Nuclear Weapons: Legal Challenges for Military Doctrines and Deterrence Policies*. Cambridge: Cambridge University Press.

Blackaby, Frank, and Tom Milne. 2000. *A Nuclear Weapon-Free World: Steps Along the Way*. Basingstoke: Macmillan.

Blechman, Barry. 2016. 'Obama Should Return his Nobel Peace Prize', *The National Interest*, 6 April. http://nationalinterest.org/feature/obama-should-return-his-nobel-peace-prize-15691 (accessed 17 January 2022).

Bolton, Matthew, and Elizabeth Minor. 2016a. 'The Humanitarian Initiative on Nuclear Weapons: An Introduction to *Global Policy*'s Special Section', *Global Policy*, 7(3).

Bolton, Matthew, and Elizabeth Minor. 2016b. 'The Discursive Turn Arrives in Turtle Bay: The International Campaign to Abolish Nuclear Weapons' Operationalization of Critical IR Theories', *Global Policy*, 7(3).

Bolton, M., H. Whall, A. Pytlak, H. Guerra, and K. E. James. 2014. 'The Arms Trade Treaty from a Global Civil Society Perspective: Introducing Global Policy's Special Section', *Global Policy*, 5(4).

Booth, Ken. 1999. 'Nuclearism, Human Rights and the Construction of Security', *The International Journal of Human Rights*, 3(2).

Booth, Ken. 1979. *Strategy and Ethnocentrism*. London: Routledge.

Booth, Ken, and Nicholas J. Wheeler. 2008. *The Security Dilemma: Fear, Cooperation, and Trust in World Politics*. London: Palgrave Macmillan.

Borger, Julian. 2020. 'US Staged "Limited" Nuclear Battle against Russia in War Game', *The Guardian*, 25 February. www.theguardian.com/world/2020/feb/24/limited-nuclear-war-game-us-russia (accessed 17 January 2022).

Borger, Julian. 2016. 'Nuclear Weapons Risk Greater Than in Cold War, says ex-Pentagon Chief', *The Guardian*, 8 January. www.theguardian.com/world/2016/jan/07/nuclear-weapons-risk-greater-than-in-cold-war-says-ex-pentagon-chief (accessed 17 January 2022).

Born, Hans. 2006. 'Civilian Control and Democratic Accountability of Nuclear Weapons', in Hans Born and Heiner Hanggi, eds, *Governing Nuclear Weapons: Democratic Accountability and Civilian Control of Nuclear Weapons*. Geneva: Geneva Centre for the Democratic Control of Armed Forces.

Born, Hans, Bates Gill, and Heiner Hanggi, eds. 2010. *Governing the Bomb: Civilian Control and Democratic Accountability and Civilian Control of Nuclear Weapons*. Oxford: SIPRI/Oxford University Press.

Borodavkin, A. 2014. 'Statement at the Plenary Meeting of the Conference on Disarmament', Permanent Representative of the Russian Federation to the United Nations Office and other International Organizations in Geneva, 21 January. www.reachingcriticalwill.org/images/documents/Disarmament-fora/cd/2014/Statements/part1/21Jan_Russia.pdf (accessed 17 January 2022).

Borrie, John. 2014a. 'Humanitarian Reframing of Nuclear Weapons and the Logic of a Ban', *International Affairs*, 90(3).

Borrie, John. 2014b. 'Changing the Discourse on Nuclear Weapons: What It Means for Campaigners and why It's Important', *ICAN Campaigners' Kit*. https://d3n8a8pro7vhmx.cloudfront.net/ican/pages/745/attachments/original/1575654831/Campaigners-Kit-Pernilla_final2.pdf?1575654831 (accessed 17 January 2022).

Borrie, John. 2009. *Unacceptable Harm: A History of how the Treaty to Ban Cluster Munitions was Won*. New York and Geneva: United Nations Institute for Disarmament Research.

Borrie, John, and Vanessa Martin Randin. 2006. *Thinking Outside the Box in Multilateral Disarmament and Arms Control Negotiations*. Geneva: UNIDIR. www.unidir.org/files/publications/pdfs/thinking-outside-the-box-in-multilateral-disarmament-and-arms-control-negotiations-329.pdf (accessed 17 January 2022).

Borrie, John, Anne Guro Dimmen, Torbjorn Graff Hugo, Camilla Waszink, and Kjolv Egeland. 2016. *Gender, Development and Nuclear Weapons: Shared Goals, Shared Concerns*. Geneva: UNIDIR. www.unidir.org/files/publications/pdfs/gender-development-and-nuclear-weapons-en-659.pdf (accessed 17 January 2022).

Borrie, John, Maya Brehm, Silvia Cattaneo, and David Atwood. 2009. *Learn, Adapt, Succeed: Potential Lessons from the Ottawa and Oslo Processes for Other Disarmament and Arms Control Challenges*. Geneva: UNIDIR. www.reachingcriticalwill.org/images/documents/Publications/BAC/chapter14.pdf (accessed 17 January 2022).

Boutros-Ghali, Boutros. 1994. 'The Landmine Crisis: A Humanitarian Disaster', *Foreign Affairs*, September/October. www.foreignaffairs.com/articles/1994-09-01/land-mine-crisis-humanitarian-disaster (accessed 21 January 2022).

Boutros-Ghali, Boutros. 1992. *An Agenda for Peace*. New York: United Nations.

Boyer, Paul. 1985. *By the Bomb's Early Light: American Thought and Culture at the Dawn of the Atomic Age*. New York: Pantheon.

Brixey-Williams, Sebastian, and Paul Ingram. 2017. *Responsible Nuclear Sovereignty and the Future of the Global Nuclear Order*. BASIC and Birmingham University. https://basicint.org/wp-content/uploads/2018/06/Brixey-Williams-and-Ingram-Responsible-Nuclear-Sovereignty-Report-PDF_FINAL-2017.pdf (accessed 21 January 2022).

Brodie, Janet Farrell. 2015. 'Radiation Secrecy and Censorship after Hiroshima and Nagasaki', *Journal of Social History*, 48(4).

Bryden, Alan. 2013. *International Law, Politics and Inhumane Weapons: The Effectiveness of Global Landmine Regimes*. London: Routledge.

Bugos, Shannon. 2020. 'CEND Establishes Two-year Work Program', *Arms Control Today*, January/February. www.armscontrol.org/act/2020-01/news/cend-establishes-two-year-work-program (accessed 17 January 2022).

Bukovansky, Mlada, Ian Clark, Robyn Eckersley, Richard Price, Christian Reus-Smit, and Nicholas J. Wheeler. 2012. *Special Responsibilities: Global Problems and American Power*. Cambridge: Cambridge University Press.

Bull, Hedley. 1980. 'The Great Irresponsibles? The United States, the Soviet Union and World Order', *International Journal*, 35(3).

Bull, Hedley. 1976. 'Arms Control and World Order', *International Security*, 1(1).

Bull, Hedley. 1961. *The Control of the Arms Race: Disarmament and Arms Control in the Missile Age*. London: Praeger/IISS.

Bulletin of the Atomic Scientists. 2015. *Nuclear Notebooks: Nuclear Arsenals of the World*. http://thebulletin.org/nuclear-notebook-multimedia (accessed 21 January 2022).

Burke, Anthony. 2009. 'Nuclear Reason: At the Limits of Strategy', *International Relations*, 23(4).
Bunn, George, and John B. Rhinelander, 2007. *Reykjavik Revisited: Toward a World Free of Nuclear Weapons*, World Security Institute and Lawyers Alliance for World Security. https://fsi-live.s3.us-west-1.amazonaws.com/s3fs-public/Bunn-Rhinelander-Reykjavik_Sept07.pdf (accessed 21 January 2022).
Burroughs, John. 2013. *Beyond International Humanitarian Law*, 22 April, NPT Preparatory Committee side-event, New York: United Nations.
Burroughs, John. 1997. *The (Il)legality of Threat or Use of Nuclear Weapons: A Guide to the Historic Opinion of the International Court of Justice*. Munster: Lit Verlag.
Burt, A. 2013. 'Statement on Nuclear Weapons', British Parliamentary Under Secretary of State for Foreign and Commonwealth Affairs, House of Commons Debate, 4 March. www.publications.parliament.uk/pa/cm201213/cmhansrd/cm130304/text/130304w0002.htm#130304w0002.htm_spnew24 (accessed 21 January 2022).
Butler, Lee. 2000. 'At the End of a Journey: The Risks of Cold War Thinking in a New Era', in John Baylis and Robert O'Neill, eds, *Alternative Nuclear Futures: The Role of Nuclear Weapons in the Post-Cold War World*. Oxford: Oxford University Press.
Butler, Lee. 1999. Speech at the University of Pittsburgh, 13 May. www.wagingpeace.org/general-george-lee-butler-university-of-pittsburgh-speech/ (accessed 17 January 2022).
Butler, Richard. 1996. *The Elimination of Nuclear Weapons: Reversing History's Greatest Accident*, The Sir Robert Madgwick Lecture, delivered at the University of New England, Armidale, 1 May. Armidale: University of New England Press.
Cahill, Kevin, ed. 1995. *Clearing the Fields: Solutions to the Global Landmines Crisis*. New York: Basic Books.
Cameron, M. A., R. J. Lawson, and B. W. Tomlin, eds. 1998. *To Walk Without Fear: The Global Movement to Ban Landmines*. Oxford: Oxford University Press.
Camilleri, Joseph, Michael Hamel-Green, and Fumihiko Yoshida. 2019. *The 2017 Nuclear Ban-Treaty: A New Path to Nuclear Disarmament*. Abingdon: Routledge.
Carlson, John. 2017. 'The Nuclear Weapons Ban-Treaty is Significant, but Flawed', *The Lowy Interpreter*, 11 July. www.lowyinstitute.org/the-interpreter/nuclear-weapon-ban-treaty-significant-flawed (accessed 21 January 2022).
Carlson, John. 2016. 'Why Australia Should Support Negotiations for a Nuclear Weapons Ban', *The Lowy Interpreter*, 30 August. www.lowyinstitute.org/the-interpreter/why-australia-should-support-negotiations-nuclear-weapon-ban (accessed 21 January 2022).
Carpenter, Charli, Sirin Duygulu, Alexander H. Montgomery, and Anna Rapp. 2014. 'Explaining the Advocacy Agenda: Insights from the Human Security Network', *International Organization*, 68(2).
Casey-Maslen, Stuart. 2019. *The Treaty on the Prohibition of Nuclear Weapons: A Commentary*. Oxford: Oxford University Press.

Cassese, Antonio. 2000. 'The Martens Clause: Half a Loaf or Pie in the Sky?', *European Journal of International Law*, 11(1).
Caughley, Tim. 2016. *Nuclear Disarmament Verification: Survey of Verification Mechanisms*. Geneva: UNIDIR. www.unidir.org/files/publications/pdfs/survey-of-verification-mechanisms-en-657.pdf (accessed 21 January 2022).
Caughley, Tim. 2012. *Humanitarian Impacts of Nuclear Weapons: Tracing Notions about Catastrophic Humanitarian Consequences*, Humanitarian Impact of Nuclear Weapons project paper no. 1, Geneva: UNIDIR. www.unidir.org/files/publications/pdfs/tracing-notions-about-catastrophic-humanitarian-consequences-en-412.pdf (accessed 21 January 2022).
Caughley, Tim, and Ghaukar Mukhatzanova. 2017. *Negotiation of a Nuclear Weapons Prohibition Treaty: Nuts and Bolts of a Ban*. Geneva: UNIDIR. https://heinonline-org.ezproxy.library.uq.edu.au/HOL/Page?collection=ustreaties&handle=hein.unl/ngnwpty0001&id=2&men_tab=srchresults (accessed 21 January 2022).
CCNR. 1996. *Statement by Generals and Admirals of the World Against Nuclear Weapons, 5 December 1996*. Reprinted by the Canadian Coalition for Nuclear Responsibility. www.ccnr.org/generals.html (accessed 21 January 2022).
Chang, Parris. 2016. 'Time is Not Right for US No First Use', *Bulletin of the Atomic Scientists*, 18 October.
Chilton, Paul. 1982. 'Nuke-speak: Nuclear Language, Culture, and Propaganda', in Crispin Aubrey, ed., *Nukespeak: The Media and the Bomb*. London: Comedia, 94–112.
Choubey, Deepti. 2010. 'Understanding the 2010 NPT Review Conference', Carnegie Endowment for International Peace, 3 June. http://carnegieendowment.org/2010/06/03/understanding-2010-npt-review-conference-pub-40910#2 (accessed 21 January 2022).
Cirincione, Joseph. 2016. 'The Historic UN Vote On Banning Nuclear Weapons', *The Huffington Post*, 27 October. www.huffingtonpost.com/joe-cirincione/historic-un-vote-on-banni_b_12679132.html (accessed 21 January 2022).
Cirincione, Joseph. 2015. 'What Happens When Our Nuclear Arsenal is Hacked?' *San Francisco Chronicle*, 17 June. www.sfchronicle.com/opinion/openforum/article/What-happens-when-our-nuclear-arsenal-is-hacked-6333739.php (accessed 21 January 2022).
Cirincione, Joseph. 1995. 'The Non-Proliferation Treaty and the Nuclear Balance', *Current History*, 94(592), 1 May.
Clinton, Bill. 1998. *Weekly Compilation of Presidential Documents*, 13 May, 853.
Clinton, Bill. 1995. White House Press Release, 11 May. 'Statement on Extension of the Nuclear Non-Proliferation Treaty', reprinted in *The American Presidency Project*. Santa Barbara: University of California, Santa Barbara. www.presidency.ucsb.edu/ws/index.php?pid=51348 (accessed 21 January 2022).
Cohn, Carol. 1987. 'Sex and Death in the Rational World of Defense Intellectuals', *Signs*, 12(4).
Cohn, Carol, Felicity Hill, and Sarah Ruddick. 2005. 'The Relevance of Gender for Eliminating Weapons of Mass Destruction', *Disarmament Diplomacy*, 80(1).

Cohn, Nathan, and Russell Rumbaugh. 2012. *Resolving Ambiguity: Costing Nuclear Weapons*, The Stimson Center, 17 September. www.stimson.org/content/resolving-ambiguity-costing-nuclear-weapons (accessed 21 January 2022).

Cooper, Neil. 2006. 'Putting Disarmament Back in the Frame', *Review of International Studies*, 32(2).

Corsi, Jessica. 2009. 'Towards Peace Through Legal Innovation: The Process and the Promise of the 2008 Cluster Munitions Convention: Recent Developments', *Harvard Human Rights Journal*, 22(1).

Craig, Campbell, and Jan Ruzicka. 2013. 'The Non-Proliferation Complex', *Ethics and International Affairs*, 27(3). www.cambridge.org/core/journals/ethics-and-international-affairs/article/the-nonproliferation-complex/1DD39ECAAD0E68093B204C5BC221CBDF/core-reader (accessed 21 January 2022).

Cramer, Ben. 2009. *Nuclear Weapons: At What Cost?* New York: International Peace Bureau.

Cronberg, Tanja. 2015. 'Why Does the EU Stay Silent on Nuclear Disarmament?', *Green European Journal*, 10, 1 March. www.greeneuropeanjournal.eu/why-does-the-eu-stay-silent-on-nuclear-disarmament/ (accessed 21 January 2022).

Crossette, Barbara, and George Perkovich. 2009. 'India: The Ultimate Test of Free-Market Democracy', in Michael Schiffer and David Shorr, eds, *Powers and Principles: International Leadership in a Shrinking World*. Lanham: Lexington Books.

Dahl, Robert. 1985. *Controlling Nuclear Weapons: Democracy Versus Guardianship*. Syracuse: Syracuse University Press.

Daley, Tad. 2010. *Apocalypse Never: Forging a Path to a Nuclear Weapons Free-World*. New Brunswick: Rutgers University Press.

Datan, Marev, Felicity Hill, Jürgen Scheffran, and Alyn Ware. 2007. *Securing Our Survival: The Case for a Nuclear Weapons Convention*. Cambridge, MA: Massachusetts. www.inesap.org/book/securing-our-survival (accessed 21 January 2022).

Davis Gibbons, Rebecca. 2018. 'The Humanitarian Turn in Nuclear Disarmament and the Treaty on the Prohibition of Nuclear Weapons', *The Non-Proliferation Review*, 25(1–2).

De Luce, Dan, and Reid Standish. 2016. 'Putin Throws Out the Old Nuclear Rules, Rattling Washington', *Foreign Policy*, 16 October. http://foreignpolicy.com/2016/10/16/putin-throws-out-the-old-nuclear-rules-rattling-washington-clinton-trump-arms-control/ (accessed 21 January 2022).

DeRensis, Hunter. 2019. 'The Danger of a Nuclear Catastrophe is Greater than during the Cold War', *The National Interest*, 7 August. https://nationalinterest.org/feature/danger-nuclear-catastrophe-greater-during-cold-war-72061 (accessed 21 January 2022).

Deudney, Daniel H. 2007. *Bounding Power: Republican Security Theory from the Polis to the Global Village*. Princeton, NJ: Princeton University Press.

Deudney, Daniel H. 1995. 'Nuclear Weapons and the Waning of the Real-State', *Daedalus*, 124.

Dewes, Kate, and Robert Green. 1999. 'The World Court Project: History and Consequences', *Canadian Foreign Policy Journal*, 7(1).

Dhanapala, Jayantha. 2013. 'The Permanent Extension of the NPT, 1995', in Andrew F. Cooper, Jorge Heine, and Ramesh Thakur, eds, *The Oxford Handbook of Modern Diplomacy*. Oxford: Oxford University Press.

Dhanapala, Jayantha, and Tariq Rauf, eds. 2016. *Reflections on the Treaty on the Non-Proliferation of Nuclear Weapons Review Conferences and the Future of the NPT*, SIPRI, September. www.sipri.org/sites/default/files/Reflections%20on%20 the%20NPT_Dhanapala%20and%20Rauf.pdf (accessed 21 January 2022).

Dhanapala, Jayantha, and Randy Rydell. 2005. *Multilateral Diplomacy and the NPT: An Insider's Account*. Geneva: UNIDIR.

Donnelly, John. 2017. 'Pentagon Panel Urges Trump Team to Expand Nuclear Options', Carnegie Endowment for International Peace, 7 February. http://carneg ieendowment.org/2017/02/07/pentagon-panel-urges-trump-team-to-expand-nucl ear-options-pub-67935 (accessed 21 January 2022).

Doyle, James E. 2017. 'On Integrating Conventional and Nuclear Planning', *Arms Control Today*, March. www.armscontrol.org/act/2017-03/arms-control-today/ integrating-conventional-nuclear-planning (accessed 21 January 2022).

Doyle, James E. 2013. 'Why Eliminate Nuclear Weapons?' *Survival*, 55(1). https:// cryptome.org/2014/08/55-1-02-Doyle.pdf (accessed 21 January 2022).

Doyle, Thomas. 2020. *Nuclear Ethics in the Twenty-First Century: Survival, Order, and Justice*. London: Rowman & Littlefield.

Doyle, Thomas. 2015. 'Moral and Political Necessities for Nuclear Disarmament: An Applied Ethical Analysis', *Strategic Studies Quarterly*, Summer.

Doyle, Thomas. 2010. 'Reviving Nuclear Ethics: A Renewed Research Agenda for the Twenty-First Century', *Ethics and International Affairs*, 24(3).

Doyle, Thomas. 2009. 'The Moral Implications of the Subversion of the Nonproliferation Treaty Regime', *Ethics and Global Politics*, 2(2). www.tandfonline.com/doi/full/10.3402/egp.v2i2.1916 (accessed 21 January 2022).

Duncanson, Claire, and Catherine Eschle. 2008. 'Gender and the Nuclear Weapons State: A Feminist Critique of the UK Government's White Paper on Trident', *New Political Science*, 30(4).

Dunworth, Treasa. 2015. 'Pursuing "Effective Measures" Relating to Nuclear Disarmament: Ways of Making a Legal Obligation a Reality', *International Review of the Red Cross*, 97(899). https://international-review.icrc.org/articles/ pursuing-effective-measures-relating-nuclear-disarmament-ways-making-legalobligation (accessed 21 January 2022).

Durkalec, Jacek. 2015. 'NATO Must Adapt to Address Russia's Nuclear Brinkmanship', *European Leadership Network*, 30 October. www.europeanleadershipnetwork.org/ nato-must-adapt-to-address-russias-nuclear-brinkmanship_3263.html (accessed 21 January 2022).

The Economist. 2015. 'The Unkicked Addiction: Despite Optimistic Attempts to Rid the World of Nuclear Weapons, the Threat They Pose to Peace is Growing', 7 March. www.economist.com/news/briefing/21645840-despite-optimisticattempts-rid-world-nuclear-weapons-threat-they-pose-peace (accessed 21 January 2022).

The Economist. 2010. 'Britain's Nuclear Weapons: Accounting and the Bomb', 30 July. www.economist.com/blogs/blighty/2010/07/britains_nuclear_weapons (accessed 21 January 2022).

Eden, Lynn. 2011. 'The US Nuclear Arsenal and Zero: Sizing and Planning for Use, Past, Present and Future', in Catherine Kelleher and Judith Reppy, eds, *Getting to Zero: the Path to Nuclear Disarmament.* Stanford Security Series, Stanford University.

Eden, Lynn. 2006. *Whole World on Fire: Organizations, Knowledge and Nuclear Weapons Devastation.* Ithaca: Cornell University Press.

Egeland, Kjolv. 2018. 'Banning the Bomb: Inconsequential Posturing or Meaningful Stigmatization?', *Global Governance*, 24(1).

Egeland, Kjølv. 2017. *A Nuclear Ban Treaty and Relations with Non-Party States*, 6 March. Geneva: United Nations.

Egeland, Kjolv, Torbjorn Graff Hugo, Magnus Lovold, and Gro Nystuen. 2018. 'The Nuclear Weapons Ban Treaty and the Non-Proliferation Regime', *Medicine, Conflict and Survival*, 34(2).

Eide, E. B. 2013. 'Chair's Summary, Conference on the Humanitarian Impact of Nuclear Weapons, Oslo, 4–5 Mar'. www.regjeringen.no/en/archive/Stoltenbergs-2nd-Government/Ministry-of-Foreign-Affairs/taler-og-artikler/2013/nuclear_summary.html?id=716343 (accessed 21 January 2022).

Eide, E. B. 2012. *Letter of Invitation to an International Conference on the Humanitarian Impact of Nuclear Weapons, from Espen Barth Eide*, Norwegian Minister of Foreign Affairs, 22 November.

Eland, Ivan. 1998. *No to NATO Expansion: Good Arguments Fall on Deaf Ears*, CATO Institute Commentary, 3 April. www.cato.org/publications/commentary/no-nato-expansion-good-arguments-fall-deaf-ears (accessed 21 January 2022).

Emmott, Robin. 2016. 'Risk of Nuclear War in Europe Growing, Warns Russian Ex-Minister', *Reuters*, 19 March. www.reuters.com/article/us-ukraine-crisis-russia-idUSKCN0WL0EV (accessed 21 January 2022).

English, John. 1998. 'The Ottawa Process: Paths Followed, Paths Ahead', *Australian Journal of International Affairs*, 52(2).

Erästö, Tytti, Ugnė Komžaitė, Petr Topychkanov. 2019. 'Operationalizing Nuclear Disarmament Verification', Stockholm: SIPRI. www.sipri.org/sites/default/files/2019-04/sipriinsight1904_0.pdf (accessed 21 January 2022).

Evangelista, Mathew. 2010. 'Stigmatize Nuclear Weapons as Genocidal, Then Abolish Them', 1 May. https://news.cornell.edu/stories/2010/03/evangelista-stigmatize-abolish-nuclear-weapons (accessed 21 January 2022).

Evans, Gareth. 1995. Testimony to the International Court of Justice, Verbatim Record.

Evans, Gareth, Tanya Ogilvie-White, and Ramesh Thakur. 2015. *Nuclear Weapons: The State of Play.* Canberra: ANU Press.

Falk, Richard A. 2018. 'Rethinking Nuclearism: Thirty Years Later', *Foreign Policy Journal*, 6 October. www.foreignpolicyjournal.com/2018/10/06/rethinking-nuclearism-thirty-years-later/ (accessed 23 January 2022).

Falk, Richard A. 2017. 'Challenging Nuclearism: The Nuclear Ban Treaty Assessed', *Asia-Pacific Journal*, 15(14). https://apjjf.org/2017/14/Falk.html (accessed 21 January 2022).

Falk, Richard A. 1995. 'Walking the Tightrope of International Humanitarian Law: Meeting the Challenge of Land Mines', in Kevin Cahill, ed., *Clearing the Fields: Solutions to the Global Landmines Crisis*. New York: Basic Books, 69–86.

Falk, Richard A. 1982a. 'Nuclear Weapons and the End of Democracy', *Praxis International*, 2.

Falk, Richard A. 1982b. 'The Political Anatomy of Nuclearism', in Robert J. Lifton and Richard A. Falk, eds, *The Indefensible Weapons: The Political and Psychological Case Against Nuclear Weapons*. New York: Basic Books.

Falk, Richard A. 1973. 'Environmental Warfare and Ecocide: Facts, Appraisal, and Proposals', *Bulletin of Peace Proposals*, 4(1). Oslo: Sage Publications.

Feinberg, Ashley. 2018. 'Exclusive: Here is a Draft of Trump's Nuclear Review. He Wants A Lot More Nukes', *Huffington Post*, 12 January. www.huffingtonpost.com.au/entry/trump-nuclear-posture-review-2018_us_5a4d4773e4b06d1621bce4c5 (accessed 23 January 2022).

Fihn, B., ed. 2013. *Unspeakable Suffering: The Humanitarian Impact of Nuclear Weapons*. Geneva: Reaching Critical Will. www.reachingcriticalwill.org/resources/publications-and-research/publications/7422-unspeakable-suffering-the-humanitarian-impact-of-nuclear-weapons (accessed 23 January 2022).

Fleck, Martin. 2016. 'PSR Builds Opposition to New Nuclear Arms Race', 20 June. www.psr.org/nuclear-weapons/blog/psr-mounts-opposition-to-new-nuclear-arms-race.html (accessed 23 January 2022).

Flockhart, Trine. 2013. 'NATO's Nuclear Addiction: Twelve Steps to "Kick the Habit"', *European Security*, 22(3).

Franck, James et al. 1945. *The Franck Report: Report of the Committee on Political and Social Problems Manhattan Project 'Metallurgical Laboratory'*, University of Chicago, 11 June. www.dannen.com/decision/franck.html (accessed 23 January 2022).

Franz, Broswimmer. 2002. *Ecocide: A Short History of Mass Extinction of Species*. London: Pluto Press.

Frear, T., L. Kulesa, and I. Kearns. 2014. *Dangerous Brinkmanship: Close Military Encounters Between Russia and the West in 2014*, European Leadership Network, November.

Freedman, Lawrence. 2013. 'Disarmament and Other Nuclear Norms', *The Washington Quarterly*, 36(2).

Freedman, Lawrence. 2004. *Deterrence*. Malden, MA: Polity Press.

Friedman, Leon, ed. 1972. *The Law of War: A Documentary History*. New York: Random House.

Friedman, Thomas L. 1998. 'Foreign Affairs: Now a Word from X', *New York Times*, 2 May. www.nytimes.com/1998/05/02/opinion/foreign-affairs-now-a-word-from-x.html (accessed 23 January 2022 [subscription only]).

Fritz, Jason. 2009. 'Hacking Nuclear Command and Control', Research Paper Commissioned by the International Commission on Nuclear Non-proliferation and Disarmament. www.icnnd.org/Documents/Jason_Fritz_Hacking_NC2.pdf (accessed 23 January 2022).

Gaillard, Emilie. 2016. *Emerging International Law: Future Generations and Ecocide*, Amicus presented at the International Peoples' Tribunal on the Nuclear Powers and the Destruction of Human Civilisation, 7 July, Sydney. www.unfoldzero.org/wp-content/uploads/Emerging-law-.EGAILLARD.pdf (accessed 23 January 2022).

Gamson, William. 1987. 'Review Essay: Nuclear Forgetting', *Contemporary Sociology*, 16(1).

Gandenberger, Mia, and Ray Acheson. 2016. 'Countries Which "Value Nuclear Weapons for Their Security" Undermine Progress in Nuclear Disarmament', *Global Research*, 6 August. www.globalresearch.ca/countries-that-value-nuclear-weapons-for-their-security-undermine-progress-in-nuclear-disarmament/5540006 (accessed 23 January 2022).

Garthoff, Raymond. 2000. 'Nuclear Weapons and the Cold War: Did Nuclear Weapons Prevent War or Increase its Risks?' in Frank Blackaby and Tom Milne, eds, *A Nuclear-Weapon-Free World: Steps Along the Way*. Basingstoke: Macmillan.

Gerson, Michael S. 2011. *The Future of US Nuclear Policy: The Case for No First Use*, Policy Brief, Harvard School of Government, Belfer Center, February. www.belfercenter.org/publication/future-us-nuclear-policy-case-no-first-use (accessed 23 January 2022).

Gilinsky, Victor. 2016. 'What If Nuclear Weapons Are Used?' *Bulletin of the Atomic Scientists*, 16 November. http://thebulletin.org/what-if-nuclear-weapons-are-used10183 (accessed 23 January 2022).

Giorgou, Eirini. 2018. 'Safeguards Provisions in the Treaty on the Prohibition of Nuclear Weapons', *Arms Control Law*, 11 April. https://armscontrollaw.com/2018/04/11/safeguards-provisions-in-the-treaty-on-the-prohibition-of-nuclear-weapons/ (accessed 23 January 2022).

Global Zero. 2016. *Nuclear Weapons Countries: Military Incidents*, March 2014 – November 2015. Updated 2017. www.globalzero.org/wp-content/uploads/2018/12/Global-Zero-Military-Incidents-Study.pdf (accessed 23 January 2022).

Global Zero. 2011. *Global Zero Technical Report: World Spending on Nuclear Weapons Surpasses $1 Trillion per Decade*, June. www.globalzero.org/wp-content/uploads/2020/01/GZ-Weapons-Cost-Global-Study.pdf (accessed 23 January 2022).

Goodby, James E. 2006. 'Looking Back: The 1986 Reykjavik Summit', *Arms Control Today*, September. www.armscontrol.org/act/2006-09/looking-back-1986-reykjavik-summit (accessed 23 January 2022).

Gowing, Margaret. 1974. *Independence and Deterrence: Britain and Atomic Energy, 1945–1952*. London: Macmillan.

Gowing, Margaret. 1973. 'Atomic Politics', *Nature*, 245, 26 October.

Graham, Thomas. 2002. *Disarmament Sketches: Three Decades of Arms Control and International Law*. Seattle: University of Washington Press.

Granoff, Jonathan. 2000. 'Nuclear Weapons, Ethics, Morals, and Law', *BYU Law Review*, 4.

Gray, Mark Allan. 1996. 'The International Crime of Ecocide', *California Western International Law Journal*, 26(2). http://scholarlycommons.law.cwsl.edu/cgi/viewcontent.cgi?article=1335&context=cwilj (accessed 23 January 2022).
Green, Leslie C. 2008. *The Contemporary Law of Armed Conflict*. Manchester: Manchester University Press.
Green, Robert. 2013. 'Shifting the Nuclear-Weapons Security Paradigm', in David Atwood and Emily J. Munro, eds, *Security in a World Without Nuclear Weapons: Visions and Challenges*. Routledge/GCSP Report.
Gusterson, Hugh. 2006. 'A Double Standard for Nuclear Weapons?' *MIT Audit of the Conventional Wisdom*, April. http://cis.mit.edu/sites/default/files/images/gusterson_audit.pdf (accessed 23 January 2022).
Gusterson, Hugh. 2001. 'Tall Tales and Deceptive Discourses', *Bulletin of the Atomic Scientists*, 57.
Gusterson, Hugh. 1999. 'Nuclear Weapons and the Other in the Western Imagination', *Cultural Anthropology*, 41(1).
Guven, Onar, and Sico van der Meer. 2015. *A Treaty Banning Nuclear Weapons and its Implications for the Netherlands*. Clingendael: Netherlands Institute of International Relations. www.asser.nl/media/2582/a-treaty-banning-nuclear-weapons-2015.pdf (accessed 23 January 2022).
Hall, Xanthe. 2012. *Ecocide: A Catastrophic Consequence of Nuclear Weapons*, International Physicians for the Prevention of Nuclear War, 28 October.
Ham, Paul. 2011. *Hiroshima Nagasaki: The Real Story of the Atomic Bombings and Their Aftermath*. New York: Thomas Dunne Books.
Hanson, Marianne. 2022. 'Power to the Have-Nots? The NPT and the Limits of a Treaty Hijacked by a Power-Over Model', *Contemporary Security Policy*, 43(1).
Hanson, Marianne. 2020. 'Think Things are Bad Now? Wait Until We Stumble into a Nuclear War', *Australian Outlook*, Australian Institute of International Affairs, 31 March. www.internationalaffairs.org.au/australianoutlook/think-things-are-bad-now-wait-until-we-stumble-into-a-nuclear-disaster/ (accessed 21 January 2022).
Hanson, Marianne. 2018. Normalizing Zero: the Humanitarian Road to the Prohibition Treaty, *Contemporary Security Policy*, 39(3).
Hanson, Marianne. 2012. 'The Advocacy States: Their Normative Role Before and After the US Call for Nuclear Zero', *The Nonproliferation Review*, 17(1).
Hanson, Marianne. 2005a. 'The Future of the NPT', *Australian Journal of International Affairs*, 59(3).
Hanson, Marianne. 2005b. 'Regulating the Possession and Use of Nuclear Weapons: Ideas, Commissions, and Agency in International Security Politics – The Case of the Canberra Commission', in Ramesh Thakur, Andrew F. Cooper, and John English, eds, *International Commissions and the Power of Ideas*. Tokyo: Nations University Press.
Hanson, Marianne. 2002. 'Nuclear Weapons as Obstacles to Security', *International Relations*, 16.
Hanson, Marianne. 1998. 'Russia and NATO Expansion: The Uneasy Basis of the Founding Act', *European Security*, 7(2).

Hanson, Marianne, and Carl J. Ungerer. 1999. 'The Canberra Commission: Paths Followed, Paths Ahead', *Australian Journal of International Affairs*, 53(1).
Hanson, Marianne, and Carl J. Ungerer. 1998. 'Promoting an Agenda for Nuclear Weapons Elimination: The Canberra Commission and Dilemmas of Disarmament', *Australian Journal of Politics and History*, 44(4).
Harknett, Richard J. 1996. 'Territoriality in the Nuclear Era', in Eleonore Kofman and Gillian Youngs, eds, *Globalization: Theory and Practice*. London: Pinter.
Harries, Matthew. 2017a. 'Nuclear Disarmament Agreements Haven't Worked: Is There Another Solution?' *Prospect Magazine*, 6 October. www.prospectmagazine.co.uk/magazine/banning-the-bomb-well-all-go-together (accessed 23 January 2022).
Harries, Matthew. 2017b. 'The Real Problem with a Nuclear Ban-Treaty', *Carnegie Endowment for International Peace*, 15 March. https://carnegieendowment.org/2017/03/15/real-problem-with-nuclear-ban-treaty-pub-68286 (accessed 23 January 2022).
Harrington de Santana, Anne. 2011. 'The Strategy of Non-Proliferation: Maintaining the Credibility of an Incredible Pledge to Disarm', *Millennium: Journal of International Studies*, 40(1).
Harrington de Santana, Anne. 2009. 'Nuclear Weapons as the Currency of Power: Deconstructing the Fetishism of Force', *The Nonproliferation Review*, 16(3).
Hashmi, Sohail, and Steven P. Lee, eds. 2004. *Ethics and Weapons of Mass Destruction: Religious and Secular Perspectives*. Cambridge: Cambridge University Press.
Hecht, Gabrielle. 2003. 'Globalization Meets Frankenstein? Reflections on Terrorism, Nuclearity, and Global Technopolitical Discourse', *History and Technology*, 19.
Helfand, Ira. 2016. 'The Growing Danger of Nuclear War and What We Can Do About It', Lecture delivered at the Judith Reppy Institute for Peace and Conflict Studies, Cornell University, 8 February. https://news.cornell.edu/stories/2016/02/nuclear-weapons-pose-greater-threat-climate-change (accessed 23 January 2022).
Helfand, Ira. 2013a. International Physicians for the Prevention of Nuclear War (IPPNW), *The Wider Impact: Long Term Effects on Health, Environment and Development*, Presentation for the International Campaign to Abolish Nuclear Weapons (ICAN), Oslo, 4 March. www.regjeringen.no/upload/UD/Vedlegg/Hum/hum_helfand.pdf (accessed 23 January 2022).
Helfand, Ira. 2013b. *Nuclear Famine – Two Billion at Risk? Global Impacts of Limited Nuclear War on Agriculture, Food Supplies, and Human Nutrition*, Physicians for the Prevention of Nuclear War/Physicians for Social Responsibility, November. www.psr.org/assets/pdfs/two-billion-at-risk.pdf (accessed 23 January 2022).
Helfand, Ira, and Robert Dodge. 2016. 'Op ed: Should we let an Unstable Person have Control of the Nuclear Arsenal?' *The Los Angeles Times*, 23 September. www.latimes.com/opinion/op-ed/la-oe-helfand-dodge-nuclear-weapon-question-20160923-snap-story.html (accessed 23 January 2022).

Helfand, Ira, and Philip Lederer. 2016. 'Administration is Wrong on Nuclear Weapons and Clinton, Trump are Silent', *CNN*, 4 November. http://edition.cnn.com/2016/11/03/opinions/nuclear-disarmament-election-helfand-lederer/ (accessed 23 January 2022).

Helfand, Ira, Arun Mitra, and Tilman Ruff. 2020. 'Will Covid-19 Save the World?', *Physicians for Social Responsibility*, 17 March. www.psr.org/blog/will-covid-19-save-the-world/ (accessed 23 January 2022).

Helfand, Ira, Tilman Ruff, Michael Marmot, Frances Hughes and Michael Moore. 2016a. 'Banning Nuclear Weapons is Crucial for Global Health', *The Guardian*, 28 September. www.theguardian.com/commentisfree/2016/sep/28/banning-nuclear-weapons-is-crucial-for-global-health (accessed 23 January 2022).

Helfand, Ira, Andy Haines, Tilman Ruff, Hans Kristensen, Patricia Lewis and Zia Mian. 2016b. 'The Growing Threat of Nuclear War and the Role of the Health Community', *World Medical Journal*, 62(3). www.researchgate.net/publication/312021837_The_Growing_Threat_of_Nuclear_War_and_the_Role_of_the_Health_Community (accessed 23 January 2022).

Hersey, John. 1946. 'Hiroshima', *The New Yorker*, 31 August.

Herz, John. 1958. *International Politics in the Atomic Age*. New York: Columbia University Press.

Herzog, Rudolph. 2013. *A Short History of Nuclear Folly: Mad Scientists, Dithering Nazis, Lost Nukes and Catastrophic Cover-Ups*. New York: Melville House.

Higgins, Polly. 2010. *Eradicating Ecocide: Laws and Governance to Prevent the Destruction of our Planet*. London: Shepheard-Walwyn.

Higgs, Robert. 1997. 'Can Nuclear Weapons be Scrapped?', *Independence Institute*, 9 May. www.independent.org/newsroom/article.asp?id=338 (accessed 23 January 2022).

Highsmith, Newell, and Mallory Stewart. 2018. 'The Nuclear Ban-Treaty: A Legal Analysis', *Survival*, 60(1).

Hilgartner, Stephen, Richard C. Bell, and Rory O'Connor. 1982. *Nukespeak: Nuclear Language, Visions and Mindset*. New York: Penguin.

Hoffmann-Axthelm, Leo. 2016. *Germany: In Defense of Nuclear Weapons?* Heinrich Boll Stiftung, 24 August. www.boell.de/en/2016/08/24/germany-defense-nuclear-weapons (accessed 23 January 2022).

Horsburgh, Nicola. 2015. *China and Global Nuclear Order: From Estrangement to Active Engagement*. Oxford: Oxford University Press.

Hubert, D. 2000. 'The Landmine Ban: A Case Study in Humanitarian Advocacy', *Humanitarianism and War Project*, Occasional Paper 42, Rhode Island: Watson Institute.

Hudson, William E. 2004. *American Democracy in Peril: Eight Challenges to America's Future*, 4th edn. Washington, DC: CQ Press.

Hulme, Karen. 2009. 'The 2008 Cluster Munitions Convention: Stepping out of the CW Process (Again)', *The International and Comparative Law Quarterly*, 58(1).

Human Rights Watch Arms Project. 1993. *Landmines: A Deadly Legacy*. New York: Human Rights Watch.

Huntley, Wade L., Mitsuru Kurosawa, and Kazumi Mizumoto, eds. 2004. *Nuclear Disarmament in the Twenty-First Century*. Hiroshima: Hiroshima Peace Institute.

Hynek, Nikola. 2007. 'Humanitarian Arms Control, Symbiotic Functionalism and the Concept of Middlepowerhood', *Central European Journal of International and Security Studies*, 1(2).

IBP/PPND/WFC. 2016. *Move the Nuclear Weapons Money: A Handbook for Civil Society and Legislators*, International Peace Bureau, Parliamentarians for Nuclear Non-proliferation and Disarmament, and World Future Council, October. www.unfoldzero.org/wp-content/uploads/pnnd-handbook-nuclear-spending-english_v04.pdf (accessed 23 January 2022).

ICAN. 2020. *Enough is Enough: 2019 Global Nuclear Weapons Spending*, Geneva. https://d3n8a8pro7vhmx.cloudfront.net/ican/pages/1549/attachments/original/1589365383/ICAN-Enough-is-Enough-Global-Nuclear-Weapons-Spending-2020-published-13052020.pdf?1589365383 (accessed 23 January 2022).

ICBL (International Campaign to Ban Landmines). 2012. *Timeline of the International Campaign to Ban Landmines*. Geneva: ICBL. www.icbl.org/media/916929/icb009_chronology_a5_v4-pages.pdf (accessed 23 January 2022).

ICC (International Criminal Court). 2016. *Policy Paper on Case Selection and Prioritisation*, Office of the Prosecutor, 15 September. www.icc-cpi.int/itemsDocuments/20160915_OTP-Policy_Case-Selection_Eng.pdf (accessed 23 January 2022).

ICJ (International Court of Justice). 1996. *Legality of the Threat or Use of Nuclear Weapons, Advisory Opinion of 8 July 1996*. The Hague: International Court of Justice.

ICNND (International Commission on Nuclear Non-proliferation and Disarmament). 2010. *Eliminating Nuclear Threats: A Practical Agenda for Global Policymakers*. www.icnnd.org/reference/reports/ent/contents.html (accessed 23 January 2022).

ICRC. 2018. Briefing Note. *Safeguards and the Treaty on the Prohibition of Nuclear Weapons*. safeguards-treaty-prohibition-nuclear-weapons-briefing-note-icrc.pdf (accessed 23 January 2022).

ICRC. 2011. Council of Delegates: Resolution 1, *Working Towards the Elimination of Nuclear Weapons*, 26 November. www.icrc.org/en/doc/resources/documents/report/nuclear-background-document-2011-11-26.htm (accessed 23 January 2022).

ICRC. 1999. *Protection of Victims of Armed Conflict through Respect of International Humanitarian Law*, Reference Document – 27th International Conference of the Red Cross and Red Crescent, Geneva, 31 October to 6 November. www.icrc.org/eng/resources/documents/misc/57jpzn.htm (accessed 23 January 2022).

ICRC. 1997. *Convention on the Prohibition of the Use, Stockpiling, Production and Transfer of Anti-Personnel Mines and on their Destruction*, 18 September, Geneva. https://ihl-databases.icrc.org/ihl/INTRO/580 (accessed 23 January 2022).

ICRC. 1996. *Anti-Personnel Landmines: Friend or Foe? A Study of the Military Use and Effectiveness of Anti-Personnel Mines*, commissioned by the International Committee of the Red Cross, Geneva. www.icrc.org/eng/assets/files/other/icrc_002_0654.pdf (accessed 23 January 2022).

ICRC. 1993. *Mines: A Perverse Use of Technology*. Geneva: ICRC.

ICRC. 1980. *Convention on Prohibitions or Restrictions on the Use of Certain Conventional Weapons Which May be Deemed to be Excessively Injurious or to Have Indiscriminate Effects*, 10 October, Geneva. www.icrc.org/applic/ihl/ihl.nsf/Treaty.xsp?action=openDocument&documentId=7A690F9945FF9ABFC12563CD002D6D8E (accessed 23 January 2022).

ICRC. 1977. *Protocols Additional to the Geneva Conventions of 12 August 1949*, 8 June, Geneva. www.icrc.org/eng/assets/files/other/icrc_002_0321.pdf (accessed 23 January 2022).

ICRC. 1925. *Protocol for the Prohibition of the Use of Asphyxiating, Poisonous or Other Gases, and of Bacteriological Methods of Warfare*, 17 June, Geneva. https://ihl-databases.icrc.org/ihl/WebART/280-380001?OpenDocument (accessed 23 January 2022).

ICRC. 1907. *Convention (IV) Respecting the Laws and Customs of War on Land and its Annex: Regulations Concerning the Laws and Customs of War on Land*, 18 October, The Hague. www.icrc.org/applic/ihl/ihl.nsf/0/1d1726425f6955aec125641e0038bfd6 (accessed 23 January 2022).

ICRC. 1899a. *Final Act of the International Peace Conference*, 29 July, The Hague. www.icrc.org/applic/ihl/ihl.nsf/Article.xsp?action=openDocument&documentId=8FCF14D950797012C12563CD00515C0A (accessed 23 January 2022).

ICRC. 1899b. *Convention (II) with Respect to the Laws and Customs of War on Land and its Annex: Regulations Concerning the Laws and Customs of War on Land*, 29 July, The Hague. https://ihl-databases.icrc.org/ihl/INTRO/150?OpenDocument (accessed 23 January 2022).

ICRC. 1868. *Declaration Renouncing the Use, in Time of War, of Certain Explosive Projectiles*, 29 November/11 December, Saint Petersburg. www.icrc.org/applic/ihl/ihl.nsf/Article.xsp?action=openDocument&documentId=568842C2B90F4A29C12563CD0051547C (accessed 23 January 2022).

ICRC. 1863. *The Lieber Instructions for the Government of Armies of the United States in the Field, prepared by Francis Lieber, Promulgated as General Orders Number 100 by President Lincoln*, 24 April. www.icrc.org/ihl/INTRO/110 (accessed 23 January 2022).

Ifft, Edward M., and David A. Koplow. 2021. 'Legal and Political Myths of the Treaty on the Prohibition of Nuclear Weapons', *Bulletin of the Atomic Scientists*, May.

IHRC (International Human Rights Clinic). 2018. 'Nuclear Umbrella Arrangements and the Treaty on the Prohibition of Nuclear Weapons', *Human Rights Program at Harvard Law School*, June. http://hrp.law.harvard.edu/wp-content/uploads/2018/06/Nuclear_Umbrella_Arrangements_Treaty_Prohibition.pdf (accessed 23 January 2022).

IPB/PNND/WFC. 2016. *Move the Nuclear Weapons Money: a Handbook for Civil Society and Legislators*, International Peace Bureau/Parliamentarians for Nuclear Nonproliferation and Disarmament and World Future Council. www.worldfuturecouncil.org/wp-content/uploads/2016/10/IBP_PNND_WFC_2016_Move-the-nuclear-weapons-money.pdf (accessed 23 January 2022).

IISS. 2015. *NPT Review: Failure Underlines Challenges Ahead*, Strategic Comments, 4 June.

Isachenkov, Vladimir. 2020. 'New Russian Policy Allows Use of Atomic Weapons against Non-nuclear Strike', *Defense News*, 2 June. www.defensenews.com/global/europe/2020/06/02/new-russian-policy-allows-use-of-atomic-weapons-against-non-nuclear-strike/ (accessed 23 January 2022).

Izewicz, Paulina. 2016. 'The Nuclear Ban Treaty and its Possible Ramifications', International Institute for Strategic Studies, IISS Voices, 1 November.

Janis, Irving. 1972. *Victims of Groupthink: A Psychological Study of Foreign Policy Decisions and Fiascoes*. Boston: Houghton Mifflin.

Japan, Ministry of Foreign Affairs. 1999. *Facing Nuclear Dangers: An Action Plan for the 21st Century*, The Report of the Tokyo Forum for Nuclear Non-Proliferation and Disarmament. www.mofa.go.jp/policy/un/disarmament/forum/tokyo9907/ (accessed 23 January 2022).

Joeck, Neil. 2016. 'Obama's Disappointing Nuclear Security Legacy', *Foreign Policy*, 12 April.

Johnson, Rebecca and Daniela Varano. 2015. 'NPT: Nuclear Colonialism Versus Democratic Disarmament', *Open Democracy*, 21 May. www.opendemocracy.net/5050/rebecca-johnson-daniela-varano/npt-nuclear-colonialism-versus-democratic-disarmament (accessed 23 January 2022).

Johnson, Rebecca. 2013a. 'Banning Nuclear Weapons: This Time Lip Service Will Not Be Enough', *Open Democracy*, 26 February. www.opendemocracy.net/5050/rebecca-johnson/banning-nuclear-weapons-this-time-lip-service-will-not-be-enough (accessed 23 January 2022).

Johnson, Rebecca. 2013b. 'Statement to the Open-ended Working Group on Nuclear Disarmament, May 21', Acronym Institute for Disarmament Diplomacy.

Johnson, Rebecca. 2012. 'Changing the Game to Achieve Nuclear Disarmament', *IPS*, 12 December.

Johnson, Rebecca. 2011. *Nuclear Weapons and International Humanitarian Law: Pursuing Disarmament as Humanitarian Action*, Presentation made at ISODARCO, Andalo, Italy, January.

Johnson, Rebecca. 2000a. 'The 2000 NPT Review Conference: A Delicate, Hard-Won Compromise', *Disarmament Diplomacy*, 46, May.

Johnson, Rebecca. 2000b. 'Summits That Cheat Security', *Disarmament Diplomacy*, 61.

Johnson, Rebecca. 2000c. *Nuclear Disarmament in the Twenty-first Century*, presentation made at the International Symposium, 29 July. Hiroshima Peace Institute. www.peace.hiroshima-cu.ac.jp/symposium/20000714/ (accessed 23 January 2022).

Jones, Frank L. 2013. '"The High Priest of Deterrence": Sir Michael Quinlan, Nuclear Weapons and the Just War Tradition', *Logos: A Journal of Catholic Thought and Culture*, 16(3).

Jowit, Juliette. 2010. 'British Campaigner Urges UN to Accept "Ecocide" as International Crime', *The Guardian*, 10 April. www.theguardian.com/environment/2010/apr/09/ecocide-crime-genocide-un-environmental-damage (accessed 23 January 2022).

Joyner, Dan. 2016a. 'US Pressured NATO States to Vote No to the Ban Treaty – Including with Legal Argument', *Arms Control Law*, 29 November. https://armscontrollaw.com/2016/11/29/u-s-pressured-nato-states-to-vote-no-to-the-ban-treaty-including-with-legal-argument/ (accessed 23 January 2022).

Joyner, Dan. 2016b. 'U.N. General Assembly Decides to Convene a Nuclear Weapons Ban Conference', *Arms Control Law*, 31 October. https://armscontrollaw.com/2016/10/31/u-n-general-assembly-decides-to-convene-a-nuclear-weapons-ban-conference/ (accessed 23 January 2022).

Joyner, Dan. 2015. 'An Alternative to Another Set of Unkept NPT Review Conference Promises – Collective Withdrawal', *Arms Control Law*, 19 April. https://armscontrollaw.com/2015/04/19/an-alternative-to-another-set-of-unkept-npt-review-conference-promises-collective-withdrawal/ (accessed 23 January 2022).

Kahn, Herman. 1984. *Thinking About the Unthinkable in the 1980s*. New York: Simon & Schuster.

Kahn, Herman. 1962. *Thinking About the Unthinkable*. Horizon Press.

Kahn, Paul W. 1998/1999. 'Nuclear Weapons and the Rule of Law', *NYU Journal of International Law and Politcs*, 31.

Kamp, Karl-Heinz. 1995. 'The Folly of Rapid NATO Expansion', *Foreign Policy*, 98.

Kane, Chen, and Gaukhar Mukhatzhanova. 2013. *What is the Israel Nuclear Capabilities (INC) Resolution? Why is it Controversial?* Center for Nonproliferation Studies/Vienna Center for Disarmament and non-proliferation, Fact Sheet #2. www.nonproliferation.org/wp-content/uploads/2013/09/130911_cns_iaea_factsheet_middle_east.pdf (accessed 24 January 2022).

Kaplan, Fred. 1983. *The Wizards of Armageddon*. New York: Simon & Schuster.

Karem, Mahmoud. 2013. 'Missed Opportunities to Rid the Middle East of WMD', *Open Democracy*, 24 June. www.opendemocracy.net/mahmoud-karem/missed-opportunities-to-rid-middle-east-of-wmd (accessed 24 January 2022).

Keating, Fiona. 2016. 'Genocide Memorial Day 2016: Nuclear Weapons Are "An Existential Threat to Humanity"', *International Business Times*, 26 January. www.ibtimes.co.uk/genocide-memorial-day-2016-nuclear-weapons-are-existential-threat-humanity-1538233 (accessed 24 January 2022).

Keating, Paul. 1998. *Eliminating Nuclear Weapons: A Survival Guide for the 21st Century*, Public Lecture, University of New South Wales, 25 November. www.keating.org.au/shop/item/eliminating-nuclear-weapons---25-november-1998 (accessed 24 January 2022).

Keck, Margaret, and Kathryn Sikkink. 1999. 'Transnational Advocacy Networks in International and Regional Politics', *International Social Science Journal*, 51(159).

Kelle, Alexander. 1995. 'The Nuclear Non-Proliferation Regime After the NPT Extension Conference: The Tasks Ahead', *The International Spectator*, 30(4).

Kelleher, Catherine, and Judith Reppy, eds. 2011. *Getting to Zero: The Path to Nuclear Disarmament*, Stanford Security Series, Stanford University.

Kellenberger, Jacob. 2010. *Bringing the Era of Nuclear Weapons to an End*, 20 April. www.icrc.org/en/doc/resources/documents/statement/nuclear-weapons-statement-200410.htm (accessed 24 January 2022).

Khan, Kamhran, and Kevin Sullivan. 1998. 'Indian Blasts Bring World Condemnation', *The Washington Post*, 13 May. www.washingtonpost.com/archive/politics/1998/05/13/indian-blasts-bring-world-condemnation/112e024f-0c41-491c-89c8-5d5f54236fa1/ (accessed 24 January 2022).

Kile, Shannon. 2016. *Global Nuclear Weapons: Downsizing but Modernizing*. Stockholm: SIPRI. www.sipri.org/media/press-release/2016/global-nuclear-weapons-downsizing-modernizing (accessed 24 January 2022).

Kimball, Daryl. 2016. 'Take Nuclear First Use Off the Table', *Arms Control Today*, 30 June. www.armscontrol.org/ACT/2016_07/Focus/Take-Nuclear-First-Use-Off-the-Table (accessed 24 January 2022).

Kmentt, Alexander. 2021. *The Treaty Prohibiting Nuclear Weapons: How It Was Achieved*. Abingdon: Routledge.

Knopf, Jeffrey. 2012. 'NGOs, Social Movements and Arms Control', in Robert E. Williams and Paul R. Viotti, eds, *Arms Control: History, Theory and Policy*. Santa Barbara: Praeger.

Krause, K. 2011. 'Leashing the Dogs of War: Arms Control from Sovereignty to Governmentality', *Contemporary Security Policy*, 32(1).

Krepon, Michael. 2016. 'The Humanitarian Pledge, Nuclear Weapons, and the Laws of War', *Arms Control Wonk*, 4 June. www.armscontrolwonk.com/archive/1201449/the-humanitarian-pledge-nuclear-weapons-and-the-laws-of-war/ (accessed 24 January 2022).

Krieger, David. 2013. *Zero: The Case for Abolishing Nuclear Weapons*. Santa Barbara: Nuclear Age Peace Foundation.

Krieger, David. 2011. *The High Costs of Nuclear Weapons*, Nuclear Age Peace Foundation. 31 October. www.wagingpeace.org/the-high-costs-of-nuclear-arsenals/ (accessed 24 January 2022).

Krieger, David. 2009. *Preventing Omnicide*, Nuclear Age Peace Foundation, 29 October. www.wagingpeace.org/preventing-omnicide/ (accessed 24 January 2022).

Kristensen, Hans. 2015. 'Nuclear Arsenals: Current Developments, Trends and Capabilities', *International Review of the Red Cross*, 97(899).

Kristensen, Hans. 2014. 'NATO Nuclear Weapons Security Costs Expected to Double', Federation of American Scientists, March. www.fas.org/blogs/security/2014/03/nato-nuclear-costs/ (accessed 24 January 2022).

Kristensen, Hans. 2009. *START Follow-On: What SORT of Agreement?* Federation of American Scientists (FAS) Blogs, 8 July. http://fas.org/blogs/security/2009/07/start/ (accessed 24 January 2022).

Kristensen, Hans, and Matt Korda. 2020a. 'United States Nuclear Forces 2020: Nuclear Notebooks', *Bulletin of the Atomic Scientists*, 13 January.

Kristensen, Hans, and Matt Korda. 2020b. 'Russian Nuclear Forces 2020', *Bulletin of the Atomic Scientists*, 9 March. www.tandfonline.com/doi/full/10.1080/00963402.2020.1728985 (accessed 24 January 2022).

Kristensen, Hans M., and Matthew G. McKinzie. 2015. 'Nuclear Arsenals: Current Developments, Trends and Capabilities', *International Review of the Red Cross*, 97(899), 563–599. https://international-review.icrc.org/articles/nuclear-arsenals-current-developments-trends-and-capabilities (accessed 24 January 2022).

Kristensen, Hans, and Robert S. Norris. 2021. *Status of World Nuclear Forces*, Federation of American Scientists. https://fas.org/issues/nuclear-weapons/status-world-nuclear-forces/ (accessed 24 January 2022).

Kristensen, Hans, and Robert S. Norris. 2014. 'Slowing Nuclear Weapon Reductions and Endless Nuclear Weapon Modernizations: A Challenge to the NPT', *Bulletin of the Atomic Scientists*, 70(4).

Kristensen, Hans M., Matthew McKinzie, and Theodore A. Postol. 2017. 'How US Nuclear Force Modernization is Undermining Strategic Stability: The Burst-Height Compensating Super-Fuze', *The Bulletin of Atomic Scientists*, 1 March.

Kroenig, Matthew. 2016. *The Renewed Russian Nuclear Threat and NATO Nuclear Deterrence Posture*, Atlantic Council Issue Brief, February. www.atlanticcouncil.org/in-depth-research-reports/issue-brief/russian-nuclear-threat/ (accessed 24 January 2022).

Kroenig, Matthew, and Walter Slocombe. 2014. *Why Nuclear Deterrence Still Matters to NATO*, Atlantic Council, 14 August. www.atlanticcouncil.org/publications/issue-briefs/why-nuclear-deterrence-still-matters-to-nato (accessed 24 January 2022).

Kutchesfahani, Sara Z. 2019. *Global Nuclear Order*. Abingdon: Routledge.

Kuznick, Peter J. 2007. 'Prophets of Doom or Voices of Sanity? The Evolving Discourse of Annihilation in the First Decade and a Half of the Nuclear Age', *Journal of Genocide Research*, 9(3).

LALN (Latin American and Caribbean Leadership Network). 2016. *Terror Unleashed: An Assessment of Global and National Impacts of a Nuclear Terrorist Attack*. Buenos Aires: NPS Global Foundation/LALN.

The Landmines Monitor. 2020. www.the-monitor.org/en-gb/reports/2020/landmine-monitor-2020/major-findings.aspx (accessed 24 January 2022).

Lang, Berel. 1986. 'Genocide and Omnicide: Technology at the Limits', in Avner Cohen and Steven Lee, eds, *Nuclear Weapons and the Future of Humanity: The Fundamental Questions*. New Jersey: Rowman and Allanheld.

Larkin, Bruce. 2008. *Designing Denuclearization: An Interpretive Encyclopedia*. New Brunswick: Transaction Publications.

Larrinaga, Miguel de, and Claire Turenne Sjolander. 1998. '(Re)presenting Landmines from Protector to Enemy: The Discursive Framing of a New Multilateralism', *Canadian Foreign Policy Journal*, 5(3).

The Laws of War on Land (The Oxford Manual). 1880. 9 September. Reprinted by the ICRC. https://ihl-databases.icrc.org/applic/ihl/ihl.nsf/Treaty.xsp?action=openDocument&documentId=40371257507EBB71C12563CD002D6676 (accessed 24 January 2022).

Lebow, Richard Ned, and Janice Gross Stein. 1995. 'Deterrence and the Cold War', *Political Science Quarterly*, 110(2).

Lee, Stephen. 1985. 'The Morality of Nuclear Deterrence: Hostage Holding and Consequences', *Ethics*, 95(3).

Lennane, Richard. 2016. 'Ban the Bomb: An Australian Response', *Bulletin of the Atomic Scientists*, 13 October. https://journals.sagepub.com/doi/full/10.1177/0096340214555079 (accessed 24 January 2022).

Lennane, Richard. 2015. 'Nuclear Addiction, Co-Dependence and Learned Helplessness', *Wildfire*. www.wildfire-v.org/p101.html (accessed 24 January 2022).

Lewis, Jeffrey. 2016. 'Putin's Doomsday Machine', *Foreign Policy*, 12 November. http://foreignpolicy.com/2015/11/12/putins-doomsday-machine-nuclear-weapon-us-russia/ (accessed 24 January 2022).

Lewis, Patricia. 2015. 'The NPT Review Conference and the Future of Nuclear Disarmament: Q&A', Comments made at the IISS/EU Non-Proliferation Consortium Conference, 12 November. www.youtube.com/watch?v=KcCIR5RVKOg (accessed 24 January 2022).

Lewis, Patricia. 2013. 'Foreword', in B. Fihn, ed., *Unspeakable Suffering: The Humanitarian Impact of Nuclear Weapons*. Geneva: Reaching Critical Will. www.reachingcriticalwill.org/resources/publications-and-research/publications/7422-unspeakable-suffering-the-humanitarian-impact-of-nuclear-weapons (accessed 24 January 2022).

Lewis, Patricia, Beyza Unal, and Sasan Aghlani. 2016. *Nuclear Disarmament: The Missing Link in Multilateralism*. London: Chatham House. www.chathamhouse.org/publication/nuclear-disarmament-missing-link-multilateralism#sthash.fwIUOCUQ.dpuf (accessed 24 January 2022).

Lewis, Patricia, Benoit Pelopidas, and Heather Williams. 2014. *Too Close for Comfort: Cases of Near-Nuclear Use and Options for Policy*, 28 April. London: Chatham House/Royal Institute of International Affairs. www.chathamhouse.org/publications/papers/view/199200 (accessed 24 January 2022).

Lieu, Ted, and Robert Markey. 2016. 'Congressman Lieu and Senator Markey Introduce the Restricting First Use of Nuclear Weapons Act', *Office of Rep. Ted Lieu*, 27 September.

Lifton, Robert J., and Richard A. Falk. 1982. *Indefensible Weapons: The Political and Psychological Case Against Nuclearism*. New York: Basic Books.

Lifton, Robert J., and Eric Markusen. 1990. *The Genocidal Mentality: Nazi Holocaust and Nuclear Threat*. New York: Basic.

Lothe-Eide, Stein Ivar. 2014. *A Ban On Nuclear Weapons: What's In It For Nato? Why Nato States Should Not Be Worried About A Ban On Nuclear Weapons*. ILPI. http://web.archive.org/web/20190517155612/http://nwp.ilpi.org/?p=2296 (accessed 24 January 2022).

Lynch, Aaron. 1996. *Thought Contagion: How Belief Spreads through Society: The New Science of Memes*. New York: Basic Books.

MacFarlane, S. Neil. 2000a. 'Preface', in Don Hubert, 'The Landmine Ban: A Case Study in Humanitarian Advocacy', *Humanitarianism and War Project*, Occasional Paper 42, Rhode Island: Watson Institute, xii.

MacFarlane, S. Neil. 2000b. *Politics and Humanitarian Action*, Occasional Paper 41, Providence: Watson Institute. https://reliefweb.int/sites/reliefweb.int/files/resources/2613C33E244F3547C1256C2500529E30-politics_brown_jul2000.pdf (accessed 24 January 2022).

MacFarlane, S. Neil, and Thomas G. Weiss. 2000. 'Political Interests and Humanitarian Action', *Security Dialogue*, 10(1). (accessed 21 January 2022).

Mack, D. 2014. *What Next? Thoughts for Global Civil Society Working On Arms Control and Armed Violence Reduction*. Sao Paulo: Souda Paz.

Maddock, Shane J. 2010. *Nuclear Apartheid: The Quest for American Atomic Supremacy from World War II to the Present*. Chapel Hill: University of North Carolina Press.

Maguire, Richard. 2007a. 'From the Guest Editor: The Nuclear Weapon and Genocide: The Beginning of a Discussion', *Journal of Genocide Research*, 9(3).

Maguire, Richard. 2007b. 'The Use of Weapons: Mass Killing and the United Kingdom Government's Nuclear Weapons Programme', *Journal of Genocide Research*, 9(3).

Marin-Bosch, Miguel. 1998. 'Europe's Nuclear Family', *Bulletin of the Atomic Scientists*, 54(1). https://books.google.com.au/books?id=xwwAAAAAMBAJ&pg=PA35&lpg=PA35&dq=come+to+mean+embracing+NATO%E2%80%99s+pro-nuclear+posture%E2%80%99,+resulting+in+%E2%80%98the+NATO-+ization+of+EU+foreign+and+defence+policies&source=bl&ots=eX0AnDTvZW&sig=x-G8ANtyQR73QQ6TOkbZjZswHa8&hl=en&sa=X&ved=0ahUKEwiBk5qiytXQAhXIRY8KHbjjBCwQ6AEIGTAA#v=onepage&q&f=false (accessed 24 January 2022).

Markey, Edward. 2021a. 'Senator Markey and Rep. Lieu Announce Reintroduction of Bill to Limit US President's Ability to Start a Nuclear War', Press Release, Ed Markey, 19 January. www.markey.senate.gov/news/press-releases/01/19/2021/senator-markey-and-rep-lieu-announce-reintroduction-of-bill-to-limit-us-presidents-ability-to-start-a-nuclear-war (accessed 23 January 2022).

Markey, Edward. 2021b. 'Sen. Markey and Rep. Blumenauer Announce Legislation to Cut $73 Billion from Bloated Nuclear Weapons Budget', 24 May. www.markey.senate.gov/news/press-releases/senator-markey-and-rep-blumenauer-announce-legislation-to-cut-73-billion-from-bloated-nuclear-weapons-budget (accessed 23 January 2022).

Markey, Edward. 2015. 'Sen. Markey and Rep. Blumenauer Introduce Bicameral Legislation to Cut $100 Billion from Wasteful Nuclear Weapons Budget', 23 March. www.markey.senate.gov/news/press-releases/sen-markey-and-rep-blumenauer-introduce-bicameral-legislation-to-cut-100-billion-from-wasteful-nuclear-weapons-budget (accessed 23 January 2022).

Markusen, Eric. 2007. 'Appendix: Article Abstract by Eric Markusen: The Genocidal Nature of Nuclear War', *Journal of Genocide Research*, 9(3).

Martin, Susan B. 2013. 'The Continuing Value of Nuclear Weapons: a Structural Realist Analysis', *Contemporary Security Policy*, 34(1).

Martin, Kevin, and Jay Coghlan. 2013. 'Days of Blank Checks are over for Nuclear Weapons Establishment', *The Hill's Congress Blog*, 26 April. http://thehill.com/blogs/congress-blog/economy-a-budget/296397-days-of-blank-checks-are-over-for-nuclear-weapons-establishment (accessed 24 January 2022).

Mathur, Piyush. 2001. 'Nuclearism: The Contours of a Political Ecology', *Social Text*, 19(1).

Matthew, R. A. 2003. 'Middle Power and NGO Partnerships: The Expansion of World Politics', in K. R. Rutherford, S. Brem, and R. A. Matthew, eds, *Reframing the Agenda: The Impact of NGO and Middle Power Cooperation in International Security Policy*, London: Praeger.

MccGwire, Michael. 2006. 'Comfort Blanket or Weapon of War: What is Trident for?' *International Affairs*, 82(4).

MccGwire, Michael. 1985. 'Deterrence: The Problem – Not the Solution', *International Affairs*, 62(1).

Mecklin, John. 2022. 'It is 100 Seconds to Midnight', *Bulletin of the Atomic Scientists*, 20 January. https://thebulletin.org/doomsday-clock/current-time/ (accessed 31 January 2022).

Mecklin, John. 2016. 'Introduction: Practical Nuclear Questions in an Unusual Presidential Election', *Bulletin of the Atomic Scientists*, 72(5), 273. http://dx.doi.org/10.1080/00963402.2016.1216495 (accessed 24 January 2022).

Mecklin, John. 2015. 'Disarm and Modernize', *Foreign Policy*, 211.

Mehta, Aaron. 2016. 'Senators Urge Obama to Cancel Nuclear Cruise Missile', *Defense News*, 22 July. www.defensenews.com/congress/2016/07/21/senators-urge-obama-to-cancel-nuclear-cruise-missile/ (accessed 24 January 2022).

Meron, Theodor. 2000. 'The Martens Clause, Principles of Humanity, and Dictates of Public Conscience', *The American Journal of International Law*, 94(1).

Merrick, Rob. 2017. 'Theresa May Would Fire UK's Nuclear Weapons as a "First Strike", Says Defence Secretary Michael Fallon', *The Independent*, 24 April. www.independent.co.uk/news/uk/politics/theresa-may-nuclear-weapons-first-strike-michael-fallon-general-election-jeremy-corbyn-trident-labour-cnd-a7698621.html (accessed 24 January 2022).

Meyer, David S. 1995. 'Framing National Security: Elite Public Discourse on Nuclear Weapons During the Cold War', *Political Communication*, 12.

Meyer, Paul, and Tom Sauer. 2018. 'The Nuclear Ban Treaty: A Sign of Global Impatience', *Survival*, 60(2).

Miller, Steven E. 2002. 'The Utility of Nuclear Weapons and the Strategy of No-First-Use', Working Paper, London Workshop on No-First-Use of Nuclear Weapons, Pugwash Meeting, 15–17 November. https://pugwashconferences.files.wordpress.com/2018/02/200211_london_nws_paper_miller.pdf (accessed 25 January 2022).

Mills, Michael J., Owen B. Toon, Julia Lee-Taylor, and Alan Robock. 2014. 'Multidecadal Global Cooling and Unprecedented Ozone Loss Following a Regional Nuclear Conflict', *Earth's Future*, 2(4). http://onlinelibrary.wiley.com/doi/10.1002/2013EF000205/abstract (accessed 24 January 2022).

Minor, Elizabeth. 2015. 'Changing the Discourse on Nuclear Weapons: The Humanitarian Initiative', *International Review of the Red Cross*, 97(899), 711–730.

Monbiot, George. 2020. 'Let's Nuke the Virus', *The Guardian*, 8 April.

Monin, Lydia, and Andrew Gallimore. 2002. *The Devil's Garden: The Story of Landmines*. London: Random House/Pimlico.

Moore, Mike. 1996. 'A Boost for Abolition', *Bulletin of the Atomic Scientists*, December.

Mortimer, Caroline. 2016. 'What is Britain's Nuclear Deterrent? Why Does it Need Replacing? How Much Will it Cost?' *The Independent*, 19 July.

www.independent.co.uk/news/uk/politics/trident-vote-submarine-nuclear-missile-deterrent-what-is-it-replacement-how-much-cost-debate-a7142881.html (accessed 24 January 2022).

Moxley, Charles J., John Burroughs, and Jonathan Granoff. 2010/2011. 'Nuclear Weapons and Compliance with International Humanitarian Law and the Nuclear Non-Proliferation Treaty', *Fordham International Law Journal*, 34.

Mueller, Harald, and Carmen Wunderlich. 2020. 'Nuclear Disarmament without the Nuclear Weapon States', *Daedalus*, Spring. www.amacad.org/publication/nuclear-disarmament-without-nuclear-weapon-states-nuclear-weapon-ban-treaty (accessed 26 January 2022).

Mueller, John. 1988. 'The Essential Irrelevance of Nuclear Weapons: Stability in the Postwar World', *International Security*, 13(2).

Mukhatzhanova, Gaukhar, and William Potter. 2012. *Nuclear Politics and the Non-Aligned Movement*, Adelphi Papers, Number 427. London: IISS.

Mumford, Lewis. 1946. 'Gentlemen, You are Mad!', *Macleans*, 1 June. https://archive.macleans.ca/article/1946/6/1/gentlemen-you-are-mad (accessed 26 January 2022).

Murphy, Tom. 2016. 'The DPRK and a Nuclear No-First-Use Policy', *The Strategist*, ASPI, 22 July. www.aspistrategist.org.au/dprk-nuclear-no-first-use-policy/ (accessed 24 January 2022).

Mutimer, David. 2000. *The Weapons State: Proliferation and the Framing of Security*. Boulder: Lynne Rienner.

Nadel, Alan. 1995. *Containment Culture: American Narratives, Postmodernism and the Atomic Age*. Durham, NC: Duke University Press.

Nadelmann, Ethan. 1990. 'Global Prohibition Regimes: The Evolution of Norms in International Society', *International Organization*, 44(4).

NATO. 2010. *Active Engagement, Modern Defence: Strategic Concept for the Defence and Security of the Members of the North Atlantic Treaty Organization Adopted by Heads of State and Government at the NATO Summit in Lisbon*, 19–20 November. www.nato.int/nato_static_fl2014/assets/pdf/pdf_publications/20120214_strategic-concept-2010-eng.pdf (accessed 25 January 2022).

Nielsen, Jenny, and Marianne Hanson. 2014. *The European Union and the Humanitarian Initiative in the 2015 Non-Proliferation Treaty Review Cycle*, EU Non-Proliferation Consortium, Non-Proliferation Paper 41, Stockholm International Peace Research Institute, 14 December. www.sipri.org/publications/2014/eu-non-proliferation-papers/european-union-and-humanitarian-initiative-2015-nonproliferation-treaty-review-cycle (accessed 24 January 2022).

Nobelprize. 1997. *The Nobel Peace Prize 1997*, Nobelprize.org. www.nobelprize.org/nobel_prizes/peace/laureates/1997/press.html (accessed 26 January 2022).

Norway Ministry of Foreign Affairs. 2013. *Conference*. www.regjeringen.no/en/dep/ud/selected-topics/humanitarian-efforts/humimpact_2013.html?id=708603 (accessed 26 January 2022).

NTI (Nuclear Threat Initiative). 2002. *Nuclear Posture Review – Report*, 31 July. https://uploads.fas.org/media/Excerpts-of-Classified-Nuclear-Posture-Review.pdf (accessed 26 January 2022).

Nuclear Information Service. 2017. *Playing with Fire: Nuclear Weapons Incidents and Accidents in the United Kingdom*, February. www.nuclearinfo.org/wp-content/uploads/2020/09/playing-with-fire-report-FINAL.pdf (accessed 26 January 2022).

Nuclear Weapons Ban Monitor. 2018. *TPNW Status and Compliance*. Norwegian Peoples' Aid. www.icanw.org/nuclear_weapons_ban_monitor_2018 (accessed 24 January 2022).

Nye, Joseph. 1986. *Nuclear Ethics*. New York: Macmillan/Free Press.

Nystuen, Gro, and Stuart Casey-Maslen, eds. 2010. *The Convention on Cluster Munitions: A Commentary*. Oxford: Oxford University Press.

Obama, Barack. 2009. *Remarks by President Barack Obama in Prague as Delivered*, The White House, Office of the Press Secretary, 5 April. https://obamawhitehouse.archives.gov/video/The-President-in-Prague#transcript (accessed 26 January 2022).

Oberleitner, Gerd. 2015. *Human Rights in Armed Conflict: Law, Practice, Policy*. Cambridge: Cambridge University Press.

Ogilvie-White, Tanya. 2014. *On Nuclear Deterrence: The Correspondence of Sir Michael Quinlan*. London: International Institute of Strategic Studies.

Ogilvie-White, Tanya. 2013. *Australia and the Non-Proliferation and Disarmament Initiative: Difficult Times for Disarmament Diplomacy*, January, ASPI Policy Analysis. www.aspi.org.au/report/australia-and-non-proliferation-and-disarmament-initiative-difficult-times-disarmament (accessed 26 January 2022).

Ogilvie-White, Tanya, and David Santoro, eds. 2012. *Slaying the Nuclear Dragon: Disarmament Dynamics in the Twenty-First Century*. Athens, GA: University of Georgia Press.

O'Hanlon, Michael E. 2016. *Order From Chaos: In Support of Nuclear No-First-Use*, Brookings Institution, 19 August. www.brookings.edu/blog/order-from-chaos/2016/08/19/in-support-of-nuclear-no-first-use/ (accessed 26 January 2022).

O'Hanlon, Michael E. 2010. *A Skeptic's Case for Nuclear Disarmament*. Washington, DC: Brookings Institution Press.

Onderco, Michael, and Leopoldo Nuti, eds. 2020. *Extending the NPT? A Critical Oral History of the 1995 Review and Extension Conference*. Washington, DC: Wilson Center. www.wilsoncenter.org/sites/default/files/media/uploads/documents/Extending%20the%20NPT%20-%20A%20Critical%20Oral%20History%20of%20the%201995%20Review%20and%20Extension%20Conference.pdf (accessed 26 January 2022).

O'Neill, Robert. 2007. *World Order Under Stress: Issues and Initiatives for the 21st Century*, Cunningham Lecture. Canberra: The Academy of the Social Sciences in Australia.

O'Neill, Robert, and David N. Schwartz. 1987. *Hedley Bull on Arms Control*. New York: St Martin's Press.

OPCW (Organisation for the Prohibition of Chemical Weapons). 1996. *Text of the Chemical Weapons Convention: Convention on the Prohibition of the Development, Production, Stockpiling and Use of Chemical Weapons and on Their Destruction*. www.opcw.org/chemical-weapons-convention/preamble/ (accessed 26 January 2022).

Oppenheimer, Robert J. 1946. 'Atomic Weapons', *Proceedings of the American Philosophical Society*, 29 January.

OSCEPA (Organisation for Security and Cooperation in Europe – Parliamentary Assembly). 2016. *Tbilisi Declaration and Resolutions Adopted by the OSCE Parliamentary Assembly at The Twenty-Fifth Annual Session*, Tblisi, 16 July. www.oscepa.org/documents/all-documents/annual-sessions/2016-tbilisi/declaration-24/3371-tbilisi-declaration-eng/file (accessed 26 January 2022).

Parrish, Will, and Darwin Bond Graham. 2009. 'Anti-Nuclear Nuclearism', *Foreign Policy in Focus*, 12 January. https://fpif.org/anti-nuclear_nuclearism/ (accessed 26 January 2022).

Paul, T. V. 2010. 'Taboo or Tradition? The Non-Use of Nuclear Weapons in International Politics', *Review of International Studies*, 36.

PAX. 2019. *Producing Mass Destruction: Private Companies and the Nuclear Weapon Industry*, Utrecht, May. www.dontbankonthebomb.com/wp-content/uploads/2019/05/2019_Producers-Report-FINAL.pdf (accessed 27 January 2022).

PAX. 2018. *Don't Bank on the Bomb*. Utrecht: PAX. www.dontbankonthebomb.com/2018_report_web/ (accessed 16 January 2022).

PAX. 2017. *Banning Investment: An Explicit Prohibition on the Financing of Nuclear Weapons Producers*, 17 March. www.un.org/disarmament/ptnw/pdf/A%20CONF.229%202017%20NGO%20WP.5%20Ban_financing_UNSubmission%20from%20PAX.pdf (accessed 26 January 2022).

PAX. 2016a. *Don't Bank on the Bomb: A Global Report on the Financing of Nuclear Weapons Producers*. Utrecht: PAX/ICAN. www.dontbankonthebomb.com/wp-content/uploads/2016/12/2016_Report_final.pdf (accessed 26 January 2022).

PAX. 2016b. *UN Resolution Calls for a Nuclear Weapons Ban*, 29 September. https://nonukes.nl/un-resolution-calls-nuclear-weapons-ban/ (accessed 27 January 2022).

PAX. 2016c. *NATO and a Nuclear Ban: Completely Compatible with Legal Obligations, Even While Delegitimizing Deterrence*, October. https://nonukes.nl/wp-content/uploads/2016/10/NATO-and-a-nuclear-ban_PAX_October-2016.pdf (accessed 26 January 2022).

PAX. 2016d. *Statement: Nuclear Weapons Ban Negotiations – Four Calls to Governments for a Human-Centered Treaty*, 26 May. https://paxchristi.net/wp-content/uploads/2019/10/170303-statement-nuclear-weapons-ban-negotiations.pdf (accessed 26 January 2022).

Payne, Keith. 2015. 'US Nuclear Weapons and Deterrence', *Air and Space Power Journal*, July/August. http://search.proquest.com.ezproxy.library.uq.edu.au/docview/1711201548?OpenUrlRefId=info:xri/sid:primo&accountid=14723 (accessed 26 January 2022).

Payne, Keith B., and Colin Gray. 1980. 'Victory is Possible', *Foreign Affairs*, 36.

Pelopidas, Benoit. 2021. 'The Birth of Nuclear Eternity', in Sandra Kemp and Jenny Andersson, eds, *Futures*. Oxford: Oxford University Press.

Pelopidas, Benoit. 2015. 'A Bet Portrayed as a Certainty: Reassessing the Added Deterrent Value of Nuclear Weapons', in George P. Shultz and James E. Goodby, ed, *The War that Must Never be Fought: Dilemmas of Nuclear Deterrence*. Stanford: Hoover Institution Press.

Pelopidas, Benoit. 2011. 'The Oracles of Proliferation: How Experts Maintain a Biased Historical Reading that Limits Policy Innovation', *The Nonproliferation Review*, 18(1).

Perry, William. 2016. 'Former Secretary of Defense William J. Perry Discusses the Dangers of Nuclear War at All Souls Unitarian Church, October 24, 2016'. www.wjperryproject.org/notes-from-the-brink/william-perry-speaks-at-all-souls (accessed 26 January 2022).

Perry, William. 2015. *My Journey at the Nuclear Brink*. Stanford: Stanford University Press.

Perry, William, and Tom Collina. 2020. *The Button: The New Nuclear Arms Race and Presidential Power from Truman to Trump*. Dallas: BenBella Books.

Pifer, Steven. 2020. 'Weapons, Opportunity Costs, Covid-19 and Avoiding Nuclear War', *The National Interest*, 11 May. https://nationalinterest.org/feature/weapons-opportunity-costs-covid19-and-avoiding-nuclear-war-153181 (accessed 26 January 2022).

Pilat, Joseph, and Robert E. Pendley, eds. 1995. *1995: A New Beginning for the NPT?* Center for National Security Studies, Los Alamos National Laboratory/Springer.

Pilat, Joseph, and Robert E. Pendley, eds. 1990. *Beyond 1995: The Future of the NPT Regime*. New York: Plenum Books.

PNND. 2017. *Prohibiting the Financing of Nuclear Weapons Production, Working Paper for the United Nations Conference to Negotiate a Legally Binding Instrument to Prohibit Nuclear Weapons, Leading Towards their Total Elimination*, Submitted by the Basel Peace Office, Parliamentarians for Nuclear Non-proliferation and Disarmament and Unfold Zero, March. www.unfoldzero.org/wp-content/uploads/Working-paper-on-prohibiting-the-financing-of-nuclear-weapons-production.pdf (accessed 26 January 2022).

Portela, Clara. 2003. 'The Role of the EU in the Non-Proliferation of Nuclear Weapons: The Way to Thessaloniki and Beyond', Peace Research Institute Frankfurt (PRIF) Reports 65. www.hsfk.de/fileadmin/HSFK/hsfk_downloads/prif65.pdf (accessed 26 January 2022).

Powell, Colin. 2010. 'Introductory Statements to the Film, *The Nuclear Tipping Point*'. www.youtube.com/watch?v=Kwz4hlEKPjA (accessed 26 January 2022).

Powell, Colin. 1995. *My American Journey*. New York: Random House.

Powers, Gerard. 2015. 'From Nuclear Deterrence to Disarmament: Evolving Catholic Perspectives', *Arms Control Today*, May. www.armscontrol.org/ACT/2015_05/Features/From-Nuclear-Deterrence-to-Disarmament-Evolving-Catholic-Perspectives (accessed 26 January 2022).

Pretorius, Joelien, and Tom Sauer. 2021. 'Ditch the NPT', *Survival*, 63(4). Price, Richard. 2007. 'Nuclear Weapons Don't Kill People, Rogues Do', *International Politics*, 44(2).

Price, Richard. 1998. 'Reversing the Gun Sights: Transnational Civil Society Targets Landmines', *International Organization*, 52(3).

Price, Richard. 1995. 'A Genealogy of the Chemical Weapons Taboo', *International Organization*, 49(1).

Price, Richard, and Nina Tannenwald. 1996. 'Norms and Deterrence: The Nuclear and Chemical Weapons Taboos', in Peter J. Katzenstein, ed., *The Culture of National Security: Norms and Identity in World Politics*, New York: Columbia University Press.

Princeton University. 2019. 'Science and Global Security Program', *Plan A*, September. https://sgs.princeton.edu/the-lab/plan-a (accessed 26 January 2022).

Proxmire, William. 1985. 'Cleaning up Procurement: Why Military Contracting is Corrupt', *New York Times*, 15 December.

Pullinger, Stephen, and Gerrard Quille. 2003. 'The European Union: Seeking Common Ground for Tackling Weapons of Mass Destruction', *Disarmament Diplomacy*, 74.

Quinlan, Michael. 2009. *Thinking About Nuclear Weapons: Principles, Problems, Prospects*. Oxford: Oxford University Press.

Quilop, Raymond. 2016. 'No First Use: Best to Maintain Ambiguity', *Bulletin of the Atomic Scientists*, 18 October.

Randin, Vanessa Martin. 2006. 'Diplomats, Civil Society and Academia: Some Thoughts on the Limits of the Discourse', in John Borrie and Vanessa Randin, eds, *Thinking Outside the Box in Multilateral Disarmament and Arms Control Negotiations*. Geneva: UNIDIR.

Rappert, Brian. 2006. *Controlling the Weapons of War: Politics, Persuasion, and the Prohibition of Inhumanity*. London: Routledge.

Rauf, Tariq. 2017. *Engagement on Nuclear Disarmament between Nuclear Weapon-Possessing States and Non-Nuclear States*, Working Paper, SIPRI, Hiroshima Prefecture, May. https://hiroshimaforpeace.com/wp-content/uploads/2019/09/sipri2017.pdf (accessed 26 January 2022).

Rauf, Tariq. 2016. 'Assessing the 2015 Review Conference', in Jayantha Dhanapala and Tariq Rauf, eds, *Reflections on the Treaty on the Non-Proliferation of Nuclear Weapons: Review Conferences and the Future of the NPT*. Stockholm: SIPRI. www.sipri.org/sites/default/files/Reflections%20on%20the%20NPT_Dhanapala%20and%20Rauf.pdf (accessed 26 January 2022).

Rauf, Tariq. 2015. 'The NPT Review Conference: Setting the Record Straight', 24 June. Stockholm: SIPRI. www.sipri.org/node/384 (accessed 26 January 2022).

Rauf, Tariq. 2000. 'The 2000 NPT Review Conference', *The Nonproliferation Review*, Spring.

Rauf, Tariq, and Jayantha Dhanapala. 2016. 'Conclusions: The Future of the NPT', in Jayantha Dhanapala and Tariq Rauf (eds), *Reflections on the Treaty on the Non-Proliferation of Nuclear Weapons: Review Conferences and the Future of the NPT*. Stockholm: SIPRI. www.sipri.org/sites/default/files/Reflections%20on%20the%20NPT_Dhanapala%20and%20Rauf.pdf (accessed 26 January 2022).

Rauf, Tariq, and Rebecca Johnson. 1995. 'After the NPT's Indefinite Extension: The Future of the Global Non-Proliferation Regime', *The Nonproliferation Review*, Fall. www.nonproliferation.org/wp-content/uploads/npr/raufjo31.pdf (accessed 26 January 2022).

RCW (Reaching Critical Will). 2021. *Bringing Feminist Perspectives to Disarmament*. www.reachingcriticalwill.org/resources/publications-and-research/research-projects/10637-gender-and-disarmament (accessed 26 January 2022).

Reif, Kingston. 2019. 'Trump Budget Boosts Nuclear Effort', *Arms Control Today*, April. www.armscontrol.org/act/2019-04/news/trump-budget-boosts-nuclear-efforts (accessed 26 January 2022).

Reif, Kingston. 2018a. *US Nuclear Modernization Programs*, Arms Control Association, Fact Sheets and Brief, August. www.armscontrol.org/factsheets/USNuclearModernization (accessed 26 January 2022).

Reif, Kingston. 2018b. 'Trump Seeks Expanded Nuclear Capabilities', *Arms Control Today*, March. www.armscontrol.org/act/2018-03/news/trump-seeks-expanded-nuclear-capabilities (accessed 26 January 2022).

Reif, Kingston. 2016a. 'The Case for No-First-Use', *Arms Control Today*, 5 October. www.thecipherbrief.com/column_article/the-case-for-no-first-use (accessed 26 January 2022).

Reif, Kingston. 2016b. 'UN Approves Start of Nuclear Ban Talks', *Arms Control Today*, November. www.armscontrol.org/ACT/2016_11/News/UN-Approves-Start-of-Nuclear-Ban-Talks (accessed 26 January 2022).

Rendall, Matthew. 2007. 'Nuclear Weapons and Intergenerational Exploitation', *Security Studies*, 16(4).

Republic of the Marshall Islands. 2014. *Application Instituting Proceedings Against the United Kingdom submitted on 24 April 2014 by the Republic of the Marshall Islands to the International Court of Justice re 'Obligation to pursue in good faith and conclude negotiations leading to nuclear disarmament'*. www.icj-cij.org/public/files/case-related/160/160-20140424-APP-01-00-EN.pdf (accessed 26 January 2022).

Reuters. 2012. 'Middle East Nuclear Talks Will Not Occur Next Month: US', 23 November. www.reuters.com/article/us-nuclear-middleast-idUSBRE8AN01L20121124 (accessed 26 January 2022).

Rieffer-Flanagan, Barbara Ann. 2009. 'Is Neutral Humanitarianism Dead? Red Cross Neutrality Walking the Tightrope of Neutral Humanitarianism', *Human Rights Quarterly*, 31(4).

Rietiker, Daniel. 2018. *Humanization of Arms Control: Paving the Way for a World Free of Nuclear Weapons*. Abingdon: Routledge.

Rinna, Anthony. 2015. *Nuclear Weapons, Financing, and Russia's Armed Forces Reform*, BASIC (British American Security Information Council), 17 February.

Ritchie, Nick. 2019. 'A Hegemonic Nuclear Order: Understanding the Ban Treaty and the Power Politics of Nuclear Weapons', *Contemporary Security Policy*, 40(4), 31 January.

Ritchie, Nick. 2017a. 'The "Real" Problem with the Ban-Treaty? It Challenges the *Status Quo*', Carnegie Endowment for International Peace, 3 April. https://carnegieendowment.org/2017/04/03/real-problem-with-ban-treaty-it-challenges-status-quo-pub-68510 (accessed 26 January 2022).

Ritchie, Nick. 2017b. 'A Rebuttal to Critics of the Nuclear Weapons Ban Treaty', *Bulletin of the Atomic Scientists*, 24 July. https://thebulletin.org/commentary/rebuttal-critics-nuclear-weapon-ban-treaty10967 (accessed 26 January 2022).

Ritchie, Nick. 2016. 'Delegitimising Nuclear Violence', in *Civil Society Engagement in Disarmament Processes: The Case for a Nuclear Weapons Ban*, UNODA. http://eprints.whiterose.ac.uk/114289/1/UNODA_civil_society_2016.pdf (accessed 26 January 2022).

Ritchie, Nick. 2015. 'UNIDIR: The Humanitarian Imitative in 2015: Expectations are Building for the Need for Nuclear Disarmament Progress', *ILPI-UNIDIR NPT Review Conference Series*, 1(5). www.unidir.org/files/publications/pdfs/the-humanitarian-initiative-in-2015-en-626.pdf (accessed 26 January 2022).

Ritchie, Nick. 2014a. *Nuclear Risk: The British Case*, Article 36 Briefing Paper. https://eprints.whiterose.ac.uk/78773/1/Nuclear_risk_paper.pdf (accessed 26 January 2022).

Ritchie, Nick. 2014b. 'Waiting for Kant: Devaluing and Delegitimizing Nuclear Weapons', *International Affairs*, 90(3).

Ritchie, Nick. 2014c. 'Nuclear Disarmament and the Humanitarian Initiative: Making Sense of the NPT in 2014', Briefing Paper, Article 36, May. https://article36.org/wp-content/uploads/2014/05/A36_Ritchie_NPT.pdf (accessed 26 January 2022).

Ritchie, Nick. 2013. 'Valuing and Devaluing Nuclear Weapons', *Contemporary Security Policy*, 34(1). www.tandfonline.com/doi/abs/10.1080/13523260.2013.771040 (accessed 26 January 2022).

Ritchie, Nick. 2010. 'Relinquishing Nuclear Weapons: Identities, Networks and the British Bomb', *International Affairs*, 86(2).

Ritchie, Nick. 2006. 'Replacing Trident: Who Will Make the Decisions and How?', *Oxford Research Group*. www.files.ethz.ch/isn/25598/0608%20TridentDM.pdf (accessed 26 January 2022).

Ritchie, Nick, and Kjolv Egeland. 2018. 'The Diplomacy of Resistance: Power, Hegemony and Nuclear Disarmament', *Global Change, Peace and Security*, 30(2).

Roberts, Adam, and David Guellf, eds. 1982. *Documents on the Law of War*. Oxford: Clarendon Press.

Roberts, Brad. 2015. *The Case for US Nuclear Weapons in the 21st Century*. Stanford: Stanford Security Studies.

Robock, Alan, and Owen B. Toon. 2012. 'Self-Assured Destruction: The Climate Impacts of Nuclear War', *The Bulletin of the Atomic Scientists*, 68(5). https://journals.sagepub.com/doi/10.1177/0096340212459127 (accessed 29 January 2022).

Rojecki, Andrew. 1999. *Silencing the Opposition: Antinuclear Movements and the Media in the Cold War*. Champaign: University of Illinois Press.

Rotblat, Joseph, and Frank Blackaby, eds. 1998. *Nuclear Weapons: The Road to Zero*. Boulder: Westview Press.

Rotblat, Joseph, Jack Steinberger, and Bhalchandra Udgaonkar, eds. 1993. *A Nuclear Weapon Free World: Desirable? Feasible?* Boulder: Westview Press.

Rowland, Matthew. 2016. *The United Kingdom of Great Britain and Northern Ireland Statement on Nuclear Weapons*, delivered to the UNGA First Committee. 14 October. www.un.org/disarmament/wp-content/uploads/2016/10/14-Oct-UK.pdf (accessed 26 January 2022).

Rublee, Maria Rost. 2015. 'Fantasy Counterfactual: a Nuclear-Armed Ukraine', *Survival*, 57(2).

Rublee, Maria Rost, and Carmen Wunderlich. 2022. 'The Vitality of the NPT After 50', *Contemporary Security Politics*, 43(1).

Ruff, Tilman. 2016. 'The More We Know, the Worse it Looks', *IPPNW Blog*, 18 May. https://peaceandhealthblog.com/2016/05/18/more-we-know/ (accessed 26 January 2022).

Ruhle, Michael. 2017. 'The Nuclear Weapons Ban-Treaty: Reasons for Scepticism', *NATO Review*, 19 May. www.nato.int/docu/review/articles/2017/05/19/the-nuclear-weapons-ban-treaty-reasons-for-scepticism/index.html (accessed 26 January 2022).

Rutherford, Kenneth R. 2011. *Disarming States: The International Movement to Ban Landmines*. Santa Barbara: Praeger.

Rutherford, Kenneth R. 1999. 'The Hague and Ottawa Conventions: A Model for Future Weapon Ban Regimes?' *The Nonproliferation Review*, Spring/Summer.

Rutherford, Kenneth R., and Stefan Brem, eds. 2003. *Reframing the Agenda: The Impact of NGO and Middle Power Cooperation in International Security Policy*. Westport: Praeger.

Sagan, Scott. 2009a. 'The Case for No First Use', *Survival*, 51(3).

Sagan, Scott. 2009b. 'Shared Responsibilities for Nuclear Disarmament', *Daedalus*, 138(4).

Sauer, Tom, Jorg Kustermans, and Barbara Segaert, eds. 2020. *Non-Nuclear Peace: Beyond the Ban-Treaty*. London: Palgrave Macmillan.

Sauer, Tom. 2016. 'Just Leave It: NATO's Nuclear Weapons Policy at the Warsaw Summit', *Arms Control Association*, June. www.armscontrol.org/ACT/2016_06/Features/Just-Leave-It-NATOs-Nuclear-Weapons-Policy-at-the-Warsaw-Summit (accessed 26 January 2022).

Sauer, Tom. 2015a. *70 Years after Hiroshima, the Humanitarian Initiative Challenges Nuclear Weapons*, European Leadership Network, 6 August. www.europeanleadershipnetwork.org/70-years-after-hiroshima-the-humanitarian-initiative-challenges-nuclear-weapons_3012.html (accessed 26 January 2022).

Sauer, Tom. 2015b 'The NPT and the Humanitarian Initiative: Towards and Beyond the 2015 NPT Review Conference, *Deep Cuts*, Working Paper No 5, April. https://deepcuts.org/images/PDF/DeepCuts_WP5_Sauer_UK.pdf (accessed 26 January 2022).

Sauer, Tom, and Claire Nardon. 2020. 'The Softening Rhetoric by Nuclear-Armed States and NATO Allies on the Treaty on the Prohibition of Nuclear Weapons', *War on the Rocks*, 7 December. https://warontherocks.com/2020/12/the-softening-rhetoric-by-nuclear-armed-states-and-nato-allies-on-the-treaty-on-the-prohibition-of-nuclear-weapons/ (accessed 26 January 2022).

Sauer, Tom, and Joelien Pretorius. 2021. 'Ditch the NPT', *Survival*, 63(4).

Sauer, Tom, and Joelien Pretorius. 2014. 'Nuclear Weapons and the Humanitarian Approach', *Global Change, Peace and Security*, 26(3).

Scarry, Elaine. 2014. *Thermonuclear Monarchy: Choosing Between Democracy and Doom*. New York: WW Norton.

Schelling, Thomas. 1966. *Arms and Influence*. New Haven CT: Yale University Press.

Schelling, Thomas, and Morton Halperin. 1961. *Strategy and Arms Control*. New York: The Twentieth Century Fund.

Schindler, Dietrich, and Jiri Toman, eds. 1988. *The Laws of Armed Conflicts: a Collection of Conventions, Resolutions and Other Documents*, 3rd edn. Dordrecht and Geneva: Martinus Nijhoff/Henri Dunant Institute.

Schlosser, Eric. 2014. *Nuclear 'Command and Control': A History of False Alarms and Near Catastrophes*, author interview, 11 August. www.npr.org/2014/08/11/339131421/nuclear-command-and-control-a-history-of-false-alarms-and-near-catastrophes (accessed 26 January 2022).

Schlosser, Eric. 2013a. *Command and Control: Nuclear Weapons, the Damascus Accident, and the Illusion of Safety*. London: Penguin.

Schlosser, Eric. 2013b. 'Nuclear Weapons: An Accident Waiting to Happen', *The Guardian*, 14 September. www.theguardian.com/world/2013/sep/14/nuclear-weapons-accident-waiting-to-happen (accessed 26 January 2022).

Schwartz, Stephen I. and Deepti Choubey. 2009. *Nuclear Security Spending: Assessing Costs, Examining Priorities*, Carnegie Endowment for International Peace, 12 January. https://carnegieendowment.org/2009/01/12/nuclear-security-spending-assessing-costs-examining-priorities-pub-22601 (accessed 26 January 2022).

Shaker, Mohamed I. 1990. 'The Non-Proliferation Treaty Regime: A Re-Reading Before 1995', in Joseph Pilat and Robert E. Pendley, eds, *Beyond 1995: The Future of the NPT Regime*. New York: Plenum Books, 7–16.

Shetty, Shatabhisha. 2022. 'Walking Away From NPT: Be Careful What You Wish For', *Korea Times*, 5 January. www.koreatimes.co.kr/www/opinion/2022/01/197_321644.html (accessed 17 January 2022).

Short, Nicola. 1999. *The Role of NGOs in the Ottawa Process to Ban Landmines*. The Netherlands: Kluwer Law International.

Shugerman, Emily. 2018. 'Donald Trump Says He Will Expand Nuclear Arsenal "Far in Excess of Anybody Else"', *The Independent*, 12 February. www.independent.co.uk/news/world/americas/us-politics/donald-trump-nuclear-arsenal-force-us-military-weapon-a8207586.html (accessed 26 January 2022).

Shultz, George P., and Sidney Drell, eds. 2012. *The Nuclear Enterprise: High Consequence Accidents: How to Enhance Safety and Minimize Risks in Nuclear Weapons and Reactors*. Stanford: Stanford University Press.

Shultz, George P., and James E. Goodby, eds. 2015. *The War That Must Never be Fought: Dilemmas of Nuclear Deterrence*. Stanford, CA: Hoover Institution Press.

Shultz, George P., William J. Perry, Henry A. Kissinger, and Sam Nunn. 2013. 'Toward a World Without Nuclear Weapons', The Nuclear Security Project/Nuclear Threat Initiative/Hoover Institution, Stanford University. www.nti.org/media/pdfs/NSP_op-eds_final_.pdf?_=1360883065 (accessed 26 January 2022).

Shultz, George P. William J. Perry, Henry A. Kissinger, and Sam Nunn. 2011. 'Deterrence in the Age of Nuclear Proliferation: The Doctrine of Mutual Assured Destruction is Obsolete in the Post-Cold War Era', *The Wall Street Journal*, 7 March. www.wsj.com/articles/SB10001424052748703300904576178760530169414 (accessed 26 January 2022).

Shultz, George P., William J. Perry, Henry A. Kissinger, and Sam Nunn. 2008. 'Toward a Nuclear-Free World', *The Wall Street Journal*. 15 January. www.wsj.com/articles/SB120036422673589947 (accessed 26 January 2022).

Shultz, George P., William J. Perry, Henry A. Kissinger, Sam Nunn. 2007. 'A World Free of Nuclear Weapons', *The Wall Street Journal*, 4 January. www.wsj.com/articles/SB116787515251566636 (accessed 26 January 2022).

Simpson, John. 1996. 'The Nuclear Non-Proliferation Regime After the NPT Review and Extension Conference', *SIPRI Yearbook*. Stockholm: Stockholm International Peace Research Institute. www.sipri.org/yearbook/1996/13 (accessed 26 January 2022).

Simpson, John, and Jenny Nielsen. 2010. 'The United Kingdom', in Hans Born, Bates Gill, and Heiner Hänggi (eds), *Governing the Bomb: Civilian Control and Democratic Accountability of Nuclear Weapons*, Oxford: Oxford University Press/SIPRI.

Smetana, Michel. 2016. 'Stuck on Disarmament: The European Union and the 2015 NPT Review Conference', *International Affairs*, 92(1).

Sokov, Nikolai. 2007. *Reykjavik Summit: The Legacy and a Lesson for the Future*, Nuclear Threat Initiative. www.nti.org/analysis/articles/reykjavik-summit-legacy/ (accessed 18 May 2021).

Solis, Gary. 2016. *The Law of Armed Conflict: International Humanitarian Law in War*. Cambridge: Cambridge University Press.

Somerville, John. 1986. 'Einstein's Legacy and Nuclear Omnicide', *Peace Research*, 18(1).

Sommaruga, Cornelio. 1997. 'Statement of Cornelio Sommaruga, President, ICRC', reprinted in Louis Maresca and Stuart Maslen, eds, *The Banning of Landmines: The Legal Contribution of the International Committee of the Red Cross*. Cambridge: Cambridge University Press, 2000.

Southard, Susan. 2015. *Nagasaki: Life after Nuclear War*. London: Viking.

Spinnaze, Gayle. 2020. 'It is Now 100 Seconds to Midnight', *Bulletin of the Atomic Scientists*, 23 January. https://thebulletin.org/2020/01/press-release-it-is-now-100-seconds-to-midnight/ (accessed 26 January 2022).

Spring, Baker, and Michaela Dodge. 2013. *Bait and Switch on Nuclear Modernization Must Stop*, The Heritage Foundation, 13 January. www.heritage.org/defense/report/bait-and-switch-nuclear-modernization-must-stop (accessed 26 January 2022).

Starr, Steven. 2009. 'Catastrophic Climatic Consequences of Nuclear Conflict', in *Nuclear Famine: The Deadly Consequences of Nuclear War*, Nuclear Famine Project. October. https://nuclearfamine.org/war-consequences/deadly-climate-change-from-nuclear-war-a-threat-to-human-existence/ (accessed 26 January 2022).

Stegenga, James A. 1988. 'Nuclearism and Democracy', *Journal of American Culture*, 11(1).

Stimson Center. 1997. *An American Legacy: Building a Nuclear Weapon Free World*. www.files.ethz.ch/isn/93672/Report22.pdf (accessed 26 January 2022).

Stimson Center. 1995a. *Beyond the Nuclear Peril: The Year in Review and the Years Ahead*. Stimson Report 15. 6 January. www.stimson.org/1995/beyond-nuclear-peril-year-review-and-years-ahead/ (accessed 26 January 2022).

Stimson Center. 1995b. *An Evolving US Nuclear Posture*. Stimson Report 19, 11 December. www.stimson.org/1995/evolving-us-nuclear-posture/ (accessed 26 January 2022).

Stoltz, William. 2020. 'How Australia Can Help the World Avoid Nuclear War', *The Financial Review*, 17 July. www.afr.com/policy/foreign-affairs/how-australia-can-help-the-world-avoid-nuclear-war-20200715-p55cdc (accessed 25 January 2022).

Stone, Jon. 2020. 'Belgian Parliament Nearly Expels US Nuclear Weapons in a Close-Run Vote', *The Independent*, 17 January. www.independent.co.uk/news/world/europe/belgium-nuclear-weapons-us-vote-result-debate-trump-a9288451.html (accessed 26 January 2022).

Stone, Jon. 2016. 'Lifetime Cost of Replacing Trident at Least 250 Billion Pounds, Latest Estimate Suggests', 12 May. www.independent.co.uk/news/uk/politics/trident-replacement-cost-nuclear-submarines-205-billion-independent-trident-commission-cnd-caroline-a7025956.html (accessed 26 January 2022).

Sullivan, Kathleen. 2016. 'Hibakusha's Hope to Ban the Bomb', in *Civil Society Engagement in Disarmament Processes: The Case for a Nuclear Weapons Ban*. UNODA. www.un.org/disarmament/wp-content/uploads/2017/03/civil-society-2016.pdf (accessed 26 January 2022).

Tannenwald, Nina. 2020. 'The Humanitarian Initiative: A Critical Appreciation', in Tom Sauer, Jorg Kustermans, and Barbara Segaert, eds, *Non-Nuclear Peace: Beyond the Ban-Treaty*. London: Palgrave Macmillan.

Tannenwald, Nina. 2007. *The Nuclear Taboo: The United States and the Non-Use of Nuclear Weapons since 1945*. New York: Cambridge University Press.

Tannenwald, Nina. 1999. 'The Nuclear Taboo: The United States and the Normative Basis of Nuclear Non-Use', *International Organization*, 53(3).

Taylor, Bryan C. 2010. 'A Hedge Against the Future: The Post-Cold War Rhetoric of Nuclear Weapons Modernization', *Quarterly Journal of Speech*, 96(1).

Taylor, Bryan C. 2007. ' "The Means to Match Their Hatred": Nuclear Weapons, Rhetorical Democracy, and Presidential Discourse', *Presidential Studies Quarterly*, 37(4).

Taylor, Bryan C., and Judith Hendry. 2008. 'Insisting on Persisting: The Nuclear Rhetoric of Stockpile Stewardship', *Rhetoric and Public Affairs*, 11(2).

Taylor, Bryan C. William J. Kinsella, Stephen P. Depoe, and Maribeth S. Metzler, eds. 2008. *Nuclear Legacies: Communication, Controversy and the US Nuclear Weapons Complex*. Lanham: Lexington Books.

Tellis, Ashel. J. 2013. 'No Escape: Managing the Enduring Reality of Nuclear Weapons', *National Bureau of Asian Research*, October. www.nbr.org/publications/element.aspx?id=698 (accessed 25 January 2022).

Thakur, Ramesh. 2016a. *Asia-Pacific and Global Nuclear Orders in the Second Nuclear Age*, APLN-CNND, Policy Brief 21, July.

Thakur, Ramesh. 2016b. 'The Eight Deadly Nuclear Sins', *The Japan Times*, 10 February. www.japantimes.co.jp/opinion/2016/02/10/commentary/world-commentary/eight-deadly-nuclear-sins/#.WQhfCtyLnIU (accessed 25 January 2022).

Thakur, Ramesh. 2015. *Nuclear Weapons and International Security: Collected Essays*. Abingdon: Routledge.

Thakur, Ramesh, and Gareth Evans, eds. 2013. *Nuclear Weapons: The State of Play*. Canberra: Centre for Nuclear Non Proliferation and Disarmament.

Thiele, Leslie Paul. 1993. 'Making Democracy Safe for the World: Social Movements and Global Politics', *Alternatives*, 18.

Thurlow, Setsuko. 2020. 'Setsuko Thurlow Remembers the Hiroshima Bombing', *Arms Control Today*, 50(6).

Thurlow, Setsuko. 2014. 'Hiroshima: A Survivor's Testimony', *Irish Studies in International Affairs*, 25.

Ticehurst, Rupert. 1997. 'The Martens Clause and the Laws of Armed Conflict', *International Review of the Red Cross*, 317, 30 April. www.icrc.org/eng/resources/documents/article/other/57jnhy.htm (accessed 21 January 2022).

Tierney, Dominic. 2016. 'Refusing to Nuke First: Why Rejecting Nuclear Pre-emption Reflects Strength, Not Weakness', *The Atlantic*, 14 September. www.theatlantic.com/international/archive/2016/09/nuclear-obama-north-korea-pakistan/499676/ (accessed 2 February 2022).

Toon, Owen B., Charles G. Bardeen, Alan Robock, Lili Xia, Hans Kristensen, Matthew McKinzie, R. J. Peterson, Cheryl S. Harrison, Nicole S. Lovenduski, and Richard P. Turco. 2019. 'Rapidly Expanding Nuclear Arsenals in Pakistan and India Portend Regional and Global Catastrophe', *Science Advances*, 5(10), 2 October. www.science.org/doi/10.1126/sciadv.aay5478 (accessed 4 February 2022).

Toon, Owen, B., Alan Robock, and Richard P. Turco. 2008. 'The Environmental Consequences of Nuclear War', *Physics Today*, 61(12).

Toon, Owen B., Alan Robock, Richard P. Turco, Charles G. Bardeen, and Luke Oman. 2007a. 'Consequences of Regional-Scale Nuclear Conflicts', *Science*, 315(5816).

Toon, Owen B., Richard P. Turco, Alan Robock, Charles G. Bardeen, Luke Oman, and Georgiy L. Stenchikov. 2007b. 'Atmospheric Effects and Societal Consequences of Regional Scale Nuclear Conflicts and Acts of Individual Nuclear Terrorism', *Atmospheric Chemistry and Physics*, 7.

TPNW. 2020. *Open Letter in Support of the Treaty on the Prohibition of Nuclear Weapons*, 21 September. https://d3n8a8pro7vhmx.cloudfront.net/ican/pages/1712/attachments/original/1600645499/TPNW_Open_Letter_-_English.pdf (accessed 2 February 2022).

Troianovski, Anton. 2018. 'Putin Claims Russia is Developing Nuclear Arms Capable of Avoiding Missile Defenses', *The Washington Post*, 1 March.

UK (United Kingdom). 2021. UK Parliament, *Global Britain: The Integrated Review of Security, Defence, Development and Foreign Policy*. https://assets.publishing.service.gov.uk/government/uploads/system/uploads/attachment_data/file/975077/Global_Britain_in_a_Competitive_Age-_the_Integrated_Review_of_Security__Defence__Development_and_Foreign_Policy.pdf (accessed 4 February 2022).

UK (United Kingdom). 2010. *UK/Norway Initiative on Nuclear Warhead Dismantlement Verification*, UK Ministry of Defence, 31 March.

UK (United Kingdom). 2006. UK Parliament, House of Commons. *Hansard Debates 4 Dec*. Column 34. https://publications.parliament.uk/pa/cm200607/cmhansrd/cm061204/debtext/61204-0004.htm (accessed 4 February 2022).

UN (United Nations). 2017. *Treaty on the Prohibition of Nuclear Weapons*, 7 July. https://treaties.un.org/pages/ViewDetails.aspx?src=TREATY&mtdsg_no=XXVI-9&chapter=26 (accessed 4 February 2022).

UN (United Nations). 2015a. *Consensus Eludes Nuclear Non-Proliferation Treaty Review Conference as Positions Harden on Ways to Free Middle East of Mass Destruction Weapons*. Meeting Coverage and Press Releases. www.un.org/press/en/2015/dc3561.doc.htm (accessed 4 February 2022).

UN (United Nations). 2015b. *Resolution adopted by the General Assembly: Taking Forward Multilateral Nuclear Disarmament Negotiations*, A/RES/30/73, 7 December.

UN (United Nations). 2013a. *Statement to the High-Level Meeting on Nuclear Disarmament on Behalf of France, the United Kingdom, and the United States, delivered by the United Kingdom*, New York, 26 September. www.un.org/en/ga/68/meetings/nucleardisarmament/pdf/GB_en.pdf (accessed 4 February 2022).

UN (United Nations). 2013b. *Statement to the UNGA First Committee on behalf of France, the United Kingdom, and the United States, Delivered by France*, New York, October.

UN (United Nations). 2012. UN Office for the Coordination of Humanitarian Affairs). 2012. *What Are Humanitarian Principles?* https://docs.unocha.org/sites/dms/Documents/OOM-humanitarianprinciples_eng_June12.pdf (accessed 4 February 2022).

UN (United Nations). 2010. *United Nations 2010 Review Conference of the Parties to the Treaty on the Non-Proliferation of Nuclear Weapons, Final Document*, volume I, May 2010. www.un.org/ga/search/view_doc.asp?symbol=NPT/CONF.2010/50%20%28VOL.I%29 (accessed 4 February 2022).

UN (United Nations). 2004. UN Institute for Disarmament Research, *Disarmament as Humanitarian Action: Making Multilateral Negotiations Work*. Geneva: UNIDIR.

UN (United Nations). 1972. UN Office of Disarmament Affairs, *Text of the Biological Weapons Convention: Convention on the Prohibition of the Development, Production and Stockpiling of Bacteriological (Biological) and Toxin Weapons and on their Destruction*. https://front.un-arm.org/wp-content/uploads/2020/12/BWC-text-English-1.pdf (accessed 4 February 2022).

UN (United Nations). 1948. *Convention on the Prevention and Punishment of the Crime of Genocide. Adopted by the General Assembly of the United Nations on 9 December 1948*. New York: United Nations.

UN (United Nations). 1946. *Establishment of a Commission to Deal With the Problems Raised by the Discovery of Atomic Energy*, 24 January.

UN (United Nations). 1945. *United Nations Charter*. New York: United Nations. www.un.org/en/about-us/un-charter/full-text (accessed 14 January 2022).

Unal, Beyza, and Yasmin Afina. 2020. *How to Deter Cyberattacks on Nuclear Weapons Systems*. London: Chatham House. www.chathamhouse.org/2020/12/how-deter-cyberattacks-nuclear-weapons-systems (accessed 23 January 2022).

Ungar, Sheldon. 1992. *The Rise and Fall of Nuclearism: Fear and Faith as Determinants of the Arms Race*. Pennsylvania: Pennsylvania State University Press.

UNODA (United Nations Office for Disarmament Affairs). 1968. *Treaty on the Non-Proliferation of Nuclear Weapons*, New York. www.un.org/disarmament/wmd/nuclear/npt/text (accessed 4 February 2022).

US Department of Defense. 2013. 'DoD is Not Prepared to Defend Against This Threat' (US 2013: 1). US. Dept of Defense. 2013. *Task Force Report: Resilient Military Systems and the Advanced Cyber Threat*, Washington, January.
US Department of Defense. 2010. *Nuclear Posture Review Report*, April. www.defense.gov/Portals/1/features/defenseReviews/NPR/2010_Nuclear_Posture_Review_Report.pdf (accessed 4 February 2022).
US Department of State. 2016. *Joint Statement From the Nuclear-Weapons States at the 2016 Washington, DC P5 Conference*. Washington DC: US Dept of State. https://2009-2017.state.gov/r/pa/prs/ps/2016/09/261994.htm (accessed 4 February 2022).
US Department of State. 1993. *Hidden Killers: The Global Problem with Uncleared Landmines: A Report on International Demining*. Washington, DC: Political-Military Affairs Bureau, Office of International Security Operations, US Department of State.
US Mission to NATO. 2016. *United States Non-Paper: Defense Impacts of Potential United Nations General Assembly Nuclear Weapons Ban-Treaty*, 17 October. https://d3n8a8pro7vhmx.cloudfront.net/ican/pages/821/attachments/original/1590165765/NATO_OCT2016.pdf?1590165765 (accessed 4 February 2022).
US Mission to the UN. 2017. *Joint Press Statement from the Permanent Representatives to the United Nations of the United States, United Kingdom, and France*. July 7. New York. https://usun.usmission.gov/joint-press-statement-from-the-permanent-representatives-to-the-united-nations-of-the-united-states-united-kingdom-and-france-following-the-adoption/ (accessed 4 February 2022).
Vilmer, Jean-Baptiste Jeangene. 2020. 'The Forever Emerging Norm of Banning Nuclear Weapons', *Journal of Strategic Studies*, June.
Walker, William. 2012. *A Perpetual Menace: Nuclear Weapons and International Order*. Abingdon: Routledge.
Walker, William. 2010. 'The UK, Threshold Status, and Responsible Nuclear Sovereignty', *International Affairs*, 86(2).
Walker, William. 2004. 'Weapons of Mass Destruction and International Order', Adelphi Papers 370, London: International Institute for Strategic Studies, 10 December.
Walker, William. 2000. 'Nuclear Order and Disorder', *International Affairs*, 76(4).
Walt, Stephen. 2016. 'What Would a Realist World Have Looked Like?', *Foreign Policy*, 8 January.
Waltz, Kenneth. 2012. 'Why Iran Should Get the Bomb', *Foreign Affairs*, July–August.
Waltz, Kenneth. 1981. 'The Spread of Nuclear Weapons: More May Be Better', *Adelphi Paper 171*, London: IISS.
Ward, Thomas (2001) *The Ethics of Destruction: Norms and Force in International Relations*. Ithaca: Cornell University Press.
Ware, Alyn. 2016. 'Prosecution Rebuttal and Closing Statement', *International Peoples Tribunal on the Nuclear Weapons and the Destruction of Human Civilisation*, University of Sydney, 7–8 July. www.unfoldzero.org/wp-content/uploads/Prosecution-rebuttal-and-closing-statement-.pdf (accessed 4 February 2022).

Wareham, Sue. 2020. 'Amid and Beyond Covid-19, it's Time to Focus on Healthcare not Warfare', *Croakey*, 8 May. www.croakey.org/amid-and-beyond-covid-19-its-time-to-focus-on-healthcare-not-warfare/ (accessed 4 February 2022).

Wareham, Sue. 2016. 'Expert Witness Testimony to the International People's Tribunal on the Nuclear Powers and the Destruction of Human Civilisation, University of Sydney, July. Reproduced by the Medical Association for the Prevention of War, Australia. www.mapw.org.au/evidence_nuclear/ (accessed 7 February 2022).

Warren, Aiden, and Philip M. Baxter, eds. 2020. *Nuclear Modernization in the 21st Century: A Technical, Policy and Strategic Review*. Abingdon: Routledge.

Weart, Spencer R. 2012. *The Rise of Nuclear Fear*. Cambridge, MA: Harvard University Press.

Weeramantry, Christopher. 1996. *Dissenting Opinion of Judge Weeramantry*. The Hague: International Court of Justice. https://fas.org/nuke/control/icj/text/iunan_ijudgment_19960708_Dissenting_Weeramantry.htm (accessed 4 February 2022).

Wells, Natalya. 2016. *Explosive Remnants of War*. Australian Institute of International Affairs. www.internationalaffairs.org.au/australian_outlook/explosive-toll-of-remnants-of-war/ (accessed 4 February 2022).

Welsh, Susan B. 1995. 'Delegate Perspectives on the 1995 NPT Review and Extension Conference: A Series of Interviews Conducted by Susan B. Welsh', *The Nonproliferation Review*, Spring-Summer.

Welty, Emily. 2016. 'The Theological Landscape of the Nuclear Nonproliferation Treaty: The Catholic Church, the World Council of Churches and the Bomb', *Global Policy*, 7(3).

Whall, Helena, and Allison Pytlak. 2014. 'The Role of Civil Society in the International Negotiations on the Arms Trade Treaty', *Global Policy*, 5(4).

Wheeler, Nicholas J. 2010. 'Nuclear Weapons in Waltz's World: More Trust May Be Better', in Ken Booth, ed., *Realism and World Politics*. London: Routledge.

Wheeler, Nicholas J., and Jan Ruzicka. 2010. 'The Puzzle of Trusting Relationships in the Nuclear Non-Proliferation Treaty', *International Affairs*, 86(1).

Wigg-Stevenson, Tyler. 2015. 'The Humanitarian Impact of Nuclear Weapons: A Problem for State Authority', *Christian Scholars' Review*, 44(4).

Williams, Heather, Patricia Lewis, and Sasan Aghlani. 2015. *The Humanitarian Impacts of Nuclear Weapons Initiative: The 'Big Tent' in Disarmament*, March. London: Chatham House/Royal Institute of International Affairs. www.chathamhouse.org/sites/default/files/field/field_document/20150331HumanitarianImpactNuclearWilliamsLewisAghlani.pdf (accessed 4 February 2022).

Williams, Jody. 1999. *The International Campaign to Ban Landmines*, Global Policy Forum, 3 September. https://archive.globalpolicy.org/ngos/campaign/landmine/1999/0804nobel.htm (accessed 4 February 2022).

Williams, Raymond. 1980. 'The Politics of Nuclear Disarmament', *New Left Review*, November.

Wilson, George. 1977. 'Slowing Pentagon's Revolving Door', *The Washington Post*, 15 September.

Wilson, Ward. 2014. *Five Myths About Nuclear Weapons*. New York and Boston: Mariner Books.

Wilson, Ward. 2008. 'The Myth of Nuclear Deterrence', *The Nonproliferation Review*, 15(3).

Wilson, Ward. 2007. 'The Winning Weapon? Rethinking Nuclear Weapons in Light of Hiroshima', *International Security*, 31(4).

Wisotzki, Simone. 2009. *Between Morality and Military Interests: Norm Setting in Humanitarian Arms Control*, Peace Research Institute Frankfurt, PRIF Report 92. www.hsfk.de/fileadmin/HSFK/hsfk_downloads/prif92.pdf.pdf (accessed 4 February 2022).

Wittner, Lawrence S. 2009 *Confronting the Bomb: A Short History of the World Nuclear Disarmament Movement*. Stanford: Stanford University Press.

Wolfenstein, Lincoln. 1991. 'End Nuclear Addiction', *Bulletin of the Atomic Scientists*, 47(4).

Wolfstahl, Jon, and Jeffrey Lewis. 2014. *Trillion Dollar Nuclear Triad: US Strategic Modernization over the Next Thirty Years*, Center for Nonproliferation Studies, 7 January. http://cns.miis.edu/trillion_dollar_nuclear_triad/ (accessed 4 February 2022).

Woolcott, Richard. 2013. 'Joint Statement on the Humanitarian Consequences of Nuclear Weapons', United Nations, General Assembly, First Committee, 68th session, 21 October. www.reachingcriticalwill.org/images/documents/Disarmament-fora/1com/1com13/statements/21Oct_Australia2.pdf (accessed 4 February 2022).

Woolf, Amy F. 2020. *Russia's Nuclear Weapons: Doctrines, Forces and Modernization*, Congressional Research Service report, July. https://fas.org/sgp/crs/nuke/R45861.pdf (accessed 4 February 2022).

Zimmerer, Jurgen. 2007. 'From the Editors: Environmental Genocide? Climate Change, Mass Violence and the Question of Ideology', *Journal of Genocide Studies*, 9(3).

Index

Page numbers including 'n.' indicate note numbers

accidents 39n.8, 59, 61–3, 204, 209
accountability 23, 25, 48
Acheson, Ray 52, 67, 123, 130n.5, 136, 137, 153, 156, 157, 163, 165, 166, 168, 169, 170, 171, 175, 183, 184, 202
acquisition decisions 27
Action Plan 85
'addiction' to nuclear weapons 44–5, 88
Additional Protocols 4, 198–9
Advisory Opinions 75
Aldrich, George H. 97
Allen, Daniel R. 55, 60
Alliance for Nuclear Accountability 46
Alperovitz, Gar 27
anti-nuclear groups 76–7, 163
anti-nuclearism 25, 36, 76–7, 84, 138, 149, 152, 163, 170
anti-nuclear nuclearism 64n.2
Arab states 73, 86, 87–8
  see also Middle East
Archer, Colin 31, 32
Arkin, William 47
Arms Control Association 32
Arms Trade Treaty (2013) 95, 113, 173
Australia 55, 57, 76, 81, 118, 125, 172, 173, 178, 193, 196
Austria 119, 124, 135, 151, 193
Axworthy, Lloyd 104

balance of risks 29, 62, 82
ballistic missiles 47, 49
Ban Ki-moon 81, 119
ban versus regulation 127
Becker, Una 24

Belarus 197
Belgium 102, 173, 174, 175, 177, 192
Benedict, Kennette 24, 153
benign practices 53–4
Bevin, Ernest 41n.22
Bhutto, Zulfikar Ali 31
Biden, Joe 189, 194
biological weapons see chemical/biological weapons
Biological Weapons Convention (1972) 87, 99, 112
Blair, Tony 34, 164
blast waves 141
Blix Report 80–1
Bolton, Matthew 137, 154, 163
Bond Graham, Darwin 64n.2
Booth, Ken 16, 18–19, 28, 61, 62, 117
Born, Hans 23, 26
Borrie, John 17, 113, 125, 136, 142–3, 149, 151, 173–4, 184
Boutros-Ghali, Boutros 101
boycotts 119, 155
Boyer, Paul 16
Britain
  initial acquisition decisions 27
  landmines 108
  managerial approach 164
  modernization 47
  moratorium on testing 71
  NPT (Non-Proliferation Treaty) 2, 33–4, 36–7, 88
  parliamentary review 23–4, 27
  reductions in nuclear weapons 32, 43–4

security doctrines 51
statistics on nuclear weapons 8n.3
and the TPNW 189
Trident 27, 32, 169
utility of nuclear weapons 169
verification systems 198
see also P5 (Permanent Five)
broken arrow incidents 63
Brussels Conference (1874) 98, 114n.7
budget scrutiny 32, 155–7
see also spending on nuclear weapons
Bull, Hedley 163, 168
bunker busters 32
Burke, Anthony 28
Burt, A. 165
Bush, George W. 49, 84
Butler, Lee 18, 77, 205
Butler, Richard 72, 162, 205

Cahill, Kevin 101
calamities of war 95–6
Canada 80, 104, 135, 173, 177
Canberra Commission Report 55, 76–7, 78, 79, 149
Carlson, John 167, 197, 199
Cartwright, James 63
Carver, Field Marshall Lord 77
Catholic Church 138
Caughley, Tim 115n.12
CCW (Convention on Certain Conventional Weapons) 100, 102–3, 108, 122
CD (Conference on Disarmament) 33, 71–2, 102, 104, 106, 107, 122
CEND (Creating an Environment for Nuclear Disarmament) 183
Chatham House, London 124
chemical/biological weapons 56, 57, 78, 87, 99, 170
Chemical Weapons Convention (1993) 76, 87, 99, 112
Chernobyl 39n.8, 59
Chilton, Paul 18
China
 landmines 104, 106, 108
 no-first-use declarations 48–9
 NPT (Non-Proliferation Treaty) 2, 37, 75
 statistics on nuclear weapons 8n.3

testing 75, 76
and the TPNW 196
see also P5 (Permanent Five)
Choubey, Deepti 85
Christianity 60, 138
Cirincione, Joseph 70, 146
Cities Appeal 159n.8
citizen oversight 23–4, 25–6, 27, 32
civilian casualties 20–1, 53, 101
civilian protection 6, 20, 21
civil society
 budget scrutiny 32
 interaction with states 124
 investment in nuclear weapons 156
 mass protest 152
 new discourses beyond security 134, 135
 in non-democracies 196–7
 pushing for disarmament 67, 75–6, 104, 113
 role in negotiations 150–1, 152–3
 and the TPNW 119, 124–5, 170, 171, 175–6, 182, 196
civil-state relations 22–3, 60
civil wars 103
climate change 31, 139, 142
Clingendael Report 176
Clinton, Bill 41n.29, 75, 164
close calls 44, 53, 207
cluster munitions 95, 113, 125, 173, 194
Cluster Munitions Convention (2008) 113
Coghlan, Jay 29–30
Cohn, Carol 18
Cohn, Nathan 30, 31
Cold War
 deterrence doctrines 43, 52, 54, 58, 60–1
 end of 68
 humanitarian principles 100
 and landmines control 101
 normalization of nuclear weapons 28–9, 36
 nuclear weapons as hallmark of 11
 weapons targets 55
collective liability 127
combatants/non-combatants distinction 97
compliance culture 169–71, 194

Comprehensive Safeguards Agreement
  see CSA
compromise 84, 111
Conference on Disarmament see CD
Conference on the Humanitarian
  Impact of Nuclear Weapons
  see HINW
confidentiality 26
congressional review 23–4, 27
consensus 71, 75, 77, 86, 102, 103, 110, 111, 209
contemplated use incidents 63
contradictions 36, 44
Convention on Certain Conventional Weapons see CCW
conventional weapons 55–7, 58, 78–9, 168
Cooper, Neil 35
corruptibility 25
Costa Rica 124
costs 14, 29–33, 155–7
covert planning 27
COVID-19 155, 185n.9
Creating an Environment for Nuclear Disarmament see CEND
cruise missiles 32, 52, 189
CSA (Comprehensive Safeguards Agreement) 198
CTBT (Comprehensive Test Ban Treaty) 52, 71, 78, 83, 84
cumulative normative effects 109–10
cyber-attacks 63

Dahl, Robert 24–5
Daley, Tad 57
Datan, Marev 91n.17
death rates 53, 110, 144
defence industry 29–30
  see also weapons manufacturing corporations
defence planning 23, 28
dehumanization 21, 143
delegitimization 3, 126, 127, 148, 156, 161, 184, 211
democracy 14, 17, 22–3, 24, 25, 26, 28, 149
deterrence doctrines 17, 19, 48, 52–61, 134, 166–7
Deudney, Daniel 24, 25
Dewes, Kate 76

Dhanapala, Jayantha 73, 74, 164
diplomacy 95, 103–4, 110, 123, 150, 162, 169–71
disarmament 16, 33–7, 58, 67–92
divestment policies 155
Dodge, Michaela 53
Dodge, Robert 63
Domesday Clock 204
Doyle, James 53, 56, 195–6
Doyle, Thomas 22, 92n.21, 179
Drell, Sidney 63
drone warfare 115n.8
dum-dum bullets 98
Dunworth, Treasa 205

East Asia 45, 51, 172
East-West relations post-Cold War 68
ecocide 143, 144–5
Eden, Lynn 27, 28, 47, 168
Egeland, Kjølv 176, 177, 180, 198
Egypt 73, 86, 87, 161–2
Eide, Espen Barth 119, 140
Einstein, Albert 142, 145
elites 13, 14, 22–9, 30, 46, 134, 138, 143, 148, 150
END (extended nuclear deterrence arrangement) 174
English, John 106, 108, 153
environmental consequences 26, 120, 139, 140, 144–5, 146
Estonia 57
ethical investment 156
ethnic cleansing 115n.13
ethnocentrism 18
EU 68, 108, 172–3, 174, 192–3
euphemism 17, 18, 135
European Leadership Network 62
Evans, Gareth 22, 47, 76, 202n.4
exclusivity 14, 22–9
experts 13, 23, 153
exploding bullets 97
export control measures 163
extended nuclear deterrence arrangement see END

faith and fear 15, 61
faith-based groups 136
Falk, Richard 11, 12, 13, 16, 22–3, 24, 37, 61–2, 101, 133, 166, 184, 190

fallout 141
false alarms 204
famine 140
fast-track processes 104, 110
fear 15, 16, 59, 139, 144, 152, 195–6
Feinberg, Ashley 51
Feinstein, Dianne 32
fetishization of nuclear weapons 44
Fihn, B. 139, 142, 184
financing 156–7
  see also spending on nuclear weapons
firestorms 140, 141
First Geneva Convention (1864) 114n.6
first-strike capabilities 41n.21, 47, 52, 189
first-use doctrines 49
  see also no-first-use declarations
First World War 99
Fissile Material Cut-off Treaty
  see FMCT
Five Point Proposal for Nuclear Disarmament 81
FMCT (Fissile Material Cut-off Treaty) 52, 71, 78, 84
food security 120, 139, 140, 146
France 2, 8n.3, 32, 37, 51, 76, 102, 108
  see also P5 (Permanent Five)
Franck Report 40n.13
Frear, T. 62
Freedman, Lawrence 53, 58
Freedom of Information 63
Friends of the Earth 39n.8
Fukushima disaster 59

Gaillard, Emilie 146
Galston, Arthur 145
Gamson, William 16
gender inequalities 120–1, 142–3
genetic damage 146
Geneva Conventions 4, 98
Geneva Protocol (1925) 90n.7, 99, 112
genocide 21–2, 28, 143–4
geopolitics 36–7, 50, 68, 166, 205
Germany 149, 173, 174, 175, 176, 192
Gilinsky, Victor 60, 65n.3
Giorgiou, Eirini 197, 199
global economic consequences 120, 139
global effects of a nuclear deployment 140

Global Financial Crisis 31
global governance 113
global nuclear disarmament 60–1, 64n.2
global nuclear order 12–14, 35, 38, 70, 117, 160–86, 205, 208
global prohibition regimes 181
global responsibility 137
Global Zero 62
Goodpaster, Andrew 69
Gorbachev, Mikhail 44, 69
Gowing, Margaret 41n.22
Graham, Thomas 75
Green, Robert 76
Greenpeace 39n.8
groupthink 42n.30
guardians of nuclear resources 46
Gusterson, Hugh 162
Guven, Onar 176, 177

hacking 63
Hague Convention 90n.7, 98, 99
Hanson, Marianne 47, 78, 81, 84, 161
Harknett, Richard J. 60
Harries, Matthew 194, 196
Harrington de Santana, Anne 47
Harvard Human Rights Clinic Report 176
Hashimoto, Ryutaro 80
health professionals' role in debate 151
health provision, effects on 140, 141
Hehir, J. Bryan 22
Helfand, Ira 63, 119, 127, 139, 140, 141, 142, 147, 151
Hendry, Judith 46, 65n.4
Henry L. Stimson Center 69
Heritage Foundation 50
Hersey, John 40n.15
Herz, John 60
Hibakusha 120, 124, 151, 195
hierarchies 34, 70, 162
high-alert status 78, 140, 212
high risk zones 45
Hilgartner, Stephen 17
HINW (Conference on the Humanitarian Impact of Nuclear Weapons) 119
Hiroshima 20, 27, 142, 151
Hoffman-Axthelm, Leo 91n.16, 176
Horner, Charles 56–7

Hubert, D. 102, 103, 107, 109–10, 112, 116n.16, 173
Hudson, William 26, 30
human fallibility 60
humanitarian advocacy 4–6
humanitarian arms control 3, 6, 121–8
humanitarian disarmament 95
Humanitarian Impact of Nuclear Weapons *see* HINW
Humanitarian Initiative
  allies of US 192
  beginnings of 3
  'big tent' 124
  Conferences 195
  effects on humanity as a whole 137
  non-nuclear states 118
  non-proliferation regime 167
  and the P5 165
  pursued by states 208
  rejecting nuclearism 133–59
  and RevCon 2010 86
  and the TPNW 117–30, 174–5
  women's voices 143
humanitarian principles
  as basis for post-2010 discourse 3, 86
  definition 4–6, 111–12
  humanitarian advocacy 4–6
  modern expectations of war 21
  and the TPNW 125–6
human rights 96, 137, 146, 172–4
Human Rights Watch 101, 106
humility 60
Hussein, Saddam 57
Hynek, Nikola 123
hyper-masculinity 143

IAEA (International Atomic Energy Agency) 72, 73, 85, 87–8, 198–9
ICAN (International Campaign to Abolish Nuclear Weapons) 84, 118, 119, 125, 151, 155, 159n.8
ICBL (International Coalition to Ban Landmines) 103, 104–5, 113, 195
ICC (International Criminal Court) 115n.13, 144, 173
ICJ (International Court of Justice) 22, 75–6, 99, 126, 147, 166
ICNND (International Commission on Nuclear Non- proliferation and Disarmament) 81
ICRC (International Committee of the Red Cross) 4, 96, 97, 98, 99, 100, 101, 104–5, 106, 112, 125, 136, 138
identity politics 172
ignition technology 47
IHRC (International Human Rights Clinic) 176
illogicality 27–8, 29, 60, 168, 205, 209, 212
ILPI (International Law and Policy Institute) Reports 176
impacts
  downplaying of impacts 16
  ecocide 143, 144–5
  genocide 21–2, 28, 143–4
  global effects of a nuclear deployment 140
  humanitarian impacts 138–48
  infrastructure impacts 139, 141
  initial effects of a nuclear weapon 141
  limitation of suffering 99
  long-term effects of nuclear weapons 139–41
  omnicide 145–6, 158
  radiation effects 120, 139, 141
  starvation 139, 140–1
impartiality 4, 5
implicit laws 98
impracticality as weapons 55
India
  costs of nuclear weapons 31
  HINW (Humanitarian Impact of Nuclear Weapons) 119
  landmines 106
  no-first-use declarations 48–9
  and the NPT 7n.1, 8n.3, 33, 71, 85, 90n.6
  nuclear colonialism 163
  security doctrines 51
  testing 79–80
  and the TPNW 196
  and the US 185n.2
indiscriminate targeting 21, 55, 102
infrastructure impacts 139, 141
inhumane, nuclear weapons as
  development of warfare 96, 114n.3
  humanitarian principles 100, 137, 139, 150, 166
  and the NPT 118

reframing 103
versus security doctrines 2, 40n.11
security doctrines 193–4
stigmatization 78
and the TPNW 127, 173
Inhumane Weapons Convention (1980) 100
see also CCW
Institute of International Law 114n.7
inter-generational justice 139, 143, 146–8
Intermediate-range Nuclear Forces Treaty 52, 69, 189
international arms trade 99
International Atomic Energy Agency see IAEA
International Campaign to Abolish Nuclear Weapons see ICAN
International Coalition to Ban Landmines see ICBL
International Commission on Nuclear Non-proliferation and Disarmament see ICNND
International Committee of the Red Cross see ICRC
International Court of Justice see ICJ
International Criminal Court see ICC
International Human Rights Clinic see IHRC
international law
  development of 96
  disregard for 20
  ecocide 144
  genocide law 143
  Hague Conventions 98
  history of applications 97–105
  humanitarian principles 3
  inter-generational justice 146
  mission civilisatrice 99–100
  modern expectations of war 21
  and natural law 99
  and the NPT 86
  states forced to declare position 171–2
  and the TPNW 125, 191
  and weapons 6
International Law and Policy Institute Reports see ILPI Reports
International Partnership for Nuclear Disarmament Verification

International Physicians for the Prevention of Nuclear War see IPPNW
international security order see IPNDV
ionizing radiation 120
IPNDV (International Partnership for Nuclear Disarmament Verification) 198
IPPNW (International Physicians for the Prevention of Nuclear War) 151
Iran 37, 59, 85, 87, 163, 167
Iraq 21, 37, 164
Ireland 124, 193
irreversibility principle 85
ISIS 55
Israel 7n.1, 8n.3, 33, 73, 85, 87, 167
Italy 175
Ivanov, Igor 204

Janus, Irving 42n.30
Japan 50, 57, 80, 81, 149, 173, 178, 193, 196
jargon 17, 19
JCPOA (Joint Comprehensive Program of Action) 37
Johnson, Rebecca 84, 88, 89n.1, 128, 158, 162, 167, 183
Joint Comprehensive Program of Action see JCPOA
Journal of Genocide Research 144
Journal of Genocide Studies 41n.18
Joyner, Dan 178
jus in bello 6, 96
justification for continued holding of nuclear weapons after TPNW 168, 184
justification for military choices 168

Kahn, Herman 16, 17
Kaplan, Fred 23
Kazakhstan 197
Keating, Fiona 144
Keating, Paul 76, 77
Keck, Margaret 5
Kelle, Alexander 72, 73
Kellenberger, Jacob 136–7, 154
Kennan, George 89n.2
Kile, Shannon 52
Kimball, Darryl 32, 49

Kim Jong-un 65n.6
Kissinger, Henry 62, 81
Korda, Matt 49, 189
Krepon, Michael 147, 185n.4
Krieger, David 13, 145
Kristensen, Hans 29, 44, 47, 49, 65n.3, 189
Kroenig, Matthew 50

Landmeter, Freel 176
landmines 95, 96, 100–12, 150, 168, 171, 173, 194, 195
Lang, Berel 145
language 14, 17–18, 35, 36, 134–6, 142
Larrinaga, Miguel de 111, 136
launch codes 25
launch on warning status 140
LAWS (lethal autonomous weapons systems) 115n.8
'laws of war' 96
League of Arab States 87–8
League of Nations 99
legitimization of war 114n.3
Lennane, Richard 44–5, 88, 161, 169, 199–200, 206
lethal autonomous weapons systems *see* LAWS
lethality, increasing 27, 45, 47, 72, 189
Lewis, Jeffrey 24, 51, 54
Lewis, Patricia 63, 139, 207
Libya 87
Lieber Instructions 97–8
Lieu, Ted 41n.21
Lifton, Robert Jay 11, 12, 16, 21, 22–3, 61, 133, 143
'limited' nuclear war 39n.4, 50–1, 134, 140, 141
lobbying 5, 30, 151
long-range missiles 32, 52
long-term effects of nuclear weapons 139–41
Lothe-Eide, Stein Ivar 176
low yield weapons 51
Lynch, Aaron 42n.30

MccGwire, Michael 47, 58
McCoy, Ron 84
MacFarlane, S. Neil 6, 108, 150, 168
McKinzie, Matthew G. 47, 65n.3
McNamara, Robert 62, 69, 77
Maddock, Shane J. 41n.26

Maguire, Richard 34
maintenance 45
managed systems of deterrence 36
Manhattan Project 27
MAPW (Medical Association for the Prevention of War) 151
Markey, Ed 32, 41n.21
Markusen, Eric 21, 143, 144
Marshall Islands 126, 202n.3
Martens Clause 98–9
Martin, Kevin 29–30
mass protest 152
material resources 29–33, 155–7
Maurer, Peter 119
Mecklin, John x, 31, 204
medical assistance, ability to provide 140, 141
Medical Association for the Prevention of War *see* MAPW
Meeting of States Parties 175, 180
metaphors 17
Mexico 119, 124, 135, 151
Meyer, David S. 117
Middle East 73, 74, 80, 85, 86–7, 167
middle powers 123, 181
Minor, Elizabeth 137, 154, 155, 163
miscalculation dangers 55, 63, 204
miscommunication 63
modernization 31, 44–7, 72, 134, 157, 167
Mongolia 149
moral considerations
  consequences of nuclear use 142
  deterrence doctrines 40n.12
  implicit laws 98
  internalized moral restraint 53
  moral code transgressions 20
  moral consequences 26
  moral persuasion 172, 173–4
  national security 112
  objections to nuclear arsenals 16
  rejection of violence 150
  risks of nuclear weapons 62
  spending on nuclear weapons 31
  stigmatization 170
moratorium on testing 71
Mukhatzhanova, Gaukhar 91n.18
Muller, Robert 104
multilateralism 84, 95, 99, 110, 111, 118, 121, 154, 172–4
Mumford, Lewis 15–16, 134

musketballs 97
mutually assured destruction 144
Myanmar 110

NAC (New Agenda Coalition) 83
Nadelmann, Ethan 181
Nagasaki 20
NAM (Non-Aligned Movement) 72–3, 86–7, 161, 167
national security 26, 125, 150
  see also security doctrines
NATO (North Atlantic Treaty Organisation)
  conventional weapons 57
  expansion 68
  no-first-use declarations 50
  and the NPT 164
  and Russia 45, 49, 51
  serious incidents 62
  spending on nuclear weapons 30
  and the TPNW 172, 174, 175, 176–8, 191, 192–3, 196
natural law 96, 99
'naturalness' of having nuclear weapons 15, 23, 184
near-use incidents 61–3
Netherlands 174, 175, 176, 192
neutral humanitarianism 138
neutrality 4–5
NewSTART process 46, 194
New Agenda Coalition *see* NAC
new threats 32, 56, 68, 78
New Zealand 118, 124, 149, 159n.5, 193
NGOs
  anti-nuclearism 39n.8, 84
  disarmament activism 75–6, 81
  investment in nuclear weapons 157
  landmines 101, 103–5, 106–7, 111, 112
  and the NPT 118, 119
  and the TPNW 124–5, 150, 153
Nielsen, Jenny 27
Nobel Peace Prize 46, 113, 125
no-first-use declarations 48–52, 54, 78, 192
Non-Aligned Movement *see* NAM
non-nuclear states
  assurances to 52
  and ban treaties 200–1

deterrence doctrines 54
disarmament 67, 83
  HINW (Conference on the Humanitarian Impact of Nuclear Weapons) 119
  Humanitarian Initiative 150
  Middle East 87–8
  and the modernization of stocks 45–6
  and the NPT 33–7, 72, 74, 75, 79, 85, 118, 164, 178–9, 180
  and the TPNW 123, 126, 129, 135, 174, 183
  World Court Project 76
Non-Proliferation and Disarmament Initiative *see* NPDI
non-proliferation regime 14, 43–66, 70, 72, 167
Non-Proliferation Treaty *see* NPT
non-signatories, effects of treaties on 110
non-state actors 55, 106
non-use discourses 17, 54, 60, 62, 166–7, 195
normalization 11–42, 134–5, 210
Norris, Robert S. 44
North Atlantic Treaty Organisation *see* NATO
North Carolina bombs 63
North Korea 7n.1, 8n.3, 31, 33, 37, 51, 65n.5, 80, 163, 193, 196
Norway 108, 118–19, 124, 135, 149, 151, 170, 174, 175, 192
NPDI (Non-Proliferation and Disarmament Initiative) 81
NPT (Non-Proliferation Treaty)
  defection from 178–9, 186n.11
  disarmament 68–71, 72, 83–8
  global nuclear order 33–7, 117
  and the global nuclear order 161–5
  history of elimination of nuclear weapons 68
  indefinite extension of 73–5
  negotiation in good faith for disarmament 44
  and the P5 2, 33–7, 75, 88, 89, 160–1, 163
  PrepCom (Preparatory Committees) 83, 87–8
  and the TPNW 122, 169, 178–80

NPT Review Conferences *see* RevCon
nuclear colonialism 162–3
nuclear compact 72
nuclear despotism 24
nuclear deterrence theory 48
nuclear ethics 22
nuclear forgetting 16
nuclearism
  definition 12–38
  first use of 12
  history of term 11
  as justification for weapons 13
nuclear monarchies 25
Nuclear Posture Reviews 48, 49, 51, 71, 189
nuclear preponderance 15
nuclear priesthood 18–19, 135
Nuclear Security Project 82
Nuclear Security Summits 66n.12
nuclear weapon-free zones 35, 76–7, 78, 81, 85, 120, 167, 198
Nuclear Weapons Ban Monitor 170
nuclear winter 40n.16, 140, 142
nukespeak 17–19, 142
Nunn, Sam 81
Nuremberg trials 98

Obama, Barack 44, 46, 48, 49, 50, 66n.12, 82, 84, 149
Oberleitner, Gerd 99, 100
OEWG (Open Ended Working Group) 119–20, 157, 180
Ogilvie-White, Tanya 81
omnicide 145–6, 158
O'Neill, Robert 77, 161
ontological acceptance of weapons 16
OPCW (Organisation for the Prohibition of Chemical Weapons) 112
Open Ended Working Group *see* OEWG
Open Skies Treaty 189
operational independence 4, 5
Oppenheimer, Robert 40n.13, 59–60
opportunity costs 31
oppositional discourse 19
Organisation for the Prohibition of Chemical Weapons *see* OPCW

OSCE (Organisation for Security and Cooperation in Europe) 50
Ottawa Convention 101, 104, 105–12, 168
overkill 27
Oxford Manual of the Laws and Customs of War (1880) 114n.7
oxygen depletion 141

P5 (Permanent Five)
  Article VI 72
  and the global nuclear order 160–1
  HINW (Conference on the Humanitarian Impact of Nuclear Weapons) 119
  landmines 106–8
  membership of 2
  and the NPT 2, 14, 33–7, 75, 88, 89, 160–1, 163
  post-Cold War 70
  security doctrines 147
  special responsibilities 205
  and the TPNW 122–3, 179–80, 183, 190, 191
Pakistan 7n.1, 8n.3, 31, 33, 51, 79–80, 85, 119, 196
paradox of indispensability 206
parity 15
Parliamentarians for Nuclear Non-proliferation and Disarmament *see* PNND
parliamentary oversight 23–4, 27
Parrish, Will 64n.2
patriarchy 143
patriotism 16
PAX 20, 156, 157, 176, 201
Payne, Keith 53, 206
peace, international 32
peace activists 16
peace and deterrence 53
peace education 121
peaceful use of nuclear technology 70, 85
peace treaties 99
Pelopidas, Benoit 23, 61, 117
perceptual shifts 136
Permanent Five *see* P5
Perry, William 62, 63, 81, 82, 204, 207

PNND (Parliamentarians for Nuclear Non-proliferation and Disarmament) 50, 156, 157
politics
  geopolitics 36–7, 50, 68, 166, 205
  humanitarian advocacy 5–6
  multilateralism 84, 95, 99, 110, 111, 118, 121, 154, 172–4
  post-Cold War 102
  revolving doors syndrome 30
Pope Francis 119, 138
Portela, Clara 173
positivism 99
Potter, William 91n.18
Powell, Colin 51, 56–7
Powers, Gerard 138
Prague meeting 149
precautionary principle 143
president of the USA 25, 27, 41n.21
prestige 1, 34, 51, 134
Pretorius, Joelien 152, 171, 179, 183, 184
Price, Richard 112, 150, 162, 168, 171, 172, 184
Principles and Objectives on Non-Proliferation and Disarmament 84
principles of distinction 6
principles of war 20
Program on Science and Global Security, Princeton University 141
prohibition versus regulation 126–8
proportionality 6, 20, 21, 53, 97, 125
Proxmire Law 30
psychology 19, 59–60, 143
public activism 39n.8, 152
public consultative committees 26
public health 139
publicity 111
public scrutiny 23–4, 25–6, 27, 32
Pugwash Conferences 69
Pullinger, Stephen 173
Putin, Vladimir 49, 51, 189

Quadrennial Reviews 71
Quille, Gerrard 173
Quinlan, Michael 40n.12, 52

radiation effects 120, 139, 141
rationality 12–13, 19, 53, 55, 59–60, 134, 163

Rauf, Tariq 73, 74, 83, 117, 163, 164, 182, 209
Reagan, Ronald 44, 69
Red Cross 4, 5
Reif, Kingston 124, 189
research and development 29–30
retaliation-only doctrines 48
Reuters 87
RevCon (NPT Review Conferences)
  1995 NPTREC (NPT Review and Extension Conference) 69–70, 71, 72, 73, 74, 75, 160
  2000 RevCon 83, 84
  2005 RevCon 81, 84
  2010 RevCon 86, 118, 128–9, 135, 136–7, 160
  2015 RevCon 85, 87–8, 117, 128–9, 161, 164, 186n.10
  2020 (2022) RevCon 177, 183, 186n.11
  decision-making processes 122
revolving doors syndrome 30
Reykjavik meeting 69, 149
'right conditions' for disarmament, waiting for 45
'right' to possession of nuclear weapons 166
risks of nuclear weapons 61–3, 136
  see also impacts
Ritchie, Nick 15, 27, 51, 127, 137, 150, 154, 156, 162, 175, 184, 196, 198, 210
Roberts, Brad 54
Robertson, George 81
Robust Nuclear Earth Penetrator 32
Rojecki, Andrew 26
Rotary International 136
Rowland, Matthew 51
Rublee, Maria Rost 185n.9
Rudd, Kevin 81
Ruff, Tilman 142
Ruhle, Michael 180
Rumbaugh, Russell 30, 31
Russia
  Chernobyl 39n.8
  conventional weapons 57
  deterrence doctrines 54
  effects of deployment of weapons 140
  and the Humanitarian Initiative 165

Russia (*continued*)
  landmines 104, 106, 108
  and NATO 45, 49, 51, 62
  no-first-use declarations 49
  and the NPT 8n.3, 37, 71
  post-Cold War 68
  reductions in nuclear weapons 43–4, 67, 71, 74, 164
  security doctrines 50, 52
  serious incidents 62
  St Petersburg Declaration 97
  tactical weapons 52
  and the TPNW 189, 196
  see also P5 (Permanent Five)
Rutherford, Ken 105, 107, 108, 110, 151

safeguards 63, 163, 197–9
safety increases 48
safety lapses 63
salience, reduction of 48–52, 177, 189, 191
salvation narratives 12
Sandoz, Yves 114n.3
SANE Act (Smarter Approach to Nuclear Expenditures Act) 32
Sauer, Tom 57, 117, 128, 150, 152, 168, 169, 171, 177, 179, 183, 184, 196
Scarry, Elaine 25
Schindler, Dietrich 98, 114n.7
Schlosser, Eric 27, 62, 63
Schultz, George 56, 63, 81
scientists' role in negotiations 151
scrutiny processes 23–4
Second World War 112
secrecy 13, 25, 26, 27
security doctrines
  continuing use of 193–4, 207–9
  global nuclear order 3
  'human security' 102
  illogicality 28–9
  and 'no-first-use' 48, 50
  rejection of 134–7, 148–9, 153
serious incidents 62
Seven Nation Initiative 81, 149
Shaker, Mohamed I. 72
short-range weapons 52
Shultz, George 81, 82, 209
Sikkink, Kathryn 5

simple ban 126–7
simple messaging 108
Simpson, John 27, 79
SIPRI Nuclear Weapons Project 52–3
Sjolander, Claire Turenne 111, 136
smaller states' involvement 123, 150, 154, 181, 182, 193
Smarter Approach to Nuclear Expenditures (SANE) Act 32
smart technology 116n.17
Smarter Approach to Nuclear Expenditures Act *see* SANE Act
smoke 140
social contract 25
soft compliance 194
soft targets 65n.3
software 12
Sokov, Nikolai 69
Solis, Gary 21
Somerville, John 145, 158
Sommaruga, Cornelio 105
South Africa 124, 162, 193, 197
South Asia 45, 51, 79–80, 83, 204
South Korea 50, 57, 178, 193, 196
South Sudan 33
Soviet Union 2, 21
  see also Cold War; P5 (Permanent Five); Russia
spending on nuclear weapons 29–33, 46, 155–7
Spring, Baker 53
SSA (Stepping Stones Approach) 183
Stanford University 82
Starr, Steven 140
START (Strategic Arms Reduction Treaty) 47, 71
starvation 139, 140–1
statistics on nuclear weapons 8n.3, 34–5, 44, 67
step-by-step disarmament processes 83–4, 88, 123, 129, 152, 165, 209
Stepping Stones Approach *see* SSA
stewardship systems 24
stigmatization 3, 78, 99, 126, 127, 167, 170, 200, 211
Stimson Center Report 31, 69, 76, 78, 117
Stockholm Initiative 183

stockpile stewardship 46–7
Stoltz, William 200
storage sites 30, 82
St Petersburg Declaration 97, 98, 99, 112
Strategic Arms Reduction Treaty *see* START
strategic doctrines 12, 15, 18, 19, 21, 28, 58, 134
submarines 47
   see also Trident
sunlight, blocking 140
super-fuze ability 47
surface devaluation 51–2
survivor testimonies 126, 142, 149–50, 155, 195
   see also Hibakusha
Sweden 183
Switzerland 124
Syria 21, 51, 87

taboos 11, 17, 39n.3, 62, 171, 196
tactical weapons 52
Tannenwald, Nina 11, 39n.3, 211
targeting of weapons 47, 55
Taylor, Bryan C. 13, 15, 17, 25, 26, 27, 46, 47, 65n.4, 207
technological failure 59, 63
technology, belief in 13
techno-strategic language 18, 136, 142
terrorism 55, 63, 80, 82, 84, 175, 204
testing 20, 40n.14, 71, 75–6, 79, 83, 89n.3, 120, 126, 195
Thakur, Ramesh 47, 154, 164, 179
thermonuclear monarchy 25
Thiele, Leslie Paul 210
think tanks 81, 124
thought contagion 42n.30
threats of use 27, 127, 130n.5, 166
Three Mile Island accident 39n.8
Thurlow, Setsuko 142
Ticehurst, Rupert 98
Tokyo Forum for Nuclear Non-Proliferation and Disarmament 80, 149
Toman, Jiri 98, 114n.7
Toon, Owen B. 140, 144, 145
TPNW (Treaty on the Prohibition of Nuclear Weapons) 117–30, 133–59, 160–86, 189–203

transnational advocacy networks 5
transparency 23, 26
Treaty on the Prohibition of Nuclear Weapons *see* TPNW
Treaty of Versailles 99
Trident 27, 32, 169
Truman, Harry S. 40n.13
Trump, Donald 37, 50, 51, 116n.16
Turkey 175

Ukraine 51, 197
UN (United Nations)
   CD (Conference on Disarmament) 33, 71–2, 102, 104, 106, 107
   Charter 31, 37, 72
   Convention on Genocide 143
   Five Point Proposal for Nuclear Disarmament 81
   General Assembly 4, 67–8, 112, 118, 119, 165
   Institute for Disarmament Research (UNIDIR) 6
   landmines 101
   ODA 169
   Office for the Coordination of Humanitarian Affairs (OCHA) 4
   Security Council 2, 31–2, 34, 44, 108, 163
   Sustainable Development Goals 31
   TPNW (Treaty on the Prohibition of Nuclear Weapons) 3, 67, 117–30
unanimity 111
Ungar, Sheldon 15, 16, 206
United Nations *see* UN
United States
   accidents and near-misses 62–3
   American Civil War 97
   budget scrutiny 32
   calls for cuts to nuclear arsenal 32
   comprehensive nuclear test ban treaty (CTBT) 83
   congressional review 23–4, 27
   Constitution 25
   control measures 163
   conventional weapons 56–7
   Convention on Certain Conventional Weapons (CCW) 100
   Creating an Environment for Nuclear Disarmament (CEND) 183

United States (*continued*)
  cyber-vulnerability 63
  defence industry 29–30
  deterrence doctrines 54
  effects of deployment of weapons 140
  focus on 14–15
  initial acquisition decisions 27
  landmines 101–2, 104, 106–7, 110
  managerial approach 164
  and the Middle East 87
  modernization 46, 47
  moratorium on testing 71
  national security state 26–7
  no-first-use declarations 48
  and the NPT 2, 35, 36–7, 74, 84, 118
  nuclear despotism 24
  Nuclear Posture Reviews 71
  president of the USA 25, 27, 41n.21
  Quadrennial Reviews 71
  reductions in nuclear weapons 43–4, 67, 71, 74, 164
  security doctrines 50, 52
  spending on nuclear weapons 30–1, 46, 155
  state leaders' power 25, 27
  statistics on nuclear weapons 8n.3
  Three Mile Island accident 39n.8
  and the TPNW 174–8, 189, 191–3
  use of nuclear weapons 14–15, 21, 27
  verification systems 198
  weapons on other countries' territory 175
  see also P5 (Permanent Five)
universality 4, 109–10, 123–4
unnecessary suffering, avoidance of 97
unparalleled catastrophe 142
'unthinkable,' the 17
upgrading 31
  see also modernization
utility of landmines 112, 126, 168
utility of nuclear weapons 78, 126, 134–5, 137, 168–9

value for money 29
valuing of nuclear weapons 15
Van der Meer, Sico 176, 177

Varano, Daniela 161, 162
Vatican 138
Verification Research, Training, and Information Centre *see* VERTIC
verification systems 85, 127, 197–9
VERTIC (Verification Research, Training, and Information Centre) 198
veto powers 34
victim perspectives 18
victims, effects on 96, 97, 105, 111, 120, 151
Vienna Conference 138

Walker, William 36, 164, 182
Wall Street Journal 81, 82
Walt, Stephen 68
Waltz, Kenneth 59
Ware, Alyn 143, 146, 147
Wareham, Susan 141
war on terror 84
watchdog roles 170
water 141
weapons bans, history of 97–105
weapons manufacturing corporations 27, 29–30, 110, 157
weapons of acceptable risk 53
weapons of mass destruction 35, 55, 99, 136, 164, 167, 208
Weart, Spencer R. 17
Weeramantry, Christopher 76, 146
Welsh, General Larry 53
Welsh, Susan B. 75
Wigg-Stevenson, Tyler 144
Williams, Heather 124
Williams, Jody 104–5, 107, 111, 113
Williams, Raymond 13
Wilson, Ward 37, 38
Wittner, Lawrence S. 39n.8
WMD Free Zone 85, 86–7
women and girls, impact on 120, 143
Woolcott, Richard 118
World Court Project 75–6
World Medical Journal 151
Wunderlich, Carmen 185n.9

Yemen 21

zero-sum security outlook 28